MASTERING MARKETING

The Complete MBA Companion in Marketing

FINANCIAL TIMES

MASTERING MARKETING

The Complete MBA Companion in Marketing

IN ASSOCIATION WITH

 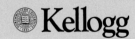

London
Business
School

Wharton
The Wharton School
University of Pennsylvania

INSEAD

INSEAD, founded in 1959, provides management education for more than 600 MBA graduates and 5,000 executives annually from all over the world. There are 113 standing faculty and affiliate faculty, from 24 countries. The PhD program is placing graduates in top business schools around the world. Extensive research assures the relevance of INSEAD's teaching in today's highly competitive and constantly changing international business environment. INSEAD recently announced the opening of a second campus in Singapore in January 2000.

 **Kellogg**

Widely recognized as one of the finest business programs in the United States, the Kellogg Graduate School of Management at Northwestern University is home to a renowned, research-based faculty and bright, ambitious management students from around the world. From its quiet beginning at the turn of the century as the undergraduate School of Commerce, Kellogg has risen to national prominence through a dedication to academic excellence, a lively spirit of innovation, a commitment to serving the needs of the marketplace, and, above all, a profound sense of fellowship.

Kellogg's Master of Management degree can be attained through three different programs, each of which is led by the same faculty using the same teaching methods. The one-year and two-year full-time programs are conducted on Northwestern's Evanston campus; a part-time evening program, called the Manager's Program, is held at Northwestern's downtown Chicago campus.

Founded in 1965, London Business School aims to be the most important and respected international business school, generating work and ideas that will have a powerful, lasting and world-wide impact on the learning and practice of management of key business leaders.

The School's thriving community consists of world-renowned faculty, culturally diverse students, global corporate partners and international alumni, all of whom work together to achieve our aim.

London Business School was recently placed number one in Europe and eighth overall in the *Financial Times'* ranking of international business schools – the only non-US school to be ranked in the top ten.

A graduate school of the University of London, we already hold the highest possible rating (5*A) for the quality of our research, awarded by the Higher Education Funding Council for England.

The Wharton School of the University of Pennslyvania, founded in 1881 as the first collegiate school of management in the United States, is recognized around the world for its innovative leadership and broad academic strengths across every major discipline and at every level of business education. With nearly 200 faculty members, 11 academic departments, 19 research centers, and leading programs at undergraduate, MBA, doctoral and executive education levels, the Wharton School is committed to creating the highest value and impact on the practice of business and management worldwide. Currently, Wharton has approximately 4,500 students enrolled in degree programs, more than 10,000 participants in its executive education programs each year, and a network of more than 70,000 alumni in more than 100 countries.

Executive editor	Tim Dickson
Subeditor	Neville Hawcock
Series commissioner	George Bickerstaffe
Editorial consultant	John Willman
Website editor	James Pickford
FT Mastering co-ordinator	Laura Scanga
Graphics	Graham Parrish
School co-ordinators	INSEAD: Tracey Gillespie and Helle Jensen
	J.L. Kellogg Graduate School of Management: Lakshman Krishnamurthi
	London Business School: Gerry Griffin, Tom Robertson, Pippa Goodman and Mika Ahsan
	The Wharton School of the University of Pennsylvania: Michael Baltes and Skip Ferguson

PEARSON EDUCATION LIMITED

London Office
128 Long Acre, London WC2E 9AN
Tel: +44(0)171 447 2000
Fax: +44(0)171 240 5771
Website: www.pearsoned-ema.com

First published in Great Britain1999

© INSEAD (The European Institute of Business Administration)
© J.L. Kellogg Graduate School of Management
© London Business School
© The Wharton School of the University of Pennsylvania

pbk ISBN 0 273 64222 7
hbk ISBN 0 273 64223 5

British Library Cataloguing in Publication Data
A CIP catalogue record for this book can be obtained from the British Library

10 9 8 7 6 5 4 3 2 1

Typeset by Land and Unwin (Data Sciences) Limited, Bugbrooke
Printed and bound in Great Britain by William Clowes Ltd., Beccles, Suffolk

The Publishers' policy is to use paper manufactured from sustainable forests.

Contents

Introduction

The *Financial Times Mastering* series is the product of a unique collaboration between the *FT* and some of the world's leading international business schools. *Mastering Marketing*, which is drawn from a weekly series that appeared in the *FT*, is the fifth book to emerge from this partnership. As with its predecessors, we believe that it combines the essential basics of the discipline with many fresh ideas for 21st century students and practitioners.

Mastering Marketing brings together more than 50 articles written by faculty at the Kellogg Graduate School of Management at Northwestern University, near Chicago; the Wharton School of the University of Pennsylvania; INSEAD, just outside Paris in France; and London Business School. The combined European and North American perspective of this outstanding writing team is what makes *Mastering Marketing* a particularly valuable resource.

There are 10 modules: 21st century marketing; Understanding consumers; Competitive analysis; Brand strategy; Advertising and selling; Market entry strategy and new technologies; Retailing and direct selling; Sector marketing; New marketing media; and International marketing.

Readers will find analysis of, and solutions to, a wide range of problems – everything from the familiar but thorny dilemmas of advertising, pricing and brand extension to the extraordinary – and often confusing – opportunities presented by new electronic media. There are articles on how companies collude (quite legally in many countries), on the pros and cons of pioneering versus later market entry, and on the ethical questions that marketing often throws up. As you browse through the text, bear in mind Philip Kotler's observation (on page 6) that "the most successful companies are already marketing their products as if we lived in 2005".

Brief introductions to each module outline its significance in a wider context and the summaries at the end of each article are designed to help readers quickly identify subjects of special interest. Lists of further reading should be helpful for those who want to delve deeper or look up particular references.

As with other *FT Mastering* books there are many people to thank. The contributors all gave generously of their time and are too numerous to list here, but special mention should go to the co-ordinators at the four business schools: Tracey Gillespie and Helle Jensen at INSEAD, Mike Baltes and Skip Ferguson at Wharton, Lakshman Krishnamurthi at Kellogg, and Gerry Griffin, Tom Robertson, Pippa Goodman and Mika Ahsan at LBS.

Finally, if you enjoy this book you will be glad to know that there are more Mastering books on the way: the next two topics in the series will be *Mastering Information Management* and *Mastering Strategy*. You can also find out more by looking at our website, *www.ftmastering.com*

Tim Dickson and Neville Hawcock
June 1999

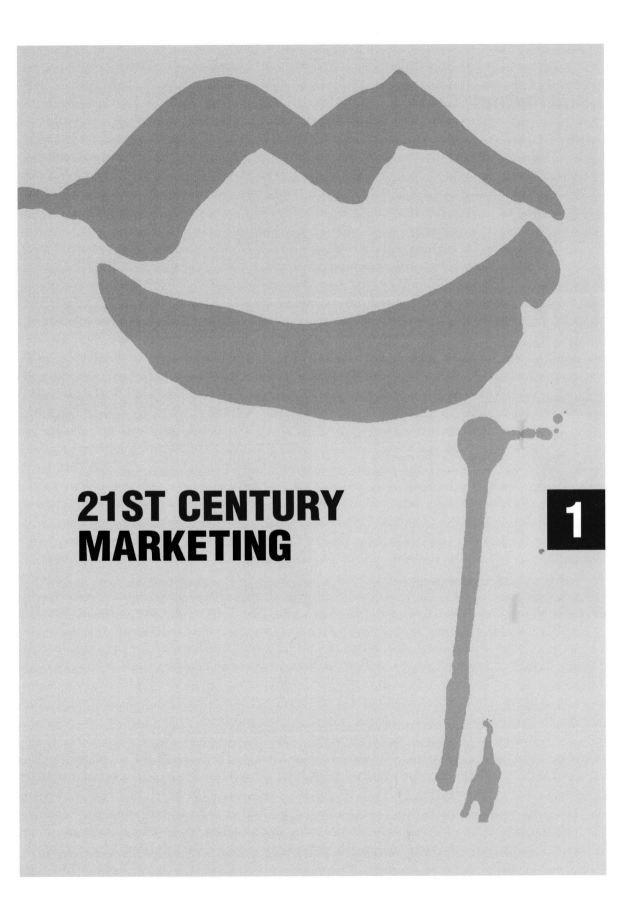

21ST CENTURY
MARKETING

1

Contributors

Philip Kotler is distinguished professor of international marketing at the J.L. Kellogg Graduate School of Management, Northwestern University.

Sean Meehan is professor of marketing and strategy at the International Institute for Management Development (IMD), Lausanne, Switzerland.

Gregory S. Carpenter is associate professor of marketing at the J.L. Kellogg Graduate School of Management, Northwestern University. His research focuses on competitive marketing strategy, with an emphasis on the role of consumer learning and decision making in creating competitive advantage.

Patrick Barwise is professor of management and marketing at London Business School, where he is also director of the Centre for Marketing and chairman of the Future Media Research Programme.

Leonard Lodish is Samuel R. Harrell Professor and professor of marketing at the Wharton School of the University of Pennsylvania. His research interests include marketing decision support systems, marketing experimentation and marketing resource allocation.

Tim Ambler is a senior fellow at London Business School, where he teaches global marketing and doing business in China. His research interests include measuring marketing performance, how advertising works and relationship marketing.

Philip M. Parker is professor of marketing at INSEAD. His research interests include marketing strategy, international management, pricing, new product diffusion, and forecasting.

Flora Kokkinaki is a research fellow at London Business School, where she works on the marketing metrics research program. Her research interests include the measurement of marketing effectiveness, consumer behavior and consumer involvement, economic psychology and social cognition.

Contents

Introduction

The business environment is changing rapidly – owing especially to electronic commerce and globalization – and the challenge for companies is to ensure that their marketing strategies and marketing skills keep pace. This introductory module looks at some of the areas in which successful marketers of the next century will need to excel: the ability to anticipate or even shape consumers' preferences, instead of merely reacting to them; measurement of the effectiveness of advertising and marketing; prioritization of overseas markets to enter; and, generally, consistent delivery of superior customer value.

Where do we go from here?

by Philip Kotler

I am pleased to write an introduction to this fine tapestry of articles featuring many new strands of thought about the present and future character of marketing. I continue to believe that marketing, correctly interpreted and practiced, is the key to company adaptability and profitability. Markets are changing at an accelerating rate. Industry boundaries are blurring. Companies more than ever need quick and reliable intelligence about their customers, competitors, distributors and products. More companies are recognizing the prescient wisdom in Peter Drucker's observation that "the customer is the business."

Here I will add my thoughts about where marketing is headed in the new millennium. I will do this by "looking back into the future."

It is the year 2005. Here are the major developments in the evolving market place/market space:

- There has been substantial disintermediation of wholesalers and retailers owing to electronic commerce. Virtually all products are now available without going to a shop. The customer can access pictures of any product on the Internet, read the specification, shop among online vendors for the best prices and terms, and click order and payment over the Internet.

- Expensively printed catalogs have disappeared. Business-to-business purchasing over the Internet has increased even faster than online customer buying. Business purchasing agents shop for routine items on the Internet, either advertising their needs and waiting for bidders or simply surfing in their "bookmarked" web sites.

- Shop-based retailers find shop traffic highly diminished. In response, more entrepreneurial retailers are building entertainment and theatre into their shops. Many bookshops, food shops and clothes shops now include coffee bars and feature lecturers and performances. Essentially these shops are marketing an "experience" rather than a product assortment.

- Most companies have built proprietary customer databases containing rich information on individual customer preferences and requirements. They use this information to "mass customize" their offerings to individuals.

  An increasing number of companies present online product platforms on which customers design products to suit their own specifications. Many automobile, computer, domestic appliance and food companies invite customers to visit their web page and design the market offering (product, service, system, program) by filling in choices on a form. The modified product is then displayed on the screen.

- Businesses are doing a better job of retaining customers through finding imaginative ways to exceed customer expectations. As a result, competitors find it increasingly difficult to acquire new customers and most companies are spending time figuring out how to sell more products and services to their existing customers.

  Companies are focusing on building customer share rather than market share. Many have thought up new ways to increase cross-selling and up-selling.

Companies are gaining segment and customer insight from their dataware-houses by applying newer and more effective datamining techniques.

- Companies have finally managed to persuade their accounting departments to generate real numbers on profitability by individual customer, product and channel and are now focusing their attention on these. They are formulating reward packages and incentives for their more profitable customers.
- Companies have switched from a transaction perspective to a customer loyalty-building perspective. Many have moved to customer lifetime-supply thinking, whereby they offer to deliver a regularly consumed product (for example, coffee) on a regular basis at a lower price per unit. They can afford to make less profit on each sale because of the long-term purchase contract.
- Most companies now outsource over 60 per cent of their activities and requirements. A few outsource 100 per cent, making them virtual companies owning very few assets and therefore earning extraordinary rates of return.

    Outsourcing companies are enjoying a boom. In the case of equipment manufacturers, most prefer to work with single supply partners who design and supply overall systems (such as the braking system, the seating system and so on in a car) in partnership with the branded manufacturer. Most companies today are networked companies, relying heavily on alliances.
- Many field salespeople are franchisees rather than company employees. The company equips them with the latest sales automation tools, enabling them to develop individualized multimedia presentations and customized market offerings and contracts.

    Most buyers prefer to meet salespeople on their computer screen rather than in their office. More and more personal selling is occurring over electronic media where the buyer and seller see each other on their computer screens in real time. Salespeople are traveling less and airlines are shrinking. The most effective salespeople are well-informed, trustworthy, likeable and good at listening.
- Mass TV advertising has greatly diminished as a result of 500 viewing channels. There are far fewer printed newspapers and magazines. On the other hand, marketers can now reach their target markets more effectively by advertising through specialized online magazines and newsgroups.
- Companies are unable to sustain competitive advantages (beyond patents, copyrights, superior locations, proprietary information and so on). Competitors are quick to copy any advantage through benchmarking, reverse engineering and leapfrogging. Companies believe that their only sustainable advantage lies in an ability to learn faster and change faster.

Back in the present, the key to competitive success is to keep your marketing changing as fast as your marketplace. The most successful companies are already marketing their products as if we lived in 2005. *Mastering Marketing* will tell you more about them and the techniques that give them competitive advantage.

Summary

The successful company is one whose marketing can keep ahead of the fast-changing global marketplace. So what will the discipline look like in the future? In this introduction to the series, **Philip Kotler** forecasts the trends that will be shaping marketing by the year 2005.

Changing the rules of the marketing game

by Gregory S. Carpenter

Driven by intense competition and increasingly sophisticated customers, organizations are rushing to "get close to their customers," to become "market driven." Industrial giants such as General Electric, consumer goods leaders such as Unilever and rapidly growing smaller organizations such as 3Com are initiating or resuming a dialog with customers, scrutinizing market research, drawing on new ideas to improve products, building stronger customer relationships and reorganizing to speed products to market. They are, in the classic definition of the marketing concept, seeking to "give customers what they want."

Though the benefits to customers have been enormous, this rush to embrace the marketing concept has produced some unanticipated consequences. In many cases competitors are speaking to the same customers, analyzing similar if not identical market research data, drawing new managers and new ideas from the same sources and benchmarking the same companies. As a result they are approaching markets with the same perspective and producing products that, while offering high value, are competitively indistinguishable.

This lack of differentiation presents an important challenge to the marketing concept. As a result, the concept itself is evolving. The current view of marketing is that it is about "giving customers what they want." Companies should learn what buyers want and devise efficient ways to deliver it. Marketing is essentially about discovery. The core assumption is that buyers know what they want.

The evolving marketing concept challenges this view. Increasingly, strategies are being created on the assumption that, at least initially, buyers do not know what they want but instead *learn* what they want. Under the conventional view of customers, how they perceive, value and select brands are the essential "rules of the game." Every competitor must play by these rules. On the other hand, if buyers learn what they want, then brand perceptions and preferences are outcomes of the learning process. The rules of the game, in other words, evolve as buyers learn. That evolution depends, in part, on what companies teach buyers. For example, Motorola, Nokia and Ericsson are shaping buyer perceptions of cellular phones, the features customers value and how buyers choose a cell phone. Brand strategies play a central role in defining the rules of the game. The emerging concept suggests that marketing is part learning – gaining an understanding of what buyers know now and of the process of buyer learning – and part teaching – playing a role in the buyer learning process. It is about being market driven *and* "market driving."

Consumer learning

At the root of much consumer learning are goals that motivate it. All individuals and organizations have goals that they seek to achieve. An individual goal might be "to look younger"; a corporate goal might be "to be number one in the industry." Individuals and organizations turn to brands to achieve those goals. Many of the brands or product categories we turn to are obvious. To provide transportation we look for an automobile and to protect ourselves from the elements we buy clothing. Over time, the goals associated with product categories and brands grow from a simple set of functionally orientated goals to a more elaborate set of functionally and emotionally orientated goals.

The recent popularity of sport-utility vehicles is illustrative. These provide their owners with valuable functionality: transportation that is safe and reliable in most weather. But they also satisfy other less obvious, though quite important, goals. For the frazzled, often anonymous, suburbanite, a sport-utility vehicle can provide a sense of independence, distinctiveness and ruggedness. Buyers have learned that these goals, although not naturally linked to the family car, can be achieved by owning a sport-utility vehicle.

Through a similar process, links are learned between brands and customer goals. The goals associated with brands differ from brand to brand in the same category. Among sport-utility brands, Mercedes-Benz provides safety and prestige, Range Rover enables its owners to portray themselves as refined individuals who are sensitive to tradition and Lexus provides peace of mind and a more modern, smart self-image. These links between brands and goals are created and nurtured over time. Some are built inadvertently. The popularity of Harley-Davidson motorcycles with motorcycle clubs has enabled Harley-Davidson to link its brand with buyers' desire to portray a rough, rebellious image. However created, these brand–goal links are a fundamental result of consumer learning.

The concept of brand–goal links has important competitive implications. The conventional view is that the customer compares brands along only one dimension, making comparisons across brands simple. In more formal economic terms, the customer seeks a single goal-utility.

The emerging view is that buyers seek many different goals and that within the same category some brands can be linked with multiple goals in unique combination. Volvo has successfully linked both "be a responsible parent" and "add excitement to my life" to the Volvo brand through its new V70 station wagons, which combine a high-performance engine, suitable for racing, with a family car, blurring the traditional distinction between "sports car" and "family car." By successfully linking these goals – along with the "safety" so long associated with the brand – Volvo has defined the brand as delivering value that no other can. Brand–goal links such as these, built through strategy and learned by consumers, make the similar incomparable.

Brand perceptions

Initially, of course, we have no perceptions of any brands. All brands are at some point novel to us. All the brand perceptions we have are learned. They have a number of important properties.

First, perceptions of brands in the same category are not necessarily equal. We may have a richer, more complex set of associations for "Coca-Cola" or "Jaguar" than we do for "Cott" or "Mitsubishi." A richer set of associations can increase the ease with which we recall a brand, affect our feelings towards it (increasing trust or confidence, for example) and affect our price sensitivity. It is hard to justify a price premium for a brand about which we know little.

Second, even brands with the same associations can be perceived differently because the vividness of those associations differs. Both Levis and Lee jeans are "American," "rugged," associated with the American West and similarly designed and priced. Yet perceptions of Levis are likely to be more powerful and more vivid. These differences are the result of brand strategy. We are certainly not born with richer perceptions of Levis or Coca-Cola.

The process of acquiring brand perceptions has important implications for the marketing concept and for the nature of competition. If consumers know what they want, then they establish the perceptual dimensions along which they perceive brands and all brands are subject to them. To be sure, Mercedes and Lexus can be perceived differently along those dimensions and one can be perceived as superior to the other. But both Mercedes and Lexus are evaluated along the same dimensions. The objective of strategy in that case is to discover and respond to the established perceptual criteria.

On the other hand, if buyer perceptions are learned and if that learning depends on the strategies of brands, then marketing has a completely different objective: to influence the evolution of perceptions in a way that competitors cannot effectively imitate. The aim is to create vast inequalities – in the richness of perception – between a brand and its competitors.

Brand preferences

In every category, our knowledge of how products satisfy different goals is learned. To see this, consider a market over its life. Initially, buyers have no idea how to value product attributes and thus no way to evaluate alternative brands. Buyers may sample a number of brands, liking some more than others. This experience triggers the process of consumer inference: "what are the characteristics of the ones I like and the ones I don't like?"

Obvious differences in brand or attributes are assumed to be the "cause" of these differences. You may conclude that you have a preference for a brand or some combination of attributes. If you prefer Starbucks coffee to other brands, you might judge that you do so because of the darker roast and particular blend of beans. In reality, of course, the source of a satisfactory outcome can never be precisely determined. Many consumption experiences are largely or even entirely ambiguous (for example motor oil, batteries and many professional services).

Nevertheless, buyers form a naive "theory" relating brand features to satisfaction, which is reinforced by advertising and repeat purchase. In the process, preferences are formed and evolve, based on the interaction of buyer experience and brand strategy. This suggests that what customers want depends on what customers have experienced. Brand strategy plays a defining role in this evolution and can have enduring consequences. Consider the case of Vaseline petroleum jelly. Introduced in 1880, Vaseline was advertised as a healing agent of unsurpassed purity. Competitors at the time offered healing agents based on black coal tar derivatives. Sampling Vaseline, a translucent, highly pure gel, buyers learned that its attributes produced an effective wound preparation and, generalizing from this observation, inferred that the effectiveness of petroleum jelly lies in its translucence and purity. Subsequent trials and advertising confirmed this conjecture, leading to translucence being favored over opacity in the petroleum jelly market. That preference structure prevails today, over 100 years later.

Decision making

Buyers learn how to choose brands. The conventional view is that buyers consider all the alternatives, evaluate their differences – making the necessary trade-offs – and ultimately choose the brand that maximizes self-interest. Implicitly or explicitly, this model of consumer decision making is the foundation for much current thought about marketing. For example, many market research methods are built on it. It implies that buyers use only one decision strategy – maximize self-interest by considering all the alternatives along all the dimensions on every occasion.

In fact, people make decisions in many ways, responding to the situation and the need. We draw on a repertoire of decision rules. In purchasing a battery we use a very different decision process than we would in buying jeans or selecting a car. In selecting a battery, use is very uninformative, so we might consider only brands we have tried, ignoring lower-priced alternatives as too risky. In the case of jeans, we might compare all brands to Levis, not to one another. In choosing a car, we might consider only brands that meet some minimum level along certain dimensions (for example, quality, safety, fuel economy) and then select among those brands along another dimension (styling, price).

The decision rules buyers learn depend on the strategies brands pursue. If all brands deliver value with respect to the same goals (for example, video recorders) and comparisons between brands are easy, buyers may simply exhaustively compare alternatives. In more complex situations, buyers may resort to strategies to simplify matters. For example, in a market with many brands, each with a complex goal structure (for example, shampoo), comparisons are difficult. Buyers may use simpler decision rules – buy the one on special offer or the one recommended by a friend.

Competitive advantage

Consumer learning has profound implications for the nature of competition and competitive advantage. If buyers *learn* what they want, competition is less a race to meet consumer needs than a battle over how perceptions, preferences and decision making will evolve in a market. It is a battle over the rules of the game. Below are two cases that illustrate this.

Pioneering advantage

In many markets, the pioneer (first entrant) outsells the others in its category, in some cases for decades. Brands such as Wrigley's chewing gum, Gerber baby food and Kleenex tissues have retained the largest shares of their markets despite numerous competitive entries.

The traditional view of the marketing concept suggests that pioneers have higher shares because they have pre-empted the "best position" in the market, leaving less attractive positions for later entrants. A consumer-learning view offers a fundamentally different account. Under this view, prior to the pioneer's entry the category is ill-defined. Buyers do not know what goals to attach to brands, how to perceive differences between them, the value of those differences or the best strategy for choosing among alternatives. The rules of the game are yet to be defined.

The pioneer plays a defining role in the market. It builds the first set of brand–goal links, defining the basis of value for the category, and it begins the process of establishing brand perceptions. As a result, the pioneer is often strongly associated, even synonymous, with the category (think of Kleenex or Xerox). Such brands come to mind more quickly and reliably than other brands. Perceptions of the pioneer are often more vivid than those of later entrants, making the pioneer the "standard." As such, it is often the brand buyers sample first or most often. All brands are compared to it and all suffer by comparison.

Attacking such a brand is a daunting proposition. A later entrant may position itself near the pioneer because that is what consumers request. It will then invariably be compared to the pioneer, but without the rich, vivid perceptions that the pioneer evokes, the competitor will be overshadowed. On the other hand, if a later entrant positions itself away from the pioneer, it will suffer because, although more differentiated, it is now less ideal. It will also evoke less vivid, weaker perceptions and have less influence in the decision process.

Pioneering advantage arises from not simply playing the game first and thus better; it arises from defining the game that later entrants must play. The challenge for later entrants, therefore, is not to play better than the pioneer but to change the nature of the game, just as Gillette is doing through technological innovations in shaving and Starbucks is doing through strategic innovation in the US coffee market.

Product differentiation

Consumer learning occurs in mature markets as well. Product differentiation is one excellent example. The classic view of product differentiation is that it is about discovery: finding a relevant, widely valued but unmet dimension. This approach implicitly assumes that buyers value some aspects of a product that have simply been ignored. Once all valuable attributes have been discovered, further differentiation is impossible.

A consumer-learning perspective suggests, in contrast, that differentiation can be successful even if no "undiscovered" dimension of preference exists. Differentiation is possible so long as a new dimension exists that buyers can learn is valuable. The differentiating attribute need not be relevant, valuable and meaningful to buyers. It can be irrelevant. This strategy – "meaningless differentiation" – is widespread. For example, Alberto Culver differentiated its Natural Silk shampoo by adding silk. It advertises that it "puts silk in a bottle." A spokesman for Alberto Culver later told the magazine *Brand Week*, however, that silk does "nothing for hair."

How can an irrelevant attribute become a meaningful basis for differentiation? First, a brand with it is distinctive and attracts attention. Facing the shampoo shelves, the consumer's eye might be caught by Alberto Culver Natural Silk's claim to contain real silk. That moment of attention might produce an inference that the product must be valuable. Using the shampoo successfully might lead to the same conclusion. Buyers may even come to believe that the silk causes the shampoo to work well. Second, an irrelevant attribute simplifies brand choice. For example, when choosing among three very similar brands of shampoo, consumers have an incentive to infer that the irrelevant attribute is valuable; by doing so, they can dismiss the two brands without it, leaving an unambiguous choice.

Conclusion

Throughout the evolution of the marketing concept, the basic notion that competitive advantage can be created by giving customers what they want has remained unchanged. All that has changed is the way in which customers are satisfied.

Today, organizations are gaining a deeper understanding of customers. They are learning about the goals they hope to achieve in their lives and then creating powerful links between those goals and their brands. Good companies are giving customers what they ask for. But great companies are creating markets, even ones that customers have never envisaged, shaping their evolution and producing in the process competitive advantage unattainable a generation ago.

Summary

As more organizations shift to being customer-orientated, more are discovering that they face similarly orientated competitors. The result is a lack of differentiation rather than the anticipated competitiveness. Here **Gregory Carpenter** argues that the marketing concept needs to evolve in response to this. Instead of taking "what the customer wants" as a given, companies must recognize that consumers' product preferences and perceptions are learned. The aim of marketing strategy then becomes to drive the market – to influence the customer's learning process to the company's advantage. If the aim of the game is to keep the customer satisfied, then the role of marketing strategy is continually to redefine the rules of the game.

When do commercials boost sales?

by Leonard Lodish

Retailing tycoon John Wanamaker once said, "I know that half of my advertising doesn't work. The problem is, I don't know which half." The statement is also attributed to Lord Lever but regardless of the source, it is, if anything, an understatement. Global companies spend billions of dollars on television advertising, always in the hope that their money will produce greater sales. Much of their money is wasted. The problem advertisers have has remained the same since long before the invention of television: what is the best way to determine the effectiveness of advertising expenditures?

Advertising is typically the largest expenditure in consumer products companies' marketing budgets. It is also the first to be cut when revenues or profits fall short. Cuts are frequently made with only the weakest information on the effectiveness of each aspect of the company's overall advertising plan. A thorough evaluation will be likely to show that some of the current advertising is simply ineffective, while other advertisements are moderately helpful and still others are very helpful. It is paradoxical that, notwithstanding the enormous sums companies pour into advertising, almost all other aspects of the marketing mix are regularly measured with considerable rigor, precision and confidence. One reason for this is simply that it is difficult to measure both the short- and long-term impact of advertising. This is particularly true of television advertising.

Are there any rules?

Many companies accept as given certain television advertising "rules." Many of these are of questionable veracity. For example, most companies believe that the following are beyond dispute:

- In order to increase market share, television advertising share of voice must be larger than current market share.
- At least three exposures per person are required to make a significant impact.
- More television advertising is better than less.
- Television advertising takes a long time to work.

These rules should not necessarily be accepted at face value. Powerful methods for evaluating advertising efficacy do exist and they show that these and other "certainties" need to be examined carefully in each unique situation. In the late 1980s and early 1990s, I and some colleagues tested some common perceptions about television advertising for consumer packaged goods. We performed an independent analysis of Information Resources' historical Behaviorscan database.

Behaviorscan is a household purchasing panel that comprizes around 3,000 demographically representative households from each of six geographically dispersed markets. Each household's supermarket purchases are recorded via scanners so that purchasing behavior can be precisely measured. Households receive all of their television transmissions via cable and advertising can be directed to or removed from individual households on a targeted basis. This has allowed the execution of numerous carefully controlled advertising experiments to test advertising variables.

We found that some factors boost sales, while many do not. For example, increasing advertising expenditure relative to the competition does not necessarily result in higher sales. This is not to say that television advertising cannot be effective. We found that effective advertisements produced considerable volume effects: a mean increase of 18 per cent in sales. Their impact emerged surprisingly fast, typically within six months, and often lasted for more than two years. But many of the long-held rules of thumb about television advertising are false, which suggests that it must be tested constantly to determine precisely what works.

We examined four different factors that tend to affect advertising: general brand and category conditions in the marketplace; the business strategies/objectives underlying the advertising; media usage (when and where commercials were shown); and copy-related measures. Our analysis was structured to allow us to isolate those factors that had an incremental impact on sales from all other factors. For example, our copy tests consisted of two groups of households that were exposed to adverts with different copy and equal weight, while our weight tests consisted of two cells with the same copy but different weight. ("Weight" in this context refers to the number and frequency of showings.) We analyzed new products separately from established products since each requires a different advertising strategy.

The fundamental question for us was why some advertising treatments affect sales and others do not. We examined changes in sales volume and in percentage of market share. We looked at particular brands that used television advertising over a one-year period, with sales measured each week. Our sample included frequently purchased, relatively low-priced consumer packaged goods.

Our findings are outlined below:

- It was easier for less well-established and smaller brands than for well-established brands to effect a change with increased weight. Among established products, less entrenched brands were more responsive.
- Standard flighted media plans (in which advertising is cycled "on" for some weeks and then "off") were relatively unlikely to increase sales. Changes in the media plan, with big increases rather than periodic flights may be more effective. Our work suggests that as category size and overall category purchase occasions increase, a new player will have more opportunities to capture sales. Advertising will then be more likely to influence switching behavior.
- Concentration of advertising appears to offer advantages over dispersion; this is particularly compelling for new products. It is important for sellers to advertise their products heavily early on to stimulate consumers to try them.
- Effects tended to be stronger when the advertising message was intended to change attitudes rather than reinforce them and also when the copy strategy had recently been changed. It is important to keep the message fresh in the minds of buyers. Our research suggests that the benefits of constant change are more likely to outweigh the risks. To justify television advertising, copy should change frequently and regularly. There is considerable danger in maintaining the status quo: it is how companies lull customers into boredom and complacency. This is critical for larger and more established brands.
- Brands in growing categories or in categories with more purchase opportunities are more likely to be able to improve sales through increased television advertising weight.
- In the case of established brands, we did not find a strong link between standard measures of television commercial recall and persuasion, and the sales impact of the copy in market. Our data suggest that it is more productive to test advertising in the market than to rely on pre-test measures of advertising recall or persuasion, or both.

New brands or line extensions tended to be more responsive to alternative television advertising plans than established products. Our data support the importance of introductory weight and prime time for new products: higher boosts in prime television advertising are correlated with larger increases in sales of new products.

Frito-Lay's experience

Frito-Lay, the US snack food manufacturer, put our findings to the test in its advertising for a single product category. The company wanted to develop guidelines for managing its television advertising and setting priorities for campaigns. Frito-Lay's experiments, carried out in the mid to late 1990s, used Behaviorscan to test the effectiveness of television advertising across brands. The basic design was an "ad/no-ad" split test in which each brand's advertising was tested in at least two markets over 12 months. Media plans for each brand were those previously approved by management during the annual planning cycle and were not modified during the year.

Households were assigned to "ad" or "no-ad" conditions by using a methodology that matched households according to a variety of purchasing characteristics, including category and brand penetration and purchasing rate. Once pairs were identified in each market, one member of each pair was assigned randomly to "ad" conditions and the other was assigned to "no-ad" conditions. For "no-ad" house-

holds, the brand's advertisements were replaced with public service advertisements. Cable, radio and outdoor advertising were not manipulated as part of the
experiment. These forms of advertising, however, represented only a small portion
of the marketing mix. Promotional activities were also not manipulated.

After four years of testing, the company found that 57 per cent of its commercials
resulted in significant volume increases in the advertising households compared to
the no-advertising households. Commercials were categorized as either "new" or
"base": "new" if their content included a significant innovation such as a line
extension, new brand or feature; "base" if they focused on existing brand attributes
of an established brand. Eighty-eight per cent of the "new" advertisements drove
significant volume increases.

The company found a big difference between the results obtained by larger
brands and those obtained by smaller brands. Among larger brands, only 27 per
cent showed significant volume increases as a result of the advertising, whereas the
figure was almost 90 per cent for the smaller brands. Simply put, it is harder to
turn a large ship around than a smaller; capturing attention for a product that is
well known is always problematic, even with advertising that is original, clever and
fresh. Frito-Lay discovered that if an advertisement had a positive effect, it was
virtually always noticeable within the first six months; indeed, in all but one case,
the effect was noticeable within the first three months. The company's other major
finding was that the average volume increase with effective advertisements was a
healthy 15 per cent.

For Frito-Lay, innovation and brand size are critical in differentiating effective
and ineffective advertising. The company also learned the importance of testing
"small" versus "big" brands without anything new in the message to determine
which advertisements work. On average, only 13 per cent of "big" brand television
advertising resulted in increased sales. But if that 13 per cent results in an average
increase of 15 per cent in gross revenues and an increase in overall margins, it may
well be worth the cost. For example, if we spend $9m on new advertising that
increases our sales 15 per cent from $300m, revenues will increase by $45m. If our
incremental gross margin is 40 per cent, we would generate $18m and net, after the
advertising expenditures, $9m. Testing several campaigns to find the most effective
one might be troublesome but would be worth $9m in gross profit.

One of the many lessons from Frito-Lay's experience is that once we have
determined which advertisement is most effective, there is likely to be a bonus in
the form of long-term impact. In a follow-on study, we found that if advertising
works in the short term, it will have a long-term impact that approximately doubles
the short-term impact. On the other hand, if television advertising does not work in
the short term, it will not work in the long term. The only way to know whether it
is working is to test constantly. Considering that an effective testing system costs a
few hundred thousand dollars, while advertisements can cost millions, the weight
is clearly in favor of building testing into television advertising strategies.

Frito-Lay gleaned three principles from its research:

- Advertise against some form of "news" for lesser brands.
- Advertising for larger brands is not likely to drive sales if it contains no "news."
- Advertising effects occur quickly and tend to last if they occur at all. Managers
  might want to rotate advertising support for key brands on the basis of the availability of news and according to brand performance in the previous year.

Test and test again

One important caveat is that the data from our initial study explain less than half of the sales changes associated with television advertising weight changes. But if managers are aware of this uncertainty, they can manage it. We found that 61 per cent of advertising was not responsive to weight changes. It would make sense to run tests to find out if the current campaign is working. If it is not, it is much easier to determine that changes need to be made. The manager should always be estimating the incremental effects of the current campaign in the real world.

The prudent manager should select certain "lead markets" for experimentation in which television advertising is reduced or eliminated. If there is no sales reduction in the lower-weight experimental market after six to twelve months, then the manager can feel confident about reducing the weight throughout the entire advertising market.

Testing can also benefit sales forces, which often point to their companies' large advertising budgets when trying to persuade retailers that consumer demand will justify more shelf space for their products. Quantitative test results can be used to win over doubting retailers.

There are many aspects of advertising's effectiveness with respect to sales that seem to be unique to a particular brand, competitive situation, copy strategy or media strategy. The key to success is constant testing. If you approach all of your advertising by questioning all assumptions, you will be that much more confident of how well it is working. Not all advertising will be effective but you may be able to modify Wanamaker's grumble and say, "I know that half of my advertising doesn't work, but at least I now know which half."

Summary

Billions of dollars are wasted every year on ineffective television advertising. Yet few companies monitor their advertising strategies with the precision with which they monitor other parts of the marketing mix. In this article, **Leonard Lodish** describes the results of research into the factors that make for successful television advertising. In many cases, sales of smaller, less well-established brands are more responsive to advertising than larger brands. But when advertising for large brands works, the rewards – in terms of increased sales and long-term impact – are considerable. Companies should therefore constantly test the effectiveness of their commercials in the market to gain the confidence that the benefits will outweigh the costs.

Suggested further reading

Lodish, L., Abraham, M., Kalmensen, S., Livelsberger, J., Lubetkin, B., Richardson, B. and Stevens, M. (1995) "How TV advertising works: a meta analysis of 389 real-world split-cable TV advertising experiments," *Journal of Marketing Research*, November.

Lodish, L. and Riskey, D. (1997) "Making ads profitable," *Marketing Research*, winter.

Choosing where to go global: how to prioritize markets

by Philip M. Parker

Imagine that your company is sitting on top of $3bn in cash and the board is asking you to invest it wisely. Your home market is near maturity. You can either put the money into a bank account or you can leverage your company's knowledge base and expand your core business into higher growth areas. This was the scenario for a European telecommunications company. Its choice? Go international, and quickly. But with over 230 countries to choose from, it became important to find a rational selection process that would be supported by the board.

The problem of national market selection is not unique to this company. Several factors have accelerated globalization: deregulation, the spread of democracy, information ubiquity, privatizations, the globalization of the value chain, improvements in infrastructure and the reduction of nationalistic entry barriers.

There are typically three phases involved in global strategic planning. First, the global environment is scanned and specific countries are prioritized. This phase not only considers the market potential for a country today but also its long-run latent demand, from which future sales will be generated. The second phase is typically more operational and involves detailed within-country analyses. The third phase involves designing optimal entry plans and monitoring approaches that can be rationalized on a regional or global basis. This article assists managers in the first phase.

Probably the most efficient way of prioritizing markets is to consider all countries on at least two key dimensions, which themselves are composites of multiple factors. Composite approaches have long been used by strategic planners. The biggest challenge in this approach is to choose the factors that are most relevant to international planners. The two measures of greatest relevance are "latent demand" and "market accessibility." Countries with high latent demand and high relative accessibility (that is, that are comparatively easy for your company to enter) are given highest priority. There is a continuum from high-priority countries to those that have low latent demand and low accessibility.

Figure 1 shows two different scenarios. In the left-hand graph, the company is driven by market potential whereas the right-hand graph represents a company that is driven by costs or an aversion to difficult markets. This article treats the reader as coming from a "generic company" – that is, neither a market-driven nor a cost-driven company. Planners must therefore augment it with their own company-specific factors that might change the priorities (for example, a Canadian company may judge Canada to be more accessible than a German company).

The globalization process

In order to understand latent demand, it is important to characterize the globalization process correctly. As shown in Figure 2 demand is often revealed in the aggregate by a global sales figure. This aggregate curve masks, however, two underlying and fundamentally different processes. The first is a country-by-country

Framework for prioritizing countries

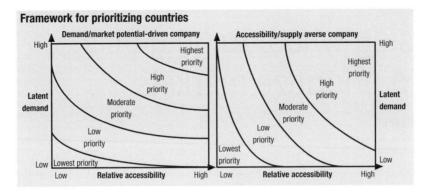

Figure 1

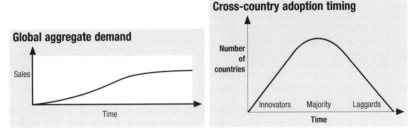

Figure 2   Figure 3

adoption process ("breadth of adoption"). The second process involves the within-country sales pattern after adoption ("depth of adoption"). The breadth process, shown in Figure 3, consists of the cumulative sequential adoption of a product or service across the world's countries. A few countries are the "innovators," followed by the "early adopters." The last countries to show any sales are the "laggards." Some countries may never adopt a product at all (snowmobiles in Jamaica).

Figure 4 shows the distinction between a "global product" and a "non-global product." The breadth process indicates where demand is likely to show up soonest. Across a number of products and services large, wealthy countries are generally innovators or early adopters and smaller, poor countries are laggards. For many

How a telco made its choice

At the beginning of this article, we met a European telecommunications company with $3bn to invest. So what did it decide to do? In its first cut, the company prioritized markets while subconsciously using the "per head" measure to indicate maturity. Licence hunters were dispatched to all corners of the earth: Vietnam, Ghana, Ireland, Hong Kong, Nepal, India, Hungary.

Resistance from the board to investments in the farther-flung markets quickly appeared. It turned out that when one controlled for the "target market" (the demand ceiling), both the home market and many neighboring countries were far from maturity, whereas many of the so-called emerging markets were about to "top out." Dividing by population turned out to be an absurd measure of penetration. Furthermore, the company had much higher levels of accessibility to neighboring markets than markets in Asia. Once all this was recognized, the licence-hunting group was disbanded and the company made greater investments in its home region.

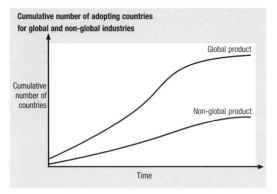

Figure 4

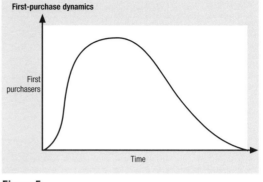

Figure 5

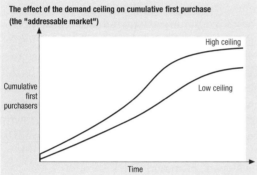

Figure 6

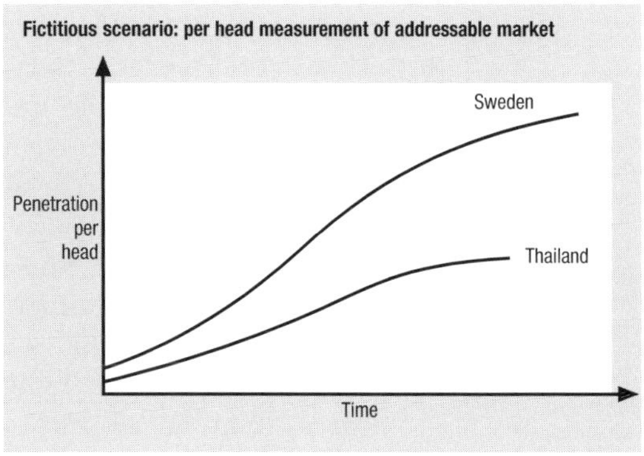

Figure 7

categories, the breadth process began over 100 years ago, while for more recent innovations, it is only now beginning.

Once a country shows initial sales, the second process becomes germane – the depth process. This tells the planner the level of sales within a country after it has adopted a product for the first time. It should be noted that an early-adopting country might have slow take-up, whereas a later country might have fast take-up. There is no general relationship between when a country adopts and how quickly sales take off thereafter.

To elaborate on this aspect of demand, it is best to decompose sales into two components: first purchases and repeat purchases. Figure 5 shows the first-purchase curve. As the product life cycle matures, a growing percentage of the market adopts the product for the first time. If this trial phase proves successful, repeat purchases follow; if not, the product dies.

Long-run demand

Long-run demand depends on two sub-factors. The first is the size of the country or social system. The second, shown in Figure 6, is the demand ceiling – the percentage of that market that is likely to adopt the product in the long run, or over the manager's planning horizon. Figures 7 and 8 make these components salient. Figure 7 shows a classic representation of demand for a fictitious category across Sweden and Thailand. Thailand has shown demand for three years and Sweden

19

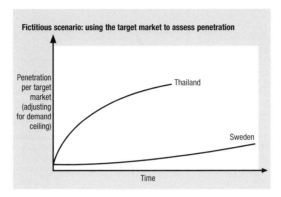

Figure 8

has shown demand for the past five years. Each country has been standardized by characterizing demand as "per head" penetration.

This type of measure is typical for the telecommunications industry, which buys and sells licences while quoting prices on a "per head" basis. This method of comparing demand across countries is often used in the popular business press too; the implication is that markets with high penetration will have lower growth in the future, whereas countries with low penetration will have higher growth.

Using this method, the graph shows Sweden as being more mature than Thailand. A global planner might conclude that the future "hot," high-growth market will be Thailand, whereas Sweden is a mature market, warranting little additional investment. Indeed, we observe in many industries a large shift in resources from "developed" to "under-developed" markets, right? Wrong!

Analyzing and comparing markets in this way can be deceptive. Planners must recognize that not all countries are created equal and that simple measures (such as penetration per head) ignore fundamental national differences. Clearly, not all persons in Thailand will, over the planning horizon, be part of the potential target market. For many categories, we can reasonably exclude young children and subsistence farming families, who are unlikely to have enough disposable income.

What latent demand is not

1 Latent demand is not a forecast of the market's sales level but rather of its long-run strategic potential. In countries where entry has occurred to its fullest and the market is served in a competitive setting, then latent demand will approach the present sales level. For many countries, a number of inefficiencies prevent this level from being realized. North Korea, for example, often has a high latent demand but political and economic policies have thus far prevented it from attaining this potential.

2 Latent demand is also not the sum of companies' sales in a given industry. Latent demand estimates often deviate from national estimates as these do not control for export sales by companies operating in that country. Latent demand reflects local consumption only. For example, if one adds up the sales of all American suppliers, this may exceed the latent demand estimate for the US. Some of these sales consolidate foreign operations, are sales to foreign entities, are exports or are re-exports. Latent demand is a "smoothed" estimate. It does not consider local demand bubbles that might appear from one year to the next due to a large order cycle.

3 Finally, latent demand is not company-specific. Total latent demand is estimated for all companies approaching a given country.

Estimating accessibility

Latent demand is only half the picture. A country may at first sight appear to be attractive due to a high latent demand but it is often less so when one considers how easy it will be to serve that potential. Accessibility will always vary from one company to another for a given country. As a minimum, the following four domains should be considered:

Demography (demand concentration)

Key demographic factors help managers gauge the extent to which a country's demand is concentrated. Demand concentration is the extent to which a country can be easily served as a whole rather than as smaller regions. Proxies for concentration include the number of large cities (having populations over 750,000) and the size of the largest city divided by the total population of the country. China, the US and Germany score low on this ratio and are typically considered to be especially difficult to cover (in terms of distribution and sales). Indeed, this handicap for China is forcing many companies to make market potential estimates by city and to reconsider China not as a country but as a region with many city-state clusters.

Economics (development and openness)

Economic factors tend to counterbalance low demand concentration. Countries with higher income levels tend to have better infrastructure and communications that allow dispersed demand to be served efficiently. Openness is the extent to which a market can be served by foreign companies. Generally, small countries lacking protectionist laws are very open to foreign entry. Larger countries with protectionist tendencies (such as Japan) are less open. Some countries have low explicit barriers yet buyers tend to favor local producers. In this case openness is low.

Culture (heterogeneity)

Culture often hinders marketing and operational entry strategies, especially in countries having heterogeneous cultures. Two proxies are noteworthy: the size of the largest language group and the size of the largest religious group (both relative to total population). In general, the larger these are, the easier it is to access the market.

Political structure (totalitarian, stable, fragmented)

Finally, political constraints can affect access. The fact that a company is American or French, for example, can play a large role in evaluating access into countries such as Iran. Concentration of political power may negatively influence entry, especially in the cases of totalitarian regimes that are less likely to adopt free market solutions. Numbers of political parties and the size of the largest power's representation in government are objective measures of this constraint.

The above factors, among many others specific to the company and industry in question, are then combined into an overall rating. Accessibility can be measured as being "company-specific" or as a generic concept independent of any particular company. Some companies (for example, French companies) can have higher levels of accessibility to certain countries (for example, in French-speaking Africa) due to historical factors. Measures provided for a generic company do not consider any specific advantage or disadvantage with respect to a national market that arises from a company's core competence. A company will always include these advantages in finalizing its estimates.

Finally, accessibility measures are difficult to predict. Political changes, especially, make accessibility assessments more likely to change than latent demand estimates, which are more strategic.

Both the size of the country/social system and the demand ceiling will vary over time and the demand ceiling will largely vary from one category/industry to another. The most important aspect of determining the demand ceiling is to "match" countries according to category/industry. In doing so, the planner may discover the graph in Figure 8. Thailand, when one excludes subsistence farmers, has nearly saturated its local potential, whereas Sweden (perhaps due to high taxes or poor marketing by a state monopoly) is far from its potential. This same principle exists for both industrial and consumer products and services. The benefit of adjusting for ceiling effects is that for some categories, small countries (for example, Belgium) may prove to have a greater latent potential than larger countries (for example, India) with ostensibly "hot" markets.

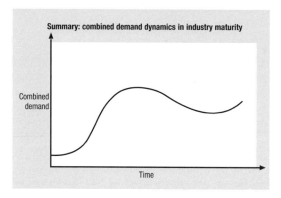

Figure 9

Once the social system and ceilings are defined and projected over the planning horizon, then the planner needs to consider the revenue stream that will result from each buyer. Combining first purchases with the stream of repeat purchases results in the aggregate product life-cycle curve for the industry. In the long run, a country's latent demand for a category or industry approaches a repeat purchase coefficient (which may vary across countries).

Provided that the coefficient is known and that social system size and ceiling have been estimated, long-term sales can be projected. At any moment, latent demand in a market is a product of these three factors; conversely, the repeat purchase coefficient is the average latent consumption rate per target consumer. As the category declines due to external shocks, the coefficient also declines.

The relationship between the factors is shown in Figure 9 and holds in maturity. Each is a function of a number of country factors. The critical question for the global planner is whether the consumption rate is converging over time across countries, or whether it is stationary in equilibrium (maturity), yet different across countries. In the consumer goods business, for example, the question might be whether adult alcohol consumption per head will converge from country to country.

Summary

When a company has the resources to enter foreign markets, how should it choose which ones to go for? According to **Philip Parker**, it must assess them along two key dimensions: latent demand and market accessibility. Latent demand is a function of the size of a country, the percentage of the population that is likely to adopt the product and likely rate of repeat purchasing. When markets are measured in these terms, it becomes clear that relatively "mature" markets in developed countries may have more potential than those in emerging economies – a result at odds with the crude "penetration per head" statistic that is often used to characterize markets. But even where latent demand is high, problems of accessibility – due to adverse demography, low economic development, cultural fragmentation or political constraints – can mean that it is not worth trying to tap it.

Do you value customer value?

by Sean Meehan and Patrick Barwise

" Market orientation" describes an organizational culture where beating the competition through the creation of superior customer value is the paramount objective throughout the business. By "customer value" we mean the customer's perception of the total benefits to be derived from a product or service versus the total perceived costs of acquisition and ownership. Although they usually have better things to think about, customers typically have some implicit preconception about the "right" ratio of benefits to costs. Having compared available alternatives, customers select the one that they think will give them best value. Value is therefore a *relative* concept; it is perceived *relative* to competitor offerings.

In a market-orientated company, the aim of providing superior customer value dominates all thinking about what its business is and which markets to serve with which products or services. It provides the rationale underpinning acquisitions and major capital investments. It drives thinking about which people to hire and how to deploy, reward and promote them.

In practice this level of absolute commitment to customers is rare; it is not to be confused with the vague mantra of "customer love" chanted with monotonous regularity in annual reports, at conferences and employee meetings. Neither is market orientation to be confused with "market*ing* orientation," which describes increased power vested in the marketing department. The marketing department is often seen as the natural champion of the customer but perception of it as an "owner" of organizational values can provoke resentment and downright opposition from other functions.

Marketing departments can play a pivotal role in making sense of marketplace dynamics and communicating them to the rest of the organization. But this does not elevate marketing to a role superior to other functions. The dominant organizational design in market-orientated businesses increasingly involves matrices dominated by customer value creation processes staffed by *multi*functional teams and supported by *all* the traditional functions.

Market sensing

A company's ability to create customer value depends first of all on its market sensing capabilities. These are its ability to understand customers' current and emerging needs and wants, competitors' capabilities, offerings and strategies, and the technological, social and demographic trends that are shaping the future market and competitive landscape. Organizations are increasingly using three main tools to improve understanding of how customers perceive value:

Market research and analysis

Esomar, the European Society for Opinion and Marketing Research, has estimated that between 1990 and 1996 company expenditure on externally commissioned market research worldwide virtually doubled to reach £7bn annually. Internal analysis of customer data (for example, from purchase records and loyalty programs) has grown even faster.

Daewoo and the art of customer focus

Daewoo entered the UK car market in spring 1995 with minimal brand recognition, a technically unimpressive product and an unfashionable country of origin (Korea). With around 40 marques the market was crowded. Less than half of these had market shares of over one per cent. Ford, Vauxhall and Rover accounted for half of all new cars sold. Good dealers were tied into exclusive relationships with established manufacturers. And many companies have a "Buy UK" or "Buy European" policy for their fleet purchases, which account for about half of all car purchases.

At the time of Daewoo's entry, no new entrant to the UK car market had broken through the elusive one per cent market share threshold since relevant data had been gathered (from the mid 1970s). Yet Daewoo did exactly that in less than a year. We believe it did so by achieving its aim of being the most customer-focused car company in the UK.

Daewoo's market sensing revealed that its best target market would be drivers primarily interested in a car's ability to get from A to B reliably and cheaply. Surveys had shown that most motorists found showrooms intimidating and salespeople pushy and believed that they were treated even worse after the sale. Further, Daewoo's research found that in its target segment, 84 per cent of motorists believed that the treatment they got from the salesman was at least as important as how they felt about the car itself.

Daewoo accordingly developed a customer value proposition with four linked pillars:

- **Direct dealing**: to save dealer commissions and to enable the company to be generous with the specifications offered.
- **Absence of hassle**: Daewoo designed its dealer network to be like a high street chain, with interactive terminals offering product information and a free café and crêche; sales people were on a fixed salary and no haggling was allowed on price.
- **Peace of mind**: the price included a three-year comprehensive warranty, three years full Automobile Association cover, three years free servicing, a six-year anti-corrosion warranty and a 30-day money-back guarantee.
- **Courtesy**: Daewoo offered free collection and delivery as well as a courtesy car during servicing.

Daewoo's competitors had been unwilling or unable to rethink the way that they did business in the face of clear dissatisfaction in the market. This created a market niche that Daewoo was able to exploit with its new customer value proposition. Subsequent product launches have enabled Daewoo to maintain its distinctive positioning while upgrading technically.

Senior executive customer contact programs

For senior executives to get out of their offices and meet customers directly has long been perceived as best practice among large companies in the business-to-business sector. Now it is also common to find top managers of consumer goods and services companies spending time with end-users and hearing about their own and their competitors' performance. The best programs bring senior executives from all functions into contact with both major customers and end-users in a formal business setting, not socially.

Competitor monitoring

We group competitor monitoring into three levels of increasing sophistication: tracking and profiling, interpreting and predicting.

Tracking and profiling competitors is not unusual; for example, it is often part of the marketing director's quarterly or annual report. Even basic descriptive data focusing on size, scope, changes in product line, big wins and so on can reveal trends and patterns if summarized intelligently.

Interpretation involves managers in explicit consideration of what has happened and why. Companies often move to this second-order analysis when they are unexpectedly beaten over a critical order or faced with an attractive new product or process innovation. They then move on from what the competitor is doing to broader analysis. For example, they encourage those in the market to monitor and feed back evidence of unexpected or idiosyncratic competitor activity. They dissect competitors' advertising activity (both creative and media choices) to deduce the underlying strategy. Like armies at war, companies use aerial photography and public planning documents to gather details of their main competitor's plant; they monitor traffic movement to provide insight into factory shift patterns; their scientists map the competitor's product formulations. Together with more readily available secondary data, this helps the company better understand the competitor's business model, capabilities and even its "game plan."

Prediction is the aim of the most sophisticated practitioners. At US consultancy Advanced Competitive Strategies, for example, cross-functional teams from client companies role-play competitors and, aided by computerized models of the market, simulate the likely actions and reactions of the key players. These "war colleges" heighten managers' market sensitivity, forcing them to make explicit and justify their assumptions about competitors' competencies, resources and intent.

Enhancing performance

Without good market sensing, a company cannot be market-orientated. But market sensing alone is not enough. Under the auspices of the Marketing Science Institute in Cambridge, Massachusetts, a growing body of research suggests that a more informed and more widely shared mental model of the marketplace simply provides the *potential* for customer value creation and superior business performance. It is important, therefore, to distinguish truly market-orientated companies from those that establish market-sensing processes only because they are fashionable or perceived as best practice.

George Day, professor of marketing at the Wharton School, identifies four "interwoven dimensions" that facilitate market focus: values, market sensing and customer linking, strategic thinking processes and aligned structures and systems (*see* Figure 1). Collectively these provide the basis for customer value creation.

Management's value system has a powerful effect on the ability of the other three dimensions to create superior customer value. The hallmarks of a market-orientated value system are flexibility, risk tolerance, entrepreneurship and the adoption of an external frame of reference. Our investigations in over 400 UK companies show that companies with such a value system tend to enjoy better competitive performance because they embrace customer value creation as the motivation for *everything* they do. Our studies show that market

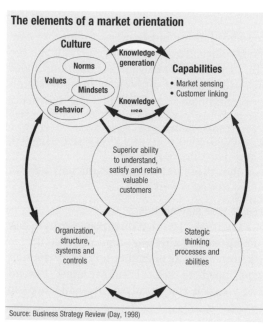

The elements of a market orientation

Culture
Norms
Values
Mindsets
Behavior

Knowledge generation

Knowledge use

Capabilities
• Market sensing
• Customer linking

Superior ability to understand, satisfy and retain valuable customers

Organization, structure, systems and controls

Stategic thinking processes and abilities

Source: Business Strategy Review (Day, 1998)

Figure 1

sensing activities are one of the most important levers for translating the value system into competitive advantage.

Another capability described by Day is customer linking. In the case of business-to-business services, most leading consulting firms identify key client service personnel to work in integrated client/customer teams. Among "capital goods" companies, best practice is to install hardware (at low or no cost to the customer) on customer sites and earn a return from its successful operation. The aim is to reduce systems costs and share with the customer the new value created.

The strategic thinking processes of a market-orientated company are distinguished by external orientation, accurate market knowledge enriched by customer contact experience and a passionate desire to beat the competition. The CEO takes an active role and involves many constituencies within the company. Moreover, the "process" is continuous and dynamic – not an annual event. Sceptics may claim that being market orientated simply means giving the customer more for less but the truth is more complex. Market-orientated businesses know which customers value their offerings and which do not. The latter are value destroyers for the business – and for other customers. Market-orientated businesses often need to prune their customer base to rid themselves of these value destroyers.

Challenges for managers

What is the engine driving your business?

Do you really believe that the ultimate driver of success is your ability to create superior customer value? If not, what is? Take out a flip chart and map the business process. Share your assumptions about what really matters with your colleagues. Work on the dissidents and don't worry too much about the other guidelines until this is resolved.

Do you understand the dynamics shaping your customers' perception of the relative importance of specific benefits and costs?

Make full use of market sensing and customer linking mechanisms to improve continuously your understanding of the marketplace. This will help you challenge the current thinking in your organization. In particular, make your assumptions about customers and competitors explicit. This will bring out differences in understanding that need to be resolved if you are to maximize your capability for delivering value. Consider:

- whether you are leveraging every contact you, your staff and your suppliers have with both customers and competitors as a learning opportunity
- how you use this resource. Do you channel these data and continuously update your view of the marketplace? Do you share this widely?

Will you rejuvenate your business system to serve your market better?

Success breeds imitation and erosion of advantage. The usual response is to tweak your business model, for example by using essentially the same architecture to achieve marginally faster response times, fewer rejects or higher labour productivity. This may be insufficient. You may need to seek breakthroughs beyond continuous improvement – to demand of yourself the standards it would take to enter the market today.

Are you prepared to lead by example?

You cannot conjure up or manufacture a company's culture but you can champion values and beliefs. For example, Sir Colin (now Lord) Marshall's drum-beating on the theme of "customer first" had a remarkable impact on British Airways just after its privatization.

Summary

Market orientation lies at the heart of marketing and business success. A market-orientated company is motivated in all its activities by the aim of creating customer value. To achieve this, say **Sean Meehan** and **Patrick Barwise**, a company must be able to do two things. First, it needs to sense what is happening in the market. The most popular tools for this are market research, contact between executives and customers and close monitoring of competitors. But second, a company must have an organizational culture that embraces flexibility and entrepreneurship if it is to convert this knowledge into enhanced performance.

How does marketing measure up?

by Tim Ambler and Flora Kokkinaki

Marketing professionals are not highly rated by their UK colleagues. In fact, according to research by Chris Radford of Synesis, other departments regard marketing as only half as good as themselves in terms of strategic thinking, creative problem solving and doing things well. But how do people arrive at such conclusions – how do they measure marketing? The present authors recently undertook research into current practice in assessing marketing effectiveness. We surveyed 531 senior marketers and finance officers using a questionnaire based on information gathered in 44 earlier interviews. So are these managers satisfied with the way the effectiveness of marketing is measured? The survey shows that marketers are slightly on the negative side (a mean of 3.97 on a 7-point scale) whereas their finance colleagues are slightly more satisfied (mean 4.28), probably because financial measures still dominate.

This article looks at some of the factors behind these ratings, in particular: the improvements that people would like to see in current measurement practice; the measures that are currently used; benchmarking; and the definition of the "marketing asset" ("brand equity").

Improvements sought

Our interviews with senior marketers and finance executives from the same companies did not show the significant divisions of opinion the cynical might have expected. In fact, the reverse was true. Both marketers and accountants welcomed one another's skills and saw themselves as sharing difficulties. The improvements both wanted were (in order of frequency of mention): more details about campaign, launch and promotions performance; faster and more regular data; predictiveness and modeling; more financial data (mostly from finance respondents); better customer information. The main difference was that accountants favored financial, internal performance measures, while marketers wanted non-financial, market measures, such as customer satisfaction. Marketing performance is assessed against plenty of measures but they are excessively weighted to internal financial figures.

In their book *Marketing Accountability: Improving Business Performance* (1997), Robert Shaw, visiting professor at Cranfield Business School, and fellow author Laura Mazur suggest that non-marketing executives' dissatisfaction with marketing arises because marketers often see measurement as a support role and accordingly outsource it to the finance department, which is left to do the job as best it can.

Yet marketers are right to put the achievement of results before the measurement of them. Making the runs matters more than adding them up. Even so, they are responsible for ensuring that marketing performance is properly evaluated. Unless they organize evaluations in line with their own marketing philosophy, they can expect to be judged less favorably by those using other criteria. Furthermore, their credibility – and the credibility of marketing as a whole – will be eroded. Marketers need to be clearer about what exactly they are trying to achieve, and to improve their presentation of the goals they reach.

Current measures

How marketing is perceived affects how it should be measured. So far, we have presented marketing as it is mostly seen by the respondents to our survey: a separate department within the company. In fact marketing is perceived in two distinct ways. "Marketing" includes both the broad sense of a company's efforts to succeed in the marketplace ("pan-company marketing") and the narrower sense of what a marketing department does. Most respondents were unable to distinguish overall business from specifically marketing objectives.

During the interviews, respondents were asked: "What measures does your firm use to track marketing, in the broad sense we are using here, performance?" The responses fell into the eight categories in the first column of Table 1, which shows the total number of measures reported in the interviews. The last two columns divide the totals by the number of respondents to provide comparability. We used these categories to develop the survey questionnaire, although we excluded

Key measures for assessing marketing performance
Based on total number of measures mentioned

	Marketers (26 interviewed)	Finance (18 interviewed)	Marketers (mean)	Finance (mean)
Financial	71	48	2.70	2.67
Consumer/end-user	50	17	1.90	0.94
Campaign effectiveness	17	3	0.65	0.17
Competitor (share)	19	13	0.73	0.72
Direct trade customer	9	2	0.37	0.11
Product performance and logistics	9	6	0.37	0.33
Employee attitudes	2	1	0.08	0.04
Econometric models	2	–	0.08	–
	179	90	6.88	4.98

Source: LBS

Table 1

Mean importance of measures for senior management
(7-point scale)

Financial	**6.51**	
Direct trade customer	**5.53**	
Consumer intermediate	**5.42**	
Competitor	**5.42**	
Consumer behaviour	**5.38**	
Innovation	**5.04**	

531 senior marketers and finance officers were asked to rate the importance that senior management attaches to different measures of marketing effectiveness
Source: LBS

Table 2

econometric models, which are a methodology rather than a measure as such. We also ruled out employee attitudes and internal measures such as production line performance, which lie on the border between marketing and general business performance.

Regarding "campaign effectiveness," we did not concern ourselves with whether the performance assessment period was a quarter, half or full year or whatever length of time the campaign took. Therefore we decided that "campaign effectiveness" muddled the time period with the metrics – the importance managers would assign to it would be likely to increase with the length of the interval under consideration – so it had to be dropped.

We decided to divide consumer/end user measures into two groups: "behavioral," such as purchases, market share and prices paid; and "intermediate" (psychological), such as awareness, attitudes and satisfaction. The resulting groups of measures form the first column of Table 2. The second column shows how frequently senior management uses these measures, according to the marketers and finance officers surveyed.

It appears that companies are preoccupied with financial measures of their marketing performance, relative to customer or competitor measures. This is fine for the assessment of business, but not for the assessment of *marketing* performance, which requires much more attention to customers. Nevertheless, there is growing interest in, and use of, customer measures, notably customer satisfaction. (See, for example, *Marketing News'* special issue on customer satisfaction measurement, October 27, 1997.) More sophisticated firms start there but recognize that satisfaction is not a reliable measure on its own. Instead, a battery of measures is needed.

Benchmarking

Success is always relative rather than absolute. Assessment requires internal and external comparison. Among our initial interviewees, a budgeted plan was overwhelmingly the dominant benchmark. For 12 respondents (27 per cent) beating the plan was "all that matters" and for 29 (66 per cent) it was a "big part." Consistent with that, the plan represents all or most marketing activity (22 per cent and 56 per cent of respondents respectively).

Companies mostly used a combination of systems for creating plans and marketing budgets (*see* Table 3). The most popular methodology was "task-based."

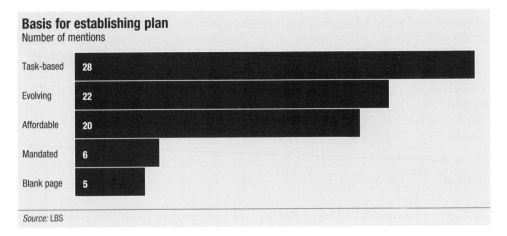

Basis for establishing plan
Number of mentions

Task-based	28
Evolving	22
Affordable	20
Mandated	6
Blank page	5

Source: LBS

Table 3

Here the marketing activities required to meet objectives are built bottom-up and then costed. There is a general movement away from "evolving" – adapting last year's plan in a Darwinian fashion – towards task-based planning. Senior management usually adjusts the "final" expenditure budget numbers. We do not know the direction of the adjustment but suspect that it is usually downwards in order to improve the immediate profit by reducing marketing investment. "Mandated" refers to a marketing budget determined by contract or third parties. "Blank page" refers to a budget calculated or modeled on a discounted cash flow. This is the theoretical zero-based approach where all items of expenditure have to be financially justified.

The "marketing asset"

There is no agreed definition of the term "brand" in the academic literature. Some authors include the underlying product(s) as part of "the brand," some do not and some switch without warning between these definitions. But it matters greatly to the valuation of a brand such as Smirnoff whether the profit stream should be inclusive or be limited to the incremental profit attributable to the branding over and above the profit that Diageo (the brand owner) makes on the vodka. There is still less agreement over the marketing asset that some companies call "brand equity" and others "reputation," "brand strength," "brand health," or "corporate identity."

The marketing asset is essential for evaluating marketing performance for a very simple reason: marketing activities in one financial period show up on the bottom line in other periods. To account – in the broad sense – for this we have to assess the state of the marketing asset at the beginning and end of each period. We can represent this by saying that marketing performance equals short-term results adjusted by the change in brand equity.

If the intended performance is to increase profits, then "short-term results" means sales less costs. This is why so many companies are seeking to put a financial value on their brands. The performance equation could then be expressed entirely in money terms. However, there are reservations about the use of brand valuation as a proxy for brand equity:

Frequency of terms used to describe the marketing asset
Where a term is specified; 331 respondents reported using one

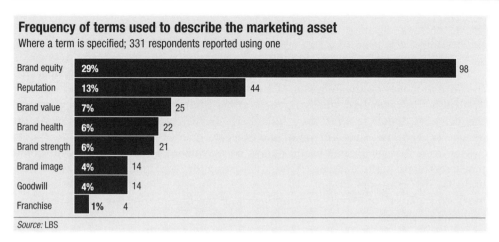

Source: LBS

Table 4

- A single number to indicate the health of anything is a poor representation of reality.
- The process of brand valuation leads to robust but not exact measures. They are suitable for purchase, sale and balance sheets but insensitive to month-to-month marketing activities. Furthermore their variability is due more to external factors such as interest rates than to marketing activities.
- Various methods of brand valuation have been developed but all are technically flawed in one or more ways. The most popular involves discounted cash flows. This treats present money values correctly but also takes into *today's* account *tomorrow's* marketing activities.

We conclude that brand valuation is a useful component of brand equity measurement but no more than that. A company should give considerable thought to how many and which measures are necessary to track brand health. These should be sensitive and predictive. In practice, measures are being collected but they are not usually perceived as being part of a brand equity whole. Thirty-eight per cent of the companies in the survey do not use a term to describe their marketing asset. Table 4 shows the most common terms. Percentages have been calculated against the 331 respondents using a term; terms used by less than one per cent of respondents have been excluded and some respondents did not specify their term. As some companies use more than one term, non-users and users sum to more than 100 per cent.

In addition, advertising agencies that have come to recognize the importance of the marketing asset are seeking to differentiate their offerings by inventing new terms. The London consultancy Brandhouse uses "Brand Soul." Young & Rubicam has registered "BrandAsset" and Leo Burnett has trademarked "Consumer Brand Equity" as the financial value of the consumer part of that asset. Quite apart from the unhelpfulness of seeking ownership of the language, these agencies are adding confusion. The asset is not the same as the valuation of that asset. The agencies' differential advantage is clear but it does not assist marketers' need for shared language, not least with non-specialists. We propose that "brand equity" should become the generic term for the unrealized asset created by marketing and not yet converted into the company's performance as profits.

Conclusion

If marketers are unclear about how marketing performance should be judged, others will apply their own standards. This explains the recent trend towards brand valuation and attempts to measure marketing in purely financial terms. But the faith in money as the language of business undermines confidence in an activity that cannot be measured wholly in such terms. Perhaps techniques will evolve but the evidence today is that they fall short. Brand valuation methodologies, in particular, are flawed both in detail and concept.

However, it is good that brand equity measurement is being addressed. Some marketers will judge internal brand valuation by the amount by which their budgets are increased or not. To misquote Stephen Leacock, the function of a marketing plan is to arrest the intelligence of the finance director long enough to take money off him.

Marketers therefore face a choice: pursue the financial route and fall short or persuade colleagues to use a wider portfolio of measures. This is not a challenge to modern shareholder value and economic value-added methods but an alarm call to marketers to have confidence in best-practice non-financial measures as well – and to "sell" them to their colleagues.

Summary

Like any business function, marketing needs to be measured. So what measures do people use? Research by **Tim Ambler** and **Flora Kokkinaki** indicates that – perhaps unsurprisingly – senior managers prefer financial indicators. If marketers would prefer more stress on indicators such as customer satisfaction, they must be prepared to promote their use.

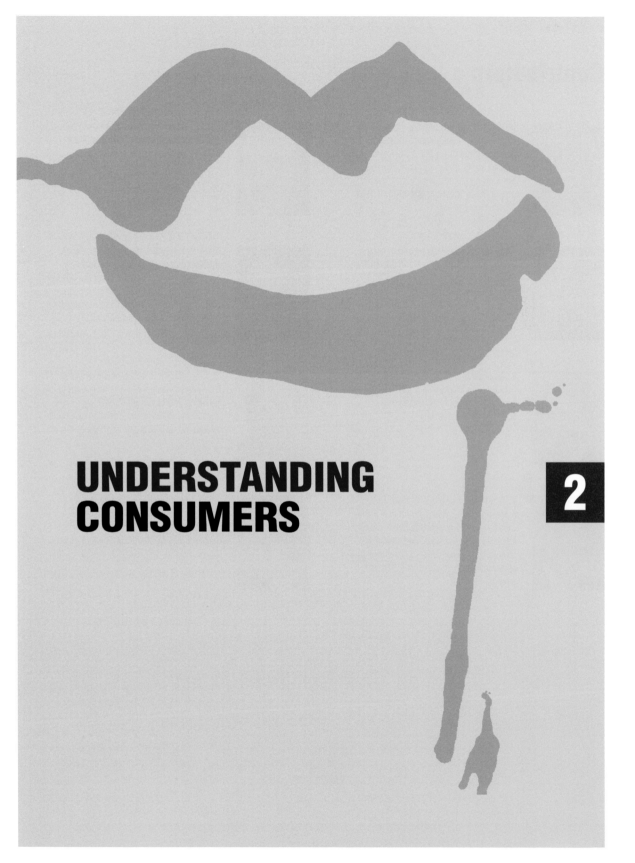

UNDERSTANDING CONSUMERS

2

Contributors

Hellmut Schütte is affiliate professor of international management at INSEAD. He has spent half of his life in Asia, both as an executive and as an academic. His new book on consumer behavior in Asia was published by Macmillan in autumn 1998.

Paul E. Green is professor of marketing and S.S. Kresge Professor Emeritus at the Wharton School of the University of Pennsylvania. His research interests include marketing research and optimal product design.

Alice M. Tybout is the Harold T. Martin Professor of Marketing at the J.L. Kellogg Graduate School of Management, Northwestern University.

Abba M.Krieger is the Robert Steinberg Professor of Statistics, Information Management, and Marketing at the Wharton School of the University of Pennsylvania. His research interests include marketing research and applied probability.

Brian Sternthal is the General Foods Professor of Marketing at the J.L. Kellogg Graduate School of Management, Northwestern University.

N. Craig Smith is an associate professor at Georgetown University Business School and a visiting professor at INSEAD. He specializes in marketing management, with a focus on business and marketing ethics.

J. Scott Armstrong is professor of marketing at the Wharton School of the University of Pennsylvania. His research interests include forecasting methods, strategic planning, research methods and communication, and expert systems for advertising copy.

Jill G. Klein is an assistant professor at INSEAD. She specializes in marketing management, with a focus on consumer decision making in international markets.

Contents

Introduction

Building a better mousetrap is only half the story; the company that does so must also ensure that people will want to buy it. It must be able to understand how consumers behave and position the product accordingly. This module looks at the elements of successful positioning – that is, aligning a product with a particular product category yet differentiating it from other members of that category – and at ways of analyzing customer segments and forecasting consumer response. It also includes a detailed analysis of the differences between Asian and Western consumers and discusses some of the ethical issues in marketing and consumer research.

Asian culture and the global consumer

by Hellmut Schütte

In recent decades, Asia has been home to many of the world's most dynamic markets. The region contains about 50 per cent of the world's population and, despite the recent economic crisis, represents a significant portion of the world's economy. For this reason few international companies can afford to ignore Asia as a market of primary importance, despite the present crisis in parts of the region. Yet there is a surprising paucity of work that establishes a marketing theory specific to Asia. Most practitioners apply marketing concepts in the region developed from a distinctly Western (and primarily US) perspective.

The underlying assumption is that consumers around the world are driven by similar needs and desires, and that consumer behavior is universal. This thinking is very much in line with the trend towards global markets and global competition. However, as consumer behavior is strongly influenced by culture and Asian culture is distinctly different from Western culture, one may doubt whether many global consumers can be found in Asia. Cultural bonds run deep and different tastes, habits and customs prevent consumers from universally preferring the same product attributes, advertising messages, packaging and presentation.

The advent of the global product, one has to remember, is not the result of consumers' preferences for products available worldwide. Global products are being *pushed* upon consumers as companies try to capture savings through standardization, rather than *pulled* by them.

The immense popularity of Western luxury goods among high-income earners and teenagers in Asia is therefore not proof that they have joined the global bandwagon. They may try the same goods but for different reasons. Brand-name goods such as a Louis Vuitton bag may be bought more for "face" reasons and the importance of the regard of others than from an individual preference for the product. Remy Martin cognac and Lafitte red wine may not be consumed because consumers really prefer it over local liquor or beer but because of peer pressure.

Strong market positions can therefore be built on foundations different from those in the West and requiring different marketing activities. In other words, an approach especially geared towards an Asian culture may be less efficient in terms of standardization and globalization but more efficient in terms of creating value for the consumers and, thus, in earning higher returns.

Asian culture

Culture has a profound impact on how individuals perceive who they are, what they are allowed to do and what their role is as a member of society. These perceptions are often so thoroughly internalized that they are difficult to express explicitly but they are revealed through behavior such as consumption. This is one means through which individuals express who they perceive themselves to be and who they aspire to be.

Although Asia is culturally more heterogeneous than, for example, Europe, the emphasis on social harmony is an overriding and unifying belief across all societies. Asian societies are fundamentally collectivist, meaning that the rights of the individual are subordinated to those of the group. This is considered necessary in order not to disturb social harmony. Such thinking, grounded in Confucianism, Buddhism and Islam, contrasts sharply with Western individualism. The difference is profound and has major implications for consumer behavior. While Asians tend to identify themselves in terms of their social frame or relationships, Westerners define themselves in terms of personal attributes or achievements.

Of course, all societies were traditionally more collectivist than individualist due to the interdependence characteristic of agrarian communities. Individualism has come to be considered a natural component of a "modern" society. However, Asian cultures are now challenging this assumption. Japan, a "modern," first-world nation by any standard, is still strongly collectivist. South Korea, Hong Kong, Singapore, and Taiwan, too, are all thoroughly modern societies that continue to have firmly entrenched collectivist orientations.

Collectivism in Asia expresses itself in a number of ways, some of which are described below.

Belongingness

Much emphasis is placed on belonging to a group, which implies an individual's identification with a collective goal. There is strong concern about acceptance by peers, anxiety about exclusion and a near compulsion to be always among the in-group. Thus, individual desires are secondary to those of the group, since belonging is the ultimate satisfaction. This strong sense of belongingness is an anchor for self-identity, which in turn demands the individual's loyalty to the group.

Reciprocity

The rules concerning reciprocity and the ways in which it is conceived tend to be far more formalized and binding than in the West. They reflect the importance placed upon relationships and social ties in a collectivist culture and acknowledge the embeddedness of individuals in groups. Gift-giving is seen as the most immediate and tangible means of cultivating *guanxi* (in Chinese cultures), or fulfilling *on* or discharging *giri* (in Japan). Whether or how well a person observes the intricate etiquette of gift-giving is essential to assessing that person's social character.

Self-esteem

Cultural differences also appear in self-appraisal of one's expertise or lack thereof and self-esteem can be correspondingly high or low. Education in the US, in particular, tries to instil in students a sense of high self-esteem in order to motivate them to achievement and self-confidence. Children are encouraged to be assertive and self-assured. Asian children, on the other hand, are taught the values of modesty and self-effacement, which are considered conducive to cultivation of the mind. This is not to say that Asians lack self-respect, rather that they do not assume that they automatically deserve to regard themselves with esteem in comparison with others.

Group conformity

Stronger pressure is placed upon the individual in Asia to conform to group norms than in individualist societies. The desire to be different, an essential element in Western culture and consumer behavior, exists in Asia too. However, it implies being different as a member of a group in comparison with other groups, while complying with the norms of the individual's group. An Asian consumer who deviates from the group norm may be treated as an outsider who does not know how to adjust to the group.

Status

Within the context of typically highly hierarchical Asian societies, individuals are always conscious of their place in a group, institution or society as a whole and of the proper behavior, dress and speech corresponding to status. They are also extremely aware of the need to maintain their own dignity, or face, and that of others.

Careful attention is given to purchasing products whose price, brand and packaging match one's social standing. In terms of personal appearance, the color, material and style of clothing should match an individual's status, which is defined by age, gender, occupation and so on. In Japan, for example, a married woman's kimono is much more subdued in color than a single woman's.

Product diffusion

In most Asian cultures uncertainty is strongly avoided, resulting in consumer behavior exhibiting high brand-name consciousness, brand loyalty, greater insistence on quality, and the active use of reference groups and opinion leaders. Shopping tends to be done in groups and new products are more slowly accepted. While consumers worldwide are concerned about monetary, functional, physical, psychological and social risks, Asians tend to be more sensitive to social risk than Westerners.

In traditional Western diffusion theory, consumers are categorized in relation to others by their speed in adopting a new product. The five categories often cited are: innovators, early adopters, early majority, late majority and laggards. These categories are generally depicted as a symmetrical, bell-shaped distribution curve (*see* Figure 1). Very few Asian consumers, however, are prepared to take the social risk of being innovators by trying a new product first. The discomfort of being left behind, however, induces them to follow suit if they think that others have tried it. Trials by early buyers thus soften the perceived risk for followers, who are then inclined to "jump aboard" hastily.

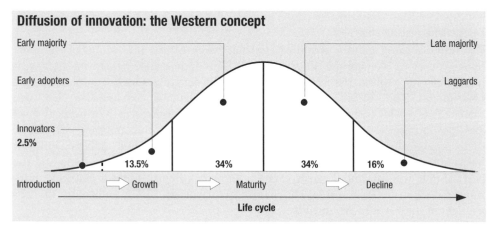

Figure 1

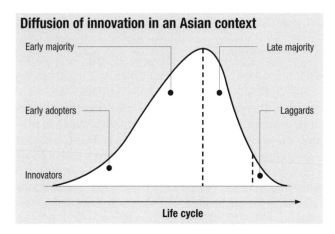

Figure 2

This suggests that the percentage of both innovators and laggards is much lower among Asian consumers, resulting in a steeper distribution curve (*see* Figure 2). The curve will also no longer be symmetrical, as it is thought to be in the West: the left tail will be longer, reflecting hesitancy to try the new product, and the right tail will drop off sharply, as consumers are ready to switch brand once the standards of their reference group change. Referral is thus a very powerful way of expanding product trials by the first wave of consumers.

Faddism

Instilled from childhood, reinforced by the educational system and solidified by peer pressure, the desire to conform is the engine behind faddism in Asia. Once risk-aversion is overcome, the speed of diffusion is dramatic, particularly in Japan, where product life-cycles can be extremely short. Faddism in Japan is facilitated by a homogeneous population and an efficient, widespread and centralized mass media. Everyone seems to be reading, watching, talking about or doing the same thing at any one time. Faddism covers not only the rapid diffusion of material culture or gadgetry such as the world-famous *tamagotchi* (an electronic pet). It also includes modes of behavior, including vocabulary. New words, typically a mix of Japanese and English, seem to be born overnight and spoken by everyone the next day.

Conspicuous consumption

The importance of gaining social recognition turns Asians into probably the most image-conscious consumers in the world. The importance of status makes it imperative to project the "right" image, which usually means up-market and prestigious. The social acceptability of conspicuous consumption in Asia corresponds with the high regard for hierarchy. Differences in hierarchical level and power are expected to be visible. Conspicuous consumption, therefore, corresponds directly with status propriety. Status-conscious Asians will not hesitate to spend freely on premium brands such as BMW, Mercedes-Benz and the best Scotch whisky and French cognac. Mercedes-Benz's highest market share worldwide is in Asian markets. The French luxury group LVMH sells more than 50 per cent of its wares to Asian consumers.

Times have changed with the economic troubles in Japan since the beginning of the 1990s and in many other parts of Asia since autumn 1997. It should not be

Maslow's hierarchy of needs and the Asian equivalent

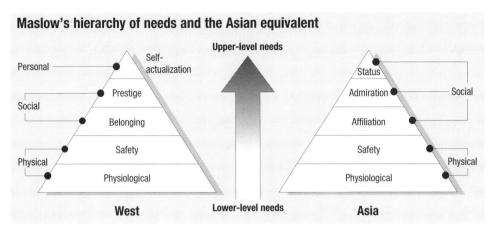

Figure 3

presumed, however, that brands have lost their lustre for the Asian consumer. The need for recognition is deep seated. Experience in Japan has proved, and reports from south-east Asia indicate, that demand for luxury products is not disappearing, although it is becoming far more selective.

Motivation and needs

Comparing some of the distinctive features of Asian culture with those in cultures of the West, we are better able to understand the motives behind consumption decisions. The two most important questions to answer are:

- *what* are the needs consumers are seeking to meet?
- *why* do they choose to meet them in the way they do?

Years ago the psychologist Abraham Maslow proposed his five-tiered "hierarchy of needs," a means of understanding motivation that has gained general acceptance. Each level of the hierarchy specifies a certain type of need, ranked in order of importance from lower- to higher-level needs: from physiological needs to safety, belonging, prestige and, ultimately, self-actualization (*see* Figure 3).

This hierarchy, although originally proposed as a means of understanding personal growth, is also an appropriate way of explaining the needs and motivations of consumers. The lowest level at which an individual experiences an as yet unsatisfied need serves to motivate the individual's behavior. Upon satisfaction of that need, a still higher need will emerge, again motivating the consumer to fulfill it. As no need is ever completely satisfied, dissatisfaction continuously creates new demands.

Maslow's hierarchy seems particularly suited to Western culture, especially with regard to his description of self-actualization as the highest category of need. In the case of the Asian consumer, however, we must question the definition of and even the very existence of such needs. As Asians, like everyone else, must first be fed and then protected in order to survive, changes are not required as far as physical needs are concerned. However, it is debatable whether self-actualization as a personally directed need actually exists for the Asian consumer. Rather, it may be a socially directed need reflecting a desire to enhance one's image and position through contributions to society.

Among the collectivist cultures of Asia, the idea that personal needs are the highest level of need would be neither readily accepted nor positively regarded by others. Indeed, the emphasis on achieving independence, autonomy and freedom characteristic of Western cultures is strikingly absent from Asian cultures. In the Asian context, the highest level of satisfaction is not derived from actions directed at the self but from the reactions of others to the individual. Therefore, a more accurate hierarchy of needs in the Asian context is one that eliminates the personally directed self-actualization need and instead emphasizes the intricacies and importance of social needs. The social needs of belonging and prestige can in fact be broken down into three levels: affiliation, admiration and status.

Affiliation is the acceptance of an individual as a member of a group. In the family this acceptance is automatic but in most other groups certain qualifications must be met in order to join. In terms of consumer behavior, the affiliation need will encourage conformity with group norms.

Once affiliation has been attained, the individual will desire the **admiration** of those in the group. This is a higher-level need and requires effort, as admiration must typically be earned through acts that demand the respect of others.

Next the individual will want the **status** arising from the esteem of society at large. Fulfillment of this need requires the regard of outsiders, whereas fulfillment of the admiration need occurs on a more intimate level. The status level most closely resembles the Western need for prestige and manifests itself in conspicuous consumption.

Modernization or Westernization?

At present, talk of a "global consumer culture" in which people are united by common devotion to certain brands, movie stars and musical celebrities, is generally understood to mean the global presence of Western culture. Western companies marketing products in Asia may be tempted to believe that, given time, consumers in Asia will become more like Western consumers. Therefore, if we were to wait long enough, marketing strategies developed in the West would be perfectly appropriate to the Asian consumer. This may be a fallacy or wishful thinking on the part of marketing gurus.

What Asian countries are experiencing is not "Westernization" or even "globalization" but "modernization." Modernization may be interpreted as Westernization because it is a social change initiated by the West. True Westernization, however, would assume that non-Western countries will become like the West. This cannot be the case because Asia prior to modernization had its own deeply rooted cultures, which continue strongly to influence people's upbringing and behavior. As Asians themselves would argue, a century of modernization cannot erase millennia of cultural development.

The high level of consumption of Western goods is typically used as an argument for the loss of Asian culture in favor of Westernization. That consumption is so visible, however, is testimony to the fact that it is not the norm but the exception. Even with the fame of McDonald's and Domino's pizza in Asia, 98 per cent of all restaurants in Asia serve indigenous food. In Indonesia, the advent of *teh botol* (bottled tea) has been to the detriment of sales of Coke and Pepsi and consumption of *kretek* clove cigarettes has not declined in the least due to the success of the Marlboro man. There may not be so many "global consumers" in Asia after all.

Summary

Asia is a crucially important market for international companies. But what sort of marketing strategy should be applied to it? Does conspicuous consumption of Western goods there indicate the presence of "global consumers," for whom Western strategies are appropriate? According to **Hellmut Schütte**, the answer is "no": despite globalization, regional culture remains the strongest influence on consumer behavior. Whereas Western consumers are motivated by a desire for individual expression, Asian consumers tend to seek status within a social group. The author details the ways in which this difference manifests itself and argues that marketers who do not recognise its strength are guilty of wishful thinking.

Connecting with consumers: the Four Ds of effective positioning

by Alice M. Tybout and Brian Sternthal

During the 1990s, a variety of hand-held electronic devices were introduced in response to the observation that consumers had more information to manage than ever before and less time to manage it.

First among these was Apple's Newton, a notepad and organizer with the distinctive feature of handwriting recognition, which meant that jotted notes could be stored digitally. Newton's sales were disappointing, an outcome attributed to the poor performance of the character recognition function rather than to the lack of market opportunity.

Undaunted by Newton's limited sales, numerous companies launched similar products. One was Motorola's Envoy, which was introduced in 1994. Envoy offered a variety of features including an agenda/calendar, an address book, spreadsheet capability and Internet access. It was unique in that faxes and e-mails could be sent without a wire-line connection via a built-in modem. Like Newton, Envoy's sales were so disappointing that the product was withdrawn from the market.

As Envoy was exiting the market, US Robotics launched Palm Pilot, a hand-sized digital personal organizer that was significantly less expensive than Newton or Envoy. Palm Pilot sold more than one million units in its first year and a half on the market, making it the most rapidly adopted computer product in history. Why did Palm Pilot have greater success than Newton or Envoy?

We contend that a key determinant was how these brands were positioned. Successful positioning involves affiliating a brand with some category that consumers can readily grasp and differentiating the brand from other products that belong to the same category. For sustained success, a brand must also be linked closely to consumers' goals. Thus successful positioning requires the performance of four tasks: careful *definition* of what the brand is; clear and meaningful *differentiation* from similar products; insightful *deepening* of the brand's connection to

Competition-based positioning triangle

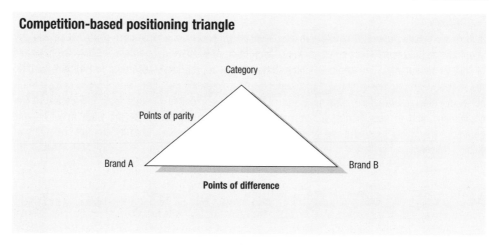

Figure 1

consumer goals over time; and *disciplined defence* of the position as competitors react and consumer tastes change. We refer to these four tasks as "the four Ds of positioning."

Competition-based positioning

Traditional approaches to positioning focus on brand definition and differentiation. Together these components emphasize the relationship between the product and its competition. The brand is defined for consumers by highlighting the features that it shares with other products – that is, its points of parity. Brand differentiation is then introduced by identifying a point of difference that allows the brand to dominate competition on a benefit important to consumers. These decisions are represented by the positioning triangle (*see* Figure 1).

For established brands, category membership is often obvious and thus does not require deliberation. Coca-Cola is a soft drink and Kellogg's Corn Flakes is a member of the cereal category.

However, when a new product is launched, there may be an opportunity to choose between category definitions and thus bases for differentiation. Slice is a carbonated beverage that is sold in the US in cans, distributed through vending machines and that contains real fruit juice. Slice might be defined as a member of the fruit juice category and differentiated from other fruit juices by its more convenient distribution. Alternatively, it might be presented as a soft drink and differentiated from other soft drinks by its real fruit juice content. Which of these categories is preferred would depend on whether the opportunity is deemed to be more substantial in the soft drink or fruit juice category.

Returning to our earlier example, a challenge faced by Motorola in positioning Envoy was to define the category in which Envoy would compete. While the manufacturer referred to Envoy as a personal digital assistant, consumers did not think of it in those terms. Rather they attempted to categorize Envoy as a member of some established category, such as laptop computers, organizers, cellular phones or pagers. Envoy lacked enough points of parity to be considered a member of any of these categories. Consumers were unable to see anything in their briefcase that Envoy could replace and thus resisted the proposition that they should spend more than $1,000 and subscribe to a radio network for the convenience of wireless fax

Challenges to effective positioning

Even when the principles of positioning are understood, there are a variety of impediments to their successful implementation.

Choosing benefits and goals

When entering a category where there are established brands, the challenge is to find a viable basis for differentiation. A frequent occurrence is that the superiority claim selected is not one that is important to consumers. Thus several analgesic brands have found limited demand arising from the claim that they are long lasting or require infrequent dosing. Most consumers have fast relief and not long lasting relief as a priority. Indeed, long lasting may imply slow acting – just the opposite of what is desired.

A variant of this problem emerges when a benefit in which a company dominates is important to some consumers but not the ones who are responsible for brand choice. For example, several cereals in the past 20 years have tried to position themselves as nutritious cereals for children. The problem is that the point of difference appeals to the purchaser in a category where demand is prompted by children's requests – and children's primary interest is in great taste, not nutrition.

One way to address the concern that any single benefit may be unimportant to some segment of consumers is to claim multiple benefits. In so doing, the hope is that the brand will offer something for everyone. This approach to differentiation may also emerge as a compromise when strategists cannot agree on an approach. Such positioning is often fraught with problems. One benefit claim might undermine another; for example, consumers are sceptical of products that claim high quality and low price. Further, claiming a variety of benefits can confound consumers' efforts to define what the product is, as we saw in the case of Envoy. Palm Pilot's success is due in part to US Robotics' understanding that, when it comes to benefit claims, less is often more.

More generally, positioning against multiple benefits invites consumers to determine the brand positioning, and consumers often do not select the one that is most advantageous to the brand.

A benefit might also lack importance because of the nature of the category. For most beverages, for example, taste is a key benefit and leading brands position themselves as having superior taste. By contrast, for sports beverages rejuvenation rather than taste is the critical benefit underlying category consumption. Thus even though All Sport was found to taste better than Gatorade in taste tests, it was problematic whether this could be used as a point of difference because it did not imply the category benefit. Emphasizing superior taste might run the risk of All Sport being classified as a soft drink rather than a sports beverage.

Disciplined defence

Once a position is developed, most activity is directed towards sustaining it in a contemporary way. For example, Grape Nuts has been positioned as the cereal that provides healthy nutrition since its introduction at the turn of the century. While this position has not changed, brand success depends on instantiating healthy nutrition in a modern way.

Sustaining a benefit over time often serves as a barrier to competitive entry. For example, Duracell supported its position as the battery with long life with an advertisement in which a Duracell-powered bunny continues to operate after similar toys powered by other battery brands have quit. When Eveready adopted not only Duracell's position of battery longevity but also used a parody of the advertising that Duracell had used for many years, tracking studies revealed that Duracell's, not Eveready's, share grew. Longevity in batteries meant Duracell to consumers.

Despite the fact that a sustained position can serve as a barrier to competitive entry, companies often abandon a position in response to some minor change in consumer preferences or in an effort to generate incremental volume for a brand. For example, the emergence of a consumer disposition against sugar in children's cereals led several brands with "sugar" in their name to adopt a new name. In effect, these brands walked away from their equity and, not surprisingly, sales plummeted.

A diet bar brand that consumers used primarily as a lunch substitute attempted to add volume by promoting itself as a snack. Consumers were puzzled by whether a product that was a snack could also serve as a meal substitute and a competitor took advantage of this confusion by claiming that *it* was the meal substitute. The new position undermined the main occasion of use by leaving consumers puzzled about the appropriate quantity to use for a snack, given that the prescribed serving was two bars for a meal.

Like an endgame in chess, defence of a brand position requires concentrated thought and a steady nerve. If careful attention is not given to this, a fifth D – decline – is apt to make an unwelcome appearance.

and e-mail transmission. Without a clear category definition, meaningful differentiation did not occur.

In contrast, the positioning of Palm Pilot as a digital personal organizer is credible to consumers because the product delivers the key benefit associated with that category, convenient organization of personal information. It is differentiated from other organizers by its ease of use, particularly with respect to synchronizing information with the user's desktop or laptop computer. Palm Pilot not only replaced the traditional organizer or secretary, it improved upon these alternatives.

While membership in a category is often determined on the basis of the brand's physical similarity to other products, such resemblance is not essential. A brand may also belong to a category with which it shares few physical features if it delivers the key category benefit. Palm Pilot may be viewed as an alternative to a secretary because it effectively delivers the key organizing benefit of a good secretary.

Once a brand's position is defined, it needs to be differentiated from other members of the category. Often this entails focusing on how the brand dominates its competitors with respect to some benefit important to consumers. The strongest position is one where a brand has a point of difference on the primary benefit that motivates consumers to buy the category.

The leader in a category usually claims this benefit, whether or not it actually has an advantage, and defends the position by relying on heavy advertising expenditures, intensive distribution or some other marketing mix vehicle. Thus Palm Pilot claims superior convenience in information organization and Tide detergent stresses superior cleaning power.

Smaller brands typically claim parity on the category-defining benefit to establish membership and focus on some secondary category feature as their point of difference. Accordingly, IBM emphasizes state-of-the-art technology as its point of difference, whereas laptop maker WinBook claims that it delivers state-of-the-art technology at a lower price.

Whatever the basis for differentiation, an effort should be made to give consumers a reason to believe that the brand possesses the benefit. Ingersoll positions itself as the company that produces superior grinding wheels because it is the only major company in the cutting-tool industry to specialize in these products. Tropicana (Orange Juice) claims to have superior-tasting orange juice because it uses only select oranges. In some cases, support for differentiation is in terms of image – who uses the brand and the occasions on which it is used. Fragrances, for example, use image as a basis for their claims.

Competition-based positioning clarifies what a brand should be compared to and why it should be preferred to those alternatives. However, it is seldom adequate on its own to produce sustained success. Deeper positioning – making connections with important consumer goals and values – enhances the chance that a brand's position will provide enduring competitive advantage.

Goal-based positioning

Goal-based positioning entails a deepening of competition-based positioning. Its frame of reference is not a product category but rather consumers' goals and values. Thus a position that focuses on some feature might be deepened by using a benefit implied by the feature as the basis for the brand's next position. In turn, the implied benefit can be used to suggest more abstract benefits. Because each of

Goal-based positioning triangle

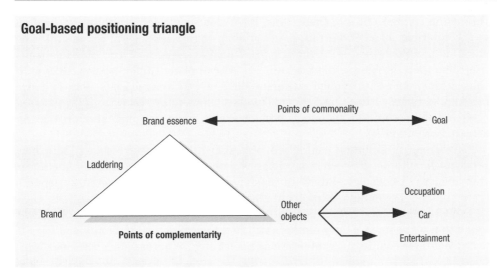

Figure 2

these inferences can be conceived of as a rung on a ladder that becomes more abstract and general as it is ascended, this technique is referred to as "laddering." At some point, laddering results in a highly abstract brand benefit that represents the brand's essence and that corresponds to consumers' goals.

McDonald's advertising illustrates the evolution of goal-based positioning. McDonald's laddered up from the cleanliness of its restaurants and the good taste of its food, to a place that was good for kids, to a trusted place in the community. These positions provided the foundation for a US advertisement that highlighted McDonald's brand essence. In it, a young man meets a blind date at her front door. He immediately attempts to manage her expectations by clarifying who he is and who he is not. He indicates that he is not a doctor, lawyer, banker or accountant, rather he is a clerk in a record store. He states that they will not be dining at a place that calls itself a bistro, casa or maison, nor will they attend a play, the opera, a symphony or the ballet. Instead he proposes McDonald's and a movie.

The points of complementarity between the brand and the young man's occupation, car and entertainment preferences imply that McDonald's has a down-to-earth, bedrock-of-the-community brand essence. Presumably, this is a point of commonality with consumers' goal of enjoying an unpretentious meal. This positioning is represented schematically in Figure 2.

Several facets of goal-based positioning warrant clarification. A brand might be positioned using an abstract benefit that implies its essence without having laddered up. However, laddering up enhances the credibility of abstract benefit claims. Goal-based positioning also does not require the association of a brand with other objects that imply brand essence, although this approach is often highly representative of how consumers view a brand. Brand essence can also be implied by representing different facets of a brand so that consumers gain a rich understanding of its nature. Finally, it is not uncommon for companies to use goal-based positioning that relies on category essence rather than brand essence. Category essence is based on a company's insight into consumers' goals in using the product category in general rather than a particular brand.

Consider a Lee jeans advertisement that depicts the tribulations consumers go through in trying to fit into their jeans. Even slender women are shown struggling to get into their jeans and a thin man's singing voice rises several octaves after he succeeds in zipping his up. Although these images make no claim that Lee jeans overcome these problems, the humorous portrayal of consumers' experiences with the category and the implied understanding of consumers' goals may enhance brand preference. Other things being equal, consumers are likely to infer that if a company understands consumers' problems and goals, it must also provide an attractive solution.

As companies embrace goal-based positioning, marketing research into how products fit into peoples' everyday lives is gaining popularity. In some instances this involves "archeological digs" in consumers' pantries while in others it entails "going native," becoming a participant-observer of consumption rituals.

Such research has yielded a variety of practical insights. For example, Kraft found that while today's busy mothers still find time to entertain family and friends over food, their goal in such interactions has shifted. Whereas such occasions were once viewed as an opportunity to demonstrate competence as a homemaker, they are now seen as an opportunity to have fun. This led Kraft to modify the positioning for Velveeta Cheese from one emphasizing taking care of others to one that focuses on being able to enjoy oneself while entertaining.

Deeper insight into consumer goals offers the opportunity to reverse the laddering process. Instead of beginning with brand attributes and laddering up to consumer goals, opportunities for positioning may be revealed by starting with consumer goals and values and laddering down to brand attributes and benefits.

Integrating positioning perspectives

The concepts underlying competition- and goal-based positioning can be integrated in a value proposition for a brand aimed at a particular consumer segment.

$$\text{Value} = \frac{\text{Product/Service Benefits + Psychic Benefits}}{\text{Price + Time}}$$

This proposition is a conceptual definition rather than a mathematical one and serves as a tool for making comparisons. Managers may examine the value propositions of brands that compete for similar consumers or may explore a particular brand's proposition across segments, either at a point in time or over time.

Differentiation in the form of product or service benefits is captured by both the average or mean performance on a particular dimension and the variance from that mean. Thus Nissan's Infiniti J30 delivers the product benefit of quality because it receives higher scores in terms of styling, comfort and engine performance than other cars in its class, as well as because consumers' perceptions of the J30 with respect to these characteristics are invariant.

The numerator of the value proposition also recognizes psychic benefits. These emerge from deepening the brand's connection to some goal important to consumers. In the context of cars, the psychic benefit might pertain to the feeling of security or prestige or some other consumer goal. In effect, the numerator captures both the functional benefits and the more abstract goals served by the brand.

The denominator of the value proposition reflects the costs of acquiring the benefits defined by the numerator. The costs include the purchase price and the time associated with acquiring and using the product. For many people, leisure time has contracted and work time has expanded during the past decade. This has resulted in time famine; consumers feel that they lack the time to accomplish the tasks they need to manage.

The predominant response to time famine is multi-tasking. People make phone calls or eat while driving, they exercise while walking to work and the like. This creates an opportunity for brands that expand the goals they serve beyond those implied by the category essence. For example, Virgin Atlantic Airways serves the basic goals of business people who need to fly. It moves them around the world punctually, comfortably and at an attractive price. What makes Virgin Atlantic special is that it has also transformed travelling into a form of entertainment. Travellers can network in an in-flight lounge or take advantage of an array of in-flight services, such as massages. The company thus serves multiple goals simultaneously.

Summary

However good your product, if it is badly positioned sales are likely to be disappointing. According to **Alice Tybout** and **Brian Sternthal**, positioning can be broken down into four basic tasks. First the brand needs to be convincingly *defined* as a member of some product category. At the same time it must be *differentiated* from other category members in a way that is meaningful to target consumers. Next, consumers' understanding of the brand's benefit needs to be *deepened*, so that its relation to their goals is made apparent. Finally, the brand's positioning needs to be *defended* over time. Like much else in marketing, positioning is an art; but if marketers give careful attention to the Four Ds they are much more likely to do it successfully.

Forecasting: principles that work

by J. Scott Armstrong

Forecasting problems are common in marketing: will the Volkswagen Beetle be a success? Will the Philadelphia Convention Hall be profitable? How will our major competitor respond if we raise the price of our product by 10 per cent? What if we cut advertising by 20 per cent? How much is Company A worth based on its future profits?

Companies need to forecast the demand for their products or services. They may also need to forecast relevant actions by decision makers outside the company, such as competitors, suppliers and government. These actions, along with policy actions by the company, will affect costs and market share. Market share and market forecasts allow a company to forecast sales.

Bad forecasts can lead to overcapacity, undercapacity, excess inventory, lost sales or other negative consequences. While we cannot completely remove errors from forecasts, we can increase accuracy through the application of well-established principles. These principles, established through research, tell us what methods to use and under what conditions they are most useful. Unfortunately, few companies use them; instead they go with their gut feelings.

Sources of forecasting principles

When I have asked practitioners what would convince them to try a new forecasting method, they often reply that they need to know what method has worked well in the past. In the past two decades, many researchers have compared the accuracy of different methods in real situations.

The most influential of the comparative studies was begun in 1979 by Spyros Makridakis, a professor at INSEAD. These became known as the M-competition studies. The fourth study in this series is currently under way, and it involves 3,003 economic, demographic and business time-series. As with previous M-competitions, an open invitation was issued to researchers and commercial forecasters to make forecasts for each series. The forecasts are submitted to an umpire who scores the accuracy of the forecaster's method. The aim is to see which methods are best for which type of data.

In 1996, along with 39 other researchers, I began a project to examine findings from such empirical research. We wanted to translate the findings into principles that would enable practitioners to select the best methods for their situation.

The task has been more complicated than expected, partly because too little attention has been paid to defining the conditions. Nevertheless, progress has been significant.

Forecasting methods

There are methods for handling judgmental information and other methods for statistical data. They are:

JUDGMENTAL	STATISTICAL
Intentions	Extrapolation
Role-playing	Rule-based forecasting
Conjoint analysis	Expert systems
Expert opinions	Econometric models
Analogies	
Judgmental bootstrapping	

Intentions studies ask people to predict how they would behave in various situations – for example, "would I switch to New Coke?" Intentions have been especially useful for predicting sales of new products but they also help to predict for existing products.

A person's *role* can have a powerful influence on behavior. So a subject might be asked to take on a role. For example: "You like Coke as it is. You learn that your favorite brand will be removed from the market. You are meeting with your friends, an active group that is loyal to Coke. How might you respond?"

If you need to know which factors affect intentions, the stated intentions can be related to the features of the new product using procedures such as regression analysis. For example, potential customers could be presented with 20 alternative designs for a new product and asked about their intentions to purchase each. This procedure, which is known as *conjoint analysis*, is widely used in business.

Experts can predict how others will act in a situation, especially if they know about similar experiences. For example, are they aware of cases analogous to the introduction of New Coke?

You can also develop a model of an expert. For example, experts could be asked to make forecasts for each of a number of alternative designs for a product. This approach, a type of expert system, is called *judgmental bootstrapping*. It is inexpensive and offers enormous benefits when one has to make many judgmental forecasts, such as in personnel selection. The Dallas Cowboys have used this procedure to select players.

Extrapolation uses earlier values of a series to predict later values. For example, knowing how many gallons of Coca-Cola have been sold in the US over the past 50 years, one can extrapolate future sales. This is the most widely used approach to forecasting for production and inventory control. Interestingly, it ignores the information that managers possess, a defect that creates serious errors, especially when changes are expected, such as the introduction of New Coke.

This defect is overcome by *rule-based forecasting*, a type of *expert system* that incorporates managers' knowledge into extrapolations. Rule-based forecasting uses managers' knowledge along with the historical time-series to decide how to weight forecasts from alternative extrapolation methods. Expert systems are typically used for data other than time-series. Assume, for example, that we need to obtain sales forecasts for items in a mail catalog. By formalizing an expert's rules, we can reduce the cost of repetitive forecasts and improve consistency. By using the best experts in the problem area (such as people known to be most successful in predicting catalog sales) we can improve the accuracy of what could be achieved by the typical expert.

Why not take all the information we have and let a statistical model such as regression tell us what is important? This popular approach has been the researchers' Holy Grail for decades. Advances in computer hardware and software have aided the development of ever more sophisticated methods. So far the efforts have produced a prodigious number of academic studies but their success in forecasting has been disappointing. Two resulting principles are: do not develop the model solely from the data at hand; and never use stepwise regression analysis.

The most successful *econometric models* draw primarily upon prior theory. They use estimates of relationships drawn from earlier research. In addition, they should integrate management knowledge. At the same time the models should be simple. How simple? Here is another principle: if, after a good effort, you cannot fully understand the forecasting method, do not use it. Econometric models represent the ultimate in the integration of judgmental and statistical sources. They have an additional advantage in that they allow us to examine what would happen if different policy decisions were made, such as "What would happen if Coca-Cola were to adopt everyday low pricing?"

The principles

Because there are so many principles, we can provide only a few examples. The full set of principles is being developed in our Forecasting Principles Project. Information about its status is available at *www-marketing.wharton.upenn.edu/ forecast*, which also has links to other relevant sites, such as the International Institute of Forecasters site.

Some principles contradict commonsense beliefs. For example:

- if you have the predictions made by someone (say, sales for items in a mail catalog) and the information used by that person, it is possible to create a model that will provide more accurate forecasts than the person can. Everyone believes there are exceptions to this but researchers have had difficulty finding them
- do not use the historical fit of a model to select the best model
- people are overconfident about their forecasts even if warned about overconfidence.

Some seemingly reasonable principles are often ignored. For example, one principle is to use long time-series when developing a forecasting model. Yet focus forecasting, one of the most widely used methods in business, does not do this. As a result it is unreliable.

Another principle is to ensure that one subject's forecasts are independent of another's when the behavior under scrutiny does not involve interaction. Focus groups always violate this principle and consequently provide poor forecasts.

Another principle is to incorporate relevant managerial judgment. Almost all extrapolation methods violate this principle. The violation is especially serious when trends in the data are opposite to the expectations of managers.

The selection of a method depends upon the conditions. If data are lacking, judgmental methods are appropriate. Otherwise one can use statistical methods. Of course, these methods can often be used together.

Judgmental forecasting

Generally, the simplest and most direct approach is to ask experts what will happen. This is relevant where one has little data, such as when forecasting for new products. How one would forecast the sales for movies-on-demand or shopping by computer or a new toy?

Some key principles for expert forecasting are:

- structure the forecasting problem so that it makes good use of the expert's knowledge (this may call for breaking the problem into a series of smaller problems)
- write out the problem and check that it is comprehensible
- prepare alternative written statements of the problem
- use at least 5 experts but no more than 20
- ensure that experts do not receive incentives that could compromise objectivity
- ask each expert to make an independent forecast
- choose experts who differ from one another
- choose experts with some expertise in the problem area (although high expertise is not necessary)
- allow the experts to revise their forecasts in light of information from other experts.

These principles are embodied in the Delphi procedure, a multi-round independent expert survey procedure. Apart from the principle concerning the number of experts, the preceding list might seem obvious. Note, however, that focus groups typically violate the principle of presenting written problem statements. That is another reason why focus groups should not be used for forecasting.

A surprising finding about using experts is that they do not need a high level of expertise. If you need a forecast of what will happen in the economy, faculty members at the local community college will do as well as the most expensive experts. One depressing finding is that students can forecast changes almost as well as professors can.

Some forecasts involve interactions among decision-makers. Examples include negotiations over contracts between suppliers and retailers, decisions by governments with respect to tariffs or other regulations, and negotiations with trades unions. If these interactions are similar to those that have occurred in the past, experts should be able to provide useful forecasts about the decisions that will be made.

When the interactions involve conflict among people or organizations, role playing is recommended. Subjects are given roles and asked to represent the parties in conflict. Although this procedure has been applied with apparent success in the military and in the law, it has had limited use in business. Yet research in this area shows substantial improvements in accuracy in comparison with traditional approaches. For example, one study examined whether a manufacturer could persuade a major supermarket chain to adopt a plan to sell appliances. Experts regarded the plan as unrealistic and only three per cent expected that the supermarket would be interested. In role playing, however, the managers agreed to the plan 75 per cent of the time. As it turned out, such a plan *was* adopted by the supermarket.

We recommend that you do not go far beyond your range of experience when making forecasts. If large changes are under consideration, it may be worthwhile to ask the people involved how they would respond (that is, to use intentions surveys). For example, imagine that you have invented a new product and you want to forecast whether it would sell. You could describe the product and ask people to state how likely they would be to buy it. Standard procedures for survey research are vital for intentions studies. New products can be designed in various ways and offered at different prices. When such variables are involved, you can use a structured procedure to assess the value of the various design elements. Conjoint analysis is one such procedure. It involves creating different designs, perhaps 20 or so, depending on the issue being addressed. It is expensive because you must identify and obtain information from many potential consumers.

Judgmental bootstrapping, by presenting experts with alternative designs, provides an alternative approach. As with expert studies, you need only 5 to 20 experts. To forecast sales for a new product, one can vary not only the design but also elements of the marketing mix such as advertising and distribution, something that cannot be done with conjoint analysis.

Statistical forecasting

Companies often have enormous volumes of data about their product sales. This allows them to extrapolate sales, a strategy that is appropriate where managers have little knowledge about the situation. There are, however, a number of extrapolation methods from which to chose. Perhaps the most useful principle here is to obtain forecasts from a set of reasonable extrapolation models. Then calculate a simple average of these forecasts.

If managers have good knowledge about the situation, rule-based forecasting is relevant. Rule-based forecasting incorporates the latest principles about forecasting time-series, along with managers' knowledge, in particular their expectations about trends.

One basic principle – which, unfortunately, many analysts violate – is to use prior knowledge. If there is empirical knowledge about the relationships between variables, use it in an econometric model. To predict the sales of Coca-Cola, for example, one should take advantage of existing knowledge about income and price elasticities.

Using forecasts

Some principles relate to the use of forecasts. For example, the act of forecasting often induces overconfidence. Managers were convinced that Ford's Edsel would be a big success, whereas outsiders were sceptical. Principles can be used to reduce overconfidence. One principle is for the experts to write down all of the reasons why the forecast will be wrong. This will lead to a more realistic assessment, though it will not completely solve the problem. Another principle is to estimate confidence by using experts who do not stand to gain or lose from the forecast.

Often it is important to evaluate alternative models in a given situation. There are principles on how to conduct the evaluation properly: for example, use the current method as the benchmark. They also show what not to do: for example, do not use the mean square error to evaluate the alternative models.

Managers tend to be overly influenced by scenarios or "stories." These tend to convince the reader that the events are likely to occur, even though the probabilities are very small. Scenarios are useful for gaining attention and for examining contingency plans. They should not be used to make forecasts.

Sometimes experts have done all the work for you. As readers of the *Financial Times* might be aware, a portfolio of shares picked by an expert performs as well as a portfolio picked by throwing darts at the page of company shares. In the darts case, the forecasts (market speculations) are prepared by a large number of unbiased experts.

And a final principle: when you see the word "focus" related to forecasting, add the prefix "out-of," as in "out-of-focus groups" and "out-of-focus forecasting."

Conclusion

By studying which methods work best in which situations, researchers have acquired basic knowledge to improve forecasting. This knowledge is now being formulated into principles. Many researchers would be willing to improve forecasts in a company at no fixed fee – just a small percentage of the savings would provide an excellent living because research-based principles produce substantially better forecasts.

Summary

Marketing managers often cite forecasting as a major concern. Numerous forecasting methods are now available. But which ones should be used in which situation? And how much confidence should one have in the results? Many companies rely on gut feelings to answer these questions, but according to **Scott Armstrong** they are making a costly mistake. Research has established – and continues to establish – principles to guide the choice of method and the use of results. Some of these are counter-intuitive, whereas others are commonsense. Companies that take the trouble to use them will make better forecasts – and larger profits.

Suggested further reading

Armstrong, J.S. and Collopy, F. (1998) "Integration of statistical methods and judgment for time series forecasting," in Wright, G. and Goodwin, P. (eds) *Forecasting with Judgment*, Wiley, Chichester, 269–93.

Gardner, E.S. and Anderson, E.A. (1997) "Focus forecasting reconsidered," *International Journal of Forecasting*, 13, 501–08.

Slicing and dicing the market

by Paul E. Green and Abba M. Krieger

Imagine you are the chief executive of a major, successful hotel chain. You operate hotels throughout the world and you are now looking for new growth opportunities. You ask yourself whether there is adequate demand for a new hotel concept in a niche in which the company does not currently operate. The concept would cater to economy-minded business and pleasure travelers.

You find yourself immediately overwhelmed with questions: What would our new chain's best competitive positioning be in terms of features and amenities? What is the best location strategy? What is the best pricing strategy? What should the new hotels look like so that they will be clearly distinguishable from our other hotels? What services should we provide beyond a room for the night?

Even within the room, what services are most important and what is the trade-off between a specific service and price (for example, a lower price for the room might mean no cable movies). What are the likely sources of new business from the competition and how much are we likely to cannibalize our own business? What should our promotional messages be? How confident are we of our market segments and overall strategy?

These are questions that the Marriott Hotel Corporation faced in the early 1980s as it sought new business opportunities. The company undertook a market-driven, customer-focused strategy as it examined opportunities. The result was its highly successful Courtyard chain, which now has more than 300 hotels, revenues in excess of $1bn and more than 15,000 employees.

Marriott based its decisions on market segmentation and conjoint analysis, two analysis methods that are widely used but whose full value is still not completely appreciated, especially by senior corporate management in other companies.

Segmentation

Market segmentation is the art and science of partitioning people or things into distinct groups. Each group will not only be distinct but ideally the groups will also be collectively exhaustive. People within each group will be more or less similar and, conversely, people across groups will be different. Segmentation can be used to find niche markets, fend off competitors and provide a base for new product design.

We can create segments on the basis of different characteristics. For example, segments might be composed of individuals, households, business establishments, postal codes or cities. We can also create segments based on things that people do in purchasing products. These segments are typically composed of brands, selected product categories, use occasions, stereotyped user profiles, benefits, needs, problems to be solved or product attributes.

The challenge for business is to segment in the most useful way. It is not enough to group people or things into distinct groups based simply on the similarity of those group members. For example, we would not find it terribly helpful to lump all readers of the *Financial Times* or all alumni of the Wharton School into one group.

We need to refine the group, a process that takes considerable time. There is a trade-off between how refined our group becomes and how much of a company's resources would be needed to define a segment and design a product or service for it. To be useful, groups must respond differently to various actions taken by the company. Groups may respond differently to how we price a product, the quality of the product, or how we promote or distribute it. By examining these reactions we can more accurately tailor our product design, pricing, advertising, distribution and so on.

Even as we "slice and dice" the market, we have to keep in mind the costs of reaching the various segments and the costs involved in implementing our plans. Finding the opinions of all *FT* readers on a given matter by using a small sample is straightforward. But when we segment the group into, for example, American women between the ages of 35 and 50 who hold executive positions in multinational companies with revenues in excess of $5bn, we can approach the market with considerably more finesse.

Thus, designing products/services and defining market segments are two sides of the same coin. For a given segment, we want to design an optimal product with optimal pricing and distribution. In addition, we want to create the appropriate advertising message and strategy. The other side of this coin is that for a given product we want to find the most attractive segments and design appropriate marketing plans.

Among the considerations we might use for market segmentation are:

- demographics and socioeconomic characteristics
- personality and lifestyle
- product usage and purchasing
- needs
- attitude to the product and its consumption
- benefits sought
- marketing-related behavior and attitude
- response to marketing variables.

One highly popular way to segment the market is in terms of buyers' needs. In the case of laundry detergent, for example, we might find that these are:

- no mess
- no smell
- "whiter whites"
- fewer trips to the shops.

Each need is distinct but they also might be combined in various ways. In response, we can assess how well our own product satisfies these needs in the marketplace compared to competing products. As a result of our analysis, we might then:

- create a liquid detergent
- create an unscented detergent
- create a detergent with bleach added
- produce our detergent in larger packaging.

Alternatively because we may decide to do nothing we cannot satisfy any of the needs in a profitable way.

How we define our segments and how we use the data we have derived from each become critical decisions. Effective segments must be created in such a way that their size and purchasing power can be effectively measured. They must be profitable and we must be able to serve them effectively. Last, and most important, we have to create segments in a way that will allow us to develop programs for attracting and serving them.

Once we gather information from the segments our choices increase. The company has to determine whether the costs of making the changes that the segments are requesting will be at least offset by the increase in revenues and profits that will presumably occur. And it needs to assess whether the best course of action is to add to the product line or delete or reposition current offerings.

Adding to the complexity is the fact that we are not performing these analyses in a static world. Competitors may well have access to similar data and may be making changes in the marketplace at the same time. And the responses we get from our segments represent opinions held at a specific point in time and might well change.

Conjoint analysis

Conjoint analysis is a sophisticated tool for implementing market segmentation strategies. It is used by virtually all of the Fortune 500 companies and measures the various trade-offs that consumers are willing to make when they buy a product. Its primary uses are in developing new products, repositioning old products and deciding prices.

Continuing with our detergent example, the consumer might be willing to pay a small premium for a detergent that has no "soapy" smell and still produces "whiter whites." The strength of conjoint analysis is that it goes beyond simply telling us what a consumer likes about a particular product; it also helps us to understand why the consumer might choose one brand or service supplier over another.

The central idea of conjoint analysis is that products and services can be described by a set of attribute levels. Purchasers attach different values to the levels of different attributes. They then choose the offering that has the highest total value, adding up all the "part-worths." Consumers' part-worths have different values, so their trade-offs vary. For example, one consumer may prefer bleach to no scent, while another might prefer "whiter whites" to "no mess."

There are four principal reasons why this technique is so useful:

1 Conjoint analysis focuses on the measurement of buyer preferences for product attributes (price, quality and so on) and the perceived benefits to the buyer that might flow from those attributes.
2 It is a micro-based measurement technique, with preferences for attribute levels measured at the individual level.
3 Conjoint studies also typically entail the collection of respondent background information, which can, in turn, be related to part-worths.

The future

Market segmentation and product positioning have recently undergone several changes. These include:

- Increased emphasis on segmentation criteria that represent "softer" data such as attitudes and needs. This is the case in both consumer and business-to-business marketing.
- Increased awareness that the bases of segmentation depend on its purpose. For example, the same bank customers could be segmented by account ownership profiles, attitudes towards risk-taking and socioeconomic variables. Each segmentation could be useful for a different purpose, such as product cross-selling, preparation of advertising messages and media selection.
- A move towards "letting the data speak for themselves," that is, finding segments through the detection of patterns in survey or in-house data. So-called "data mining" methods have become much more versatile over the past decade.
- Greater usage of "hybrid" segmentation methods. For example, a beer producer might first segment consumers according to favorite brand. Then, within each brand group, consumers could be further segmented according to similarities in attitudes towards beer drinking, occasions where beer is consumed and so on.
- A closer connection between segmentation and new product development. Computer choice models (using information about the attribute trade-offs that consumers make) can now find the best segments for a given product profile or the best product profile for a given market segment.

- The growing availability of computer models (based on conjoint data) to find optimal additions to product lines – products that best balance the possibility of cannibalization of current products with competitive draw.
- Research on dynamic product/segment models that consider the possibility of competitive retaliation. Such models examine a company's vulnerability to competitive reactions over the short term and choose product/segment combinations that are most resistant to competitive encroachment.
- The development of pattern-recognition and consumer-clustering methods that seek segments on the basis of data but also respect managerial constraints on minimal segment size and managerial weightings of selected clustering variables.
- The development of flexible segmentations that permit the manager to loosen a clustering based only on buyer needs (by shifting a small number of people between clusters); the aim might be to increase the predictability of some external criterion measure such as household profitability to a company, say, selling mutual funds.

Much of the recent research on product positioning/segmentation has been tailored to the continued growth of the service sector and the associated need for high levels of customer satisfaction and loyalty. Segmentation and conjoint analysis are as applicable to services as they are to products.

4 Even the most rudimentary studies usually include a buyer-choice simulation stage, in which the researcher can enter new or modified product profiles and find out who chooses your product and who chooses your competitor's.

Once a company gathers information on buyer needs, it then must assess both how potential purchasers are likely to react in the marketplace to any changes and, of equal importance, how competitors are likely to react.

The first step in creating a successful conjoint analysis is to examine the competitive marketplace and develop a set of product/service attributes and levels. Typically, we use focus groups, consumer interviews and in-house expertise to define these.

Complexity comes when we realize that we have, for example, nine attributes and within each attribute three or four levels. In such a case we would find ourselves with thousands of possible combinations – a market researcher's nightmare. Conjoint analysis can use statistical design techniques to select a small set of possible profiles from which the user can predict results for thousands of combinations not actually tested.

Once we work through the models we find ourselves with two outputs: profiles of products, along with expected returns to each company; and a description of each buyer who chooses a particular product profile from the array of choices.

Summary

Every business wants more consumers to buy more of its products or services. Unfortunately, no business can afford to splatter the market with exhaustive product variants; instead companies must come up with precisely targeted offerings every time. In this article, **Paul Green** and **Abba Krieger** describe two techniques that help companies to do this: market segmentation and conjoint analysis. Segmentation is the art of defining groups in a way that will be useful for marketers; conjoint analysis is a technique for optimizing the products that will be offered to different segments. The authors conclude with an overview of some of the latest developments in these areas.

Adding ethics to the marketing mix

by N. Craig Smith and Jill G. Klein

Many people believe that "marketing ethics" is an oxymoron. In surveys of ethics in the professions, marketers generally are ranked towards the bottom of the list. This unsavory view stems in part from frequent media reports of unethical or illegal conduct in marketing. There is a persistent belief that much of marketing is hucksterism. One reason for such perceptions is the visibility of many marketing activities. Because we all come into contact with marketing as consumers, we are more exposed to the misconduct that does occur, at least compared to that of other business functions. Nonetheless, marketing managers do encounter many ethical issues. For instance, marketing decisions can have effects upon product safety, truth in advertising, fairness in pricing, and the equitable treatment of distributors.

It is possible that marketers are more likely to be faced with ethical issues than managers in other functions because of their "boundary-spanning" role: that is, the requirement to deal with multiple parties, often external to the company, who may have conflicting interests. This is increasingly the case in the age of "relationship marketing." However, the greater potential for ethical challenges in marketing does not mean that marketing is unethical in itself. That said, marketers do need to be alert to the possibility of ethical issues in their decision-making.

Managing ethical issues

It is not uncommon for marketing managers to give little attention to their moral obligations – at least until it is too late. This may be due to a lack of awareness of their importance. In other cases, there may be a belief that ethics is not a relevant consideration – the myth of amoral business.

The idea that businesspeople should not consider moral values in their decision-making comes from a narrow view of economic activity, a perspective that suggests that managers can and should make business decisions solely on the basis of financial criteria such as profitability. However, in practice, business decisions can never be value-neutral and, indeed, moral values are critical to the effective functioning of business. Consider the fact that most business relationships require trust, or the fact that there would be little point in advertising in a situation where most advertisers lied. Another flaw in the myth of amoral business is the false notion of a separation between our business and our personal lives. The person who would claim to live a moral life can only do so if that extends to the business sphere.

Many ethical issues that come to prominence are the result of insufficient attention to marketing ethics. A basic requirement, then, is for "ethical sensitivity" – awareness of moral obligations in marketing decision making and of the potential for ethical issues to arise. For example, the code of ethics of the American Marketing Association states that marketers should conform to the basic rule of professional ethics not to do harm knowingly, and that they should offer products and services that are safe and fit for their intended uses.

Because marketers frequently deal with multiple parties or "stakeholders," they should be aware that their obligations to them may conflict. For instance, incentives to retailers might encourage them to push unsuitable products on consumers.

Given ethical sensitivity, many managers avoid potentially unethical actions by reference to their own sense of right and wrong. Often this is intuitive; one has a clear sense, say, that overstating the potential benefits of a product would be wrong and thereby one avoids questionable puffery. In less straightforward cases, managers use ethical maxims, such as the Golden Rule, "Do unto others as you would have them do unto you." However, these are not always so useful and cannot provide specific guidance on many of the more complex issues that marketers face.

Many ethical issues in marketing may be viewed as a conflict between the company and its customers. In these situations, marketers have obligations to the company that conflict with their obligations to consumers. For example, should a salesperson disclose negative information about a product to customers, such as supply shortages or the pending introduction of a superior product? Some might argue *caveat emptor* (buyer beware). However, this has become an increasingly inadequate explanation for unethical practices and often has proved detrimental to the company attempting to justify its behavior on these grounds.

It has been proposed that marketers are obliged to ensure that consumers can exercise informed choice. This has been described as the "consumer sovereignty test" (CST; *see* Table 1). According to the CST, marketers may evaluate their decisions along three dimensions: consumer capability, sufficiency of information, and consumer choice.

Although dependent on the facts of any specific case, the CST suggests that the previous example would be judged unethical because it violates the information

The consumer sovereignty test from Smith 1995	
Dimension	**Establishing adequacy**
Consumer capability	**Vulnerability factors** Age, education, income and so on
Information	**Availability and quality** Sufficient to judge whether expectations at time of purchase will be fulfilled
Choice	**Opportunity to switch** Level of competition Switching costs

Table 1

dimension. Failure by a salesperson to disclose the supply shortages or the new product introduction would be unethical if the customer's expectation on purchase is of timely delivery or the best product that the company has available.

Tobacco marketing generally fails on two, if not all three, dimensions of the CST. Research shows that most people start smoking in their early teens (violation of consumer capability) and, because of the addictive nature of nicotine, have great difficulty quitting (violation of choice). Most consumers in developed countries are well aware of the harmful effects of smoking on health (which is why, as adults, they attempt to quit) but consumers in developing countries – where tobacco marketing efforts increasingly are focused – are often less informed about the harm from smoking (violation of the information dimension).

The CST is a useful way of examining ethical issues arising in the relationship between the company and its customers. It is particularly appropriate to consumer marketing and where *caveat emptor* historically has been advanced as a justification for suspect marketing practices.

However, ethical issues may arise involving other stakeholders. Accordingly, marketing ethics requires that marketers engage in "stakeholder analysis"; that is, they should consider not only the effects of their decisions on consumers but also on other affected parties. Stakeholder analysis might suggest multiple conflicting obligations. For example, the marketer may have to weigh consumer preference for effective washing detergents against evidence of environmental harm from phosphates in the product. As these problems become increasingly intractable, greater reliance may need to be placed on ethical reasoning informed by moral philosophy.

Two prominent theories of moral philosophy that, at the very least, improve understanding of such issues are consequentialism and deontology. Simply put, consequentialist theories require marketers to examine the goodness of the consequences of their actions. This type of thinking is predominant in business, not least because it is closely parallel to cost–benefit calculations.

In contrast, deontological theories require the marketer to examine whether a decision is right in itself, regardless of consequences; instead, reliance is placed on duties or obligations. For example, a deontological analysis of tobacco marketing could claim that it is unethical because of the marketer's obligation to do no harm. Arguments about goodness of consequences, such as the pleasure derived by smokers would be irrelevant.

In applied ethics fields, such as business, ethical reasoning is often informed by multiple theories of moral philosophy. A compelling argument is sought that would demonstrate the superiority of analysis based on one theory over another, where (as here) they are in conflict.

Marketing research

Research is an important activity in marketing and it too has its fair share of ethical issues. Stakeholder analysis provides a useful framework for understanding them. The primary stakeholders are the researcher, the respondents and the client. Major ethical issues affecting researchers arise when there are threats to research integrity – for example, because the brand manager pressures an in-house researcher to interpret data in a way that will support the brand manager's strategy.

Another set of issues arises when research clients invite bids from research agencies. Are all the bids sought in good faith or are some agencies asked to bid when the client has already chosen a supplier and is simply fulfilling company procurement policy? Or is there no intention of going outside with the project? Is the company merely picking the brains of more experienced researchers?

Particularly challenging are issues involving respondents. Although they might be consumers of the company's products, the CST is less applicable in determining researchers' obligations to them.

Respondents, who typically provide their time for free, have various rights, including the right to be informed about the study, the right to choose whether to be involved, the right to privacy, the right to safety and the right to be treated with respect. Codes of conduct that recognize these rights include the codes of the Marketing Research Society (in the UK) and the Council of American Survey Research Organizations (Casro).

These codes notwithstanding, there is evidence to suggest that some researchers are engaging in unethical practices. Not surprisingly, this is considered to be a factor in declining research participation rates (other factors include "inconvenience," increased time pressure and the rise in telemarketing). Casro has estimated that survey refusal rates are 35–38 per cent and rising. Some sources put refusal rates as high as 60 per cent.

In our research, we have conducted studies with both researchers and respondents. In a US study, a sample of 128 research practitioners identified practices that respondents might find irritating, upsetting and unethical. These included: sales under the guise of research ("sugging"), lying about the length of the survey, inconveniencing the respondent (for example, by calling at dinner time), creating difficulties for the respondent (for example, poorly written surveys), overly long interviews, privacy violations (for example, calling unlisted numbers), poor treatment by interviewers and hidden taping or observing of respondents.

More than one in four practitioners suggested that some of these practices were unavoidable, often for economic reasons. For instance, calling people at inconvenient times was said to be necessary because it was the best time to reach them.

In a study conducted in a US shopping mall, 110 respondents described a recent market research experience. A third reported at least one negative feeling about the experience and more than a quarter characterized it as unethical or unfair.

While the problematic issues identified by practitioners and those experienced by respondents overlapped, practitioners appear to underestimate people's concern about being asked personal questions (for example, about income).

In our continuing research, we are attempting to find ways in which researchers might manage better some of the more difficult ethical issues. Some practices clearly are wrong and should be avoided. For example, there is no justification for violating promises of confidentiality or for failure to deliver promised payment for participation.

However, some practices present dilemmas. For example, while there is an obligation to ensure the informed consent of participants, this might require telling them about the purpose or sponsor of the study. This in turn might bias responses violating the researcher's obligation to the client. We have found that in such situations there may be remedial measures that will improve respondents' evaluations of the research. One such measure is to forewarn people when not all details of the study can be provided in advance and to supply a fuller account afterwards.

Conclusion

Attention to marketing ethics is important because we all have a duty to live a good, moral life. This duty has as much application to our business lives as to our private lives. However, marketing professionals also know that good ethics is good business. In our studies of marketing research, we have found that treating respondents with respect is likely to improve the chances of their future participation in research. This conserves an increasingly scarce resource.

More broadly, unethical conduct often has negative consequences, ranging from adverse publicity, to diminished corporate reputation, to lower employee morale, to consumer boycotts and even legal sanctions. Conversely, ethical conduct can contribute to a good corporate reputation, heighten morale and increase repeat business. Which would you choose?

Summary

Marketing is not seen as the most ethical of professions. This may not be fair – marketing may be no worse than any other business function – but its essentially public profile means that any misconduct is highly visible. And marketers' "boundary-spanning" role means that obligations are more likely to conflict. Here, **Craig Smith** and **Jill Klein** suggest how marketers can deal with ethical issues. In straightforward cases, referring to one's own moral sense or to simple maxims should suffice. But where things are more complex, assessment of consumer sovereignty or even recourse to moral philosophy may be necessary.

Suggested further reading
Smith, N.C. (1995) "Marketing strategies for the ethics era," *Sloan Management Review* 36 (4) 85–97
Smith, N.C. and Quelch, J.A. (1993/1996) *Ethics in Marketing*, Irwin, Homewood, IL

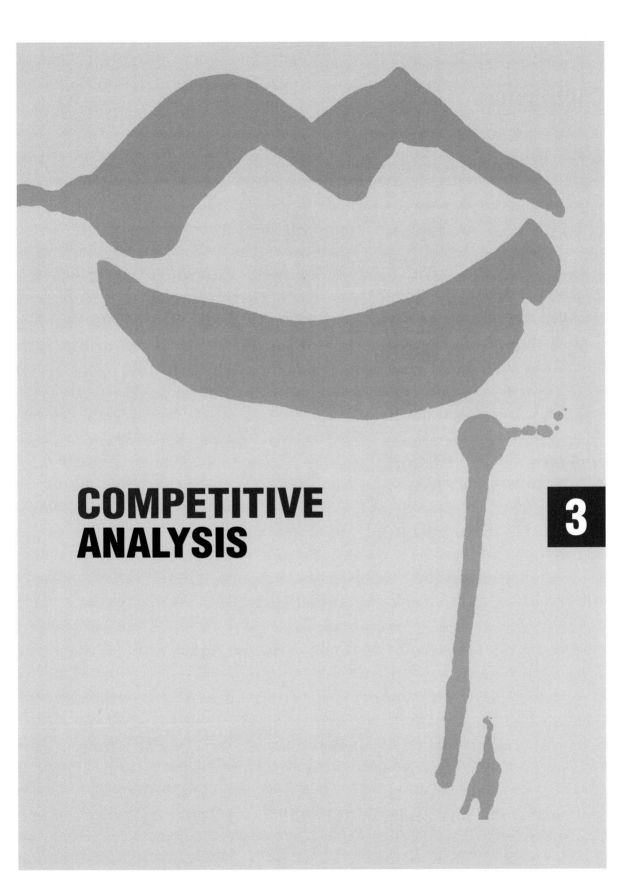

COMPETITIVE ANALYSIS

3

Contributors

George S. Day is the Geoffrey T. Boisi Professor and professor of marketing at the Wharton School of the University of Pennsylvania. He is the director of the Huntsman Center for Global Competition and Innovation and of the Emerging Technologies Management Research Program.

Arvind Sahay is assistant professor of marketing and international business at London Business School. His research interests include marketing strategy, technology and innovation, technology licensing and strategic alliances, new product development and international marketing.

Lakshman Krishnamurthi is the A. Montgomery Ward Professor of Marketing and chairs the marketing department at the J.L. Kellogg School of Business, Northwestern University. His research focuses on choice models and new product strategy.

William P. Putsis, Jr, is associate professor of marketing at London Business School. His research interests include the analysis of competition, consumer choice and international marketing.

Philip Parker is professor of marketing at INSEAD. His research focuses on marketing strategy, international management, pricing, new product diffusion and forecasting.

Contents

Introduction

Companies do not operate in a vacuum, and nor should their marketers. Understanding the competitive context is a critical part of marketing. This module examines some of the marketing implications of the fast-moving, highly interconnected markets of the "information age," and describes research into how companies respond to their competitors. It also analyzes two very different types of competitive strategy: customer-responsive strategies, in which a company aims to build durable relationships with its most valuable customers, and collusion – which, although frowned upon in Anglo-American markets, is regarded as a natural business practice in most countries. And there is a discussion of the tricky art of pricing, in which customer requirements and the competition are just two of the factors to be balanced.

Building relationships that last

by George S. Day

As markets mature, most competitive advantages are lost or greatly diminished. While rivals strive to catch up with the leader, customers have a greater range of choices. They react to the homogenization of alternatives by becoming more price-sensitive and less loyal. This scenario is common but not inevitable, so the question is how to combat the forces of uniformity and regain an advantage that customers will value.

Increasingly, the answer is found with customer-responsive strategies that seek to forge close relationships with valuable customers. The thrust of such strategies is to add value by augmenting the core offering with service enhancements, incentives and tailored interactions that reflect differences in the prospective lifetime value of each customer.

Organizations with successful customer-responsive strategies are alike in a number of ways. There is a willingness to serve customers differently, with the best customers getting the best treatment. The airline industry, for example, has created multi-level frequent-flyer programs, with dedicated reservation lines, priority upgrades, rapid check-in privileges and so on to recognize the best customers.

Decisions are based on fine-grained information about customers. Databases pull key data from internal operating systems (such as a retailer's transaction system) and merge it with descriptive information from external sources. This enables database marketing and "micromarketing" campaigns.

A "have it your way" mindset prevails. This can range from tailoring messages to micro-segments – such as the binding of *Parents* magazine in the US, which is customized according to the age of the buyer's children – to Nordstrom's allowing its clerks to range through the entire store to put together clothing ensembles for their customers. Core processes are flexible and facilitate many different ways of producing and delivering the product or service. Measures and incentives are aligned so as to prioritize retention.

Customer-responsive strategies are far easier to conceive and implement within organizations whose history inclines them towards a relationship mindset or that have the luxury of a clean start without the drag of history and past practice.

Managers who have matured and prospered in a transaction environment will subtly resist the transformation. Marketing may feel threatened as product managers lose their autonomy to segment managers; advertising may feel uncomfortable with micromarketing campaigns targeted at hundreds of segments; the systems group may argue that the legacy systems cannot handle flexible approaches to data capture; and financial people may be sceptical about efforts to estimate probable lifetime customer value.

In short, these strategies are difficult to implement. But when they work they are the source of a powerful competitive advantage that is very difficult for rivals to imitate or leap-frog.

A customer-responsive strategy is likely to gain an advantage if it:

- delivers superior customer value by personalising the interaction

- demonstrates trustworthiness
- tightens connections with customers
- requires co-ordination of complex capability elements.

Conversely, if the strategy does not satisfy these criteria the results are bound to be disappointing. This includes many programs launched under the guise of relationship marketing that involve micromarketing by tailoring communications to narrow segments or product-line extensions that aim to offer greater variety to fragmented markets.

Too often these are only warmed-over traditional mass marketing efforts that overwhelm consumers with a proliferation of products, messages and appeals for personal information. Often they are badly conceived, as when a bank's "privileged" customers were sent solicitations with offers of special credit card rates that were normally available only to new customers. A lot of money has been wasted on short-term rewards through gifts or one-time rebates for loyal customers. These are nice to receive but do nothing to strengthen the relationship.

Many frequency marketing programs that provide rewards for frequent patrons, flyers or guests have also been disappointing. Because they were often rushed into place to match a competitor there was no discernible market impact but significant new costs were incurred.

At the beginning of 1995 there were no loyalty schemes in the UK grocery market (with the exception of Co-op's stamp scheme) but once Tesco broke ranks, all the others were forced to follow suit. No doubt Tesco benefited because it was first but for the rest the frequency rewards became a costly burden. Once everyone has a program, most customers are able to accumulate credit with whichever shop they patronize and loyalty patterns remain unchanged.

Delivering superior value

The difference between repeat behavior and loyalty is that the former is for sale while the other is earned. This sums up why gifts and other one-time rewards have little lasting impact – they are not relevant to the brand's value proposition and demonstrate neither more benefits nor lower costs than the competition.

Relationships that add value to customers require some form of personalized interaction. They are built on the recognition that every relationship is different, that it is based on two-way communication and that it should continue to develop over time. Some hotels, such as the Ritz-Carlton, build relationships by accumulating and remembering information about guests' preferences and interests so they do not have to keep asking the same questions at every check-in. Successful life insurance salespeople have always understood the need to personalize relationships by staying in touch, anticipating the impact of family life-cycle events and demonstrating responsiveness.

Value is often delivered through coaching that combines instruction with encouragement to help a customer deal with a difficult task. One such problem is choosing flowers that will suit the person and the occasion, will not perish quickly and will not cost too much. One alternative is to find a local florist who can be trusted and who will provide guidance. But that means a special trip, there is no assurance the florist will have the right flowers to hand and, because of inefficiencies in flower distribution, the flowers could be seven to ten days old before they even reach the store.

Calyx & Corolla in the US devised a new direct marketing approach that allowed

Defending the customer relationship

Engage the entire organization – both minds and hearts

No company can prevail for long if its culture is unsupportive. There must be broad belief that every interaction matters – what Jan Carlson of SAS Airlines called the "million moments of truth" that determine success. To capitalize on this belief all functions must be part of the program. The Hertz #1 Club Gold program in the US would have been much less successful had operations not been fully involved in rebuilding systems and facilities to save customers going to a counter and to provide covered pick-up spots that identify customers by name.

Tighten organizational alignment

A capability emerges from a complex interaction of many elements and will only be as good as the weakest link. Every element must be scrutinized for improvement. For example, the commission system has the power to encourage sales people to chase the next easy conquest or alternatively to carefully screen prospects on the basis of their likelihood of defecting. Many companies no longer pay commissions on new accounts that last less than 12 months.

Make learning a priority

There are always ways to improve. The best-of-breed companies are never satisfied. Instead they use pilot tests and "hothouses" to try out new approaches and learn more about what their target customers really value. To exploit this learning it is necessary to keep key people on the team long enough for them to have real impact. Solid relationships require continuity, both inside and outside.

Refresh and maintain databases and records

As soon as a database is created it is obsolete – just keeping up with the 20 per cent of US households that move every year is a daunting task. But if it is not done conscientiously the program will soon falter. Companies that have strong relationships with their customers are in the best position to do this because the customer has an incentive to stay in touch.

---

growers to ship flower arrangements to the end consumer by FedEx in as little as one day from the time they were cut. To keep customers coming back the company added a number of services that made buying flowers simple, satisfying and appealing. The key was to provide informative catalogs and understanding telephone service staff. They were trained to ask tactful questions that would help customers get what they wanted without feeling they were being judged.

Demonstrating trustworthiness

Once the capabilities are in place to ensure that the value proposition is clearly superior then a virtuous circle of relationship building can begin. Only when the customer is completely satisfied will initiatives to demonstrate trust and tighten their connections to the company be cost-effective. In fact, if you cannot deliver on the basic promise of reliable performance those efforts are likely to be counterproductive.

Xerox followed this sequence to regain its leadership in the office copier market. By the mid-1980s it had lost ground to Canon and other Japanese competitors. The turnaround required wholehearted commitment to total quality management, rigorous benchmarking against competitors, a customer satisfaction program that introduced new methods of measurement, and team-based field organizations. Sales, service and operations took collective responsibility for customer problems;

previously the sales people dropped out of the picture once the machine was sold while regional service and operations people did not communicate with each other.

These efforts paid dividends as customer satisfaction steadily rose and Xerox share losses were arrested. Only then was the company in a position to forge stronger relationships. The first step was to demonstrate both its confidence in its own copiers and their trustworthiness by offering a strong guarantee.

Xerox chose a "no questions asked" guarantee whereby customers could decide they wanted the copier removed and the company would replace it with another of equivalent performance. The key was to give the customer the discretion, rather than to offer a replacement only at the company's discretion, which was what the competitors offered.

When properly used, guarantees build trust by symbolizing a company's commitment to fair play with its customers. They also maintain the pressure on the entire organization to continue to improve performance in order to avoid the costs and conflicts created by frequent payouts and replacements. Guarantees can also put intolerable pressure on competitors if they cannot match the terms. Xerox gained 4.5 share points when it introduced its performance guarantee because none of the competitors had Xerox's service coverage and consequently could not offer anything equivalent. As one of the conditions of the guarantee, the copiers had to be serviced by Xerox, which immediately put a crimp in the efforts of low-cost service competitors to steal away this lucrative business.

Frank and frequent personalized communications are an effective means of demonstrating trustworthiness. This is especially important with high involvement, long-term service commitments such as car or life insurance. Many customers are not trustful of their insurance companies because they only hear from them when a premium is due. That is when they find out the rates have been raised, usually with no explanation. When they need the service they bought – after an accident, say – the insurer seems bent on canceling the policy or making it very costly.

Life insurance customers are even more removed. Because of high turnover among agents, they are likely to have lost their initial point of contact. To build trust and confidence some companies are carefully crafting individual mailings that explain the policy benefits, describe the current status and make proposals for changing the coverage to make it more useful. They do not presume that the customer has the interest or ability to wade through a confusing policy. As a result, when the time comes to renew or expand coverage the policyholder is much more inclined to stay with his or her present insurer.

Tightening the connections

Once the relationship has a solid foundation in superior value and trustworthiness it is time to tighten the connection. The objective is to make it more attractive for the customer to remain loyal and more difficult to defect.

Incentives to remain loyal run the gamut from frequency marketing programs, epitomized by American Airlines' frequent flyer program, to providing membership in clubs. For example, Nintendo, the Japanese video-game company, has enrolled 2m members in its Nintendo Club. For an annual fee they receive a magazine with "inside" tips on how to win, previews of new games and so on, as well as access to a helpline they can call with questions or problems. Such incentives work when they enhance the core value proposition but if they are simply a "me too" response to competitive moves they become an added cost burden. Their main function is to avoid market share losses because of a competitive disadvantage.

Another effective inducement is the reward scheme that offers more reward points for each dollar spent, so each successive purchase becomes more valuable. This also introduces a disincentive to switch to a competitor because the opportunity cost is too high. Here the principle is to increase the buyer's switching costs.

The closest connections come when the solution to the customer's requirements is designed into the delivery system. The resulting web of financial, systemic and even social connections is very difficult for competitors to penetrate. Federal Express uses this approach to tie its customers ever closer. It has placed automated shipping and invoicing systems in the offices of its highest-volume customers. This "Powership" system can assign the correct weight to each package, combine package weights by destination to obtain volume discounts and print address labels. The customer gets other benefits by being able to trace packages and analyze shipping expenses. The more experience customers have with the system, the less likely they are to drop it in favor of someone else's approach.

Co-ordinating capabilities

The completion – and beginning – of the virtuous circle of relationship building requires enhancing and strengthening the underlying capability. The more successful the program, the greater is the risk of imitation. Some would argue that no relationship advantage can be sustained. The best defence is to stay ahead by continuously learning and innovating – and then to make it as difficult as possible for rivals to grasp the organizational recipe. The defence plan must address every element of the capability. Below are some suggestions for elements of the plan.

The incentive for companies to forge close relationships is that loyal customers are more profitable. They are easier and cheaper to service. Because they are familiar with the products and service they have fewer questions, are less likely to make mistakes and have adjusted their behavior to simplify their relations with the supplier. They tend to buy more as time passes, either because they learn about other parts of the product line or because they give a higher proportion of their spending to the favored source. They tend to become less price-sensitive and may even pay a premium. As the relationship strengthens over time they are less susceptible to competitors' appeals and because they appreciate the value they are getting they are prepared to pay more. Finally, loyal buyers are more likely to pass on favorable recommendations to others who also tend to be better prospects. This helps reduce the high costs of new customer acquisition.

It is not news that some customers are more profitable than others or that it costs a lot more (up to five times as much) to attract new customers than to keep the existing ones. What has captured managers' attention is research showing how much leverage an increase in loyalty has on profits. In a study of 100 companies in two dozen industries it was found that companies could improve profitability by between 25 and 85 per cent with each five per cent reduction in customer defections; that is, reducing defections from, say, 20 per cent a year to 15 per cent a year. Here is a case where a competitive advantage is rewarded with superior profitability.

Summary

Loyal customers are a valuable asset. This is particularly so in mature markets, where other sources of competitive advantage can be quickly eroded. Hence it is not surprising that many companies are adopting customer-responsive strategies, which use detailed information about customers to tailor products or services for them. The aim is to ensure that the most valuable customers receive the best treatment. Here **George Day** outlines the elements of such strategies. Excellence of product or service is fundamental; once that is established, personalized interactions with customers, initiatives to demonstrate trustworthiness and incentives for customers to remain loyal can come into play. But all too often companies rely on poorly tailored mass marketing communications or mimicry of competitors' strategies.

Competitive strategy in the information age

by Arvind Sahay

The objective of any competitive strategy is to gain advantage in the marketplace. Competitive advantage has two dimensions – superior customer value and lower relative cost. A company is able to deliver superior customer value when it satisfies the needs of customers better than its competitors. Value-delivery tools include pricing, communications and delivery. The question is: why should competitive strategy for electronic markets be any different from "normal" or "physical" markets?

Consider the case of pricing. In the agricultural age, most of a producer's costs were variable. Fixed costs were low (for artisans) to negligible (for landowners). In the industrial age, a back-of-envelope estimate suggests that between 40 and 60 per cent of costs were fixed and the remaining costs were variable. This gave rise to the well-known marginal pricing model, where price = marginal cost.

However, in the information age nearly all costs are fixed, as is the case with those icons of the age, software and semiconductor chips. The marginal costs of producing an additional unit are very low to negligible. Can companies still apply marginal cost or other variable cost-based pricing to compete where the cost of each additional unit produced is close to zero? Or is a model like the one that Netscape is applying more appropriate?

Netscape is not just giving away its browser; it is also giving away the source code for the browser. Independent software vendors and users can add applications to the browser to enhance its value and, indirectly, the value of the product package that Netscape offers to the market.

This kind of pricing does not conform to the pricing models that were constructed for the industrial age. Have we reached an information age? In 1995, the value of information-related products such as computer hardware and software, telecom products, Internet products and so on produced in the US exceeded, for the first time, the value of products from or associated with that exemplar of the 20th-century industrial age, the car industry.

Consider another example. In a typical product launch or share-of-voice exercise up to the 1970s, an organization would use television, radio, hoardings, print media and/or trade shows as vehicles for its advertising. Over time, these messages would build and maintain interest among consumers. In the 1990s, an organization can interact in real time with consumers and deliver tailored products and services almost in real time. Dell, for example, delivers made-to-order computers in two days for a customer accessing Dell through an on-line advertisement on PointCast. Toyota delivers made-to-order cars in 14 days. The entire process of awareness, interest, trial and purchase can be telescoped into a very small time-frame. At the same time, consumers have more access than before to information about competing products and services. How does an organization compete in a landscape where the old rules are breaking down or being stretched?

The electronic market

Both the above scenarios illustrate a change in the competitive arena of companies – they suggest that competitive strategy in electronic markets is likely to be different from that in "industrial" markets. Increasingly, companies are competing in a marketplace that is information-based and electronically mediated.

An electronic market is an agglomeration of producers, buyers, intermediaries and electronic infrastructure providers. Between them they provide an electronic medium within which producers and buyers can carry out exchange transactions. Users gain access to the electronic medium via new interactive multimedia. These are two-way, real-time, audio-visual communication systems that give access to content stored on computers, enabling consumers and businesses to:

- provide and interactively access content
- communicate through the medium
- conduct exchange transactions in real time.

Companies are starting to use the new media for a wide range of activities: product development; gathering information from customers; exchanging information with customers, suppliers and complementary product providers; promoting, advertising and distributing products and services; and exchange transactions. New entrants use the new media extensively to compete with established companies that rely more on traditional media. Experts perceive the new media and electronic markets as both an opportunity and a threat. They lower costs for companies and lowered costs can then be passed along to customers as lower prices.

The stock markets are implicitly beginning to recognize this change by giving unheard-of valuations to new companies that symbolize it. For example, Tobin's Q (the ratio of a company's market value to the book value of its assets) is close to 1 for companies such as General Motors and AT&T; it was 6.5 for WorldCom in November 1997; and Microsoft's Q value has hovered in the mid-teens. The financial markets have started rewarding companies that are *expected* to have leading-edge future performance rather than those that have good *present* financial statements.

Changes in how companies compete

The changes for companies competing in electronic markets can be divided into marketplace changes, changes within companies and changes within the tactics that companies use.

Changes in the marketplace

Perhaps the most significant indicator of the advent of the electronic market is that companies are no longer lone rangers. Products of all kinds are using an increasing number of technologies and rare is the company that possesses all.

Even the most "low-tech" products such as breakfast cereals are beginning to incorporate chips on the packaging that automatically lower the price as the cereal nears its expiry date and simultaneously update the retailer's records. This requires co-operation between cereal makers, chip makers and retailers. It also makes information (about product expiry) a very explicit part of the product offering. No longer can a cereal maker simply hand over a batch of cereal to the retailer and consider its job done.

In the 1980s Procter & Gamble's Pampers Division entered a strategic partnership with the Wal-Mart supermarket chain that sells so many of its disposable nappies. Wal-Mart agreed to transmit daily Pampers sales data from each of its nearly 2,000 locations to Procter & Gamble. Using this data, Procter & Gamble restocks Wal-Mart's stores with no action needed by Wal-Mart. The result almost doubled Pampers' inventory turns in the first year to nearly 100 and saved Wal-Mart inventory and staff costs – a prime example of software-based integration of point-of-sale data with a manufacturing and logistics system.

If this example is symptomatic of a trend across industries, what are the implications?

- The boundaries between companies are blurring. Cisco Systems, Dell, Sainsburys, Asda and Yoko-Itado are other examples of this increasing porosity in company boundaries.
- The nature of transactions with customers is changing. In the industrial age:
  - companies sold a product and received money
  - companies held nearly all the information in the exchange; the resulting asymmetry in information made the seller more powerful
  - companies "broadcast" messages to a mass audience of buyers – advertisements during the annual Super Bowl broadcast in the US represent the high-water mark of this genre; the audience that can be reached in this way is showing signs of declining in developed economies
  - transactions were conducted during business hours in shopping centers, to which the buyer went in person; to buy a stock an investor had to call a broker, who then bought the stock during trading times only.

Now a company provides product benefits through functionalities and information about functionalities and services. It attempts an interchange of emotions with the customer using new interactive multimedia. When CDNow sells a recording it is able to obtain a detailed profile of the customer that it uses to alert the customer to new music of his or her preferred genre. Anticipating consumer desires increases the affinity that the consumer is likely to have for the service provider.

Information access is more symmetrical – witness the change in attitudes among car dealers with the advent of Auto-By-Tel on the Internet. Auto-By-Tel aggregates data from geographically dispersed dealers and offers potential car buyers with prices that are, on average, 10 to 15 per cent lower than those obtainable at the

Industrial age and information age transactions

	Industrial age		Information age (electronic market)
	Seller	Buyer	Exchange
Value received	Money	Product or service utility	Economic, informational and emotional value
Nature of communications	Sender	Receiver	Both send and receive - bilateral interaction
Nature of information exchange	Seller has greater access; large information asymmetry	Consumer or buyer has limited access	Lower information asymmetry; shared information access
Place where transaction takes place	The "physical" marketplace	The "physical" marketplace	Anywhere
When transaction takes place	Business hours	Business hours	Any time
Transaction orientation	One-time transaction; optimise company profits on the transaction	Get a good deal on the transaction	Repeated transactions over time
Feedback time	Slow	Slow	Real time

Table 1

nearest dealer. Auto-By-Tel decreases the search costs for the consumer and enables comparison that was not possible before. Consumers do not haggle with car dealers; dealers bid to get the consumer's business.

Another point of difference with the industrial age is that customers can use filters to choose which company messages to receive. PointCast subscribers, for example, get messages that reflect the channels that they receive. Telephone subscribers in France can choose to listen to a 15-second advertisement if they want to make a free local call; or they can make a local call with nominal charges. The trend is towards paying customers to look at advertisements.

Guidelines for companies

Table 2 summarizes the differences between competing in the industrial age and in electronic markets. Listed here are some guidelines for companies:

- Be clear which economic web your company is part of and its role in the web. Also, is your company's objective to enlarge the revenue-generating pie or to enlarge its share of the pie? Develop appropriate marketing strategies according to the objective.
- Have a partnering strategy ready; otherwise your company will end up in bed but with the wrong partner.
- Bring other players in the economic web closer through tight feedback loops; increase their switching costs.
- Innovate to move to the next base of competitive advantage before rivals have caught up with the present one.
- Recognize that while a five-forces analysis is still a useful tool, electronic markets are dynamic not static; suppliers can become customers and competitors and vice versa, which can complicate things.

Industrial age and information age competition

	Industrial age	Information age (electronic market)
Players in the competition game	Members of the "industry"	Anyone
Partnering orientation	Partnering not a preferred option; companies prefer ownership of the means of production - to "integrate vertically"	Partnering is a preferred, even required, mode; choice of partners is critical to success; partnerships tend to be temporary
Bases of competitive advantages	Sustainable (over longer periods)	Short-term advantages that erode quickly; company needs to create a new source of advantage continuously
How to compete	Be market- and customer-driven; deliver better (than competition) value to the customer	Find the balance between being market-driven *and* driving the market to deliver superior value

Table 2

Transactions take place anywhere and at any time. A consumer can withdraw cash at any time; eventually investors will be able to buy and sell stocks on Nasdaq at any time whether they are in Austin, Texas or New Delhi or London.

Table 1 illustrates the changes in exchange transactions between the industrial age and the information age, between the "physical" market and the electronic market.

■ Competition can appear from anywhere. Barnes & Noble, the bookseller, was outflanked by Amazon.com for two years before it set up its own online channel. Such strategies by new companies that use the properties of electronic markets are being repeated in other industries where incumbent companies have established methods of doing business that do not involve electronic markets. Incumbent companies are especially vulnerable if their methods deliver profits and the new media offer benefits that are uncertain and difficult to quantify.

Changes within companies

Information is available in real time to all parts of the organization (although caveats about who is allowed access to what still apply in many organizations). Whether the information gets used is, of course, a different question. A corollary is that information about customers and suppliers no longer goes up the marketing ladder and then down the hierarchy in other functions – it flows laterally. Similarly, production information also flows laterally to marketing and finance.

Access to information can potentially be at all levels of the organization, not just at the top. This is already the norm in companies such as Procter & Gamble, Dell and Cisco Systems. More and better information is now available at the periphery of companies, where they connect with customers, suppliers and complementary product providers. A sales representative from Dell calling on a present customer has real-time information on what the customer has bought from Dell, when the product was bought, its service history, Dell's present production and technology plans and so on.

As the richness of information grows so do the links between the organization's parts and between the organization and customers, suppliers, competitors and complementary product providers. This implies cost savings and efficiencies.

Innovative businesses have quickly capitalized on the advantages such "connectedness" can convey. The Italian clothier Benetton, for example, has substituted information for inventory by collecting daily sales data from around the world. This allows it to make manufacturing decisions based on purchases rather than having to rely on stock made months in advance. This new system has created a direct feedback loop from the customer to the manufacturer, circumventing the delay of information transfer through retailers and wholesalers. In addition to cutting inventory, carrying costs and retail markdown expense, the new connection provides better input about customers' design preferences.

Changes in tactics

A lack of all required technologies, the blurring of company boundaries and an increase in connectedness means that partnering decisions gain importance for companies. Partnering decisions, perhaps, become the single most important determinant of a company's competitiveness.

A corollary is that competition is not just between individual companies; it is also between economic groups or webs of companies. Some companies can then choose to hedge their bets by being part of more than one web. To compete more effectively with other groups, a company will need to make it more expensive for important and/or long-term partners to switch to other webs.

Many partnerships will not be long term. Companies will need to define for themselves the length of each potential partnership to avoid turning partnerships into liabilities. For temporary partnerships, companies must be able to part amicably, especially when there is a probability of future partnerships with the soon-to-be-ex-partner.

A company's reputation as a partner in its existing partnerships then becomes a key element in attracting new partners and a means of providing a benefit package to the consumer that is better than competitors'. Such changes imply that a standard five-forces analysis of the market (as advocated by Michael Porter) would be insufficient. Customers, suppliers and complementary product suppliers can change roles in this dance of partners. What if a company plays more than one role at any given point in time?

A related question that will need to be addressed by companies in electronic markets is as follows: if a company is part of an economic web, then does it benefit more by contributing to expanding the associated revenue-generating "pie" (the end-user/consumer base, the usage of the end-product and so on), thereby obtaining increased revenues from its constant share of a growing pie? Or should the company increase its share of the pie at the expense of other partners in the economic web? More importantly, what is a company's position in the web with respect to its partners, suppliers and customers?

Wider access to information implies that companies now need to compete on the assumption of information symmetry. This means markets that are closer to being "friction free." Friction-free markets imply that the speed of competitive processes increases. Products are delivered faster; information about products is delivered faster; feedback about products is available more quickly – sometimes without the customer knowing about it; new entrants are able to scale many entry barriers in a shorter time than ever before; competitive reactions and counter-reactions get telescoped into less time.

The outcome is that there will be no one sustainable base of competitive advantage. Test marketing as we have known it in the consumer packaged goods sector will disappear. This trend is already evident in software and cars, where companies get together with suppliers and consumers to develop products.

Companies can at best have a temporary advantage and they need to move on to the next temporary basis of advantage as the competition catches up. Therefore they need to scan constantly the market and their own resources to identify the next source of competitive advantage.

Owing to faster information flow and consequently tighter feedback loops, opportunities to shape markets increase. Dell not only builds to order; it also continually uses the channel it has established with its customers to educate them about the latest developments in technology. It often develops products using inputs from those same customers. Thus Dell is able not just to respond to the environment; it is also able to change the environment that it operates in. Recent research suggests that it is possible to "drive the market" through the use of, for example, technology licensing in computer hardware and software markets and in telecom markets. Previously, only a General Motors or a Nestlé could determine the shape of a market. Today, a start-up such as Junglee – founded in 1996 – has the potential, according to many analysts, to change the structure of the online market. Junglee is creating software that will be able to do intelligent searches for information from any electronic database. Consumers will then be able to move from Boolean searches on HotBot.com to natural language searches. Such a product multiplies the potential advantages of the new interactive media for the consumer.

The caveat is that the shape of an emerging electronic market is not clear at the outset. This uncertainty results from the increase in connectedness of companies, of companies with individuals and of individuals with individuals. Theory suggests that increasing connectedness makes it more likely that discontinuities will occur in the market because of the emergent properties of adaptive systems. An adaptive system is one that consists of independent "agents," each capable of making decisions using a few rules. Agents can be people, circuit breakers, trading instructions or DNA – any entity whose decisions can be defined in terms of rules.

Companies are agglomerations of people and can be thought of as super-agents with their own set of internal connections. Because they are connected, the actions of one agent affect the choices of another. Simulations with large numbers of interacting agents show that they behave in ways that are often unpredictable; the properties of such systems are said to "emerge" from the behavior of the connected companies and individuals. Often these emergent properties are "non-linear" – that is, they are volatile, like the stock market. Companies, therefore, will need simultaneously to adapt to and shape the market. They will need to find the balance between evolving with the market and influencing the market's direction of evolution to deliver superior value to customers.

Summary

Information technology is changing the way that markets operate. The truisms of the industrial age are buckling and giving way. Here **Arvind Sahay** considers the implications for competitive strategy. Overall, he argues, the ease of information transfer – for companies, consumers and, indeed, all players in the marketplace – means that markets will exhibit a greater degree of "connectedness." Company boundaries are becoming more porous. The need for carefully thought-out partnership strategies will grow as strategic webs become the optimal mode of competion. The speed of information flow means that opportunities to shape markets will be greater than ever; but by the same token, electronic markets are likely to behave in highly unpredictable ways.

Suggested further reading

Sahay, A., Gould, J. and Barwise, P. (1998) "New interactive media: experts' perceptions of opportunities and threats to existing businesses," *European Journal of Marketing* 32 (7/8): 616–28.

Sahay, A., Srivastava, R.K. and Kotabe, M. (1998) "Using technology licensing to drive the market: an exploratory study," Working Paper, London Business School.

Pricing: part art, part science

by Lakshman Krishnamurthi

Pricing a product or service correctly is one of the most difficult things for a company to do. Marketing research can be used with reasonable success to find out what features customers would like and how important the features are. But when it comes to asking customers questions about how much they would be willing to pay, things get much more difficult. Why is this the case? This article will

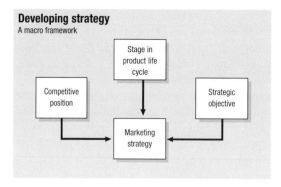

Developing strategy
A macro framework

Figure 1

first explore the strategic role of price and then discuss the different factors that influence price. It will pay particular attention to customer benefits as the key driver of price.

The strategic role of price

In pricing a product or service, your relative competitive position, your strategic objective for the product or line and the stage of the product life cycle are key macro determinants (*see* Figure 1).

If your prime strategic objective is profitability rather than market share, you will price less aggressively and seek market segments that are willing to pay your prices rather than cut prices to appeal to a larger segment. It is not very realistic to expect to maximize both profits and market share in highly competitive markets.

In the web browser market, Microsoft gives away its Internet Explorer product – an unbeatable strategy for building market share. Netscape, which used to charge for its browser, is now providing it free in a struggle to survive. Clearly, you must bear in mind short-term and long-term objectives as well as cross-subsidization. If giving away a product helps build the customer base for other products in the future, the short-term hit could turn into a long-term bonanza.

Is your main aim customer satisfaction? Do you believe that satisfied customers will result in market share and profits? Then the pricing implication is to take a long-run view of the customer and realize profits over a more distant horizon.

The stage of the product life cycle affects price as well. In the introduction and rapid growth stages, prices tend to be high because demand is strong and there are fewer competitors. As the product enters the slow growth and maturity stages of the life cycle, relative price becomes a pressing issue.

Who is your customer? If you cannot answer this question clearly, you cannot articulate a coherent pricing strategy. The fundamentals of marketing are knowing *who* you are going after (segmentation and targeting), *how* you are going after them (positioning) and *what tools* you should use (the marketing mix, which includes pricing). Figure 2 depicts the key elements of strategy design.

Factors that influence price

The customer channel

The channel is a factor when players in the same industry use different ways of reaching the end customer. For example, Dell sells its computers directly to the end customer whereas Compaq uses intermediaries in addition to selling directly.

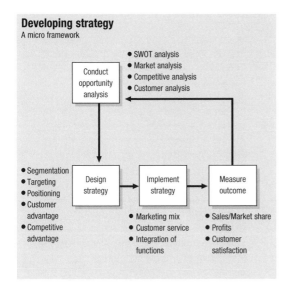

Figure 2

Assuming the same efficiencies and same end-user prices, Dell will earn more profit on each machine because Compaq has to provide incentives to the channel. Dell does not participate in the mass market retail environment and hence does not have to be as aggressive in pricing as Compaq.

Regulation

Whether this is a factor depends on the business. In some countries, regulation affects the price that can be charged – for example, to provide a targeted rate of return.

Costs

A product's variable cost is the pricing floor. The ceiling is whatever the customer is willing to pay. Consider the following example. A company manufacturing jeans sells 50,000 pairs at $10 a pair. The manufacturing plant has capacity for 80,000 pairs. The total manufacturing cost is $350,000, which includes a fixed manufacturing cost of $100,000. There is also a fixed selling cost of $50,000. The company gets an order for 20,000 pairs at $6.50 a pair, which is below the manufacturing unit cost of $7 a pair. Should it accept the order?

From a purely financial point of view it should because the variable cost of manufacture is only $5 per pair ($250,000/50,000); so each pair will make a positive contribution to profits of $1.50, yielding a total additional profit of $30,000. The company will not incur any additional fixed costs because there is excess manufacturing capacity of 30,000 units and the special order is only for 20,000 units.

Three costs need to be kept in mind:

- the *variable manufacturing cost of goods* of $5 per pair
- the *absorption cost*, which is the variable manufacturing cost plus the fixed manufacturing cost of goods; here the fixed cost is $2 per pair, so the absorption cost is $7 per pair
- the *full cost* or *fully distributed cost*, which is the absorption cost plus the fixed selling cost; here the fixed selling cost is $1 per pair, so the full cost is $8 per pair.

If the total fixed costs are allocated on a unit basis, they will change with volume. It

How to estimate price sensitivity

To estimate how customers would react to a price change, one must have some feel for their price sensitivity. The higher the value customers place on a product, the lower their price sensitivity.

There are several ways of measuring price sensitivity. Before introducing brand new products and services, one can resort to: judgment; using analogous products and making adjustments to reflect the uniqueness of the new product; focus groups, where the concept is described and a prototype-demonstrated; surveys, where again the product is described; and conjoint analysis, where different versions of the product are created hypothetically and customer reactions are obtained. Other options are limited experimentation and beta testing. For existing products and services where historical data are available, statistical methods such as regression analysis can be used.

In research that I have conducted with a colleague, we have found that an increase in mood-type, non-price advertising can reduce price sensitivity. Of course, the cost of the advertising must be compared with the increased revenue arising from the higher price that can be charged.

In other research we found that although loyal customers select the brand they are loyal to even if the price goes up, they decrease the quantity that they purchase.

That is, loyal customers are not very price sensitive in the choice decision but are price sensitive in the quantity decision.

Here is something you could do yourself to get an estimate of price sensitivity. Ask the product managers in your company how much in percentage terms sales are likely to change in response to an x per cent price increase or decrease (where x is incremented in some fashion, say two per cent, four per cent and so on up to ten per cent). Obtain responses from several informants for each product. Ask them to justify their response. If you have multiple products, it would be very instructive to compare the price elasticity estimates across products. You should be able to relate characteristics of the different products to the varying price elasticity estimates. For example, you would be likely to find greater price elasticities in more competitive markets, when many substitutes are available, when relative marketing spending is low and when the expenditure outlay by the customer is large.

If your markets are geographically separated or relatively self-contained, you could even experiment in one representative area to learn about price response.

Pricing is both a science and an art. Theory will get you some way in understanding the science; but only by practice will you learn the art.

is better to treat fixed costs as a lump sum and subtract them from total contribution to calculate profits than to allocate them on a unit basis.

The point of this simple example is that fixed costs are not relevant when you have to take a pricing decision under existing plant capacity, equipment and basic operating conditions. Maximizing contribution is the only way to cover fixed costs to the maximum extent possible. So if you have an option to manufacture product A or product B and if A yields a greater *total* contribution than B you should pick A from a financial point of view.

Going back to the jeans example, what are the consequences of accepting the new order? What if the first buyer, who paid $10 a pair, finds out that someone else paid only $6.50 a pair? The jeans manufacturer must make sure that there is no spillover from the secondary market into the primary market. Selling to an overseas buyer is one way. Making sure that the special order is sold under a different brand name is another way. Slightly altering the jeans for the special order is a third way.

If you are a low-cost producer should you price your products lower? No! Costs are an internal matter, prices are an external matter. The price you can charge depends on prevailing competitive prices and on the value your customer segment places on your product.

Customer value

Consider the personal computer market, which could be divided into the following segments: corporate, business professionals, small office/home office, government, military, education, scientific computing and family/home. Is price the most important driver of purchase in every segment? Probably not. Everyone wants the best value but that does not mean the lowest price. One should not confuse price with value.

So what is value? Value is idiosyncratic. One person may have high value for a particular Mazda car; another may have no value for it. Value is relative; there are no absolutes. It is this factor that makes pricing an art as well as a science. Value is derived from the economic, functional and psychological benefits provided by a product. Economic benefits are driven by price and increased productivity. Functional benefits are obtained through product features. Examples of psychological benefits are satisfaction, comfort, security, peace of mind, control, power and so on.

Suppose the Social Security Administration wants to buy 500 computers. Price is likely to be the most important factor in the purchase. As a computer manufacturer you might try to sell them a CD-Rom drive at a small premium over the cost of the drive. The SSA will reject this feature. For it the CD-ROM drive is worth zero. On the other hand the same CD-Rom drive can be sold at a high premium when it is packaged in a multimedia computer sold to the family/home segment. The latter segment is also price sensitive but the value derived from the CD-Rom drive is greater than the price of the drive.

Figuring out what customers value is not easy. If your product is going to replace a product that the customer currently uses, a value-in-use analysis can demonstrate the additional benefits. These benefits can be translated into monetary terms. The price of the product currently used serves as the reference price. The net benefit, which is the difference between the benefits gained and the additional costs incurred by using the product (training costs, for example), added to the reference price is the value of your product.

The astute marketer returns some of the surplus benefit to the customer and charges a price lower than the value. Combining beta testing (where the product is given to selected users to try out) and value-in-use analysis is one way of assessing customer value and the price to charge. For example, Xerox used some 20 beta sites in launching its very successful Docutech Production feeder product.

For brand new products, customer education and trials are critical in enabling the customer to understand what the product can do for them. But setting the price of new products even after the customer understands the value is still hard. Unlike existing products, which serve as a benchmark, brand new products satisfy needs that customers could not articulate on their own.

Competition

No one is immune to competition, at least in the long run. The extent to which competitors should affect your price depends on the following factors:

- What is your brand equity? How loyal are your customers?
- How substitutable are the products?
- What is the extent of market concentration?

If you are the market leader you are less vulnerable to competitive pricing actions. Compaq is less affected by Gateway than vice versa. This means the cross-price elasticities are asymmetric. Regardless of the asymmetry, however, the higher the cross-price elasticity the closer the product is to a commodity.

Smaller players are usually the hardest hit when the leader or one of the major players cuts prices. Their "me too" strategy is founded on the price advantage they have, which is eroded by the major players' price cut. The smaller players have to cut their price further but they do not have much of a cushion since they operate on very small margins. This does not mean that all is lost. The name of the game is differentiation. You may be unable to differentiate on the basic core product but might be able to differentiate on the augmented product. Better response time, reliable delivery and customized services and support are all ways in which one player can build differentiation over another.

In the laser printer market, Hewlett-Packard has a market share of over 60 per cent and its printer prices are a little higher than the competition. This is the power of brand equity. Of course, HP's power did not arise by accident nor did it come cheap. HP has devoted a lot of marketing dollars to building the Laserjet brand name. This equity insulates it from pricing actions by competitors. By constant innovation and extension of the product line to cover a wide price range, HP has acquired a commanding position in the printer market.

Compaq, which is so successful in personal computers, exited the printer market after only two years when it realized that it could not make a dent in HP's share. HP has become the technical and psychological standard when it comes to laser printers. The value that the customer derives from the psychological benefit of owning an HP printer is greater than the higher price of the printer relative to the competition.

Advantages based on functional innovation tend to be short lived. But a psychological advantage, properly nurtured, can live on for a long time. It is brand equity that makes cross-price elasticities asymmetric and favorable to you.

If value is relative then obviously competitive prices matter. The customer does not make a choice in a vacuum. The smart marketer builds in differentiation, real or perceived, to try to make comparisons across products more difficult. The smart marketer also finds the market segment that will value these differentiating features.

Store brands and generic products placed right next to national brand products on US supermarket shelves are cheaper yet have had little success in many product categories. Among the best examples are over-the-counter pain relievers: generic aspirin is outsold by Bayer aspirin and generic acetaminophen is outsold by Tylenol and so on. Customers do not swallow the brand name. But the psychological cost of making a mistake is greater than the price difference, so customers select the trusted branded product.

Such examples, where perceptions play an important role, are not just found in the consumer domain. In business decisions involving the purchase of mainframe computers and large copiers, say, or the selection of consulting companies and so on, perceptions are important too. In all these cases, particularly when the financial outlay is large, there is a reluctance to choose the lowest-priced vendor or supplier. Saving money is only one of the three benefits, the economic benefit, that contributes to value.

Research conducted by Xerox among customers for its large copiers found that the large Fortune 500-type accounts cited reliability and ease of operation as far more important than price in the equipment purchase decision and technical expertise and guaranteed repair time as more important than price in the service purchase decision. Government and education accounts, by contrast, cited price as most important in both decisions. This does not mean that price is not important to the Fortune 500-type accounts. What it means is that a copier manufacturer that bids low – and sacrifices functional and service benefits – may not win the account against a higher priced bid.

So what is the bottom line? Given the targeted market segment, you have to stay within the price range of your competition. IBM learned this to its chagrin when the prices of its PCs were out of line with market prices in the early 1990s. You also have to differentiate your product. It could be through distribution, as Dell has successfully done. It could be through product functionality, like digital copiers from Xerox. It could be through low price, as South West Airlines in the US and Virgin Atlantic in the UK have done. It could be through an overpowering brand name and ubiquity, like Nike. It could be through highly personalized service, as several stand-alone opticians have done, despite charging higher prices in the face of enormous competition from chain operations. And so on. The point is to *do something!*

Summary

Setting the right price for a product is one of the most difficult marketing skills. In this article, **Lakshman Krishnamurthi** describes the many factors that marketers must consider. Balancing them is as much an art as a science. Costs obviously need to be covered but sometimes the overall business strategy means that this can be left to the long term; thus Microsoft gives away its Internet Explorer in order to build market share. Pricing also depends upon the value that customers assign to a product; the higher the value the lower their sensitivity to price rises. This in turn depends on the product's perceived economic, functional and psychological benefits – which are particularly hard to gauge in the case of brand new products.

Exploring the rules of the competitive game

by William P. Putsis, Jr.

Much of the research conducted in marketing over the past 20 years or so has been devoted to understanding sales response. We know a great deal about how promotions work and about their relation to sales response. Researchers have measured the way consumers respond to price changes across numerous product categories.

However, from a managerial perspective, understanding sales response alone is often not enough – anticipating and understanding the impact of rivals' moves can be a critical part of decisions about the marketing mix. If Procter & Gamble decides to reduce the price of its offerings in a given category, the effect on sales, share and profit will depend not only on how consumers respond but also on how its competitors react.

For example, recent price cuts in the ready-to-eat cereal category in the US by Post and Nabisco initially increased their market share from about 16 per cent to over 20 per cent. In response, Kellogg's announced a 20 per cent across-the-board price cut due to declining shares of its major brands. General Mills and Quaker Oats also subsequently reduced prices. In the end, Post and Nabisco's share was up only slightly – the ultimate consumer response was significantly lower than if their competitors had not reacted. A central characteristic of competition is that companies are mutually dependent – the outcome of a company's marketing action depends to some extent on the reaction of its competitors.

Theoretical research into competition generally uses game theory to draw conclusions about how companies are likely to behave and what the market outcomes will be. While the theoretical assumptions that are made about company behavior often seem quite reasonable, there is little empirical evidence about the competitive interaction that actually occurs in the marketplace. What little empirical research there is suggests that, across product categories and marketing mix instruments, there are significant variations in the type of interaction that takes place.

This article describes the techniques used in empirically measuring competitive interaction and summarizes the information available on the type of interaction actually found in the marketplace.

Measuring competitive interaction

In previous research, four different approaches have been used to measure the competitive interaction between market players: reaction function estimation, menu approaches, conjectural variation models and time series causal approaches.

- **Reaction function estimation** begins with mathematical models of demand and company behavior. Each company's optimal response function, called a "reaction function," is derived from these models. It describes, under various assumptions, each company's best response to a change in rivals' marketing activity. Statistical techniques are used to simultaneously estimate the company's reaction function and consumer demand.

- **Menu approaches** begin with the assumption that a certain type of behavior characterises the market interaction between companies. Market equilibria are derived for a variety of assumed behaviors (for example, "independent" and "leader–follower"). Based upon relatively sophisticated hypothesis tests, the objective is to test statistically which form of assumed behavior best fits the observed data. Since researchers infer company behavior by deciding which form of interaction fits the data best from a menu of competing possibilities, this approach is often referred to as the "menu approach."

- By contrast, the **conjectural variation approach** treats company conduct as a single parameter to be estimated. Rather than assuming various behaviors and testing which best fits the data (as in the menu approach), this approach entails the estimation of a conjectural variation or "conduct" parameter. For example, if both companies in a duopoly have estimated conduct parameters equal to zero, then independent behavior is inferred since this implies that neither company responds to its rival's actions. Alternatively, if one company has an estimated conduct parameter greater than zero while the other company's conduct parameter is equal to zero, then a leader–follower relationship is inferred. An advantage of this approach is that it does not assume a specific type of market interaction; instead it allows the data to describe it.

- **Time series causal approaches** use time series data to deduce chains of cause and effect in competitive interaction. The intuition is simple: if company B reacts to changes in company A's marketing, then company B's reaction will be observed *after* company A's action. Such a sequence of events would imply that A is the leader and B the follower. One valuable use of this approach is to confirm leader–follower relationships estimated by the other approaches.

Types of interaction

Previous research has attempted to classify or categorize competitive interaction, specifying three basic forms. First, as mentioned above, *independent* behavior implies a lack of competitive response. Second, *co-operative* behavior implies that companies' actions move together in a co-ordinated fashion. Finally, *competitive* behavior implies that companies maximize their own profits by responding competitively to rivals' actions.

Such interactions are not always easily inferred from actual market data: while simultaneous price increases might be evidence of co-operation, simultaneous price cuts might be indicative of "retaliatory" behavior.

Recently, a more detailed set of interactions – comprising three forms of *symmetric* and three forms of *asymmetric* behavior – has been specified. We begin by discussing symmetric forms.

Co-operative promotions imply that promotional decisions are made in a co-ordinated fashion – if one company increases its promotional intensity, the other reduces its promotional intensity to accommodate. Examples of this type of interaction might include the alternating promotions run by Coke and Pepsi. Alternatively, *non-cooperative* promotions imply that an increase (or decrease) in one company's promotional intensity is met by an increase (or decrease) in its rival's. Two companies competing for end-of-year market share with extensive coupon drops would be an example of such behavior. Finally, a lack of a response by

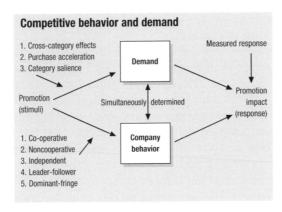

Competitive behavior and demand

Figure 1

both rivals is also symmetric. Such *independent* behavior might be expected in markets where demand substitutability is weak. Since there will be little or no cross-promotional response, the competitive response is also likely to be quite small.

Competitive behavior can also be *asymmetric*. Two forms of asymmetric behavior are *leader–follower* and *dominant–fringe firm* behavior. Leader–follower (also known as "Stackelberg") behavior occurs when one company (the "follower") reacts to the other's actions, whereas the other (the "leader") does not. For example, private labels are often thought to follow national brands' marketing efforts. In dominant–fringe interaction, two companies' competitive strategies take opposite directions – one company may behave co-operatively while the other behaves non-cooperatively. For example, a weaker or "fringe" company may simply not be willing to tackle a dominant company directly and may thus accommodate its larger rival's promotional efforts. But a company with a dominant market share might fiercely defend its position, adopting a non-cooperative stance.

With this outline of competitive interaction in mind, we can put together a complete picture of, say, promotion response. Given a company's decision to promote, competitive behavior and demand will interact as depicted in Figure 1.

On the consumer side, issues such as cross-category effects, the possibility of stockpiling the promoted item for future use and how salient the item is influence the demand response. In addition, the company's rivals will be likely to respond in one of the ways described above.

It is only after the demand- and supply-side responses are put together that we can get a complete picture of market behavior. The key is to be able to identify and estimate each separately.

Research to date

So what do we currently know about the nature of competitive interaction between companies? Recent research suggests that there is significant variation across categories and marketing mix instruments. For example, research has found cigarette advertising to be co-operative, while regular pricing (that is, excluding temporary price reductions) in the soft-drink market is not. Related research suggests that laundry detergent pricing exhibits a leader–follower pattern.

In one of the more comprehensive studies of competitive interaction to date, we looked at the interaction between private label and national brand grocery products

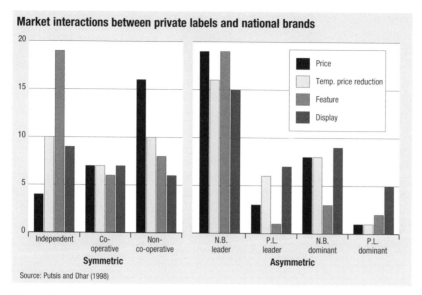

Market interactions between private labels and national brands

Source: Putsis and Dhar (1998)

Figure 2

across 58 categories. As is common in such studies, we used scanner data from US grocery retailers.

In each category, we focused on four marketing mix variables: usual price, temporary price reductions, feature advertising and display. Using a conjectural variations approach, we categorized each variable in terms of the five forms of competitive interaction discussed above.

Figure 2 summarizes our results, which reveal significant differences in competitive interaction across categories and promotional instruments. This is consistent with the broader literature.

With respect to private labels and national brands, our results suggest that national brand leadership is the most common form of competitive interaction for each marketing mix variable. However, this form of behavior describes – at most – 19 out of the 58 categories studied, while private label price leadership character-izes behavior in three categories – milk, frozen plain vegetables and fresh bread.

Not surprisingly, a relatively large number of categories (16) were characterized by non-cooperative price interaction. Aggregating across the four marketing mix variables, national brand leadership was the most common form of interaction (69 observations) and independent behavior the next most common (42), followed by non-cooperative interaction (40), dominant–fringe relationships (37), co-operative interaction (27) and private label leadership (17).

Although this characterization is quite detailed, it represents just the start of a broader understanding of how companies interact in practice. Overall we have little empirical evidence of the interaction that takes place across a wide array of industries and across a wide set of circumstances.

Conclusion

There is no one pattern of competition between companies in any industry in any setting. The pattern of interaction is often quite complex, with significant variation across instruments within a category. Most of the empirical research to date supports the notion that competitive rivalry is not symmetric and that not all marketing mix actions require a similar response.

This suggests that competitive interaction in any category is the result of a complex set of variables. As outlined in Figure 1, demand-side factors, market and industrial structure, company "personality" and category characteristics interact in a complex fashion to determine strategic behavior. Further, each marketing mix instrument is likely to be used as a strategic weapon for different objectives, which suggests that companies may very well take different competitive stances with each instrument.

There has been little research that attempts to explain why companies act as they do. When is a co-operative stance optimal? What circumstances encourage independent response? Clearly, managers need to consider the direction and size of the competitive response when evaluating the likely impact of a change in their firm's marketing mix. The information they require is only just beginning to emerge from research.

Summary

In making decisions about the marketing mix, managers must consider not only the likely response of consumers but also the competitive response of rival companies. The impact of a price cut, for example, may be diminished if rivals follow suit. In this article, **William Putsis** describes various techniques for investigating competitive interaction in the marketplace. Recent research indicates that companies' competitive strategies vary significantly across product categories and elements of the marketing mix. A company that has an independent strategy with regard to promotion, for example, may follow rivals' pricing decisions; this pattern may be very different in another category.

Suggested further reading

Putsis, W.P., Jr, and Dhar, R. (1998) "The many faces of competition," *Marketing Letters*, 9 (3). (Provides additional detail on many of the issues discussed in the present article.)

How do companies collude?

by Philip Parker

Question: In which of the world's 192 countries are anticollusion, antitrust or price-fixing laws *seriously* enforced? The answer is "none," except six, depending on the prevailing government. The six exceptions are Australia, Canada, New Zealand, the UK, the US and "Brussels." I say "prevailing government" because in the US, for example, the level of enforcement has often varied depending on whether appointments in the Federal Trade Commission or other regulatory bodies are made by a Republican or a Democratic administration.

With so few countries having or enforcing anti-competition laws, why do so few, if any, management textbooks discuss collusion? The answer probably lies in the fact that most textbooks are written for the North American market by North American academics. A manager there can go to prison for engaging in a collusive agreement with a competitor – and may even face criminal penalties if caught colluding with a non-US company in a country where collusion is commonplace (for example, Switzerland).

Lawyers in the US will often attend strategic planning or pricing discussions and warn the participants not to use phrases like "dominate the market" or "wipe out the competition" for fear that these words might come back to haunt the company in an antitrust suit.

This same level of caution exists in the free-thinking halls of North American business schools. If the *Wall Street Journal* were ever to publish an article saying that a professor at a leading business school was teaching MBA students how to price-fix with competitors, the career of that faculty member would probably be short lived.

But collusion is such a non-issue in most countries that there are no translations for the word in the local language – at least not with the pejorative force that it has in English. Ask a German for an equivalent expression, for example, and he or she will stumble around a bit until coming up with an expression like "agreement" or "understanding." In fact, Germany has elaborate competition laws but loopholes and culture result in these being ignored or ineffective.

The French definitely can translate "collusion," since it is also a French word. But to the French it does not signify fixing prices with a competitor and risking a jail sentence. Instead, the word is more likely to be applied to situations such as a man having an affair and keeping it hidden from his wife with the knowledge of others. Rather than talking about "price fixing," the French will simply say that competitors have a "common understanding."

Swiss people generally do not know that their country only recently came up with serious antitrust laws; nor do they know that such laws exist elsewhere. When they are told that their country has generally allowed companies to "consult each other on prices," they find this to be perfectly natural.

How can there be such a divergence of perspectives across democratic capitalist countries? Most countries, especially developing nations, lack the legal and judicial institutions to enforce laws against collusion but many of those that can have never found it useful to take the Anglo-American route. While many North Americans are now openly criticizing current antitrust laws as being inefficient and unenforce-able, the topic has rarely come up in Europe (until recently in the European Union institutions in Brussels). Even in France, where capitalism is seen by many as a necessary evil, there has never been a groundswell for laws against collusive practices.

Historical reasons help explain this divergence. Americans have long held the attitude that "whatever is good for the consumer is good for the country." In many European and Asian countries, on the other hand, "consumerism" is dominated by "firmism": "whatever is good for the firm is good for the country."

Competition, however, is inherently bad for the firm. Of the many lessons we learn from microeconomics, the most discouraging to companies is the long-run fatality of it all. Profits lead to entry by competitors, which leads to a reduction of profits (marginal cost pricing). In the long run, companies earn low or non-existent returns – many companies will go bankrupt, salaries will be driven down, jobs will be lost. In most economic models of competition, joint optimization across competitors yields higher profits, alleviating the rigors of competition.

Laws in countries such as Germany reflect the firmist mentality. For example, trade association laws in the US generally prevent closed-door meetings among

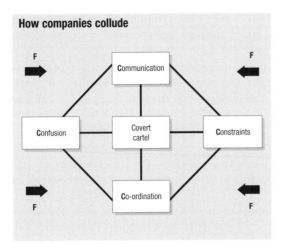

How companies collude

Figure 1

competitors and industry statistics are part of the public record. But try calling a trade association in Germany and asking for detailed industry statistics – you will be lucky to get a list of members (unless, of course, you are a member).

The four Cs of collusion

In theory, companies cannot strategically collude; the prisoners' dilemma tells us as much. In the prisoners' dilemma, a famous specimen of game theory, two suspected criminals are interrogated separately by the police. Both know that if they both say nothing they will each be sentenced to a year in prison; if they both confess they will each be jailed for five years; and if one confesses but the other says nothing, the confessor will be released and the other will be jailed for seven years. Collectively, the best strategy is to say nothing, thus minimizing time in jail. Yet for each individual, it is rational to confess, in the hope of immediate release – or, at the least, of not suffering a seven-year sentence. So both confess, yielding the worst outcome – a collective total of ten years in prison.

Similarly, collusion in the long run should break down as players will have an incentive to cheat. Yet in fact many companies *have* colluded in the long run. So how do they go about it? Based on a study of over 7,000 cases of collusion over the past five years across a broad spectrum of industries, I have found that four factors are needed to make collusion work – the "four Cs" (*see* Figure 1). These are communication, constraints, co-ordination and confusion. They are managed using "facilitators," labeled "Fs" in the diagram, which ensure that the Cs can survive in the long run – that is, that companies can *strategically* collude.

The ultimate goal for colluders is a covert cartel. A cartel is a publicly known agreement among companies selling substitutes (for example, Opec). A *covert* cartel is the same thing, except that the public is unaware of the arrangement; even in countries lacking laws against collusion, for obvious reasons it may not be desirable for consumers, or even employees, to know that such an arrangement exists. Unless the colluders manage the four Cs carefully, using the right doses of Fs, the cartel will break down. Price wars, research and development wars or marketing wars will then be likely to ensue.

The four Cs framework can be seen as a substitute for a competitive strategy model which assumes that competitors are independent players (like Michael

Porter's five competitive forces model). Nothing in it is really original. Research on the economics of industrial organization has already covered many of the findings of my study. The framework simply ties these ideas together in order to explain the success or failure of the cases I looked at.

Communication

To collude effectively, companies must send information to each other. If they cannot communicate with each other, the cartel will fall apart.

In most countries, communication is easy – managers can simply call a "competitor" on the telephone or meet in an office or some more discreet location, such as a downtown hotel, restaurant or country club.

Companies have also used a number of less obvious means of communication, sometimes successfully. These include: announcing pricing plans over online networks (US airlines were caught doing this using their reservation systems); using "meet or beat" pricing announcements over public broadcasting media – these serve to establish price floors; organizing joint trade events, symposiums, workshops and association meetings.

What do the parties communicate to each other? Here the second C is critical:

Constraints

Consider the following optimization problem faced by the companies in a covert cartel:

$$\int_0^T e^{-rt} [(Price - Cost) * Sales - Fixed]$$

$$\text{subject to}$$
$$Sales = f (price, advertising, etc.)$$

Each company has its own perception of this classic profit maximization problem. Each company has its own time horizon, T; each has its own discount rate, r; each has its own fixed costs and perception of the sales response function, which can be driven by any number of factors (prices, advertising, competitors' actions, new product development, distribution and so on).

In order for the cartel to survive, it is essential that all of the players have a similar sense of what this function looks like. Consider the simple case where the actual sales potential for a given market is $500 million. Company A correctly perceives the potential as $500 million, but Company B perceives the potential to be at least $900 million. Each of the two companies starts with a 50 per cent market share. Company B will be erroneously tempted to engage in aggressive marketing in order to expand its total revenue to absorb some of the perceived excess demand. In doing so, it will cut into the share of Company A. Company A may retaliate and the covert cartel will crumble.

A number of facilitators help to ensure that market constraints are similarly perceived by competitors. These include the formation of trade associations, workshops, seminars, industry-level training courses and other forums open to all players within the same industry. These lead to discussion of historical and future industry prospects and even in some cases to the publication or sharing of data among cartel members. In essence, the goal is to not keep all cost and marketing data secret; instead, colluders must reveal enough to ensure that all cartel players can adequately gauge market constraints.

In some cases, accounts and sales information is shared – perhaps by using common agents (sales forces, advertising agencies and so on). In other cases, third parties supply constraint information, including data vendors who collect and then resell to the industry pricing, sales and shipment data.

When communication channels are open and there is a common understanding of market constraints, the players can co-ordinate their conduct.

Co-ordination

Co-ordination of research and development activities, distribution, production, positioning or even pricing can help companies split the market, block further entrants or obtain cartel-level prices despite there being multiple suppliers.

A good example is provided by the two soda companies that were caught in the famed "Cola Payola" case, in which they used retailers to help co-ordinate pricing so as to block a third entrant. Brand A would be on promotion at retail from January 1 to February 23; Brand B would be on promotion from February 24 to April 16; Brand A would be on promotion from April 17 to May 4; and so on. Since retailers promote only one brand at a time there was simply no room in the calendar for a third brand to be promoted. In this example, the calendar is the facilitator.

Other facilitators include having board members sit on several companies competing in the same industry. Cross-ownership also facilitates co-ordination. This involves Company A and Company B both owning shares in Company C. Such arrangements are often called "joint ventures" or "consortiums." Company C's management helps A and B co-ordinate their market strategies. With Lars Roller, I have shown how cross-ownership can even exist and be successful in markets where collusion is criminal; our case in point was cellular telephone services in the US.

Finally, to achieve optimal co-ordination, companies need confusion, the last C.

Confusion

Confusion requires that consumers, employees, regulators and potential entrants should not fully understand the workings of the cartel (otherwise it fails to be covert). This typically involves elaborate use of peripheral cues or signals. One of the most common co-ordination schemes – round-robin collusion – generates such signals. This scheme (which is similar to the *dango* schemes common in Japan's construction industry) works as follows.

Imagine a covert cartel of seven companies, say, in the chemical industry. All of the companies sell to clients around the Pacific Rim. This is a case of multi-market contact. The same companies compete against each other at different, rather disparate locations.

Company A – a Swiss company, say – organizes a meeting of senior managers from all seven companies in a hotel suite in Singapore. The club decides to increase prices throughout the region to monopolistic levels – perhaps because demand elasticities or marginal costs have shifted. Company A will volunteer to increase its prices in Indonesia; the other competitors will, for the moment, stay put at their current price levels.

Of course, Company A's market share will fall in Indonesia and its customers will be upset; everyone else's shares will rise. What will Company A say to its customers in order to justify the price increase? The typical story involves costs. Company A will say, for example, that much of its product is based on dollar-based petroleum imports. The rise in the dollar relative to the Swiss franc has driven up its costs. Or, if the dollar is falling, it can claim that its overhead costs are in Swiss francs and that the recent appreciation of the Swiss franc has driven up its export prices. Whether the dollar goes up or down, Company A claims a cost increase.

The "round robin" part of this story comes from the fact that the other competitors use the same story in other Pacific Rim countries; each takes its turn as the "bad guy" who has to increase prices. Of course, within any given country the other competitors will also eventually be hit with this cost shock; they too will have to increase their prices a few months later. Prices throughout the Pacific Rim eventually increase across all competitors. Since no one Pacific Rim country tracks pricing strategies throughout the region, each country is under the illusion that the price rise was a one-off, uncoordinated event.

This game is played out across Africa, Latin America, Europe and the rest of the world. In each case, there will be a plausible explanation or cue that will make the price increases appear to be justified rather than the result of a covert cartel.

In retail markets for private label products, the cue is often the price difference between the national brands and the private labels; yet prices are nevertheless co-ordinated across the supposedly competing brands in order to monopolistically price-discriminate (the retailers, who sell one of the competing brands, internalize the competition across all of the players).

The collusion illusion

With the four Cs in place, a number of companies have been able to maintain the illusion that there is no collusion in their sector for a long time. They have been so successful that citizens in countries where no price-fixing laws exist often do not realize that price fixing is a daily event for most of the products they purchase.

Does this type of collusion exist in the US or the UK? Yes. It is just that the players need to be all the more clever in order to avoid being caught. High-profile cases brought by the US Justice Department or the Federal Trade Commission often turn out to be useful to collusive US companies: they serve to confuse the general public, who become convinced that covert cartels do not exist in the US and that price hikes are therefore due to competitive market forces.

It is relatively easy to learn about collusive behaviors. A casual conversation with an executive in a bar usually works. Otherwise, thousands of cases are documented in the trade press (F&S Information Access, Lexis-Nexus, BPO-ABI and Reuters Business Briefs all report cases). As for country-level laws or practices, the Economist Intelligence Unit publishes overviews in its Investment, Licensing and Trade reports and Icon Group publishes (via Dialog's Profound online service) an annual survey of the world's antitrust practices.

Summary

"Collusion" is a dirty word – at least, it is in the UK, the US, Australia, New Zealand, Canada and certain EU institutions. In the US, a manager can be jailed for colluding with a competitor. Yet elsewhere collusion is not a crime and is regarded as a natural business practice. According to **Philip Parker**, there are divergent perspectives: the US view is that whatever is good for the consumer is good for the country; the collusionist view is that whatever is good for the company is good for the country. Competition hurts companies, so collusion is reasonable. The author also explains in detail the strategies that companies use to collude.

Suggested further reading

Parker, P. and Roller, L. (1997) "Collusive conduct in duopolies: multi-market contact and cross ownership in the mobile telephone industry," *The Rand Journal of Economics*, summer.

Parker, P. and Namwoon Kim (1997) "National versus private label brands: an empirical study of competition, advertising and collusion," *European Management Journal*, May.

BRAND
STRATEGY

4

Contributors

Alice M. Tybout is the Harold T. Martin Professor of Marketing at the J.L. Kellogg Graduate School of Management, Northwestern University.

Karl Ulrich is associate professor of operations and information management at the Wharton School of the University of Pennsylvania. His research interests include product design and development.

Gregory S. Carpenter is associate professor of marketing at the J.L. Kellogg Graduate School of Management, Northwestern University.

Taylor Randall is a doctoral student of operations and information management at the Wharton School of the University of Pennsylvania.

Barbara E. Kahn is professor of marketing at the Wharton School of the University of Pennsylvania. Her research areas include consumer choice, brand loyalty and the purchase process.

Peter S. Fader is associate professor of marketing at the Wharton School of the University of Pennsylvania.

David Reibstein is William Stewart Woodside Professor and professor of marketing at the Wharton School of the University of Pennsylvania. His research interests include competitive marketing strategies and brand equity.

Bruce S.G. Hardie is assistant professor of marketing at London Business School. His research interests include market response analysis, choice modeling and marketing research methods for new product development.

Contents

Introduction

Good brands, it is sometimes said, can take years to build and (if you're careless) just days to destroy. Brand building and brand management are at the heart of modern marketing. Here we examine the evolution of brands since World War II and the growing range of goals that consumers hope to achieve through them. The pros and cons of different brand strategies are explained, as are the methods that supermarket shoppers use to make purchase decisions in the face of overwhelming amounts of product information. This module also looks at the dilemmas of product line extension – should an existing brand be extended or a new one set up? – and describes how to model consumer choice among stock-keeping units (SKUs).

Meeting the challenge of the postmodern consumer

by Alice M. Tybout and Gregory S. Carpenter

The pressure on brands today is intense. Products are functionally equivalent in many categories and new product development cycles are shortening so that functional innovations can be quickly imitated. The squeeze on margins in many categories has led some companies to leap conventional product market boundaries, making it increasingly difficult to anticipate who future competitors will be and how they will play the game.

New channels are emerging and power within conventional channels has shifted from the manufacturer towards the retailer as a result of both industry consolidation and the growth of private label brands (that is, retailers' own brands). Private labels now account for as much as 70 per cent of sales in some categories. Against this backdrop, it is not surprising that even powerful brands such as Coca-Cola, McDonald's and Levi's are struggling to sustain leadership positions. Some observers contend that these changes mark the end of the era of great brands.

However, such a simplistic view is contradicted by the fact that many brands continue to thrive. Consider the Swiss watch manufacturers. Japanese corporations, such as Seiko, Citizen and others offer highly accurate watches at ever-lower prices; yet buyers spend more globally on Swiss watches than on all other watches combined. Similarly, many good-quality, inexpensive pens are available. Yet Waterman's newest entry, the Edson line, includes a $400 ballpoint pen and a $700 fountain pen. Sales are brisk. Haagen-Dazs continues to have a significant impact in the growing super-premium ice cream segment. Toyota's Lexus sports-utility vehicle sells well despite its $60,000 price tag and the availability of many fine, similar alternatives at half the price.

The success of these brands reflects a growing realization that, as consumers and competitors have changed in fundamental ways, so must the nature of brands. Many of today's troubled brands were built a generation ago, an era of vastly different expectations on the part of consumers and another world in terms of competition. Today's "postmodern" buyers see these brands as irrelevant. Indeed, many of today's buyers do not see consuming brands for the sake of it as an objective, as previous generations might have done. Instead, postmodern buyers see brands as a means to an end.

The evolution of branding

As buyers, we seek to achieve the goals that motivate us. To achieve many of those goals, we turn to brands. The role of brands with respect to consumers' goals, however, has evolved, as have the goals themselves. These changes are sketched below.

Classic brands

After World War II, consumers turned their attention to their personal lives. While many factors, including mass production and television, facilitated the building of mass-market brands, the general concept of branding succeeded because it was compatible with goals that were widely shared at the time.

Consumers were anxious both to achieve and to belong. Branded products signaled that one had the economic means to purchase goods produced to consistently high standards, simplified decision-making and provided a common bond with others in the community.

This era produced many "classic" brands. These brands were typically linked to a single buyer goal, which was largely defined by the product function. Buying Tide or Ariel ensured that homemakers would achieve their goal of clean laundry. Eating at McDonald's guaranteed a predictable, hot, hassle-free meal. Detergents were for cleaning clothes and branded detergents competed to offer the cleanest wash. Fast-food restaurants were for satisfying one's appetite with a minimum of fuss and the best fast-food establishments did this more consistently and faster than others.

Contemporary brands

With basic functional needs met, buyers turned to a wider range of goals. While all consumers expect detergents to clean clothes, some value detergents that do so as efficiently as possible, whereas others seek an environmentally-sensitive solution. Recognizing this development, brand managers segmented markets according to the benefits buyers sought. Benefit segmentation produced remarkably successful "contemporary" brands. These brands, broader than classic brands, are built around functionality *and* associated benefits. Volvo cars, for example, most certainly serve the basic transportation function associated with motor vehicles. But the Volvo brand does not just stand for reliable transportation. Volvo is the car for that segment of consumers for whom the protection of self and family is a primary concern.

The link between Volvo the brand and self-preservation the goal has been carefully built over time. Consumers have been taught about the reinforced steel beams in the car's roof and side panels that protect the driver and passengers. The association with safety is further supported by the car's boxy styling. Advertisements feature crash survivors who testify to their belief that their Volvos saved their lives. As a result, consumers for whom safety is a salient goal are likely to buy a Volvo, much as those who seek high performance and status are likely to be drawn to a BMW.

Apple, the computer manufacturer, also practiced this contemporary approach to brand building and effectively challenged IBM's market position for many years. Apple focused not on processing power, which was IBM's strength, but on ease of use. This benefit connected with consumers' goals of achievement and independence.

Postmodern brands

The "postmodern" buyer presents a serious challenge to classic and contemporary brands. Volvo's US sales have suffered as safety features have become standard on most cars. Apple is struggling to reconnect with consumers who have succumbed to the dominance of Microsoft for the sake of convenience (because of extensive systems support and software availability, for example). While some companies, such as Gillette, continue to grow by constantly raising the standard of product performance with respect to a single benefit (for example, ever-closer shaves), it is also obvious that the contemporary approach to brand building offers no guarantee of success with postmodern buyers.

Postmodern buyers seek to use brands to attain a remarkably broad array of goals – much broader than contemporary consumers' goal sets. This larger array of goals is, in part, a reflection of the larger number of roles postmodern buyers play. Working parents, for example, play two obvious roles. Downsizing has forced many organizations to "do more with less," eliminating positions without eliminating the work done by them. Specialists have been replaced with generalists. Working fathers are playing more active family roles and working mothers are pursuing more active careers.

Some of the goals we seek are timeless – achievement, good health, love, membership in a larger community, intellectual stimulation, spirituality, recognition, freedom, responsibility. Others reflect our changing lives – status, convenience, stress reduction. A striking characteristic of postmodern buyers is their willingness to turn to brands to satisfy many of these goals. For example, status, frugality, social acceptance and individuality can all be achieved in some measure with the purchase or consumption of a brand of bottled water such as Evian.

Aiming for a variety of goals simultaneously creates conflict and stress. A new mother may seek to ensure her new family's health and safety but she also may have contradictory longings for self-expression and stimulation. Likewise, the executive longs for achievement and recognition but actions that serve those goals may undermine other goals, such as having a loving relationship with one's family.

The pursuit of multiple goals at once is complicated by the "time famine" that many people now experience. The perception that we are severely pressed for time often leads us to neglect important goals. We spend too little time with family, ignore friends, exercise too little and have too little fun. We all cope with this differently. Some people integrate goals or attempt to pursue several goals simultaneously. For example, an executive may conduct business by mobile phone while watching her child's soccer game. Another may take the family along on business trips so that "quality time" with loved ones can be squeezed in between meetings.

Building postmodern brands

The emergence of postmodern buyers creates opportunities for building brands that will meet their goals. Brands have evolved from serving specific, functional goals to playing a central role in consumers' efforts at goal-management. In essence, the brand manager becomes the consumer's assistant goal-manager. This new mindset suggests a variety of new strategies for building brands. Three appear to be having success.

Satisfy multiple goals

As buyers have sought to achieve an increasingly large number of goals, brands can help by enabling the consumer to satisfy several goals at once. Products that convert "down-time" to productive time, such as mobile phones and laptop computers have flourished. Pagers, which enable consumers to focus on achievement in the workplace while remaining connected to loved ones (or vice versa), have also gained widespread consumer use. However, to date, these responses to time famine have produced high-growth product categories rather than strong brands.

In less technology-intensive markets, some brands have delivered multiple goals with considerable success. Consider the example of Waterman pens noted earlier. The company's success in marketing $400 pens is, in part, attributable to the fact that these products are linked not only to the single goal – status – that is typically associated with luxury items but to multiple goals. Yes, the pen's high price undoubtedly conveys status and membership in the elite club of successful people but it is not merely self-focused consumption. The pen is of heirloom quality and can thus serve as a connection to one's children and grandchildren.

Resolve goal conflict

An alternative strategy for postmodern brands is to reconcile seemingly conflicting goals. Levis Dockers brand illustrates this point. Levis actively encouraged and helped some companies implement the concept of "casual Fridays," on which workers could forgo suits and wear more casual attire. Levis motivation for this strategy is obvious: on casual Fridays men would wear the Levis Dockers that they normally wore only on weekends and sales of Dockers would increase dramatically.

The reason that this strategy, which would have been unlikely to succeed a decade earlier, worked was that employers recognized that the longer hours they required conflicted with employees' goals of relaxing and expressing themselves. Wearing casual clothes at the office is one means of blurring the line between business and leisure, thereby integrating those goals.

Similarly, an important element in the successful repositioning of Sears, the US retailer, was the recognition of the goal conflict and role strain experienced by many homemakers over Christmas. On the one hand, the Christmas holiday presents an ideal occasion for achieving goals that revolve around family and friends. At the same time, meeting the expectations of these significant others for perfect presents, special meals and so on is time-consuming. As a result, the homemaker may actually spend little time relating to loved ones and feel disappointed and worn down.

Sears, with its broad selection of merchandise, has positioned itself as saving the harried homemaker time that might otherwise be spent running from store to store. It thereby enables its customers to achieve their goals. The message: brands can be built by helping consumers cope with goal conflict.

Satisfy neglected goals

Today's time famine often results in consumers focusing on goals such as financial security, social responsibility and social acceptance instead of more internal, self-orientated goals. Brands may forge strong bonds with consumers by focusing on intense, concentrated satisfaction of these neglected goals.

Harley-Davidson's following among successful professionals illustrates this point well. During the working week these people submerge their desire for individuality and freedom in order to meet professional goals and personal responsibilities; they are achieving conformists. On the weekend, these professionals (sometimes referred to as "Rolex riders") connect with their neglected individuality and rebel spirit by riding Harleys. This concentrated consumption directed at a neglected goal is facilitated by Harley-Davidson's clever brand extensions. Everything from black leather, spike-studded jackets to stick-on tattoos can be bought to complete the temporary transformation from button-down executive to Hell's Angel.

Parents also often neglect personal goals because their role requires them to focus on others. They too reward brands that help them to meet neglected personal goals. Indeed, the desire for autonomy and adventure has helped to fuel the rapid growth of sales of sports-utility vehicles, such as Rover Group's Land Rover and Chrysler's Jeep. These vehicles introduce an element of adventure into mundane tasks.

Conclusion

Sophisticated, time-pressured postmodern consumers respond to brands that address the goal-management challenges they face. They seek brands that allow them to pursue multiple goals at the same time. Brands are evolving to reflect this new reality. Volvo is expanding its traditional safety-focused positioning to encompass goals of individuality and self-expression. Volvos, we are now told, not only protect the physical person, they also contribute to one's psychological well-being by enabling escape to remote, pristine settings. Consumers also respond to brands that offer "extreme" consumption experiences, thereby compensating for the relative neglect of an important goal. Thus brands associated with self-indulgence, such as Haagen-Dazs ice cream and Starbucks coffee have also enjoyed healthy sales.

However, the goal-focused consumer also presents special challenges to the brand manager. When purchases are driven more by abstract goals than by functional product properties, the nature of competition can be difficult to understand and it can shift – sometimes all too quickly.

A competitor is any brand that satisfies some of the same goals. This presents both opportunities and threats. On the positive side, this broader market definition expands a brand's potential market. Thus Waterman pens may attempt to capture money that might otherwise be spent on jewellery or art. Further, the definition implies that brand extensions should be guided by a brand's link to goals rather than by similarity in product features. Leather clothing has few features in common with motorcycles but the Harley-Davidson name on both types of product makes good sense to the consuming public.

At the same time, competition across categories expands the set of potential competitors and increases uncertainty about how those competitors will behave. Waterman, for example, is likely to have a poorer understanding of the economics and likely strategies of art dealers and jewellers than of other pen manufacturers.

The notion that brand managers need to focus on underlying, enduring consumer goals rather than on the physical products they sell is not a new one. It is at the heart of the marketing concept. What is new is that the nature of brands, like the people who consume them, is changing in fundamental ways. The postmodern buyer plays multiple roles and has a wide variety of goals but little time to achieve them. While these changes threaten some brands, those that rise to the challenge are likely to reap substantial rewards because buyers need brands now more than ever.

Summary

Since World War II, brands have gone through three stages of evolution. First came classic brands. These typically positioned themselves as helping buyers to achieve simple goals such as cleaner clothes. Next came contemporary brands, which enabled consumers to attain additional goals – cleaner clothes without harming the environment, say. Finally, say **Gregory Carpenter** and **Alice Tybout**, we have entered an era of postmodern brands, in which time-starved consumers strive to attain a greater range of goals than ever before. Successful brands will be those that enable consumers to achieve many goals simultaneously, reconcile conflicting goals or satisfy neglected needs.

Brand strategies and consumer behavior

by Barbara E. Kahn

Once a consumer decides to buy a product from a particular category on a shopping trip, he or she then has to decide which specific brand to buy. Sometimes the brand decision and the product category decision are made simultaneously – the shopping list may specify "Tide" rather than just "detergent," for example – but often this is not the case. When the brand choice is made later, the consumer generally makes the decision in stages.

First, the consumer considers a set of brands that are acceptable on the basis of relatively simple criteria. Then the consumer chooses one from this set to purchase, usually applying a more detailed analysis. Observations of consumers' shopping patterns reveal that consumers spend an average of 12 seconds from the time the shelf is approached to the time the item is placed in the trolley. They examine only 1.2 brands on average. The rapidity with which consumers decide suggests that they rely primarily on memory in making their choices.

Consumers acquire information about the alternatives available to them before they enter a shop. Advertising, of course, is the dominant method for conveying product information to the consumer.

The way that consumers characterize their particular shopping needs can affect the way they go about acquiring information. For example, they can classify needs by product category, such as "fruit" or "ketchup." Such classification schemes are "natural"; they contrast with "ad hoc" classification schemes, which are constructed spontaneously for use in special instances. An example of an ad hoc scheme might be "foods for a Mexican dinner" or "things to take on a picnic."

In purchasing for an ad hoc goal, consumers are more likely to be influenced by in-store promotional cues and less likely to rely on memory, unless they have extensive experience with the particular goal. If a consumer is looking to buy products described by a natural classification scheme, the reverse tends to be true. These differences are more pronounced when the consumer is under time pressure.

In-store factors

Since consumers respond more to in-store cues when they are thinking about ad hoc categories, supermarkets have begun to organize some of their departments in accordance with these categories. For example, some supermarkets create an "Italian Food" aisle or prepare special "Fourth of July" or other holiday displays. Even within natural or traditional categories, the way brands are displayed on the supermarket shelf can affect how consumers gather information about them, and thus whether or not they consider a particular brand. For example, most supermarkets cluster products together by brand; thus, in the yoghurt category, all the flavors that Danone offers are displayed together, then all the flavors that Yoplait offers, and so on. This type of display encourages consumers to think first which brand they want to choose and then which flavors they want within that line.

The other option is to display yoghurts by flavor, so that customers first decide what flavor they want and then select a brand from that flavor category. The first

A healthy response for Kelloggs

An interesting opportunity to study how health information presented in advertising affects behavior arose in the US in October 1984, when the Kellogg Company, with the co-operation of the National Cancer Institute, began an advertising campaign to point out the benefits of dietary fiber in reducing the incidence of colon cancer. This was a telling campaign because previously it had been illegal to make such health claims for foods. The relaxation of the ban was a major event in the cereal market and was sufficiently isolated to facilitate study of how information in advertising may influence behavior.

Kellogg's not only attempted to educate the public about the health benefits of fiber but also promoted its own fiber cereal, "All-Bran." By the end of 1985, Kellogg's had extended the campaign to some of its other cereals and competitors had also begun to focus on the fiber theme. New fiber-based cereals appeared on the market.

The Federal Trade Commission analyzed this period to see how consumers reacted to the new health information. It looked first at consumers' response to the scientific information when producers were forbidden to advertise and then at the consumer response a year after the advertising had been in place. The FTC found that before Kellogg's campaign began consumers had to overcome

significant obstacles in order to respond to the new health information. First, they had to find out about the information, then understand it and then change their eating habits.

The study found great variation in the value individuals placed on health, which affected their desire to collect and use the relevant information. All else being equal, people who were more concerned with health were more likely to eat high-fiber cereals in any event. The newly released scientific information did not change their behavior. Consequently, in the pre-advertising period, the consumption of high-fibre cereals was relatively constant.

Once the ban on health-claims advertising was removed the consumption of fiber cereal increased. The data indicated that the advertising reduced the cost of acquiring information for consumers who were not likely to read about the health benefits in other media.

More generally, the study shows that consumers are likely to respond to information provided by advertisers that has value to them but that would otherwise be costly to acquire. Consumers are not likely actively to seek out such information but may respond to it if the cost of acquiring it is reduced.

type of display is likely to encourage consumers to buy the same brand for different flavors, while the second type of display is more likely to result in consumers purchasing different brands.

These differences in choice patterns as a result of how items are displayed within a category can be illustrated by comparing the way meat is merchandized in the US and Australia and Japan. In the US, meat is generally displayed by animal (chicken, beef, lamb and so on) and then by cut. In Australia and Japan, the meat department is arranged by usage or preparation – microwave, braise or grill, say – and the labeling is more descriptive. For example, a cut might be described as a "10-minute herbed beef roast." Recipes are visible on or near the package. Such merchandizing exposes shoppers to a greater variety of meat within a particular cooking style and results in more varied purchasing.

Brand familiarity and line extensions

Consumers' familiarity with brands affects which ones are considered. They are far more likely to notice familiar brands on the shelf first and to include them in their consideration set. Brands that are noticed first tend to inhibit the recognition of other brands. These factors are particularly important if a consumer is under time pressure.

Since a brand's familiarity affects whether or not it is considered, the brand name itself is one of the key factors in purchase decisions. A brand is said to have positive customer-based equity if consumers react more positively to marketing activity for it than they would to the same marketing activity applied to an unnamed or generic product.

Given that a strong brand name can influence purchase, many companies spend a lot on advertising to build up their brand names. Once a company has a successful brand name, there is usually a temptation to extend it to other products. This can be quite successful, even strengthening the original brand by clarifying the business definition. However, there are dangers.

Sometimes the extension can threaten the benefits associated with the original product bearing the brand. The risks appear to be greatest for extensions consistent with some expectations about the original product but not others. For example, Carnation considered extending its Friskies brand name to a new contraceptive dog food, to be called Lady Friskies, until tests showed that the new product would adversely affect sales of the original Friskies dog food.

Brand extensions can also dilute the power of the brand name if it is used on too many products. They can also confuse the consumer if the new product connects associations to the brand name that are different from the original product's associations.

Three factors need to be in place for a brand extension to be effective. First, the consumer must perceive that the brand's associations fit the new product. Using the Kodak brand name for a new ice cream would not be an effective extension. Second, the new item must be at least comparable, but preferably superior, to other items in the category. Putting a strong brand name on a copycat product may not be enough to persuade consumers to try the product. Third, the benefits that are being transferred from the brand name to the new item must be desirable in the category. Thus Campbell found that it was not a good idea to put its brand name on a new spaghetti sauce because consumers thought the sauce would be thin, like a soup.

Co-branding

Co-branding or partnering around new products is a growing trend in the supermarket. Two powerful brand names doubling up can seek greater influence. Arrangements vary, but generally the partners share research and development costs, slotting fees (paid to retailers to get better shelf placement), advertising and promotion budgets.

There are different degrees of partnership. Some arrangements are one-offs, such as when Disney promoted *The Lion King* by allowing Nestlé to print scenes from the movie on its chocolate bars. There are promotions that run for a limited time, such as when Grey Poupon mustard was promoted in advertising for Subway sandwiches in the US. There is also ingredient branding, such as Skippy peanut butter in Delicious cookies, or Kellogg's Pop Tarts with Smucker's fruit filling.

As with brand extensions there are both benefits and hazards to co-branding. Consumers expect the advantages of both brands to be evident in the product, which is potentially a strong selling point. Combining brand names can also expand product-market boundaries.

For example, if Pizzeria Uno decided that it wanted to increase consumption of pizza by promoting it as a breakfast food, it might make a deal with Kellogg's to name its new breakfast pizza "Eggo Pizza by Pizzeria Uno." By capitalizing on the "Eggo" brand name, which is associated with breakfast waffles, Pizzeria Uno may have an easier time convincing consumers to experiment.

On the other hand, if the co-branded product fails, then the reputation of the original brand name may suffer. Another potential problem is customer confusion – if the two brands have different images the customer may not understand the relationship. Finally, there is always the risk of overexposure.

Private label brands

Private label brands – or "store brands" or "own brands" – are retailers' own brands. Many chains, such as Safeway, offer different tiers of private label brands: Safeway's Bel-air, Town House and Lucern brands compete with premium products while its Marigold and Gardenside lines are more price-orientated. Private labels can be exclusive retailer programs such as US retailer A&P's Ann Page, or they can be manufactured by a third party, such as Loblaws (so the brand is not explicitly linked with the retailer's brand).

Private labels are different from generic brands. Generic brands are the no-name products that frequently appear in nondescript black and white packaging. Although when generics were first introduced in the early 1970s they received a lot of attention, they were never a serious threat to national brands because of their perceived inferior quality and packaging. Private labels, on the other hand, have achieved much greater success.

Private labels usually mean higher profits for the retailers. Margins on private labels can be 20 to 30 per cent higher than on national brands. Store brands can also build loyalty to the store: any retailer can sell Procter & Gamble products but only A&P can sell its private label brands. In addition, private labels are the only brands that occur throughout the store across many product categories. They are guaranteed full distribution in all the stores in a chain and are frequently given good shelf placement.

The popularity of private labels is growing in the US. Their market share has generated about 14 per cent of total supermarket revenue over the past decade and they represent 18 per cent of all units sold.

In Europe, private labels have made even greater headway. By some accounts, private labels represent as much as 32 per cent of supermarket sales in the UK and 24 per cent in France. In Canada, private labels account for 25 per cent of sales. The largest selling brand of chocolate chip cookies in Canada is Loblaw's private label, President's Choice.

One reason store brands have a greater market share in Europe and Canada than in the US is that the major supermarket chains in Europe and Canada are national. In France and the UK, the top five chains represent 65 per cent and 62 cent of grocery sales respectively. In Canada, Loblaws alone controls 27 per cent of the supermarket business. In the US there is less concentration. The top five chains in the US account for less than 20 per cent of the overall supermarket business, which is more regional and dominated by many medium-sized chains.

There are fewer national brands in the European and Canadian markets and their product range (sizes, packaging, flavors and so on) is smaller than in the US. The US market is much bigger than European markets, offering manufacturers better economies of scale for advertising and production.

These factors suggest that competition among manufacturers is more intense and the retail chains are individually weaker in the US than in the UK, France or Canada. This in turn suggests that the growth of private labels, although strong in the US, will probably remain lower there. But as the supermarket business begins to fall to national mass merchandisers, such as Wal-Mart – ranked the fourth largest food retailer in *Supermarket News'* top 75 list in 1996 – then the US market may begin to resemble the European.

In spite of the success of store brands, and in spite of their lower prices, US consumers continue to prefer national brands. However, the performance of private labels varies a great deal by category. In 1989, store brands accounted for 65 per cent of sales of frozen green and wax beans but for only 1.1 per cent of sales of personal deodorants. In some categories, the share of private labels is growing dramatically: in the disposable nappy market, the share of private labels rose from 21 per cent to 31 per cent in just two years (1991–93).

Several research studies have tried to identify the factors that contribute to the success of private label brands in a category. One study, using aggregate-level store data across 180 categories, found that the success of private labels in any particular category depended upon two factors: the quality that consumers attributed to them, and the activity of the retailers and manufacturers. Private labels appeared to perform better in categories where the objective quality of the private labels was higher and relatively constant. Interestingly, the study found that the cheapness of store brands, as compared to national brands, was not significant. In addition, promotional intensity had no impact.

Supply-side activities affect the success of private labels as well. Since retailers have to promote, brand and co-ordinate production for store brands, they are more likely to take on these additional costs in categories where there is more expected profitability. Thus, all else being equal, retailers are more likely to develop and support private labels in large categories with high profit potential.

The manufacturers of national brands also play a role. In categories where national brands are heavily advertised and where there is strong price competition among many national brands, private labels are less likely to succeed. On the other hand, if there is strong price competition between national brands and store brands, then store brands are more likely to succeed.

An experiment conducted on 1,500 shoppers found that one reason for the continued advantage of national brands over private labels is that consumers seem to evaluate brands primarily by extrinsic cues (such as price, brand name and packaging), rather than by intrinsic characteristics (such as ingredients and taste).

In the experiment, the shoppers tasted various products that were identified as either a national brand or a store brand. What they did not know was that half of the private label brands were actually labeled as national brands, and vice versa. The results showed unequivocally that the consumers evaluated the private labels as of lower quality even when the actual products tasted were national brands. Conversely, they rated the national brands as of higher quality even when those brands were actually store brands in disguise.

These results indicated that consumers use extrinsic factors to guide their choices and infer that the quality of private label brands is low because of the low price and lack of national brand name. The study also revealed that consumers seemed by and large to be more interested in quality than in value for money.

This suggests that private labels might perform better if they were positioned on

Checklist for marketers

- High-speed, highly focused shopping is the norm. The average consumer inspects just 1.2 brands per purchase. If consumers make most of their decisions before entering the store, are you doing enough advertising outside the store? And is your brand salient enough to capture attention inside?
- Consumers often use "ad hoc" product classification schemes – for example, "cocktail ingredients." Are there any such schemes for which your product is an obvious candidate? Can you encourage retailers to run suitably themed promotions or displays?
- Are retailers displaying your products by brand or product type? If your line is extensive, brand displays will be likely to maximize your sales; smaller lines are likely to benefit from product displays in which all brands are mingled.
- Brand extensions can boost your brand's strength provided they do not overstretch it. New product categories must be suited to the associations that your brand has and the products that carry it must be at least as good as competitors' offerings.
- Co-branding is potentially a powerful strategy provided that the brands in question reinforce each other rather than cancel one another out. Is it clear what benefit each brand can bring to the product? If not, customers will be confused.
- Competition between private label and national brands is increasing. National brands still predominate in many categories because consumers perceive them as being of higher quality. The task for private label brands is to confront this head on by positioning themselves on quality at least as much as price.
- Consumers need to assimilate a vast amount of disjointed information in making purchase decisions. If your product performs well in areas that the public is concerned with (it contains relatively few artificial ingredients, say), can you inform the public of this or encourage retailers to do so?

their quality rather than on their low price. Today's store brands can generally hold up to this kind of positioning. *Consumer Reports* magazine, for example, has repeatedly tested and compared private labels to other brands and found them to be of comparable, if not higher, quality.

Many supermarkets are now trying to capitalize on the high quality of some of their own labels. For example, in one New Jersey supermarket, consumers are invited to test the taste of the private label and the national brand in the store. The store manager has found this a very effective way to convert customers.

Gathering information about brands

In addition to brand name, there is other information that consumers may need in order to decide which brand to buy. Sometimes they get information about the characteristics of brands before they enter the store through advertising, word-of-mouth or direct experience. At other times they get this information at the point of sale.

Legislation in the US has standardized the presentation of some types of information. Retailers started to give unit price information in the 1970s. In 1990, manufacturers started to provide nutritional information about their products in a standardized way. When information is not standardized, consumers need to infer or interpret the facts in order to form judgments. In addition, collecting information costs time and effort, so consumers are only likely to do so if they perceive some likely benefit.

Although unit price information is supposed to be presented to customers on the shelf underneath each brand, it is frequently difficult to use. Sometimes brands are not located directly above the proper unit pricing label. Even if labels are accurately placed, it is still difficult for the customer to get the relevant pricing information about all the alternatives and then make the appropriate trade-offs.

Customers would use pricing information much more if the procedure were made easier. For example, if all the pricing information about brands within a category was listed in one place, with the unit prices ranked from lowest to highest, consumers could much more easily choose.

However, retailers may not always want to make choices easy for the consumer. Products that yield higher margins are likely to be the ones that fare poorly if pricing information is made transparently clear. On the other hand, when pricing comparisons are to the advantage of the retailer, as when retailers are trying to convince consumers of the worthiness of a store brand, then pricing information is generally more systematically conveyed. The store brand is frequently placed to the right of the competing national brand, with the difference in prices highlighted.

Another study tested how posting a simple list of nutritional information affected purchase behavior. Most evidence indicates that shoppers perceive sugar in cereal to be undesirable and try to reduce their sugar consumption. Therefore the researchers posted, right in the cereal aisle, information about the sugar content of all the breakfast cereals. The information was listed both alphabetically and in order of how much sugar each cereal contained. The average sugar content of all the cereal brands sold, and the market shares of high- and low-sugar cereals were measured before, during and after the information was posted. The results were compelling. While the posters were up in the store, consumers bought cereals with less sugar than before. Surprisingly though, the consumers returned to their old habits after the posters were removed. The information was only influential when it was present at the time of purchase.

Summary

Once a consumer has decided to buy a particular type of product, he or she then has to decide on the brand. Consumers typically consider only a restricted set of brands out of the many available. So the question for manufacturers, retailers and marketers is how brands get into consumers' consideration sets. Whatever the objective qualities of the product itself, consumers can be decisively influenced by extrinsic factors such as whether it is a national or a store brand. The accessibility of contextual information – about relative price or health benefits – can also be critical. Here **Barbara Kahn** discusses the factors that influence brand choice and the implications for tactics such as line extensions and co-branding.

Suggested further reading

Richardson, P.S., Dick, A.S. and Jain, A.K. (1994) "Extrinsic and intrinsic cue effects on perceptions of store quality," *Journal of Marketing* 58 (4) October, 28–36. (An investigation into why consumers prefer national brands.)

Ippolito, P. and Mathios, A.D. (1990) "Information, advertising and health choices: a study of the cereal market," *Rand Journal of Economics* 21, 459–80 (autumn). (The source for the cereal example above)

This article has been adapted from the author's *Grocery Revolution: The New Focus on the Consumer* (Reading, MA: Addison-Wesley, 1997), a review of academic marketing research.

Brand equity and line extension: how low can you go?

by David Reibstein, Karl Ulrich and Taylor Randall

Imagine that you are the managing director of Mont Blanc, a very successful brand in the premium pen market. Your marketing manager observes that while the company has been very prosperous at the top end of the market, most pen purchases are at the mid to lower end, currently occupied by such brands as Papermate, Sheaffer, Scripto and Pilot.

She argues that the company could be very successful in these other markets with the brand equity associated with the Mont Blanc name. Your general manager argues just as strenuously that Mont Blanc should not venture into other markets because of the potential damage to Mont Blanc's image and position at the premium end of the market.

Now shift your office to the Pilot brand, where your managers are wrestling with the question of introducing a high-end model. While the market is not nearly as large as the "utility" segment in which the company currently operates, there is the distinct possibility that not only will the new entry bring in revenue from the premium segment, it might also enhance the Pilot brand image and even further improve its share of the mid- and lower-end markets.

These two scenarios raise three main questions:

- *What are the costs and benefits of offering economy products within the product line of a premium brand?* This assessment is critical because product strategists often wish to exploit the equity of premium brands in the lower-priced parts of the market, where there is typically more product volume.
- *What are the implications of offering premium models within the product line?* Even if these products are not profitable when viewed in isolation, can they be justified when viewed in the context of their positive overall brand equity?
- *When should premium or economy products be offered within an existing brand and when should these products be offered under separate brands?* Potential benefits of separate brands include the equity a high-end brand could develop and the preservation of the equity of a premium brand when a set of economy products is offered under a distinct brand.

Why is brand equity so important? Companies invest in creating a brand preference that results in sales today but also adds value to the brand name. A strong brand equity will manifest itself generally in a price premium, an increased market share, reduced costs of introducing new products or a combination of these three benefits.

Often brands are extended to other versions of a product within the same category, such as Hewlett-Packard extending its name from InkJet printers into LaserJet printers. It has also become common practice to facilitate the introduction of new products by extending the brand name into related categories, such as when Hewlett-Packard made its transition from computers to computer printers or when Ivory Soap introduced Ivory Shampoo.

As brands offer additional products in their line or additional stock-keeping units that increase the span of their price/quality range, there is the question of whether to use the existing brand name or to create a new name. The higher the brand equity the easier it is to carry out such "vertical extensions" using the existing name.

When we look at vertical extensions in the marketplace, we can see that they have an impact on the underlying products. The presence, for example, of a high-end model in a product line may contribute to an image of prestige and exclusivity. Mercedes, as an obvious example, is seen as a prestigious brand in the US primarily because of its high-end models. This prestige persists to some degree even for the middle-market models offered under the Mercedes brand.

The corollary concern is that offering a low-end product will tarnish the prestige of the parent brand. Maintaining an image of prestige and exclusivity while simultaneously offering products at the low end of the market under the same brand may be difficult if not impossible.

Bicycles and brand extent

To determine the impact of extending a product line in either direction, we examined the bicycle market in the US. This market consists of approximately 12m units sold each year. Total sales have been fairly consistent over the past decade but recent trends in mountain biking increased that segment's portion of total unit sales from 12 per cent in 1985 to 66 per cent ten years later.

Approximately 75 per cent of all bikes in the US are sold through mass merchandizing channels. The remaining 25 per cent are sold through independent bicycle dealers. Ninety-five per cent of bikes sold through independents retail for $200 or more, while mass merchandisers sell bikes that typically retail for under $200.

In the over-$200 category, we found 75 different brands of mountain bikes, with an average of ten models per brand. With minor exceptions, we found that all of the brands in the industry are focused exclusively on cycling. There have been virtually no brand extensions into other product categories and we have not discovered that established brands have entered from other categories.

There is intense competition at all price points and companies pursue widely divergent product line strategies. Some manufacturers offer only high-end bikes, while others compete at every price point.

We worked with the manufacturer's suggested retail price as a function of brand and of eight product attributes: frame material, component group, front suspension, rear suspension, high-performance components, colors per model, sizes per model and whether or not the bicycle was made in the US.

We found a strong association between the quality extent of the product line and the brand price premium. Put simply: companies with low-quality products in their lines tend to have lower brand premiums while companies with high-quality products in their lines tend to have higher brand premiums. The lower the quality level of the line is extended, the lower the brand equity; and the higher the quality of the lowest-quality model, the higher the brand equity.

Brand equity also increases with the quality of the highest-quality model in the product line, although this equity manifests itself primarily in the lower-quality segments of the marketplace. To illustrate this point, we developed two fictitious brand names and showed a catalog of these brands and their product lines to a set of potential customers. The two brands differed in the range of their lines, with one carrying bikes from $400 to $900 and the other having bikes from $800 to $2,000. At the $850 price point both brands had a model that was technically comparable. We asked the respondents which of the $850 models they would be most likely to buy. Consistent with our previous results, most respondents preferred the bike that came from the higher-range product line.

We presented our findings at the Interbike trade show in autumn 1996 to a group including marketing managers, general managers and chief executives from a dozen of the leading bicycle brands. There was widespread agreement with our general findings, with several managers commenting that our results were consistent with their experiences.

What determines brand equity?

Our research raised many questions. For example, is product-line quality determined only by the lowest- and highest-quality products?

Perhaps other properties of the product line are important in creating an impression of a brand. Consider two brands, each with ten models and each with the same lowest- and highest-quality level. The brand with the remaining eight products concentrated near the upper-quality level should have greater brand equity than the brand with the remaining eight products concentrated near the lower-quality level. We do not take the strong position that the only features of a product line that contribute to the brand equity effect are the highest- and lowest-quality model.

Another crucial question is: if our results indicate that the presence of high- or low-quality models in a product line is associated with brand equity, what exactly is required to achieve this effect? Does merely listing a single high-end product in a catalog create an association with brand equity? Or is a larger set of activities connected with offering high- or low-quality models needed to give rise to the association?

Because brand equity is ultimately expressed in the marketplace, we suggest that the marketplace – dealers and consumers – must be aware of the structure of the product line for the effect to be active. This awareness probably requires more than a catalog entry alone but probably does not require that sales of the models at the high and low extremes of the product line be large.

If the marketplace is not aware of the extent of a product line, then the extent is unlikely to be associated with brand equity. We expect that a brand's activities to communicate the extent of its line to the marketplace will modulate the effect that the extent has on brand equity.

Brand equity may also be influenced by the market's perception of where the brand focuses its marketing efforts. For a given product line, we might expect that a company that chooses high-end distribution channels and that advertises in media targeting the high end would develop more brand equity in the middle of the market than a company focusing its marketing resources on mass channels and mass media. Part of the exclusivity and prestige of a brand may be associated with its marketing emphasis at the high end.

However, a paradox arises here. The value of a focus on the high end of the market actually accrues in the middle of the market. So a company may simultaneously have to commit resources to create the impression of high-end focus while communicating this impression to the middle of the market. Conversely, we would expect low-end brands not to develop greater brand equity until some time after they extend their product lines upmarket.

We also suspect that brands moving their product lines downmarket may enjoy higher brand equity than brands moving their product lines upmarket, even if both brands ultimately arrive at similar product lines. This implies that managers may wish to launch new brands higher than they ultimately expect to settle rather than lower.

Of course, competitive dynamics may also be important. As a brand extends its line, this may precipitate a competitive response. Both the extension of the line and the competitive offerings would have an impact on the originating brand's equity.

Balancing costs and benefits

The findings of our study imply that the costs or benefits of adding a new item also include an impact on brand equity. This can have both negative and positive consequences for the entire product line.

According to our results, a company should choose to offer only high-quality products under a brand if its objective is to maximize brand equity. However, maximizing brand equity is rarely a company's sole objective. Brand equity is a means to achieving higher profitability, which may arise from higher margins, greater market share or decreased costs of launching new products.

For a brand considering extending its product line upmarket, the trade-off is between the investment and support costs associated with the new models and their resulting sales and profits on the one hand and, on the other hand, the increase in profits that may arise from enhanced brand equity across the rest of the product line (in addition to any profits generated by selling the premium models).

For a brand considering extending its product line downmarket, the trade-off is between the increased profit contribution from the presumably large new sales volume in the lower-quality segment and the lost profits due to diminished brand equity across the rest of the product line (in addition to any investment costs required to introduce the new models).

The cost-benefit analysis is further complicated by the option of using a new brand to introduce models at the high or low end of the market. This practice is common in other industries and is starting to be adopted in the bicycle industry. A company wishing to enhance its total brand equity may choose both to extend the models of its existing brand upmarket and to introduce a new brand offering only high-end models. This is the strategy we observed with Trek.

Trek has acquired and invested substantially in several premium brands – Gary Fisher, LeMond, Bontrager and Klein – but has carefully managed their identities; it is not generally known in the marketplace that Trek owns them. Such a strategy is also followed in the car market – for example, Toyota has its Lexus line and Nissan its Infiniti line.

An alternative to extending an existing brand downmarket is to preserve the structure of the existing product line while using a new brand for the low-end models, perhaps with its own premium models to enhance its brand equity. This strategy was first adopted in the bicycle industry in 1996.

Specialized introduced a new brand, Full Force, which was aimed at the lower part of the market and supposed to be sold through mass merchandisers. However, Specialized's initial strategy of labeling the brand "Full Force by Specialized" backfired due to a strongly negative reaction from dealers concerned that this would tarnish the equity of Specialized products sold through the traditional bicycle retail channel. The company responded by downplaying the relationship between the two brands.

Our analysis is of a single product category in a single industry. An important question is the degree to which our results apply to other situations. Our theory suggests that these results apply in categories where vertical product line extent is present, where there are difficult-to-observe attributes (as, for example, in the case of wine and bicycles) and where the product category is associated with prestige (for example, cars and watches).

The mountain bike category is relatively young, having emerged within the past 10 to 15 years. To date, there has been little segmentation within the category other than by performance quality and therefore by price. Because of our focus on the role of the vertical extent of the product line, we would expect our results to be applicable primarily to categories in which a clear ordering of products by quality is possible. Packaged goods, for example, are rarely differentiated vertically within a brand but consumer durables are often arranged within a brand according to "good-better-best" logic.

One of the most significant implications of this research is that product-line managers need to be mindful not just of the possible cannibalization or stimulation of sales of products that are the immediate neighbors of an extension to the product line. They must also consider the effect of such an extension on the brand equity in other, possibly quite different, parts of the product line.

The implication of this work is clear: while it might appear attractive to introduce an extension at the bottom end of your product line to fight competition or to appeal to a more price-sensitive customer, this comes at a considerable cost to the brand equity of the entire line. Brand equity is a very important asset that companies spend years trying to develop. It allows a company to command a premium in the marketplace over comparable products with lesser names.

Diluting this equity should only come after careful consideration of the magnitude of the incremental sales relative to the lowering of the brand's equity. The alternative – if the lower, or more price-sensitive, market is so attractive – is to introduce the product under a different brand name. This, too, obviously comes at an additional cost.

Similarly, to move upmarket may not seem as attractive at times because of the lower volumes that tend to exist at higher price points. This is looking at the entry too narrowly, as the value of simply having the higher-quality item will be felt throughout the entire product line. To some extent, models at the upper end can be viewed as a form of advertising or a testimonial to the quality products that can be produced by the company.

Returning to the pen companies, our unsolicited advice to Mont Blanc is that if it finds the lower end of the market so attractive that it cannot afford not to "go for it," it has to be willing to take a hit at the top end. This appears to be too risky. Hence, we suggest that it should use a new brand name altogether. As for Pilot, our advice is to go after the top end with the Pilot name. It may not be profitable at the high end but it is likely to enhance sales at the lower end.

Summary

Extending a product line upmarket or downmarket clearly has implications for brand equity. Should a premium-brand company that wants to capture lower market segments use its existing brand? Or would it be safer in the long term to go to the expense of creating a new one? In this article, **David**

Reibstein, **Karl Ulrich** and **Taylor Randall** report on their research into line extension strategies. This indicates that a company with low-quality products in its line will tend to have lower brand premiums than a company that makes higher-quality products. Even if two companies have products with exactly the same specification, consumers will tend to buy from the company whose line extends higher. The authors discuss the implications of this and other findings for product extension strategies.

SKUs: taking stock of more than brands

by Peter S. Fader and Bruce S.G. Hardie

Companies that manufacture consumer packaged goods face a twofold challenge in the marketplace: they have to manage brand image effectively while also managing stock-keeping units (SKUs). Brands may be differentiated on a few perceptual dimensions that convey image and reputation but consumers typically discriminate among SKUs on the basis of a set of tangible product attributes. For example, when buying toothpaste, a consumer might regularly choose a 50ml tube of mint-flavored, tartar-control Crest gel. However, the same person may sometimes choose another item in response to a special promotion.

The resulting choice reflects not only a preference for the promoted brand but also a preference for package size and type (medium-sized tubes), product form (gel), formula (tartar control) and flavor (mint). Brand choice is rarely a final decision by itself; rather, SKU choice is where much of the consumer's deliberation occurs.

A typical brand manager makes relatively few product-related decisions that directly involve the brand itself. In most cases, a brand's name is essentially a permanent, unchanging characteristic. Instead, the manager generally spends more time on those product attributes that distinguish SKUs, such as packaging, product form and flavor. These and other attributes comprise the overall product. Many of these decisions may result in the development of line extensions, which are new SKUs that fall under a pre-existing brand name.

Focus on SKUs rather than brands is even more marked with retailers. While most try to carry an appropriate selection of different brands, their primary concern is how to use shelf space most effectively for a category as a whole. Managing the mix of SKUs is an essential part of the retailer's job. Virtually all publications, advertisements or pieces of research aimed at the retailer acknowledge the status of the SKU as the basic building block.

The importance of SKUs in manufacturer–retailer relationships has recently attracted a great deal of attention in the business press. For example, as part of its move towards everyday low pricing, Procter & Gamble sought to reduce its total number of SKUs by about 25 per cent. Many of these reductions were achieved by trimming product lines (for example, by eliminating slow-selling detergent package sizes) but several brand names were consolidated as well (for example, White Cloud and Charmin bathroom tissue).

With such significant changes taking place in many markets, it is important that managers understand how consumers evaluate and integrate different SKU attributes in making purchase decisions. It is ironic that these aspects are so vital to the decisions made by consumers, manufacturers and retailers yet receive so little attention in formal choice models. The irony is magnified by the fact that the descriptive characteristics that distinguish SKUs are readily available from sources such as retail scanner data that most managers routinely collect and analyze for other purposes.

Modeling consumer decisions

Our research has focused on the gap between current models and marketing practice in order to measure the benefits of modeling consumer choice among SKUs. We have developed a modeling approach that can include all the distinguishing attributes that characterize a product category's set of SKUs.

For most consumer packaged goods, SKUs are described in terms of a set of physical attributes that uniquely identifies each item. For example, our toothpaste scenario uses six different SKU attributes (brand, package size, package type, product form, formula and flavor) to portray the toothpaste market. Several of these attributes, especially brand and package size, are common to virtually all product categories. Others vary from one category to another.

We use the term "attribute level" to denote each of the distinct offerings that together comprise an attribute. For example, Crest, Colgate and Aquafresh are some of the levels under the attribute "brand" in the toothpaste category.

Marketing research companies typically use several criteria to determine what can be treated as an SKU attribute. The most important criterion is that the attribute must be recognisable to consumers. That is, a consumer must be able to distinguish an SKU attribute by casually examining the front of the package.

If two packages appear to be identical – regardless of whether or not the actual products are indeed the same – then these items should not be treated as separate SKUs. And if a manufacturer changes one or more attribute levels for a certain item, it thereby creates an entirely new SKU.

SKU attributes should also be objective: for each item, there should be no ambiguity about the level of any attribute. For example, a suitable SKU attribute for bottled water might be fruit flavoring (unflavored versus orange flavored versus lemon flavored and so on). But this attribute should generally measure only the presence of these flavorings, not their intensity. Similarly, for product categories in which sweetness is an important SKU attribute, an objective measure might be unsweetened versus naturally sweetened versus artificially sweetened rather than degree of sweetness.

The number of levels per attribute tends to be modest, usually no more than four. Perhaps the biggest exception is flavor, which can reach 20 or more in several product categories (for example soup, yoghurt, catfood). Another attribute with many levels is brand, which has ten or more distinct entries in many categories.

An SKU attribute has to be collectively exhaustive: it must apply to every SKU in a product category (although of course the levels may differ from item to item). Many SKU attributes are defined simply as the presence or absence of a particular

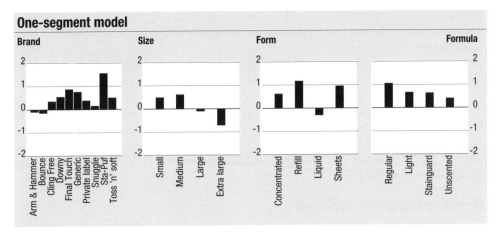

One-segment model

Figure 1

product characteristic; this gives the defining attribute two levels. For example, even if only a small number of pasta sauce brands have "homestyle" varieties, all of the other items would be represented by a "not homestyle" or "regular" attribute level.

It is easy to see how the number of SKU attributes and levels can explode to an unmanageable size for a complex product category. Much of the analyst's skill, therefore, is to define a minimal number of distinct attributes that capture all of the relevant traits within a category. For example, if "homestyle" applies to only one brand in the category, it might be viewed as an irrelevant SKU attribute. The key is that each SKU should embody a unique combination of SKU attributes.

All of this begs the following questions:

- how important are SKU attributes?
- which SKU attributes matter?
- how often do they make a meaningful difference in a choice model?

A comprehensive answer to these questions would require extensive testing across numerous datasets. Here we demonstrate our approach by examining the interrelationship and relative importance of four different attributes for a typical product category: fabric softener. We calibrated our models using scanner data for fabric softeners in the US. Because this product is sold in multiple formulations, package sizes and so on it is well suited for our proposed analysis.

We examined only two models: the one- and two-segment attribute-based models. We focus our discussion on the "part worths" (that is, contributions to utility) for each of the attribute levels present in the dataset.

The attribute-specific preferences for the one-segment model are shown in Figure 1. Each bar chart measures relative preferences. Looking at the combinations of brand, size, form and formula, we see that the most popular item would be Sta-Puf, Medium, Refill and Regular (although such a combination does not exist in the market).

The relative importance of each SKU attribute can be ascertained by determining the range of preferences – from the highest to the lowest part worth – for each attribute. By this criterion, the most important attribute is brand and the least important is formula. While this is the simplest way to infer attribute

Two-segment model

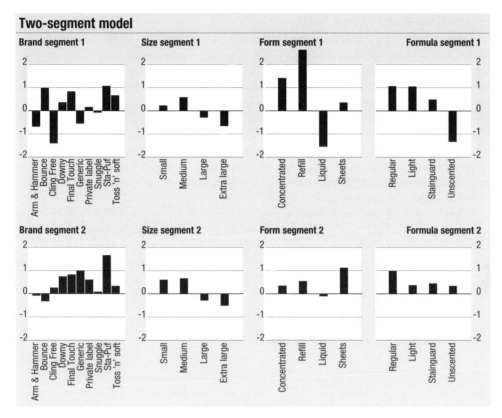

Figure 2

importance, there are also more complex (and theoretically more appealing) alternative approaches.

The one-segment model may provide a reasonable first pass towards understanding consumers' underlying preferences for each attribute level but it certainly does not provide the complete picture.

Figure 2 shows the attribute-specific estimates for the two-segment model. In some ways, the two-segment model merely confirms the findings of the one-segment model – for example, extra-large package sizes and unconcentrated liquids are consistently disliked. But in other respects, the two-segment model reveals patterns that are masked in the one-segment model. The most striking example is that of refills versus sheets. In the one-segment model, both forms are similarly favored but in the two-segment model we see a clear division between a group of consumers who prefer refills (segment 1) and a group that prefers sheets (segment 2).

It is also interesting to note that the relative importance of form is substantially greater in segment 1 than in segment 2. This suggests that if a manager can segment the market on only one attribute, he or she might choose form over the others. In a complete application of the model, the segment profiles would be accompanied by demographic and socioeconomic summaries of the households assigned for each group.

123

Forecasting sales of new SKUs

In most consumer packaged goods categories, a continuous stream of new SKUs enters a given market throughout the sort of time period used in most scanner data applications. Our model enables the analyst to forecast sales of new entrants if they combine SKU features that currently exist in the market. Such new SKUs have been termed "imitative" or "filling-in" line extensions.

An imitative line extension is a new SKU that is based on an attribute level that was previously not associated with any SKU for the brand launching the extension, but that is established in the product category (for example, Crest was the third major brand to introduce baking soda toothpaste). A filling-in line extension uses a new combination of attribute levels, all of which are currently associated with the brand launching the extension.

A line extension that introduces a new attribute or attribute level to the product category is classified as "innovative." Around 70 per cent of new consumer packaged goods are line extensions.

We can demonstrate our model using the fabric softener example. Our dataset includes a six-month forecast period (January–June 1992), which was not used for our initial test. During this period, two line-extension SKUs appeared in the market (*see* Figure 3):

Fabric softener line extensions in the US January–June 1992		
	A	**B**
Brand	Private label	Sta-Puf
Size	Medium	Small
Form	Liquid	Refill
Formula	Light	Regular

Figure 3

Both of these new SKUs can be classified as imitative line extensions. SKU A was the first private-label "light" formula fabric softener; this attribute level was previously associated with Downy and Snuggle. SKU B was the first "refill" SKU for Sta-Puf; this attribute level was previously used by three Downy SKUs.

Our model predicted a volume share for A of 0.11 per cent; the actual share was 0.26 per cent. Our prediction for B was 2.75 per cent; the actual share was 2.66 per cent. Thus our model gave us a reasonable approximation of actual performance. These results offer considerable encouragement for the use of attribute-based methods to forecast the market share of imitative and filling-in line extensions.

Conclusion

The large number of SKUs associated with most consumer packaged goods categories places an excessive burden on most existing modeling methodologies. Recognizing that SKUs can be described in terms of a small set of discrete attributes and that consumer choice is often made on the basis of these attributes, we propose that researchers should model preferences over SKU attributes rather than the SKUs themselves.

We obtained estimates of consumer preferences for different attributes. These offer useful diagnostics for the SKUs currently available in the marketplace. An additional benefit is the ability to forecast the performance of line extensions. Our initial results are very encouraging.

Our approach has a number of advantages. First, our model describes and uses actual products in the marketplace. Second, we can explicitly accommodate explanatory variables (for example, price and promotion), which collectively have a large impact on consumer choice. These variables generally change over time, across attributes/alternatives and, in some cases, across households. Third, the activity that we focus on (routine grocery purchasing) is more natural and requires less obtrusive investigative methods than any laboratory-based experiment. The artificiality of the laboratory environment is a major source of concern for researchers who perform experimental analyses of consumer choice.

Our model has close ties with conjoint analysis and in certain respects it improves upon it, especially when the realism of the decision situation is a major concern for the researcher. But in most situations, the two approaches are quite complementary and can be used in parallel.

Our model's other novel benefit – the ability to forecast sales of different types of line extension – also has important practical ramifications. Owing to the perception that many line extensions are a low-risk proposition, the cost of most pre-test-market analysis methods and the problems of applying some of these methods to line extensions, few companies carry out such formal analyses.

The SKU attribute-level preferences determined by our model are all readily interpretable and may be very helpful. For example, line extension opportunities can be identified by comparing the value that consumers attach to various attribute levels with the proportion of SKUs in the category possessing each level. A highly favored attribute level that lacks SKU depth could be ripe for line extension.

Conversely, how should a company go about eliminating SKUs in a profitable manner? Is it sufficient to drop the slowest-selling items or is it wiser to eliminate all items sharing an ineffective attribute level (for example, a particular formula or package size)? Our model lends itself nicely to such "what if" analyses.

Our analysis is only the beginning; by no means are we saying that our approach is the last word on the topic of SKU choice. We hope that our observations will encourage others to examine this neglected area from various perspectives.

One very promising avenue would be to gain a deeper understanding of how retailers use SKU attribute information to organize items on the shelf. As category management issues grow in importance in the marketplace, this and related topics will continue to be high priorities for retailers and manufacturers alike.

Summary

Brand managers spend relatively little time managing the brand itself. Most of their decisions are concerned with the stock-keeping units on which the brand appears. Yet according to **Peter Fader** and **Bruce Hardie**, many consumer choice models pay little attention to SKUs. In this article they outline a method for modeling how consumers choose among SKUs. The relative importance that consumers attach to different product attributes can be measured, making it possible to identify lucrative gaps in the current market and to predict the success of line extensions.

This article is adapted from a longer article that appeared in the *Journal of Marketing Research* (November 1996). The original won the journal's Paul E. Green Award for the year's best article that "demonstrated the most potential to contribute significantly to the practice of marketing research and research in marketing."

How consumers cope with information overload

by Barbara E. Kahn

The amount of information that consumers confront in the supermarket can be formidable. In the US, for example, there are approximately 150 national brands of instant breakfast cereal on the market and the typical supermarket carries anywhere between 60 and 90 brands. Each package in turn contains pictures or graphics in addition to almost 100 separate items of information.

Although information is helpful, the decision-maker can be flooded with too much, which may reduce the quality of the decision. Empirical evidence suggests that too much information can cause consumers to become confused or stressed.

However, consumers do not actually experience information overload in most supermarket contexts. Instead they just evaluate a small amount of the information available when making decisions. The key question therefore is: since consumers are not likely to take in all the information available to them, what information do they process? Do they look at the most relevant attributes?

Research suggests that experienced consumers are better able than inexperienced consumers to focus on attributes that are predictive of product performance. However, there are still biases in the way experienced consumers take in information.

Interpreting information

One problem with information provided for consumers, either through advertising or in-store cues (such as packaging or shelf markers), is that it is not always recalled or interpreted correctly.

Sometimes this is because information is deliberately misleading, as when a manufacturer's statement that a product is "less fattening" than a substitute is true only because the portion sizes are much smaller. In other cases information is purposely vague and the consumer interprets it in the most positive light. For example, a manufacturer may call a product "not expensive," which the consumer interprets as "inexpensive."

Even when information is clearly and accurately presented, consumers do not always understand it or believe it. Only one-third of the consumers surveyed by the US Food and Drug Administration understood that the ingredients recorded on a food product label are listed in order of weight.

Consumers may also infer information about products that is not always accurate. For example, based on an overall evaluation of a brand, a consumer may infer that it has certain characteristics (sometimes termed "halo effects"). Thus if consumers evaluate a brand overall as of high quality, they may infer that it is nutritious even if it is not.

Error can also arise when consumers evaluate a brand on the basis of its similarity to another brand. Thus a consumer may assume that a new or unfamiliar brand has the same ingredients as a more familiar brand. Likewise, consumers may infer that a brand has certain characteristics because they believe that certain attributes are likely to occur together. For example, consumers often think that higher prices are associated with higher quality. This is not always true.

Consumers sometimes say one thing and do another. For example, 94 per cent of Americans say that they are at least somewhat concerned about nutrition. In particular, they are concerned about fat, salt, cholesterol and sugar and want healthy alternatives made available. But the presence of healthly alternatives does not necessarily affect purchase behavior. As a Wendy's executive stated in a Forbes article: "Folks feel better eating a bacon cheeseburger when they're looking at a healthy salad bar with fresh vegetables."

There are also biases in the way consumers take in information. Confirmation bias, or the tendency for people to take in information that confirms what they already think and to disregard information that challenges preconceived notions, is a very strong phenomenon.

Consumers are more sensitive to very vivid, unique or otherwise salient information and may neglect more subtle cues. They may thus wrongly place more importance on the more salient cues. Similarly, consumers overestimate the relative risk of events if they are more newsworthy. This can explain the extreme reactions consumers may show to relatively minor hazards while continuing to expose themselves to greater risks.

Changes in the way items are described can affect consumers' judgments. Researchers found that when respondents were asked to choose between the same ground beef that was labeled either as "75 per cent lean" or as "25 per cent fat," they chose the "75 per cent lean." This pattern persisted even after they tasted the meat, although the magnitude of the effect decreased.

These biases in information gathering are very common and can be very strong. However, it has been demonstrated that consumers who are made aware of the potential for bias in their judgments – by reports in consumer magazines, say – often dramatically improve their decision making. This is especially the case where the discrepancy in information is large rather than slight.

Making decisions

At some point, the consumer has to choose which brand to put in the shopping trolley. When there is no clear dominant alternative to pick, the normative rules of decision making suggest that a consumer should use all of the relevant information available and make explicit trade-offs between different product attributes.

Instead, consumers typically use simplifying choice rules. During a single shopping trip, a consumer has to make many decisions and is unlikely to want to spend too much time on any single one. Besides, it is not that important to most consumers to make the best decision.

Generally consumers just want to make a decision that meets some minimum requirements. One way of doing so is to use a "satisficing" rule. Using such a rule, consumers consider the items in their consideration set one at a time as they come across them on the shelf. They then evaluate the first brand relative to some minimum standard. If it meets the standard on each important attribute, then it is chosen and no other brands are evaluated. If it is below the minimum cut-off, then the next brand in the consideration set is evaluated.

Another common rule is "elimination-by-aspects," where options are totally eliminated if they perform poorly on a certain attribute. Someone who is allergic to nuts, for example, will screen out all alternatives with nuts and consider only the remaining options.

Conversely, a consumer might consider one attribute – cheapness, say – to be the most important and then pick the option that is the best with respect to that attribute. If more than one option is best on that attribute, then the consumer might consider the second most important attribute – type of package, maybe – and then pick the brand that is best on that attribute and so on. This rule is known as a "lexicographic" rule.

Another decision strategy is to rely on memory, a process known as "affect referral." In this kind of decision making, consumers form attitudes or impressions on first receiving information. These first impressions are then stored in memory and later retrieved as a basis for judgment. The consumer thus does not consider all the information that might be available.

Where decisions are made repeatedly and the consumer does not care much about making an optimal choice, then researchers theorize that the consumer develops choice "tactics." Initially the consumer uses a simplified rule, such as "buy the cheapest brand" or "buy the brand my friend recommended." If, on sampling, the product is found satisfactory, there is an increased likelihood that it will be chosen again. Through a series of trials, the post-purchase evaluation will stabilize and a very simple decision rule will emerge.

To test this theory, researchers observed 120 shoppers in a supermarket in a metropolitan area. They focused on the way consumers bought laundry detergents, a category that comprises lots of brands, has large supermarket displays and is generally considered to be a low-risk purchase. On average, consumers examined a very small number of packages (1.42) and 72 per cent examined only one; 83 per cent picked up only one package and only 4 per cent picked up more than two. The data suggest that most consumers engaged in very little pre-purchase decision making.

Consideration sets

If supermarket consumers made optimal decisions, carefully considering all trade-offs, then the process of forming a consideration set prior to making a final choice would not affect that final choice. Consumers would always choose the optimal brand regardless of which other brands they considered in the process. Researchers have found, however, that the probability of purchasing a specific brand depends upon how many – and which – other brands are in the consideration set.

Consideration sets are often formed using very simple criteria, such as "consider all the brands that are less than £1" or "consider all cereal brands that are low in sugar." Given such less-than-optimal criteria, it is obvious that the final purchase will be likely to be sub-optimal.

Even when consumers are less arbitrary in forming consideration sets, the composition of the set can subtly affect choice. In many product classes, consumers' preferences are not fixed and may change in response to different ways of presenting the alternatives, or to differences in the timing of purchase and the amount bought. Therefore, brand choices can be influenced without changing a consumer's preference for a brand in itself merely by changing the contents of the consideration set.

Two generalizations are helpful in understanding this. First, consumers tend to prefer an alternative if it fares well in comparison with others in the consideration

Challenges for "in-store" marketers

- Consumers' recall or understanding of product information is often biased. Does your packaging compensate for this? And if bias runs in your favor, you are not necessarily safe: as consumers become more sophisticated they may be more critical of the information you offer.
- Is what consumers say they want reflected in their behavior? Giving people what they say they want may not be as profitable as giving them what they really want.
- Do you know enough about the decision-making strategies that consumers use in your category? Which attribute is typically top of the list when people use, say, lexico-graphic rules?
- In what context is your product being considered? If other brands are added to your consumers' consideration set, how will your brand fare?

set; their preference may shift if the item is put into a set in which it does not look so good in comparison. Second, consumers do not like to choose an extreme option when trade-offs are involved. They generally prefer an option with intermediate attributes to one that is extreme.

Both of these generalizations are less likely to hold when consumers have very strong preferences within a category. But in many categories, consumers' preferences are not so well-formed and – consciously or not – they use the choice context to determine which item is the "best buy."

Empirical testing has shown that adding a dominated alternative to a consideration set can increase the likelihood that a consumer will buy the alternative that dominates it. For example, consider a simple two-item food category. One item, the "high-end" item, has a high price, fancy packaging and a taste to match. The other item, the "generic" item, has a low price, plain packaging and does not taste quite so good.

If another high-end brand is added to the set but is not quite as good as the original high-end brand there is some evidence that the likelihood that the consumer will choose the original high-end product will increase. Similarly, if a dominated low-end product is added – it is more expensive, say – then the original generic will be more likely to be chosen. Adding the dominated alternative makes the item that dominates it appear more attractive. This idea was tested in the marketplace by a mail-order company. The company had traditionally offered a bread-baking machine for $279 in its catalog. When it added a $429 machine of comparable functionality, few customers bought the new, more expensive alternative but sales of the original doubled.

Some research has shown that even adding a similar – and not necessarily dominated – item to a consideration set can increase the likelihood that the original item will be chosen. For example, assume that the consumer considers just two items in the potato crisp category: plain crisps and ripple crisps. The research suggests that if the retailer can merely convince the consumer to consider another brand of ripple crisps (by using a special display, say), the consumer's desire to purchase the original rippled crisps is likely to increase.

Compromise effect

Empirical testing has also shown that when decisions are difficult to make because a consumer has trouble trading off one attribute for another, the inclusion of a "compromise" brand can help. For example, if a consumer is considering whether to buy an expensive shampoo with special ingredients or a cheaper brand without, the decision centers on whether he or she thinks the ingredients are worth the extra money. If the consumer finds it difficult to calculate how much the ingredients are worth then he or she may instead choose a compromise brand with an intermediate amount of special ingredients and an intermediate price.

Choosing a compromise brand reduces the conflict associated with giving up one attribute (say higher quality) for another attribute (say lower price). And any error (such as paying too much or not getting enough quality) is minimized. Consumers may also choose middle brands because they often determine their needs by comparing themselves to other consumers. Generally, consumers think of themselves as "average," so when they do not know their own preferences, they infer that their tastes will be consistent with the "average" brand.

Summary

Consumers are bombarded with information. A typical supermarket contains thousands of brands, whose packaging in turn conveys scores of pieces of information. As a result, says **Barbara Kahn**, consumers do not have time to trade off all the different product attributes to make optimal purchase decisions. Instead they use strategies such as "satisficing" – evaluating brands one-by-one and picking the first that meets some minimum requirement. Even so, people often interpret information incorrectly; highly salient package features, for example, may swamp less obvious – but perhaps more important – information.

This article has been adapted from the author's *Grocery Revolution: The New Focus on the Consumer* (Reading, MA: Addison-Wesley, 1997), a review of academic marketing research.

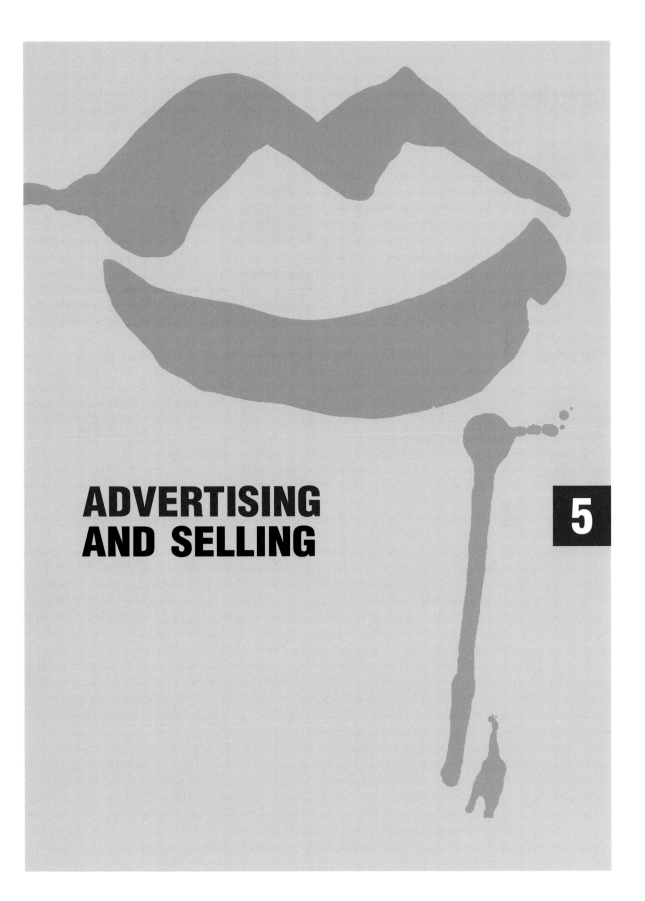

ADVERTISING AND SELLING

5

Contributors

 **Andris A.Zoltners** is professor of marketing at the J.L. Kellogg Graduate School of Management, Northwestern University. His research focuses on sales force productivity enhancement and entrepreneurship.

 **Angela Y. Lee** is assistant professor of marketing at the J.L. Kellogg Graduate School of Management, Northwestern University.

 **David Schmittlein** is the Ira A. Lipman Professor and professor of marketing at the Wharton School of the University of Pennsylvania, where he chairs the marketing department.

 **Kent Grayson** is assistant professor of marketing at London Business School. His research focuses on issues of authenticity and deception in marketing, and on network marketing ("pyramid selling").

 **Brian Sternthal** is the General Foods Professor of Marketing at the J.L. Kellogg Graduate School of Management, Northwestern University.

 **Svetlana Kirillova** is a PhD student of marketing at London Business School. Her current research concerns cross-cultural aspects of consumer behavior and global brand management.

Contents

Introduction

A company's sales force and its advertising are perhaps the most public faces of its marketing strategy. Here we look at ways of ensuring that both are up to scratch. This module explains how to ensure that the sales force is the right size and is structured appropriately for its market, and how to seize the opportunities that arise when sales forces merge. On the advertising side, different ways of evaluating the effectiveness of copy are assessed, and there is a discussion of the regulatory issues around misleading communications. The module also describes how to establish an effective customer database, a tool that is playing an increasingly important role in marketing communications.

Creating a sales force to be reckoned with

by Andris A. Zoltners

Sales forces represent a major investment for most companies. In the US alone there are approximately 14m people involved in full-time selling, of which about 5m are in direct sales and 9m in retail sales. This is about 11 per cent of the total workforce. With approximately $475bn spent annually on sales forces and sales force materials, field selling is an important factor in the US economy. The same is true of many other large economies. Sales forces cost companies anywhere from 2 per cent to 40 per cent of the money they earn from sales.

The significance of the sales force goes beyond its cost. The sales force is possibly the most empowered organization within the company. It represents the company publicly and is entrusted with its most important corporate asset: the customer. Frequently the only connection the customer has with a company is the salesperson. To the customer, the salesperson *is* the company.

The sales force drives the top line and not just the expense line. More salespeople will create higher sales than fewer salespeople. A motivated sales force will sell more than an unmotivated sales force. A well-trained, well-coached sales force will sell more than its undisciplined counterpart. The ingenuity of the selling organization has a direct effect on the company's sales and profitability.

The sales force is a force. There is not a sales force anywhere that could not seriously hurt its company's performance. At the same time, there is not a sales force anywhere that could not significantly enhance its company's position.

Corporate management typically pays careful attention to its selling organization. Frequently, the first questions asked are: is our investment appropriate? Are we the right size? Are we structured correctly? Are we getting the right coverage? Does the field force give us a strategic advantage?

Making the right decision

A sales force that is structured correctly uses the appropriate selling process for every targeted market segment. Its selling and maintenance effort is as effective as possible and uses resources in the most efficient way. It directs its selling effort appropriately across the company's product line.

A properly sized selling organization gives customers and prospects appropriate coverage, and company products proper representation; the sales force is stretched but not overworked and the company makes the appropriate investment for its sales resource. Sales force investment increases with the size and complexity of the force. Since senior management generally wants to contain costs and enhance productivity, it finds size and structure decisions to be highly salient.

The following insights should be useful for anyone having to decide how to size or structure their selling organizations. They are based upon several hundred sales force size and structure studies across several industries in North America, Europe, South America and Asia that have been conducted by the author in conjunction with the consulting company ZS Associates.

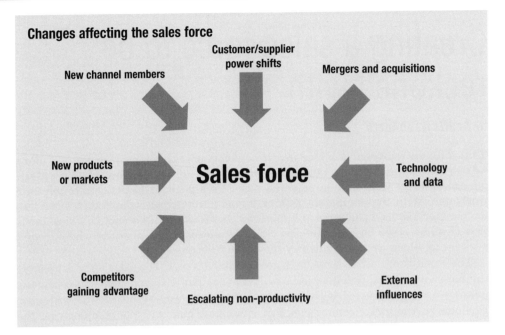

Figure 1

■ *The need to re-evaluate the size and structure of a sales force occurs more frequently than most sales force management teams foresee.*
The modern business environment changes constantly. Several factors that have a direct impact on the selling organization appear in Figure 1. Since adaptability is a source of competitive advantage, progressive managers re-evaluate the size and structure of their sales force every two to four years in response to such factors.

■ *Sizing based on cost containment does not maximize profit.*
"Keep the cost of the sales force at the historical rate" is a common sales force sizing rule. The chief financial officer knows that if it is obeyed, the company will be profitable. Regrettably, this is not a profit-maximizing rule. Table 1 serves as an example. It is a shame that so many CFOs are willing to give up profits ($1m in this case) in order to preserve the cost-of-sales ratio (8 per cent in this case). The author has seen companies forgo hundreds of millions of dollars in sales when their sales force sizes have been managed very conservatively with financial ratios. This tends to be the case when market opportunities suggest that an aggressive sales force investment would be more appropriate. Sales force sizes should be managed using the incremental return rule: expand the sales force until the expected incremental profitability exceeds the incremental cost by the desired rate of return on the sales force investment.

■ *Watch out for the size/productivity trap.*
Companies frequently use productivity programs such as automation, targeting, time management and more effective selling protocols to justify sales force reductions.

   The argument goes like this: "Our productivity program will increase our sales force's productivity by 10 per cent. Therefore, our sales force can be reduced from 100 to 90. This reduction will actually pay for the program."

Monitoring the size of the sales force			
Sales force status	Number of people	Cost	Results
Current sales force	**100 salespeople**	**$10m** This assumes that the fully loaded sales force costs are $100,000 per person	**–$125m in sales** is forecast –$1.25m in sales per salesperson **–$40m in marketing contribution** This assumes a gross production margin of 40 per cent and a sales force cost of $10m **–8 per cent is the cost-of-sales ratio**
A slightly larger sales force	**10 more salespeople** Sales force size is 110	**$1m in incremental sales force cost**	**–An extra $5m in sales** is generated by the new salespeople This is a reasonable increase since increasing the sales force size will increase the company's sales but at a diminishing rate **–An extra $1m in marketing contribution** is generated –This is a **100 per cent return** on the $1m investment **–8.5 per cent is the cost-of-sales ratio**

Table 1

What is likely to happen, however, is that the program will reduce selling costs. A lower cost per call will enable the company to call profitably on more accounts and prospects. Customers who were too expensive to call on directly will be profitable to call on. Hence expanding the sales force may actually increase profitability.

Sizing and productivity enhancement are independent decisions. Productivity should be increased regardless of the sales force size. Sales force reduction should not be used as a justification for productivity programs.

■ *Phased growth is rarely optimal.*
Too frequently, companies launching new products or expanding into new markets increase the size of their field force at the wrong time. They do so when the sales opportunity has been realized instead of investing in the prospective opportunity. These companies grow their sales forces over time as their revenues grow.

Money is left on the table when companies pursue this risk-free strategy. Profits are usually maximized if all the required salespeople are hired at once – prior to the product launch or market expansion. They will be fully trained when they are needed, morale will be higher and any disruption will be less prolonged.

The quick build up strategy is not very risky because often employee turnover rates are fairly high – an average of 18 per cent in the US. If the market opportunity does not fully materialize, management can rely on employee attrition to trim the force.

■ *The sales force is a resource allocator.*
The sales force is the "potential energy" of the company. It is the sum total of all the personal interactions between the company and its customers. Since it makes daily decisions about whom to call on, what products to sell and what activities are important it is a resource allocator. The variety of these decisions is illustrated in Figure 2.

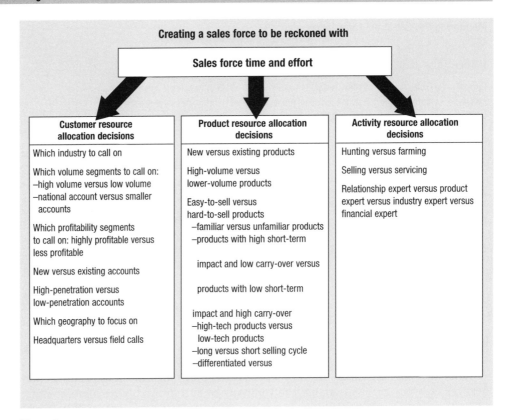

Figure 2

Faced with aggressive sales objectives or declining sales opportunities, most sales executives think first of resizing the sales force. But what is less apparent is that optimal deployment of the sales force has a bigger impact on sales and profits than optimal sizing.

Recently, ZS Associates reviewed 50 cross-country sales force sizing studies to establish the relative impact of decisions about sizing and about sales force resource allocation. The review showed that 71 per cent of any improvement could be derived from smarter resource allocation and 29 per cent from a better sales force size. It is better to work smarter than to work harder.

Unfortunately, sales forces often do not deploy their resources optimally. Compensation systems can reward short-term sales achievement at the expense of effort devoted to strategic products and markets. Consequently, salespeople go to easy accounts. Product managers pursuing aggressive marketing strategies get disproportionate effort for their products as salespeople know that more of their work has been done for them. At the same time, the selling organization may not know how responsive various products and markets are to sales force effort. Thus it may encourage an inappropriate allocation of effort.

Sales force effort is optimally deployed when two conditions are fulfilled: the incremental return on additional effort is equal for all products and markets; and the incremental return is equal to the incremental cost of that effort. It is much easier to state this rather complicated rule than to obey it.

Do some of the following statements describe your field force?

If several of these ring true, then your sales force may be undersized.

- Key customers wonder where your sales representative is.
- Your sales force does not seem to have enough time to take orders, let alone determine how customer needs might be changing.
- Because of neglect, customers are considering switching suppliers.
- New business development is down.
- The sales force feels overworked; their territory goals seem like a considerable stretch.
- A number of your salespeople are circulating their CVs.
- Company costs seem under control and the company should still make its top-line results because of the increased efforts of the field force.
- Management is happy with the sales results and lauds the productivity of its sales and marketing organization.

To determine the optimal resource deployment, the analyst must be able to measure incremental returns. In most industries this is possible with some historical data and a lot of ingenuity.

- *When launching new products, launch hard but protect your strengths; this usually requires adding salespeople.*

Companies often want to launch new products while using the current sales force to promote strong existing product franchises. However, a successful new product launch usually demands a sizeable selling investment. The sales force is a fixed resource in the short term, so any sales effort allocated to the new opportunities must come at the expense of current products and markets.

If a company has strong existing products, these will suffer with a reduction in selling effort. Assuming that existing products will maintain their sales for long without selling effort is dangerous. Almost every product will suffer in the long run if its selling effort is reduced.

New product launches and market entries can capture up to 50 or 60 per cent of a sales force's selling effort. The effort allocated to existing products usually halves. This explains why some existing products fail to make their sales goal.

The author's experience suggests that the best strategy is to launch hard and protect strengths. The only way successfully to accomplish both is by expanding the sales force. However, this strategy has a risk of its own. What if the company only needs the expanded capability for a short time?

Short-term sales force requirements can be met by borrowing or renting selling capacity. For example, other divisions can help out, "rent-a-rep" forces are sometimes available or part-time sales forces can help. Expansion is another reasonable strategy. In the worst case, attrition can be used systematically to reduce the size of the force.

- *Specialize the sales force when this will significantly increase effectiveness.*

Efficiency and effectiveness are two key concepts for developing and evaluating sales force structures. They are illustrated in Figure 3.

A company invests money in a sales force. This money is used to employ salespeople and sales managers who generate calls and interact face-to-face with customers and prospects. The calls are directed at a marketplace, which responds by buying the company's products and services.

Do you observe any of the following?

If you do, then your selling organization may not be structured appropriately.

- Your customers are complaining that your sales force doesn't know their products very well, nor does it seem to understand the customer's business.
- Your customers are concerned that their needs are not being met.
- Your salespeople are feeling uncomfort-

able, finding themselves in situations where customers and competitors know more than they do. They feel ill-equipped to do their jobs.

- Alternatively, they may not be getting access to the decision makers.
- Product managers see that their product growth and market penetration objectives are not being achieved.

Sales force structuring

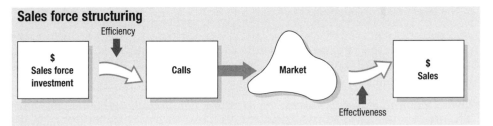

Figure 3

Efficiency reflects the rate at which the sales force converts its money investment into calls. A highly efficient sales force has a high level of call activity for its investment. Effectiveness represents the buyer's response to the calls. Highly effective sales forces have high impact per call. They generate high levels of sales for their call investment.

The geographical, or generalist, structure is a basic sales force structure. Companies that use this structure assign salespeople to territories comprised of a list of accounts or a group of geographical areas, such as counties or postal codes. Each salesperson is responsible for all selling activity in his or her territory.

Sales territories tend to be at their most compact in a geographical structure. Consequently, geographical sales forces usually generate more call activity and more face-to-face selling effort than forces with alternative structures. Why aren't all sales forces structured geographically if it is the most efficient structure? The heterogeneity of the market, product and activity provides an answer.

A company's market typically has many participants. Some are customers. Others are prospects. Some customers are price-sensitive, whereas others desire customization. Some need immediate delivery, others need 90-day dating. Some provide high sales and profit opportunity, whereas others may not even pay for the sales force effort. The variety of these needs can require a sales force structure that is designed structured to accommodate heterogeneity.

The company's products also introduce heterogeneity. Some companies, such as Lego, sell a limited product line. Other, such as Grainger and Baxter, sell thousands of products. Different products may require that the sales force visit buyers who all have different needs and a different way of doing business. Different selling skills may be needed as well as a wider knowledge of the product line. A broad, diverse product line may be difficult for a single salesperson to sell successfully.

Do the following sound familiar?

If some of them do, then your sales force may be too large.

- Your favorite customers are asking, "Didn't I just see you?"
- Overall, your customers seem to be getting plenty of attention.
- Some of them are beginning to wonder about the size of your margins because

the cost of your sales must be high.

- Your field force seems to have plenty of free time and doesn't seem sufficiently stimulated.
- The company's cost of sales is getting out of line with industry norms.
- Perhaps you have missed your profit objectives for several quarters.

Sales force activity is a final source of heterogeneity. The sales force needs to find customers, identify their needs, solve customer problems and sell, service, maintain, partner and expand their business. Technical problem-solving and selling are examples of two activities that some companies find incompatible. Skillful sellers who are also expert technicians are comparatively rare.

Excessive heterogeneity on any of these dimensions can create a need for specialization if a company wants to add value for its customers. A geographically organized sales force is likely to lose effectiveness in such circumstances. It may be impossible for a single salesperson to possess all the skills and knowledge to accommodate market, product or activity heterogeneity. Focus is necessary – and specialization provides focus.

Specialization is the mechanism that deals with heterogeneity. Salespeople specializing by market, product or activity will generate higher levels of sales for each call. A sales force with a specialized structure manages heterogeneity by focusing its resources against the causes of the heterogeneity.

Conclusion

The difference between the sales and profits produced by a properly sized and structured selling organization and those of an average sales force can be significant. An assessment of the 50 studies mentioned above revealed that good decisions on these issues were projected to increase three-year sales and profits by 4.5 per cent on average. It pays to make these decisions wisely.

Summary

As the public face of the company, the sales force has the power directly to influence sales and profitability. Hence decisions about its size and structure are critically important. A force that is the right size will cover customers appropriately – which includes identifying developing needs – and represent the company's product line fully. A correctly structured force is also able to cope with market and product complexity in the most effective and efficient way. In this article, **Andris Zoltners** provides some guidelines for managers. Common mistakes are to seek simply to contain costs, to grow only as revenues do or to use the existing force for new launches. Such caution often results in suboptimal decisions.

The power of the well-managed database

by David Schmittleïn

Sit down with a successful car salesman and ask him what he considers the key to his success. Don't be surprised if he takes a box of three-by-five cards from his drawer and tells you that this is his most important tool. You open the box, eager with anticipation, convinced that powerful secrets of marketing and sales success lie within. Instead, what you find are cards arranged alphabetically with information on every customer, prospect, and referral source the salesman has had throughout his career.

The information on each dog-eared card seems almost pedestrian: the customer's name and address, the date of purchase, which model, the final selling price, what he traded in and the last time he brought the car in for service. You note that there are dates at the bottom of the card including the customer's birthday and the date three months before the lease contract on his current car expires. The salesman explains to you: "I don't sell cars, I build relationships." And his most formidable tool is the database you are holding in your hand.

As global competition grows more fierce and products and services become more commoditised, companies are paying increasing attention to building relationships with their customers. Advances in technology now provide companies with the opportunity to create sophisticated databases which capture detailed customer information. Through the effective use of such databases, companies can build strong relationships by understanding each customer's needs more completely and then designing products, services and communications to match those needs.

Companies can use databases to develop loyalty and relationship marketing programs, integrated marketing communications, electronic commerce capability, and database marketing and mass customization. Catalog and credit-card companies have been among the most aggressive and successful in building their customer databases. These companies have created effective strategies for managing customers as strategic assets.

This type of asset management requires a considerable change in how the company operates. It is one thing to manage tangible assets, quite another to manage intangible, constantly changing assets. Customers move, have changing needs and experience other changes that may not be reflected in a company's database. Keeping a database current is an enormous task. But a growing number of highly sophisticated companies are finding that investing in the hardware, software and staffing necessary to build and maintain a useable and useful database typically amounts to a small fraction of their overall marketing expenditure and is well worth the time and money spent.

A consumer products company such as Procter & Gamble can use information it gathers about its customers to improve its target selling, introduce new products, reward loyalty or cross-sell across its product line. Each positive contact works to build a lasting relationship with each customer. The company is able, for example, to have within its overall database a category for new mothers who use Pampers disposable nappies, another for those who buy Crest toothpaste and another for those who use Tide laundry detergent. As the company builds its database with more specific information about each customer, it is building a valuable asset. Volkswagen builds loyalty with its customers through its Volkswagen Club. In addition to various benefits offered directly to customers, the program also captures information about purchasers which the company then sends to its research and development department as well as its marketing arm.

The classic example of how successful such a strategy can be is AT&T's use of its telephone customer database when it entered the credit card market in 1990. Three months after introducing its Universal card, the company had signed up more than one million customers. Mass mailings inviting individuals to apply for a new credit card are commonplace. AT&T's unique advantage was that it had carefully selected from its enormous database those prospects deemed to be the best candidates for the card, thus minimizing the possibility that it might find itself with a significant number of bad accounts.

Database marketing has profound implications for how a company creates its communication strategy. Broadcast marketing is just that: broadly cast. Database marketing sends a direct, specific message to each customer.

Technology allows your company to capture data about each customer: spending habits, size of average purchase, particular likes and dislikes and so forth. Capturing and using this information can provide a powerful competitive advantage. Each time a customer transacts any type of business with your company, you have a unique opportunity to gather essential information that can strengthen your company's relationship with that customer.

Companies can grow to be far more responsive in how they develop products and services as they capture more detailed customer information. For example, Amazon.com, the innovative internet bookseller, gathers information about a customer's book preferences each time he or she makes a purchase. As the database grows, it will make suggestions to each customer as soon as he or she logs on. If the customer purchases books on cooking or travel, for example, or shows a penchant for mysteries or literature, each time he or she signs on the company will provide specific recommendations in those particular areas.

The database is more than simply a mailing list; it is a repository of very specific customer likes and dislikes. As companies grow more responsive to individual customers, they are more likely to hold on to those customers over longer periods of time. Each customer becomes a significant asset. Marketing managers can target customers with increasing precision, allowing companies to exploit smaller niches even in a global marketplace.

Companies spend considerable time, money and effort to create brand image and awareness. This is perceived to be an asset which has value. But the equity created by a database with exacting information and knowledge about customers has the potential to become a company's most valuable asset.

Integrated communications

Companies are beginning to develop a more integrated approach to marketing, beginning with the way they use their databases. Integrated communication provides your company with the opportunity to co-ordinate all three major communication decisions: the what, the when and the how. The goal is to influence potential and current customers more effectively and to use marketing resources more efficiently.

Strategies for customizing communication				
	Message timing (when)	**Product focus (which)**	**Cross-selling (where)**	**Benefit focus (why)**
Strategic role	– Provides reminder – Prevents customer attrition – Customer reacquisition	– Maximises individual product sale – Matches product with customer interest	– Deepens customer relationship – Moves customers towards high value-added products	– Builds customer loyalty: "customer orientation"
Basis for matching communication with customer	– Hiatus in purchasing – Change in spending pattern	– Historical products purchased – Inferred customer "life cycle" within product category	– Product(s) currently/ recently bought – Typical customer migration patterns across the company's products	– Specific product benefits known to be highly important
Common key selling point	– Reminder of key differential product advantages – Highlight switching costs – Tap into tendency for "loss aversion"	– "The right product for you"	– Product synergies – One-stop shopping	– Connection of particular product benefits to customer-specific needs
Common risks/pitfalls	– Providing incentives to some customers who do not need them – May spark interest in competition or switching	– Need to identify key decision-makers – Change in product preferences/life cycle acceleration	– Which corporate entity "owns" the customer? – Potential to alienate customer/lose base product sales	– Change in benefits sought – May seem intrusive or overly familiar
Examples of use	1-800-Flowers gift registry	Amazon.com recommendations	Banks and other financial services	Personal selling (for example, car sales)

Table 1

As your company makes the transition from mass marketing to interactive marketing you have the opportunity to refine its marketing strategy from one based on average demographics and lifestyles to one based on detailed customer purchase histories. New product or service development should improve considerably as well. The driver becomes mass customization, a concept that appears to be oxymoronic, yet has the potential for leading the company into new and more profitable directions.

Mass customization allows your company to develop products specifically for the customer base, rather than developing general products for an average customer. Advertising can move from standardized, broadly cast executions to customized messages and vastly more accurate targeting. Promotional policies will be based on a customer's past behavior rather than on universal offerings.

Customizing a company's database requires considerable strategic changes within the company. The sales force will not simply be motivated by greater incentives to "go out and sell." Instead, salespeople will become customer service representatives; they will be trained to help each customer define needs and to develop a communication plan to propose products or services that will satisfy those needs.

Historically, targeted marketing programs have been built upon knowledge of customer demographics and lifestyles. Yet direct marketers have repeatedly found that actual past purchasing behavior is a much better predictor of future purchasing behavior. Indeed, in my own research I have found that customer history information is literally ten times better than geodemographics in identifying prospective customers.

For each customer, the company has at its command detailed information on frequency and recency of purchase, amount spent and class of product or service sought. The more frequently a customer does business with a company, the greater the "equity value" of that customer.

The US-based florist 1-800-Flowers makes effective use of its database through its electronic Gift Registry, which gives each customer the option to list with the company as many as 50 special occasions. Five days before each occasion the company sends the customer an e-mail reminder asking if he or she wishes to send flowers. While customers do not make a purchase every time, the company does capture more business this way and it finds that the typical order is $10 more than its average order. Customers who make regular purchases are far less likely to take their business elsewhere.

Building a database

The key to success is building a useful database. Your company needs to capture essential customer-specific information and maintain it in a way that allows easy access. We begin with the obvious: demographic data, such as name and address. From there we build in information gleaned from customer service encounters, such as when a customer fills out a warranty registration card. Other opportunities include marketing program contacts (returned rebate forms, for example), survey responses, order forms, customer inquiries and so forth.

For companies that create a database marketing capability, the key consequences for the communication program are usually answers to the following questions:

- When should we contact the customer?
- Which product should we market to the customer?
- Which benefits do we want to stress to the customer?
  (Which attributes has the customer indicated to be most compelling?)

The information then allows you to create customized communication programs that offer far more cost-efficient ways to sell products or services. The result is that offerings, sales calls and contacts, cross-selling, customer reactivation programs, relationship loyalty programs and new product development can all become highly targeted.

A market-driven customer database maintains customer histories that should include:

- transactions/orders and timing
- type of product or service ordered/purchased
- dollar volume

- profitability
- payment record
- communications with the customer, including timing, type of product or service offered, and offer price and/or payment conditions
- communications from the customer, including requests for information, location visits, and complaints.

We can break this down further into more detailed information about consumers. For example, is the customer a frequent, occasional or infrequent customer? Another type of grouping might include information on what motivates the customer to make a purchase: is he or she prompted by specific offerings, price or the general variety offered by the company? Other groupings might include information on whether the customer is a program, relationship or transaction buyer, or a bargain hunter.

We will want to know which factors influence purchase decisions. Information we should capture will include:

- what are customers doing now?
- what do we want them to do?
- how might we go about reinforcing favorable behavior?
- how might we go about creating other favorable behavior?

There is, of course, no limit to the amount of information we can capture about our customers. Customer databases can become overloaded, expensive to maintain and cumbersome to access. The key is to construct a database that provides us with essential information about each customer that will help us build a better relationship with him or her and provide better products and services.

There are seven keys to the successful implementation of database marketing:

1 Construct a marketing database
2 Segregate prospects, current customers and lapsed customers
3 Design user-friendly data access tools (query-based)
4 Measure contacts as well as responses (responsiveness versus response)
5 Assess the lifetime value of customers
6 Start with a pilot project
7 Ensure a meaningful connection with those responsible for communications and product/service design.

It is important to be aware that there will always be impediments and roadblocks that will hinder the effective use of our databases. Among the challenges are:

- *Mixing modalities/clash of cultures*. Many different groups within a company will seek information. Those information needs will often be different and at times will clash. Companies must exercise strong central control over the database and manage it for the benefit of the overall business.
- *Conflict in customer data access and control*. Who has access to the information? Which product managers or business units get access to the customer database for communication purposes? When and how often? Much of the information companies gather is highly confidential and customers want assurances that it will remain confidential.
- *Startup costs and requirements*. Investment in hardware, software, staffing and training will be necessary. This is not the time to skimp.

- *Who is responsible for the database?* The IT department? Customer service? Finance? A specific product department? The database should be a corporate asset and managed as such.
- *Selection of software.* There are many choices available for analysis software. Take time to learn what your options are and what are the advantages and disadvantages of the various products available.

Conclusion

Table 1 summarizes the strategies a company should follow to build and use a database successfully. It captures the key aspects of when to communicate, which products to focus on, how to take advantage of cross-selling opportunities and what the benefit focus should be.

The key consideration to keep in mind is that the database is a significant corporate asset. More to the point, each record – each customer – is an asset. Each customer is the reason for your company's success. Each customer assures your company a profitable future. As your company builds, refines and enhances the database, your company will also be enhancing its asset base and its competitive position.

Summary

As competition intensifies, more companies are seeking to build relationships with their customers. The key to this is information – the more a company has about each customer, the more finely it can tailor its products, services and communications. The ultimate goal, says **David Schmittleïn**, is to be able to manage customers as strategic assets. To achieve this, companies must develop databases that capture detailed customer information yet are easy to use. The implication for salespeople is that their role will be as much to define customers' needs and devise communication strategies as to go out and sell. The author also describes the type of information that should go into databases and some of the obstacles to their successful use.

Putting copy-testers to the test

by Brian Sternthal and Angela Y. Lee

Advertisers have a lot of choice when it comes to deciding which television copy-testing service to use. Unfortunately there is less variety in the types of test that are used. Most services use traditional copy-testing techniques, where consumers watch television programs in which the advertisements to be tested – as well as control advertisements – are inserted. Before viewing the programs, consumers are asked to indicate their brand preferences in several categories, including those to be advertised.

When the presentation is over, the audience is asked to recall the advertising. If respondents fail to recall the target advertisement, they may be prompted with its category (for example, "Do you remember seeing an advertisement for cars?"). The recall data are typically supplied in the form of the respondents' verbatim responses together with a score representing the percentage of viewers who recalled critical message information. The score is used in establishing norms for all the advertising tested by the service.

Viewers are also asked again to select their preferred brand in various categories. These responses are compared to the pre-presentation preferences to assess advertisements' switching power. Other data that copy-testers gather include respondents' predictions of which elements of the advertised information they will remember, their evaluations of the advertising and the brand, and their suggestions for improving the advertising. Some services ask respondents to record their moment-by-moment enjoyment of the presentation and some even measure viewers' physiological responses.

Clients of copy-testing services use the test results to assess the likely impact of their advertising. They understand that the recall and brand-switching scores do not offer perfect forecasts of advertisement performance. Rather, they use the scores to compare different executions at a point in time, to evaluate new creative material relative to old or as a variable in models for predicting sales.

Copy-testers can provide norms to be used as benchmarks in evaluating the advertisements' effectiveness. They also frequently advise clients on how copy-testing scores might be improved. If respondents' moment-to-moment reactions have been measured, the information can be used to eliminate relatively uninteresting passages. Conversely, it can suggest which facets of the message should be elaborated upon.

Such tests can provide valuable insights into consumers' reactions to advertising and into how creative executions may be revised. However, there are potentially serious limitations to the current approaches of measuring advertising responses. In this article, we shall first assess current measures of advertising effectiveness and then suggest ways of enhancing the value of copy-testing procedures.

Current measures

Explicit measures

Most copy-testing measures are based on the assumption that when consumers make purchase decisions they attempt to recall advertising as well as other brand knowledge. The success of their attempt is supposed to depend upon how well they have "learned" advertisements. Thus the commonest measure of advertising effectiveness is verbatim recall of the advertising message. This is an "explicit" measure of memory because it focuses on the extent to which people can retrieve the content of an explicit message.

While message recall indicates the extent to which learning has occurred, there are problems in using this measure to assess the impact of advertising. One is that consumers often have difficulty in tracing the origin of their knowledge. People respond to advertising by relating what they know to the content of the advertisement. What they store in memory is a combination of the message information and their own thoughts.

When asked to recall the contents of a specific advertisement, people have difficulty in determining whether their recollection is based on the message being asked about, some other message they might have seen for the brand, or other knowledge. Thus people frequently misreport what they have learned from advertisements.

But even when consumers report accurately, a second problem with explicit measures of memory arises. This is the fact that brand evaluations and choice are often determined not by the information recalled but by the associations that the information has for consumers. For example, consumers might exhibit good recall of a carmaker's claim that its car came with a complete toolkit. But this might be because they associated the claim with the thought that the toolkit will be needed to fix the car's frequent breakdowns. Good advertising recall would be associated with a disinclination to purchase.

Implicit measures

Consumers make purchase decisions based on what they know about a brand rather than just on what they remember from a commercial. Thus advertisers are interested in what people know about their brand. Implicit measures of memory are useful in this regard. These explore what people know without reference to the origins of their knowledge.

Brand recall is an implicit measure because people are asked to tell what they know about a brand. Measuring the effect that exposure to advertising has on brand recall is often more valuable than measuring advertisement recall.

Another useful implicit measure is top-of-mind awareness. This involves using a category cue to prompt the retrieval of brand names – for example, consumers might be asked to list the brands of beer they would consider buying. A copy-tester might find that people who have seen a commercial for, say, Miller beer, include it in their list more often than those who have not. This would suggest that the advertisement was effective.

While brand recall and top-of-mind awareness are useful indicators of what people know about brands, advertisers are generally most interested in how advertisements influence consumers' dispositions towards their brands. To some extent, dispositions can be inferred from these measures – for example, enhancing top-of-mind recall often increases preference for a brand. However, because this measure is of limited diagnostic value advertisers use other measures designed to reflect dispositions.

Perhaps the most-used measure of dispositions is attitude. Attitude questions probe how people feel about a brand rather than what they know about it. They are asked to evaluate the brand generally ("like/dislike," "good/bad" and "superior/inferior") and in terms of more specific characteristics (such as feelings about its price and quality).

Attitude measures are typically implicit – no mention is made of prior advertising exposures. An advertisement has impact if people who have seen it are more favorably disposed to the brand than people who have not. Attitude measures offer insight into why people have various preferences.

Copy tests often include measures of choice. A commercial's brand-switching potential is assessed by the change in brand preference that results when it is shown. However, if the goal is to sustain current user loyalty, the use of choice requires the assumption that the same execution that best promotes switching also best sustains loyalty.

At a minimum, it would be useful to test this assumption. Alternatively, if the goal is to maintain loyalty, it might be useful to examine the extent to which advertising boosts consumers' resistance to competitors' overtures. This would entail testing whether loyalty is sustained when a commercial is shown in the context of other commercials in the same category.

Developing effective copy tests

Advertisers are interested in what consumers know about their brand and how favorable this knowledge is. Whether or not consumers can recall the contents of a specific advertisement is generally not germane to assessing advertisement effectiveness. Indeed, because consumers are often skeptical about the veracity of advertising messages, messages may have greater impact if consumers cannot remember that the origin of their knowledge was advertising.

Several procedures seem appropriate to improve the measurement of advertising effectiveness:

- *Knowledge and disposition should be measured using implicit memory measures.* Consumers' knowledge can be tapped by asking message recipients what brands they can recall, what brands they would consider in a category and what they know about the target brand. Consumers' dispositions can be assessed using overall and brand-specific attitudes as well as brand choice. When consumers' ability to perceive information such as brand names is of interest, perceptual measures such as fragment completion might be used.

- *Procedures used to examine advertising effectiveness currently focus on brand switching.* However, because many advertisers use advertising to retain current customers, it would be useful to incorporate procedures to assess brand loyalty. Including competitive advertising along with the target would provide a means of determining whether brand loyalty is sustained under competitive attack.

- *Procedures are needed to estimate the elasticity of response to advertising exposures.* At issue is whether increasing exposures to advertising will enhance or diminish impact. This will offer insight into whether the superiority of one execution over another in copy testing is likely to be sustained when different levels of exposure are used in everyday settings.

- *The context in which advertising is evaluated may bias the outcome towards a particular type of execution.* Procedures in which advertising is assessed in the absence of television programs and other commercials may be inadequate. It is important to select test contexts that correspond to those in which advertisements will appear.

Some copy tests attempt to bolster attitude and choice measures with indicators of consumers' physiological responses to commercials. Pupil dilation and voice stress have been used for this purpose. However, pupil dilation reflects both changes in attention and changes in luminosity and thus may be impossible to interpret unequivocally. And voice stress does not appear to correlate with other physiological indicators, so again its interpretation is elusive.

While the use of physiological measures appears to be on the decline, moment-to-moment measures of consumer response are more popular than ever. These measures typically entail having respondents turn a dial to indicate their level of interest from moment to moment. Parts of an advertisement that yield high interest are usually considered effective, whereas parts corresponding to weak interest are deemed ineffective. As intuitive as this approach is, there is evidence that other parameters are more useful in interpreting moment-to-moment responses.

Indeed, the trend in interest over the length of the commercial and the level of peak interest may be more indicative of effectiveness than is the specific response to a portion of the copy. There is also the possibility that providing moment-to-moment responses might prompt respondents to focus on their own thoughts and thus interfere with their processing of the advertised information.

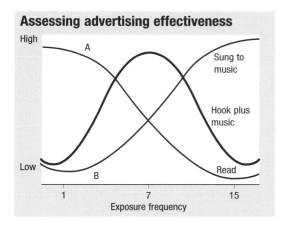

Assessing advertising effectiveness

Figure 1

Finally, some copy tests involve asking consumers how they would increase the impact of advertising. This approach is problematic because consumers' responses mostly take the form of what is generic in the category. If the advertisement is for a beer, the suggestion often is to add a bar scene or to include women – which would make it indistinguishable from many other beer commercials.

Perceptual measures

The measures discussed so far are relevant to situations where choices are based on information retrieved from memory. But there are a growing number of situations where the goal of advertising is limited simply to making consumers familiar with a brand name. Signs at sporting events and roadside hoardings are often used for this.

In these cases, perceptual measures are useful. These test how far advertising enhances consumers' ability to recognize the brand name. One such measure is fragment completion. For example, if respondents complete "B–l–-e" as "Bullseye" after seeing an advertisement for that brand, there would be evidence of perceptual learning.

Testing procedures

Copy-testing procedures usually involve showing the target advertisement once or several times within the context of other ads. The assumption is that if execution A is superior to execution B, this relationship will be preserved when the advertising is aired or printed, regardless of whether the number of exposures is different from that in the test.

This assumption is only likely to be true if the alternative executions require similar processing effort. When this is not the case, inferences from copy tests may be inaccurate. To illustrate this, consider the impact of three different executions for the same brand. In this illustration, the effort people need to put in to grasp the message depends on how the message is presented.

The hardest advertisement to process is the one in which the message is sung to music. As shown in Figure 1, increasing the number of exposures to this advertisement increases the likelihood that people will comprehend the message and thus become favorably disposed towards the brand.

A different outcome emerges for the easiest advertisement to process, which is read dramatically. The simplicity of the advertisement allows people to learn its contents after a single exposure. Further showings prompt people to think for themselves about the product and their thoughts are likely to be less favorable than the ones they were left with after the first exposure. This causes the advertisement's effectiveness to decline.

Finally, there is an advertisement that is moderately difficult to process because viewers are told the main theme of the message before hearing the message sung to music. In this case, people first learn the message content over a few showings and then think for themselves. The result is that the advertisement's effectiveness initially increases and then declines.

This pattern of outcomes has been documented in a number of investigations. It illustrates the problem with point estimates of advertisement effectiveness. For example, suppose that a copy test indicates that at three exposures each the read message (A) is more effective than the sung message (B). The assumption is that A will be more effective than B whatever the number of exposures. However, if the average number of exposures planned for the campaign is more substantial, say 10, then A is the wrong choice. Clearly it is important to assess exposure elasticities when evaluating the effectiveness of different executions.

In developing procedures to measure advertising effectiveness, it is important to consider the context in which an advertisement will be shown. The context used in most copy tests consists of television programs and advertisements for products from categories unrelated to the target advertisement's. There is evidence that this context may be biased in favor of advertisements that feature a brand's image rather than brand attributes.

Consider two advertisements for a camera. The attribute-focused advertisement enumerates attributes such as the flash and shutter speeds and shows pictures of these features. The image-focused advertisement enumerates the same attributes but instead of picturing them, it shows holiday pictures taken by the camera. The image advertisement is likely to be more persuasive than the attribute advertisement when shown in a context of unrelated commercials. This is because it prompts recall of the fact that there was an advertisement for a camera by relating it to holidays; the unrelated context makes it easy to recall the camera's features because it was the only brand advertised in that category. In contrast, the attribute-focused advertisement is more persuasive within a context of other camera advertisements. This is because it facilitates recall of the camera's specific features, a task made difficult by the presence of other camera advertisements. Thus the correspondence between the test and real-world context is an important consideration for copy-testers.

Summary

Advertising costs a lot of money so it is important to get it right. Many companies use copy-testers to identify the best execution. These services focus on explicit measures of effectiveness such as recall, where consumers are asked what they can remember from a commercial. Much greater insight would emerge, say **Angela Lee** and **Brian Sternthal**, if implicit measures were used to assess what consumers know and feel about a brand. More informed evaluation would also emerge if the test context were adjusted to match the everyday context in which commercials will appear. The authors suggest some ways in which copy tests might be improved.

Suggested further reading

Anand, P. and Sternthal, B. (1990) "Ease of message processing as a moderator of repetition effects in advertising," *Journal of Marketing Research*, 27, 345–53.

Baumgartner, H., Sujan, M. and Padgett, D. (1997) "Patterns of affective reactions to advertisements: the integration of moment-to-moment responses into overall judgments," *Journal of Marketing Research*, 34, 219–32.

Horvath, F. (1978) "An experimental comparison of the psychological stress evaluator and the galvanic skin response in detection of deception," *Journal of Applied Psychology*, 63, 338–44.

How to make sales force mergers work

by Andris A. Zoltners

1998 was a remarkable year for the merger and acquisition industry. In the first six months of 1998 deals worth a total of $1,200bn were announced worldwide. This compares with $1,600bn in all of 1997. In the US alone there were $813bn in the first six months of 1998, compared with $920bn in all of 1997.

Mergers and acquisitions involving separate companies are called external mergers. Internal mergers occur when divisions or product groups within the same company merge to rationalize resources or deliver more value to a common set of customers. These happen at least as often as external mergers. The total business affected by both internal and external mergers easily doubles the 1998 six-month deal figure of $1,200bn.

Mergers and acquisitions force organizations to blend. No one is spared – certainly not the sales forces. Corporate mergers and acquisitions usually require significant cost reductions. Individual sales forces are scrutinized to make sure that they contribute to these savings.

A sales force merger creates significant opportunities for the company

Status quo is usually not an option when selling organizations are merged. Mergers imply change. The product portfolio is expanded and new market segments are added. The customer attraction and retention process is redefined. The new organization is resized and restructured and selling support systems change accordingly. A new sales force is created. Sales force mergers provide an opportunity to create a vital, highly productive selling organization. Unfortunately, it is sales force creation with baggage – each existing force brings its history, style and people to the integration.

Integration can take one of two very different paths. First, the selling organizations can be pasted together as quickly and cost effectively as possible. Financial objectives are jeopardized if cost savings are not realized and "feet are not on the street" very soon. Or second, the company can try to design the most appropriate

Support systems and processes for a new sales force	
Sales force decisions, processes and systems	**Description**
Sales force strategy	Determine how the sales force will execute the corporate strategy effectively.
Product/market prioritization	Determine the best products to promote and the best market segments to service using the new sales force.
Selling process	Develop a customer attraction and retention process that is effective and meets customer needs.
Size and structure	Derive a profit-maximizing size and an efficient organizational structure so that the selling organization can implement the desired selling process effectively.
Territory alignment and personnel selection	Retain high-performing salespeople and determine their new account assignments.
Compensation	Develop a recruiting process to attract high performing salespeople.
Recruitment	Develop a recruiting process to attract high performing salespeople.
Training	Develop a training program that enables salespeople to develop the knowledge, skills and capabilities to be successful.
Performance evaluation systems	Develop evaluation systems that provide salespeople with the appropriate feedback and coaching so they grow professionally and feel connected with the organization.
Sales force support systems	Implement field force automation, goal setting, lead generation and customer targeting systems.
Sales force culture	Create a success culture.

Table 1

sales force for the merged product portfolio and the redefined customer base.

The first path is reactive; the second path is proactive. The first path usually results in a contest – over who will survive – whereas the second starts from scratch and views the merger as an opportunity to create a sales force that will add the most value to the company and its customers. The best merger combines elements of both – proactive creation accomplished quickly.

Regardless of which path a company takes, it will need to make a number of decisions and develop a number of support systems and processes for the new sales force. The most important of these are listed in Table 1.

Since each organization in the merger already has a sales force with an established culture, selling process and sales support process, the merged organization should at least adopt the best practices from each participant. The best strategy is to approach the merger as a sales force creation and develop a selling organization that is better than the sum of the parts. Regrettably, most organizations settle for less.

The sales force merger opportunity is rarely realized in the short term

Sales force merger results do not usually meet the company's expectations in the short term. Figure 1 sets out some of the most common reasons for this.

Sales force mergers

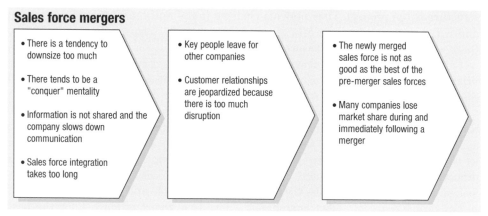

Figure 1

There is a tendency to downsize too much. A merger typically promises at least two benefits. First, the organization will realize market synergies and, second, it will achieve cost savings. Since cost savings are always easier to see and measure, companies are under significant pressure to downsize the entire organization aggressively.

Since everyone must "share the pain," the sales force is a prime candidate for downsizing as well. Further, the company needs to realize the cost saving immediately. This logic overlooks a fundamental fact about the sales force: the sales force drives the top line. Excessive downsizing results in an immediate sales loss and jeopardizes future product and customer development needs.

There tends to be a "conquer" mentality. A sales force merger affects everyone. Change is in the air. Downsizing is anticipated. "The sales force is scared stiff" is a common refrain. Survival is usually at the expense of someone else in a merger environment, especially when downsizing is taking place. The acquiring company or the stronger company usually survives and wins. Consequently, its people assume positions of power, design the resulting sales force and establish its culture.

Since decisions need to be made quickly, the new sales force is usually compatible with the history and habits of the "winners." People in the acquired company either leave or accept less powerful positions. The conqueror's sales force becomes the new sales force. Practicable ways of improving the sales force are not fully evaluated, even though the conqueror's sales force design and systems are usually not appropriate for the expanded product line and customer base.

Information is not shared and the company slows down communication. Rumors start as soon as the deal is announced and spread quickly, while accurate information is communicated much more slowly. Typically, this is because there is nothing to tell until leadership is established and integration teams are organized. This can take time. Meanwhile the sales force waits, anticipates and worries.

Information flows slowly even after the integration teams are assembled. There are two main reasons for this. One is that management does not want to give employees false expectations and thus guards information until its decisions are final. Besides, if employees learn details of the decision making process, managers may lose the flexibility to make exceptions to the "rules" they are using.

The other reason is that management does not want to involve the field in the decision process. This could be because managers themselves are unsure as to the structure of the process. They may also believe that employees lack strategic vision and will put their own interests above the company's – especially if it looks like there will be "winners" and "losers."

External communication slows down as well. This is a more dangerous communication interruption. Customers begin to worry about whether their needs will continue to be met after the merger.

Sales force integration takes too long. The integration process requires leaders to be chosen, integration teams to be formed, sales force design questions to be answered and all members of the new force to be selected. These activities consume a lot of time. Meanwhile an entire sales force waits in anticipation. Morale degenerates proportionately with the length of the integration process. Customers get overlooked. Aggressive competitors try to steal the best people and poach customers.

Key people leave for other companies. There is a vigorous market for the best people in any industry. Recruiters recognize the vulnerability of salespeople working for an organization that is merging and possibly downsizing, and they start calling immediately. The best people leave when they get good outside offers because there is too much uncertainty over their options in the newly merged organization. Companies offering exit packages to accelerate downsizing often provide the extra nudge their good performers need to leave. It is essential for the integration process to establish incentives to keep the best performers.

Customer relationships are jeopardized because there is too much disruption. Downsizing and restructuring create disruption. Salespeople may be required to change the products that they sell or the customer segments that they sell to. They may be asked to perform different selling tasks – hunters may be asked to farm and farmers to hunt. Relationship sellers may be asked to become technical sellers, and technical sellers may be asked to become more intuitive.

Customers may have become comfortable with "their" salesperson. Frequently, customers feel they have trained their salesperson on their business and how they use the sellers' products. A new salesperson will require an investment of time and energy and hence creates apprehension for the customer.

Because a lot of accounts are reassigned during a sales force merger, customer frustration is to be expected. This is especially true when a customer greets a salesperson from the other side of the merger who does not have the knowledge needed to communicate effectively with the customer. The merged selling organization must try to minimize the reassignment of key customers. Where customers do have to be reassigned, it must craft an effective account transition program to protect them.

The newly merged sales force is not as good as the best of the pre-merger sales forces. The pre-merger sales forces have a history of adapting to their environments. They have been redesigned many times in response to product launches, new market segments, customer consolidations, new distribution channel options, new technologies, competitive attacks and government regulations. Now these sales forces will be integrated and will sell an expanded product offering to a larger customer base. Major design decisions are made quickly with a "conquer" mentality. The forces are likely to be downsized and will lose some good people. Downsizing guarantees that incremental sales will be lost. Since a sales force is only as good as its people, customer relationships will be jeopardized by the loss of key individuals. Only the best integration will yield a sales force that is, in the short term, as good as the sum of its parts.

The sales force integration time line

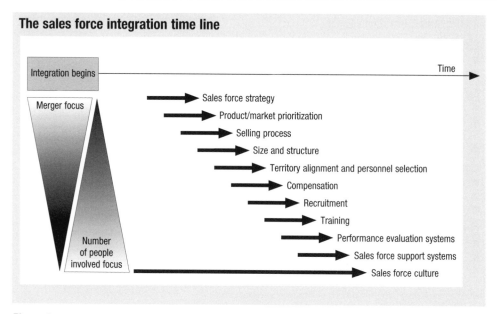

Figure 2

Many companies lose market share during and immediately following a merger. The short-term market share decline can be due to many factors. The sales force's contribution to the decline results from underinvestment in it, the loss of good people, a suboptimal design, loss of focus as people worry about losing their jobs, disruption in customer relationships, and the opportunism of competitors. The market share will bounce back, as all of these conditions are corrected over time.

A sales force integration process

Figure 2 describes the steps needed to create a merged sales force. The steps are ordered sequentially in terms of the timing of their implementation. Regrettably, only the strategy, size and structure, and territory alignment and personnel selection steps are certain to be implemented in a typical merger. Once transition teams are formed, the company is usually under great pressure to implement the new selling organization. Executing the three steps just mentioned will finalize the personnel decisions and put "feet on the street." The other integration steps require more sales force involvement and are usually deferred until later.

The sales force integration team has several challenges:

- Keep the best people.
- Make the best decisions for each of the sales force integration steps.
- Move as many of the integration steps forward in time as possible.
- Create merger-related synergies.

Table 2 is intended to help sales forces plan their mergers. The advice it contains has helped many companies create good post-merger selling organizations. The selling organization is rarely consulted when companies decide to merge. Usually salespeople first hear of the merger or acquisition when they read the morning newspaper. Yet they are called upon to participate constructively in the creation of a new sales force that may significantly alter the work that they will do for the next

---

A sales force integration advisor

Sales force strategy
- Implement the strategies that gave impetus to the merger.
- Focus on strategic revenue synergies as well as cost reduction.

Focus on the customer
- Focus on customer needs when making critical decisions about the integrated organization.
- Resolve conflicts by assessing the impact on customers and striving for the most efficient and effective coverage of those customers.
- Create short-term goals and contests to maintain customer focus.

Cross-company teams
- Develop cross-company teams with clearly defined roles and responsibilities.
- Encourage a "merger" as opposed to "conquer" mentality during the integration process.
- Encourage input and objective, critical assessment from both companies.

Establish strong leadership
- Identify leaders and managers with a "can do" attitude for key post-integration positions.
- Target the involvement of key individuals in the merger process.
- Staff the integration teams with individuals who are organized, task-orientated, objective and fair, and who have a positive attitude.
- Encourage tough decision making and support sub-team decisions.

Rapid transition
- Instill a sense of urgency to integrate quickly.
- Keep the focus on customers: do not let it migrate to the politics of internal change.
- Make personnel decisions as soon as possible.
- Retain good people who otherwise may get frustrated with a lengthy process.

Communicate, communicate, communicate
- Minimize unproductive rumors and speculation by providing timely, accurate information.
- Send constant messages from senior management about process, timing and progress to maximize a spirit of co-operation
- Reduce uncertainty and overcome resistance to change.

Targeted third-party involvement
- Use outside organizations as appropriate to structure, monitor and facilitate the integration process; they can also mitigate conflict between companies.
- Use outside organizations to bring in best-practice sales force expertise.

Table 2

few years. The integration can be done well or it can be done poorly. Many careers depend on how well it is accomplished.

Summary

Mergers provide an opportunity to create a new and superior selling organization. Unfortunately, says **Andris Zoltners**, the opportunity is often missed. There are several reasons for this. One is a "conquer" mentality on the part of the stronger company. Instead of the best of both sales force cultures being blended, one dominates, even though it is unlikely to be suitable for the expanded product line or customer base. This is exacerbated by pressure to make cost savings quickly, which means that insufficient effort is devoted to crafting the new selling organization. Another cost-driven error is to downsize the sales force in proportion with the rest of the company; but because the sales force drives the top line, there is a disproportionate effect on sales revenue. The author reviews these and other problems in detail and provides guidelines for overcoming them.

Monitoring the market misleaders

by Kent Grayson and Svetlana Kirillova

The authors thank Tim Ambler, Bill Lennon and Gil McWilliam for their comments.

Misled customers are a serious business concern. Products that do not last as long, taste as good or work as quickly as expected increase the possibility of customer complaints and hurt repeat business. And dissatisfied customers are more likely than satisfied ones to tell others about their experience.

Customers can be misled for a number of reasons. These range from carelessness on the part of the customer to negligence or deliberate deception on the part of the marketer. When a customer feels that he or she has been misled, legal procedures are available in most countries but self-regulatory organizations (SROs) usually offer faster and cheaper redress. Generally these are impartial, independent bodies funded by advertising agencies for the purpose of regulating marketing communications. In Europe some SROs have existed for more than 50 years.

The main purpose of this article is to consider such regulation from the point of view of business and to discuss the wider issues involved when customers make complaints.

Modes of communication

SROs focus primarily on advertising because it is generally the most explicit way that marketers communicate with customers. However, it is not the only way consumers can end up with a false belief.

Every market offering is made up of a number of attributes that "say something" about the product or service. To assist with marketing planning and management, marketers divide these attributes into four categories, which are widely known as the "Four Ps." They are:

- **product:** the product or service offered to the consumer
- **price:** the cost to the consumer of getting the product or service
- **place:** the way in which the product is distributed
- **promotion:** verbal, auditory or visual information communicated about the product by the marketer

It is important to recognize that communication is accomplished via all of the Ps, not just promotion. Take the physical attributes of the *product* itself. Its color, shape, design or size inherently provides information. Research has shown, for example, that some customers judge the quality of bread by relying more on its color than on its nutritional label. Furthermore, the *price* of a market offering can communicate more than just its cost. For instance, some customers will avoid buying a low-price product because they believe – sometimes incorrectly – that the low price means low quality. How a market offering is *distributed* can speak volumes. When a product is available only in speciality shops or when it is

What should marketers do?

A tempting solution to the problem of misleading advertising is simply to place all responsibility for it on marketers. But however simple this approach may be, it places unreasonable demands on business. As we have argued, an advertisement can be truthful and well intentioned but still mislead a customer. Thus it is appropriate that marketers, consumers and regulators negotiate, usually on a case-by-case basis, whether or not an advertisement is misleading.

A case-by-case regulatory system – especially one that is dependent in part on customers' motivation to complain – is by nature flexible, and skillful marketers can easily take advantage by stretching the rules as far as they will go. Some marketers have even found that the publicity generated by incurring the wrath of regulators helps to enhance their company's image in some customers' minds.

Although testing regulatory limits has its place, such tests should be undertaken with due regard for the costs. Experience has shown that the more marketers are seen as not playing their role in keeping advertising reasonably honest, the more regulators and consumers argue for less flexible controls on advertising.

Most marketers know that simply following the basic principles of good marketing goes a long way to keep marketers from naïvely misleading customers. Advertisements are pre-tested for consumer response and are adjusted if there are misunderstandings. Many campaigns are aimed at specific customer groups via the appropriate media, thus keeping the message from being seen by those who may not share the same social facts as the target audience. Lastly, keeping information about research and strategy can assist in verifying a marketer's intent to regulators and consumers.

Many marketers also recognize that, even when the best information is kept, consumers and regulators may still view the advertisement as deceptive and may request that it be removed. The nature of a three-way negotiation between consumers, regulators and marketers is that the marketer's view does not always win.

In such situations, many marketers reluctantly agree that both they and the regulatory system are generally best served by prompt assent. Of course, it is difficult to say "you win some, you lose some" when production costs, media plans and client goodwill may all be at stake. But unless the regulatory system develops a pattern of prohibition that is widely seen to be inappropriate or unfair, questioning or testing the legitimacy of the system's decisions may amount to questioning the value of an imperfect umbrella in the middle of a rainstorm.

displayed prominently in a supermarket, this in and of itself communicates information.

Promotion includes not only advertising but also brochures, press releases, instruction manuals, sales pitches and words written on packaging. Because promotion includes words and pictures it communicates with customers more explicitly than the design of a perfume bottle or the appearance of an automobile dealership. In this article we will focus primarily on promotion, although the points we raise are generally applicable to communication accomplished by all of the Ps.

Are marketers to blame?

The general opinion seems to be that customers are misled because marketers wish to mislead them. For instance, a majority of the 38,000 customers surveyed by Roper Starch Worldwide in 40 countries reported that advertising exaggerates product benefits, health benefits and product sizes – and that advertising in general does not provide accurate information. In a CLA Medialab Sensor survey,

60 per cent of UK customers aged 15 to 24 agreed that products frequently fail to live up to their promises. Given these results, it is not surprising that US customers contacted by Gallup rated selling and marketing jobs lowest in terms of honesty and ethics.

But are marketers always to blame when marketing is misleading? Indeed, some marketing communication may be unintentionally complex, purposefully vague or deliberately extreme – all of which will mislead at least some consumers. However, even when a marketer communicates clearly and accurately, consumers may not do a good job of interpreting it.

Customers can be "misled" when they read too quickly, make unreasonable assumptions or fall victim to their own wishful thinking. So the cause of misleading marketing can range from deception on the part of the marketer to delusion on the part of the consumer. Because of this, a potentially important issue for regulators is determination of the marketer's intent.

From a strict consumer protection standpoint, a marketer's intent should not be relevant. A marketer who purposefully misleads will often have the same negative impact as one who inadvertently does. And intent can be difficult to determine – people who deliberately deceive are unlikely to confess their intention.

Despite these issues, regulators often operate on the assumption that a company acting in good faith should not be judged by the same standards as someone acting in bad faith. Therefore marketers can protect themselves from potential regulatory action by making it as easy as possible for regulators to determine intent when it falls under question. In most instances, it is the marketer alone who has access to the information and documents that can shed light on the issue.

The collection of evidence is a responsibility that marketers must shoulder in order to facilitate the regulatory process – and this is a requirement stated in many SROs' codes. Without clear assurances from the marketer, a regulatory body is left to make judgments based only on the evidence of the marketing communication itself. Even if this evidence is debatable, the marketer's unwillingness to provide counter-evidence may be taken as indicating an intention to mislead.

With the right information, however, marketers may be able to show that they have naïvely – rather than deliberately – misled customers. Consider, for example, an advertisement for a travel company that described an itinerary for a boat tour of the Yangtse. When a customer was able to complete only part of the cruise, he complained to the UK's Advertising Standards Authority (ASA). In response, the company explained that it had changed the itinerary because of exceptionally low water levels. It was able to show that these circumstances were indeed exceptional and not seasonal, thus supporting the claim that the marketer naïvely misled the customer. When the advertisement was published, the marketer believed that the information provided was truthful. The ASA did not uphold the customer's complaint.

Social facts and SROs

When a question arises about marketing activity, it is important to ascertain not only the marketer's intent but also the facts. Without this knowledge, it is impossible to determine whether or not the customer has a false belief about the product. However, most of the "facts" we use in our everyday lives are based more on social agreement than on objective truth and thus are prone to ambiguity.

For example, consider the following case, which is based on a complaint raised with the ASA in 1997. A magazine advertisement for an airline-branded credit card reported that card holders could earn a mile for every £1 spent on the card. A complainant objected that the "miles" earned did not correspond to the nautical miles traveled on the free trips offered. For example, the 15,000 "miles" required for a trip from London to selected European destinations were significantly more than the actual miles flown to Europe and back. In many airline loyalty programs the "miles" earned are more like "points" that can be exchanged for rewards. However, these programs are most familiar to frequent flyers and it is unlikely that all consumers know the rules.

This case raises two difficulties associated with determining social facts. The first is that they can differ from group to group. What is a social fact to a seasoned airline loyalty program customer may not be a social fact for a less experienced traveler. The second difficulty is that, almost by definition, social facts do not start out as facts. When the first airline loyalty program used the word "miles" as a way of referring to points, it was just one company's approach and it was incumbent on the company to be explicit about its terms. What is less clear is how many frequent flyer programs must adopt the same system – and for how long – before these terms become a social fact.

Although determining the nature of social facts is not always easy, SROs – as the bodies that must decide whether marketing claims match social facts – should endeavor to keep track of them. To this end, many SROs establish consultative councils with consumer groups, use their regional offices to keep in touch with local views, and undertake direct consumer research. For example, the UK's Independent Television Commission (an SRO that regulates television advertising) spends £1m per year on consumer research.

As a postscript, the ASA did not uphold the complaint about air miles on the grounds that because similar schemes' "miles" did not correspond to exactly to travel miles, readers were unlikely to be misled.

Summary

When customers complain that a purchase does not live up to expectations, who is at fault? Many would blame the marketer – a Gallup survey in the US indicated that people rate marketing and selling jobs lowest in terms of honesty. But **Kent Grayson** and **Svetlana Kirillova** argue that this is too simplistic. While there are undoubtedly dishonest marketers, many misunderstandings are down to mere carelessness on the part of the marketer or the customer. And because of the slippery nature of "social facts" – established by convention rather than objectively – it is not always clear whether a marketing communication is misleading or not.

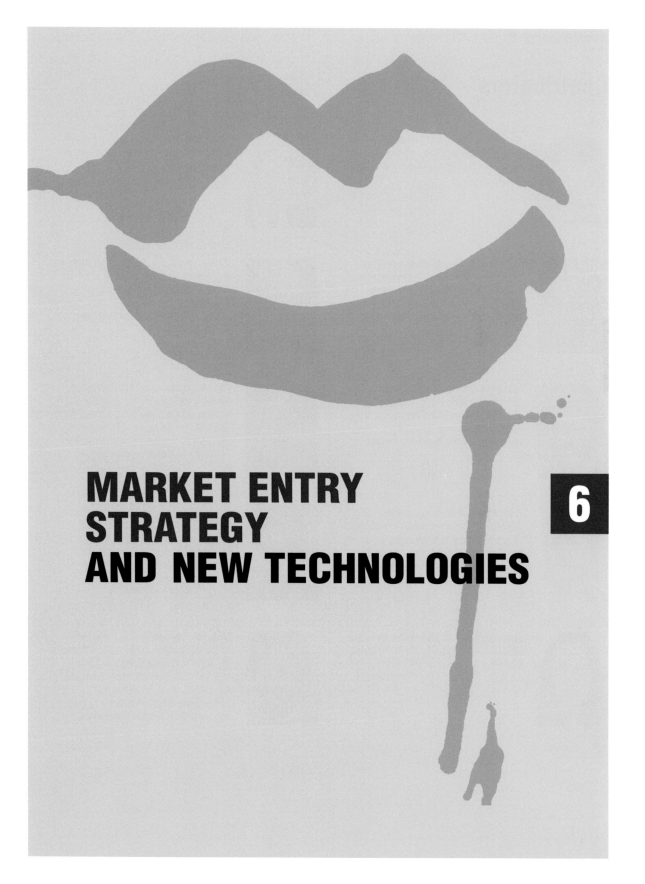

MARKET ENTRY STRATEGY AND NEW TECHNOLOGIES

6

Contributors

Markus Christen is assistant professor of marketing at INSEAD. His research focuses on managerial information and decision making.

Thomas S. Robertson is dean at Emory University's Goizueta Business School. He was formerly deputy dean at London Business School.

Venkatesh (Venky) Shankar is assistant professor of marketing and director of the Quality Enhanced Systems and Teams (Quest) program at the Smith School of Business, University of Maryland.

Paul E. Green is professor of marketing and S.S. Kresge Professor Emeritus at the Wharton School of the University of Pennsylvania. His research interests include marketing research and optimal product design.

Lakshman Krishnamurthi is the A. Montgomery Ward Professor of Marketing and chairs the marketing department at the J.L. Kellogg Graduate School of Management, Northwestern University.

Abba M. Krieger is the Robert Steinberg Professor of Statistics, Information Management, and Marketing at the Wharton School of the University of Pennsylvania. His research interests include marketing research and applied probability.

Sabine Kuester is visiting assistant professor of marketing at the Stern School of Business, New York, on leave from Essec Management School, France. Her research focuses on technology marketing.

Vikas Mittal is visiting assistant professor at the J.L. Kellogg Graduate School of Management, Northwestern University. His research centers on issues related to customer satisfaction, retention and profitability management.

Elisa Montaguti is a post-doctoral fellow at INSEAD. Her research deals with issues of technology and sales acceleration.

Mohanbir Sawhney is assistant professor of marketing at the J.L. Kellogg Graduate School of Management, Northwestern University. His research interests include marketing strategy for technology companies and cross-functional co-ordination in product development.

Contents

Introduction

Launching a new product, particularly one that incorporates new technology, is one of the marketer's toughest responsibilities. A key dilemma – and the theme of two of the articles in this module – is whether to be a trailblazer, carving out and cornering a new market, or a "free-riding" follower. Also discussed is the related problem of achieving rapid market acceptance for new, unfamiliar technologies; the slow growth of the video recorder market, in which VHS and Betamax fought for dominance, is a case in point. Other issues considered here are the use of conjoint analysis to assess consumer response to new products, and ways in which manufacturers of online information products can secure consumer attention.

Does it pay to be a pioneer?

by Markus Christen

The timing of market entry is critical to the success of a new product. A company has two alternatives: it can compete to enter a new product market first or it can wait for a competitor to take the lead and then follow once the market has been proven viable. Companies such as Sony, Intel, Merck and 3M are examples of companies that try to enter new markets first. They aggressively search for new products and markets and invest heavily in research and development to support their strategic objectives. By contrast, Matsushita typically follows Sony in introducing consumer electronic products. AMD and Cyrix let Intel introduce new processor generations and then follow quickly with lower-priced alternatives. Many pharmaceutical companies, such as Novopharm or Ratiopharm, do not invest in developing new drugs but focus instead on generic versions of existing drugs.

All this raises an intriguing strategic question: is it generally better to take the lead and pioneer a new product market or to wait and follow a pioneer? "Be first to market" is one of the more enduring strategic principles in marketing. It is based on the belief that pioneers have persistent advantages in the form of higher market share and superior distribution, product lines and quality. However, during the past few years the wisdom of this principle has been increasingly criticized despite generally strong empirical support.

The criticism typically centers on three issues:

Survivor and reporting bias

The various databases used to study the effects of pioneering only contain data for surviving companies. Further, the classification of companies as pioneers or followers relies on responses from current employees. These problems are suspected to lead researchers to overestimate the pioneering effect.

Causation versus correlation

The conclusion that pioneers have an advantage has been based on observed differences between pioneers and followers. In the Pims (Profit Impact of Market Strategies) database, market shares for a large cross-section of business units are approximately 29 per cent for pioneers, 20 per cent for early followers and 15 per cent for late entrants. However, this observation alone is insufficient to conclude that pioneering causes a market share advantage. Let us assume that well-managed companies are more likely to be pioneers. At the same time, we would expect well-managed companies to achieve higher market shares. This situation would lead to the same observed market share pattern but the differences would not be caused by pioneering.

Market share versus profit

Research has focused on market share and paid little attention to the effect of pioneering on profitability. Higher market share does not automatically lead to higher profits.

The purpose of this article is to reconsider the validity of the "be first to market" principle. It uses recent research results to draw a more differentiated picture of the impact of pioneering on company performance.

Customer-based sources of pioneering advantage

Despite the limitations of existing research, nobody denies that there are potentially advantages to being a pioneer. Over the years, a long list of sources that could yield an enduring performance advantage for pioneers has been developed. These can be divided into two main types: customer-based sources and operation- or cost-based sources. We shall consider customer-based sources first.

Customer learning and preference formation

For many new products, customers are initially uncertain about the contribution of product attributes and features to the product's value. Preferences for different attributes and their desired levels are learned over time. This enables the pioneer to shape customer preferences in its favor. It sets the standard to which customers refer in evaluating followers' products. The pioneering product can become the prototypical or "original" product for the whole category, as exemplified by Walkman, Kleenex, Polaroid or Hoover.

Access to customers

The pioneering product is a bigger novelty when it appears on the market and is therefore more likely than followers to capture customer and distributor attention. In addition, a pioneer's advertising is not cluttered by messages from competitors. Even in the long term, followers must continue to spend more on advertising to achieve the same effect as pioneers.

The pioneer can set standards for distribution, occupy the best locations or select the best distributors, which can give it easier access to customers. For example, in many US cities Starbucks, as the first entrant, was able to open coffee bars in more prominent locations than its competitors. In many industrial markets, distributors are reluctant to take on second and third products, particularly when the product is technically complex or requires large inventories of products and spare parts.

Switching costs

Switching costs arise when investments are required that would be lost when switching to another product. For example, many people have developed skill in using the traditional qwerty keyboard. Switching to the presumably more efficient Dvorak keyboard (Figure 1) would require relearning how to type, an investment that in many cases would exceed the expected efficiency gains.

Switching costs also arise when the quality of a product is difficult to assess. People who move abroad often experience this "cost" when simple purchase decisions such as buying detergent, toothpaste or coffee become harder because the trusted brand from home is no longer available. Pioneering products have the first chance to become this trusted brand. Consequently, followers must convince customers to bear the costs and risks of switching to an untried brand of unknown quality.

Network externalities

The value to customers of many high-technology products depends not only on their attributes but also on the total number of users. For example, the value of a videophone depends on the number of people using the same or a compatible system. A pioneer obviously has the opportunity to build a large installed base before competitive entry. This reduces followers' ability to introduce differentiated products. There are other advantages from a large user base, such as the ability to share documents with other computer users. Thus, software companies are often willing to give away products to build the market quickly and set a standard.

The Dvorak keyboard

Figure 1

Operation- or cost-based sources of advantage

Operation- or cost-based sources of pioneering advantage fall into three main categories:

Experience effects and economies of scale

Being first means that pioneers can build production volume and accumulate research and development and market experience before any other competitor. This potential cost advantage can be used to achieve higher margins or to protect customer-based advantages through lowering prices to discourage competitors from entering the market. A pioneer can maintain this advantage only when it is able to keep the accumulated experience proprietary. However, different studies have shown that inter-company diffusion of technology and knowledge occurs rapidly in most industries. Mechanisms for diffusion include reverse engineering, research publications, plant tours, workforce mobility, use of external consultants and so on.

Patents

Patents offer a means of keeping experience proprietary and limit imitation. However, they offer a significant barrier in only a few industries, such as pharmaceuticals. On average, patents are imitated within about four years at about 65 per cent of the innovator's cost. Moreover, filing for and enforcing patents is time-consuming and costly and requires the release of detailed information that could be useful to potential followers.

Pre-emption of scarce resources

Pioneers have the opportunity to acquire scarce resources when demand for them is still low and they are therefore cheaper. In some cases, they might be able to monopolize an important input factor. For example, Minnetonka, a small US manufacturer of consumer goods, was able to protect Softsoap, the first liquid soap, against competitors such as Procter & Gamble by buying up a full year's supply of the small plastic pump required for the dispenser. Subsequently, however, P&G's size told and its Ivory brand ousted Softsoap.

However, if a resource remains scarce, its value increases and so do incentives to search for alternative sources or substitutes. And it is often unclear at the time of entry which resources will be critical. A scarce resource also provides its owner with the opportunity to extract the benefits from the pioneer. For example, Drexel, Burnham & Lambert was a pioneer in junk bonds but one of its employees –

Why be first to market?

The research cited above calls into question the "be first to market" principle, which is based on the expected long-term effects of pioneering. So if it yields lower long-term profits than following, why should companies continue to pioneer?

There are four main reasons. First, according to the study just mentioned, pioneers may not have a long-term profit advantage but they enjoy higher profits in the early years after entry. With high enough discount rates, long-term profits could play only a limited role in the entry timing decision. In other words, pioneering may be justified by its short-term rather than its long-term benefits. Some companies plough the short-term profits of pioneering into research and development that will form the basis for another bout of pioneering. The idea is to generate a continuous cycle of pioneering – to never wait for followers to catch up and profits to sag. Gillette pursues a strategy of this sort.

The second reason for pioneering is that, while it may not be best for an individual product or business unit, it can be the optimal strategy for a company to implement across all its markets. For example, 3M builds its long-term success less on a single pioneering product such as Post-it notes than on a continuous stream of new, innovative products. Its corporate goals are set accordingly. 3M wants 30 per cent of sales to come from products that are less than five years old and 10 per cent from products that are less than 12 months old.

Third, deciding on market entry timing requires an assessment of the advantages and disadvantages associated with pioneering and following. Among the companies considering entering a market first, the one that expects the biggest gain from doing so is likely to invest more resources and to take more risks to beat the competition to market. Unfortunately, this company is also more likely to overestimate the magnitude of the obtainable advantages. This phenomenon is known as "the winners curse" and has been observed, for example, in auctions of oil drilling licences.

Finally, while pioneering may not pay off on average, under specific conditions the advantages may exceed the disadvantages. For example, when customers are unmotivated or unable to learn about alternatives once a first product has been adopted, pioneers can build lasting profit advantages. Customers may be unmotivated to learn because the product is not considered important enough to justify the effort of a renewed product evaluation. Certain habit purchases fall into this category. Customers are unable to learn when a product's quality is not observable, it is relatively expensive and it is purchased infrequently. This description applies to many consumer durables. In contrast, industrial buyers are often better able and more motivated to evaluate different alternatives before purchase. This is one explanation of why the effects of pioneering are generally weaker for industrial products.

Michael Milken, who was the driving force behind the company's success – earned more than his employer at one point.

Sources of follower advantage

Potential sources of follower advantage fall into two categories: free riding and incumbent inertia.

Free riding

By definition, pioneers are the first to invest significant resources into such areas as research and development, market infrastructure, buyer education and employee training. These investments cannot always be kept proprietary. In other words, followers can free-ride on them. For example:

- IBM, although not the pioneer, was the first to push its personal computer (PC) as a standard for the whole product category. This offered clone makers such as Compaq, which followed IBM, a larger market without bearing the cost of market development.
- Convincing retailers to carry a second brand in a successful new product category may require less effort than to induce them to use limited shelf space for an unproven new category.

- Before Starbucks, few Americans were willing to pay a premium for good-tasting coffee. Today, any coffee bar can benefit from the consumer education effort by Starbucks.
- The widespread use of electric cars will require a network of battery recharging stations. Early market entrants will be likely to carry these investments disproportionately.

Incumbent inertia

When followers enter the market, they have significantly more information than pioneers had at their time of entry. They can worry less about customer or technology uncertainty. They can imitate best practices and avoid the pioneer's mistakes. Before a market exists, market research is often unreliable. Once customers have gained experience with a product, they can better describe what they like.

For example, before entering the US market, Toyota interviewed owners of Volkswagens, the leading small car at the time, to learn what they liked and disliked about small cars. Though pioneers have access to the same new information, they are often less able or willing to take advantage of it.

Inertia is not necessarily irrational. Companies have investments in specific assets. Thus, switching costs faced by pioneers may make new practices less attractive to them than to followers. With fixed assets, incremental changes often look more attractive than radical changes. For example, IBM was afraid that PCs would cannibalize its mainframe business, a concern that clone makers did not share. Dell can take better advantage of the Internet to sell directly to customers than PC manufacturers such as IBM or Compaq, which must consider how their existing retailers will be affected. But even when economic arguments favor radical changes, many companies and their employees are highly resistant to change.

The long-term impact of pioneering

The existence and persistence of customer-based sources of pioneering advantage is strongly supported by theoretical, empirical and experimental research. Customer-based sources enable the average pioneer to achieve and maintain higher market shares. Recent re-examinations of research have shown that this finding holds even when survivor and reporting bias and the causation versus correlation problem (*see* p. 167) are taken into account.

In contrast to customer-based sources, the operation- or cost-based sources of pioneering advantage do not yield a long-term cost advantage. While the average pioneer cannot build a persisting advantage from these sources, followers are generally able to leverage their own sources to achieve and maintain a cost advantage. This pattern holds especially for consumer product markets.

In summary, the average pioneer obtains higher market share, while the average follower counters this advantage with lower cost. This raises the question: which of the two advantages is stronger? Or are they equally strong?

One way to answer this is to examine the long-term effect of pioneering on profitability (net income or return on investment, say). If the market share advantage is stronger, pioneers should be more profitable; and if the cost advantage is stronger, followers should be more profitable. In 1997, the present author and a colleague carried out a study of the Pims database to determine which was the case. We found that the average follower is more profitable than the average pioneer. A pioneer's profit handicap is generally smaller in business markets than in consumer markets. However, in the first few years after entry the average pioneer has higher profits, especially in consumer markets. This advantage evaporates over time and then turns into a disadvantage.

Conclusion

Firms considering pioneering a new market should base their decision on a careful evaluation of the potential sources of advantage and disadvantage. Expectations of a sustainable long-term advantage due to pioneering should remain moderate. Market share advantages are often more easily established but generally at the expense of operational efficiency. Pioneers should remain operationally flexible and not hesitate to learn from followers.

Summary

Markus Christen questions the "be first to market" principle. The thinking behind it is that companies that pioneer a market benefit from both customer- and operations-based sources of advantage. Pioneers attract more attention, shape customers' preferences and can become the category standard. On the operational side, they can secure patents, pre-empt scarce resources and accumulate valuable market experience. However, research shows that, in the long term, the average late entrant is more profitable than the average pioneer; late entrants can free-ride on pioneers' trailblazing efforts, copy their operational expertise and take advantage of their inertia. Despite this, pioneering yields higher short-term profits and, in certain circumstances, is the optimum strategy.

Suggested further reading

Boulding, W. and Christen, M. (1997) "Sustainable pioneering advantage: at what cost?" research paper, INSEAD.

Bowman, D. and Gatignon, H. (1996) "Order of entry as a moderator of the effect of the marketing mix on market share," *Marketing Science*, 15, 222–42.

Kerin, R.A., Varadarajan, P.R. and Peterson, R.A. (1992) "First-mover advantage: a synthesis, conceptual framework, and research propositions," *Journal of Marketing*, 56, 33–52.

What are the options for later entrants?

by Venkatesh (Venky) Shankar and Lakshman Krishnamurthi

It is not easy for a company to decide whether to pioneer a market or to enter later. Both strategies have the potential to offer substantial benefits. Research shows that pioneers obtain better returns for advertising and promotion and can charge higher prices than later entrants. If consumer preferences are ambiguous in a new category, a pioneer can shape them to suit. In cases where uncertainty about the performance of a new product is high or switching costs are large, the pioneer is

To pioneer or to enter?		
Questions	**Answers**	**Decision**
What is the likely life of the product category?	Long	Enter later
	Short	Pioneer
What are the expected costs of limitation?	High	Pioneer
	Low	Enter later
What are my resources?	High	Enter later
	Low	Pioneer
What are the expected switching costs in this market?	High	Pioneer
	Low	Enter later
How important is brand equity in customer choice?	High	Pioneer
	Low	Enter later
What are the likely costs of market education?	High	Enter later
	Low	Pioneer

Table 1

also at an advantage. Later entrants, on the other hand, can free-ride on the pioneer's efforts to build a new category. They can also learn from the pioneer's mistakes and enjoy a greater response to perceived product quality. For those companies with innovative products, the benefits of later entry are even greater. They can grow faster than pioneers, making pioneers' marketing efforts less effective, and can enjoy higher repeat purchase rates.

How then should companies plan their entry strategies? When should they pioneer? When should they follow? The decision will depend on the answers to the questions in Table 1.

To pioneer or enter later?

What is the likely life of the product category?
One benefit of pioneering is the potential for profits during the monopoly period. The shorter the life of the category, the longer is the monopoly period relative to it. In product categories with a short life cycle, it pays to be the first mover. Certain software products fall under this classification. Year 2000 software, for example, has a very short business horizon.

What are the expected costs of imitation?
In many product categories, the cost of imitation may be quite low compared to the pioneer's cost of development. For example, a study of chemical, drugs, electronics and machinery industries shows that, on average, imitation costs are only 65 per cent of the pioneer's development costs. If this is likely to be the case, it may be better to enter later than to pioneer. In some cases, however, pioneers may gain valuable patents that substantially increase the cost of imitation. For example, Polaroid benefited from large margins on its pioneering instant cameras thanks to its long-running patent.

What are my resources?
A company with large resources need not be a first mover. It may be a better idea to let some other company undertake the risk of pioneering a new market. By waiting

and entering later, it can cash in on the pioneer's effort and muscle the pioneer out.

Corporate history contains many examples of large companies pushing aside small pioneers. Minnetonka produced the first dispenser soap in the US market but was ousted by Procter & Gamble's Ivory brand. Microsoft is another company that has succeeded in many markets by entering later with greater resources.

What are the expected switching costs in this market?

In some markets, it is highly expensive for customers to switch from one brand to another. A pioneer can lock customers in before later entrants. This creates an uphill task for later entrants, which are often reduced to competing only for new customers to the market. This is particularly true in many industrial and business-to-business markets.

How important is brand equity in customer choice?

Brand equity can be critical in some markets but is far less important in others. Consider the Personal Digital Assistant (PDA) market. Palm Pilot, built by US Robotics (now 3Com), was a late entrant, following products such as Apple's Newton and Motorola's Envoy. Both Apple and Motorola are better known and have greater brand equity. However, these earlier entrants lacked high-quality handwriting-recognition software, which is critical for the functioning of a PDA. Palm Pilot was the first to use this software and improved on other features as well. By producing a better product, it overcame the brand equity handicap. The other brands subsequently tried to match Palm Pilot on quality but many customers still preferred Palm Pilot.

Brand equity matched with reasonable product quality does favor pioneers. Hewlett-Packard pioneered laser printing in the desktop market. The power of the HP name along with high product quality has made the HP Laserjet the technical and psychological standard in the market.

What are the likely costs of market education?

If it costs a lot to educate customers in a new market, the chances are that later entrants will free-ride on the pioneer. Hence later entry may be preferable. The Cat scanner market is a good example. EMI went to a lot of trouble to teach medical institutions about the usefulness of the Cat scanner that it pioneered in 1972. To encourage trials, it agreed to service newly purchased Cat scanners at no extra cost for a year so that customers could learn more about them.

General Electric entered the market in 1976. It did not have to sell the idea of Cat scanners. It simply had to persuade customers that its model was better than EMI's, which is just what it did. GE's task was made easier by the fact that it already supplied traditional X-ray equipment and thus had access to the market. It also helped that GE's third-generation scanner succeeded whereas EMI's failed. EMI had a solid 50 per cent market share at the time of GE's entry. In 1978, however, GE surpassed EMI to become the market leader.

The answers to these questions may not always point in the same direction. Companies will have to weigh them carefully. Successful companies will be those that are able to think clearly about all these issues before making a final decision.

Late entrant strategy

For many companies, pioneering is not an option. In many markets, some company always beats others to the market to become the pioneer. So what can later

Drivers of later entrant strategy

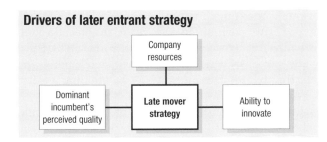

Figure 1

entrants do to compete with the pioneer or, more generally, the dominant incumbent?

A later entrant's strategy will depend upon the answers to three questions (*see* Figure 1):

- How substantial are my resources?
- How able am I to come up with an innovative product?
- What is the perceived quality of the dominant incumbent's product?

A company's resources are typically reflected by its financial position, capital, cash and other assets. Its ability to innovate depends on its research and development expertise. A dominant incumbent's perceived quality can be heavily influenced by its marketing efforts. Depending on the combination of these factors, a late entrant has eight strategic options (*see* Table 2). An innovative, well-resourced late entrant that faces a dominant brand with low perceived quality has the easiest challenge.

The best strategy is to come up with a product that is innovative compared to the

Later entrant strategies for competing with dominant incumbents				
Dominant incumbent's perceived product quality	**Resources**			
	Low Ability to innovate		High Ability to innovate	
	Low	**High**	**Low**	**High**
Low	**Be an early follower** (for example, Lycos web search engine)	**Innovate product** (for example, Ticketmaster computerized ticketing service)	**Outspend and/or undercut incumbents** (for example, Microsoft Office suite)	**Develop innovative products** (for example, Gillette razors)
High	**Be a niche marketer** (for example, Hon Industries office furniture)	**Differentiate your product** (for example, Amazon. Com bookshop)	**Be an early follower and outspend and/ or undercut incumbents** (for example, Microsoft, Excel spreadsheet, Microsoft, Internet Explorer)	**Develop innovative products and outspend and/or undercut incumbents** (for example, Zantac antiulcer drug)

Table 2

incumbents' offerings. A good example of a company that has adopted this strategy is Gillette, which has built a powerful position in the razor market through continuous innovation. This has enabled it to overtake the pioneer in the US, Star, and many others. Similarly, Boeing surpassed the UK's De Havilland Comet 1, the pioneer in commercial jet aircraft, through product innovation – by building a safer, larger, more powerful jet.

The role of innovation is particularly strong in evolving or so-called "high-technology" markets, such as the video cassette recorder market, in which the pioneer Ampex was overtaken by Matsushita. Another example is the microwave market, in which the pioneer Amana was eclipsed by Samsung. Innovation also plays a role in so called "low-technology" markets. In the US, Tide dominates the liquid laundry detergent market pioneered by Whisk, and Eveready is the leader in the flashlight battery market launched by Bright Star.

At the other end of the spectrum, the most daunting task falls to a late mover with scarce resources and little research and development expertise that faces a dominant incumbent with a high perceived quality. Such a late mover may have to settle for a lower market share but could remain very profitable – sometimes more profitable than the dominant player – by focusing on niches.

Hon Industries is a good example of a successful niche marketer in the office furniture market, which is dominated in the US by Steelcase. Although it is only the fourth largest office furniture manufacturer in the US, Hon is the leader in the $4bn "medium-priced" niche, where it has a share of over 20 per cent. Although Steelcase is three times larger than Hon, Hon generates about twice its rate of return. How did Hon achieve this position? It has developed an excellent reputation for offering good products at attractive price points and backs this with a broad product line in its market niche. Unlike Steelcase, it focuses on distribution through office products wholesalers. It can offer quick delivery from a nationwide network of 135 wholesalers.

Many later entrants are small companies with a limited ability to innovate but which face markets where the dominant brand's perceived quality is low. Their best strategy is to enter soon after the pioneer, when the market is in the growth stage. One such company is Lycos, which entered the market for web search engines after Yahoo!, the pioneer. Although the search offered by both these brands is rated as less powerful than that offered by Altavista (for example), today Lycos enjoys a market share that is close to Yahoo!'s.

Some later entrants may have the ability to produce a superior product but lack resources. If they face a dominant incumbent with a low perceived product quality, their best strategy is to innovate. An example is computerized ticketing services, which were pioneered by Ticketron, a subsidiary of Control Data. Ticketmaster, a start-up company, competed by making innovations around the basic product: it helped customers promote shows, carried out demand analysis for them and offered superior customer service. Ticketmaster also stressed continuous product improvements. It kept improving its ticketing software by increasing the speed of processing and adding features such as translations into other languages to serve foreign markets. With all these, it took only five years for Ticketmaster to dethrone Ticketron, a pioneer that had been a market leader for over ten years.

By understanding consumer preferences better than incumbents do, even a later entrant with limited resources can identify a superior but overlooked product position and differentiate itself. Consider the bookselling sector. In 1995

Amazon.com was a start-up company with few resources. It succeeded by differentiating its product (selection of books) from the highly rated US incumbent, Barnes & Noble. It accomplished this by offering its products on the internet, allowing customers to browse its selection electronically and customizing book suggestions for individual customers. Today, with a market capitalization of over $31bn, it is one of the biggest start-up success stories of recent years.

When a later entrant has plenty of resources but little capacity for innovation, it should try to beat the incumbent at its own game by out-advertising or out-distributing it.

When the dominant brand's perceived quality is low, the later mover simply has to outspend or undercut it; but when its perceived quality is high, the later mover should enter as soon as possible. Microsoft has successfully pursued this strategy. In the market for software suites, it has eclipsed Corel Suite, which is widely seen as of lower quality, by out-advertising and out-distributing it. In the market for spreadsheets, it has beaten Lotus 1-2-3, which is generally perceived as a high-quality incumbent, by entering early and outspending it. Interestingly, Lotus 1-2-3 is itself another example of a successful later entrant that surpassed the pioneer, Visicalc. Microsoft is pursuing a similar strategy in the web browser market. It is steadily gaining market share for its Internet Explorer at the expense of the market pioneer, Netscape.

While Microsoft has mainly outspent its rivals, Sunbeam is an example of a later entrant that overtook the dominant brand by undercutting its price. In the food processor market Cuisinart, the pioneer, is known for its high quality. Sunbeam capitalized on an increasingly price-sensitive market by offering a no-frills compact processor at a low price. In contrast, Cuisinart continued selling a high-end processor at a substantially higher price.

When a later entrant is resource-rich, is renowned for its technological expertise and faces an incumbent whose product is perceived to be of high quality, it should innovate and outspend or undercut the incumbent. Glaxo's Zantac in the anti-ulcer drug market is a classic example. The pioneer, SmithKline Beecham's Tagamet, was a highly rated product that took the market by storm. Glaxo followed with Zantac, which was effective in smaller dosages and had fewer side-effects. Further, Glaxo teamed up with Roche's sales force and outspent Tagamet in marketing. The result was that Zantac became not only the highest-selling anti-ulcer drug but also the best-selling prescription drug in the world by 1986.

Although pioneering advantage is real and seemingly insurmountable, all is not necessarily lost for later entrants. By adopting the right strategies, they may be able to turn the conventional wisdom of pioneering advantage on its head.

Summary

The strategic advantages and disadvantages of being a pioneer or a later market entrant were set out in the previous article. Here **Lakshman Krishnamurthi** and **Venkatesh Shankar** explain how companies can choose their optimum market entry strategy. The factors they need to consider include the likely life of the product category, the costs of imitating the pioneer, the resources available and the cost of educating consumers about the new product. Companies with high brand equity can certainly benefit from pioneering but the quality of their offering is decisive. For a late entrant, strategy for competing with a dominant incumbent should be determined by the size of the late entrant's resources, its research and development capacity and the perceived quality of the incumbent's product.

Suggested further reading

Shankar, V., Carpenter, G.S. and Krishnamurthi, L. (1998) "Late mover advantage: how innovative late entrants outsell pioneers," *Journal of Marketing Research*, 35, 54–70, February.

Shankar, V., Carpenter, G.S. and Krishnamurthi, L. (1998) "The advantages of entry in the growth stage of the product life cycle: an empirical analysis," *Journal of Marketing Research*.

How new technologies can take off fast

by Sabine Kuester, Elisa Montaguti and Thomas S. Robertson

Most senior executives understand the necessity for constant innovation. Companies that rely on their present portfolio of products or services risk being overtaken by new offerings from competitors. Yet most new products fail, or fail to produce acceptable profits, because market acceptance takes longer than anticipated. Sometimes new products merely open the door for competition that leapfrogs the innovator. Even though Xerox pioneered the huge market for plain-paper copiers, for a long time Japanese producers enjoyed the profits.

The problem of gaining acceptance for new products is particularly acute in high-technology markets that are characterized by high levels of product and market uncertainty. The question in such markets is whether the product can be brought to market at reasonable cost and whether anyone will want to buy it.

Hand-held computers, network computers, video conferencing, smart cards and digital cameras are all technologically feasible and standard configurations are emerging as competitors modify their forms and functions. Yet there is a great deal of market uncertainty surrounding such technologies compared with fast-moving consumer goods. For example, Larry Ellison of Oracle sees the "network computer" as a stripped-down computer appliance that can access intelligence on the internet and on intranets. His competitors, however, have quite different conceptions. More importantly, it is not evident how quickly the technology will be accepted by customers, whatever the product form.

Much has been written about the need for companies to hasten the process by which new products are developed and brought to market. Indeed, examples of shortened technology development cycles are abundant. IBM, for example, has cut the development time for PCs from 48 to 14 months and General Electric has cut that for jet engines from 84 to 48 months.

In this article we pick up where that concern leaves off: how can new market entrants as well as incumbents speed market acceptance after a new-technology product is developed? We focus on consumer technology markets, although the underlying processes we discuss are relevant to business-to-business technology products as well.

Generally, emerging technology markets are characterized by complex products, large numbers of entrepreneurial competitors, a confused customer base and rapid technological change. Clearly the marketing of emerging technologies is by no means an easy matter. Marketing managers need to design marketing programs that will make their products attractive to consumers – and that will do so quickly. This involves some difficult decisions. For example:

- Which customer segments should be targeted first, in order to gain quick sales and establish a base of innovators who may be the opinion leaders for later customers?
- How can we ensure that our product crosses the chasm between innovating technophiles and more mainstream customers who wait for a new-technology product to show its merit?
- How can we move customers away from products and technologies that serve them now? For example, it took longer than expected for automated teller machine sales to take off because banks and customers were slow to relinquish face-to-face contact in bank branches. Similarly, sales of computers for home use have lagged behind projections; the result is a litter of failed manufacturers around the world and a glut of supply that promises only thin margins for most survivors.
- How can we secure a market position that will pre-empt later competitive offerings or discourage at least some potential competitors from entering our market?
- In the case of more discontinuous technology products – that is, those that represent a considerable break from existing products – how can we help customers understand their greater benefits?

What slows market penetration?

To achieve accelerated take-off, we need to understand why slow market penetration often occurs. Customers defer technology adoption or do not adopt at all in the following circumstances:

The product is of value only if other people also have it

This refers to situations where a product becomes valuable to a user only as other users adopt the same product or compatible ones. Examples include video systems, personal computers and many telecommunication services. Economists refer to this as "network externalities." In general, for products with high network externalities, it is difficult for marketers to achieve initial acceptance and take-off is slow.

The technology needs a common standard

Technology standards may be mandated by government or industry committees but a lot of standardization is left to the marketplace and is sponsored by dominant companies. Markets where a dominant standard fails to emerge are characterized by low penetration. When Matsushita's VHS format for video recorders (VCRs) gained industry acceptance as the dominant standard, driving Sony's Betamax format off the shelves, the market for VCRs took off. Today, the rapid worldwide growth of internet usage is due in no small measure to the fact that it is nonproprietary. Anyone with virtually any kind of computer or operating system can "surf."

The product's value depends on complementary products

A technology's usefulness to consumers may depend on its availability and fit with complementary technologies. For example, VCR sales only accelerated after movie

Different market entry scenarios

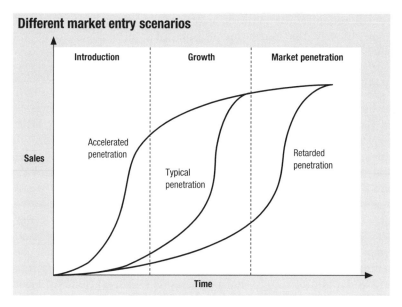

Figure 1

producers made titles available for rent on videotapes. In business-to-business markets, sales of some hardware products languish because not enough independent software vendors write applications.

The switching costs of the product are high

Especially in the technology domain, consumers incur costs in changing from one product to another. This includes purchase costs but greater costs may be incurred in learning new systems (as in software) or in having to modify homes or factories to install new equipment. For example, the main cost of a dishwasher for many people is the cost of reconstructing their kitchen. Switching costs were the initial problem with microwave ovens until they became small enough to fit on a worktop.

It is difficult for consumers to engage in product trial

The challenge for the marketing manager is to stimulate or encourage trial. Whereas in grocery products, trial opportunities are relatively easy to provide (through coupons, sampling and so on), in technology markets it is relatively difficult. However, in emerging technology markets companies have discovered the benefits of trial in triggering purchases. Some (for example, AOL and Compuserve) have mailed software "samples" to potential users to jump-start the market penetration process. On the assumption that profits can be realized later, when a technology secures an installed base, companies may even give away their products or bundle them "free" with other products. In the well-publicised case of Microsoft's internet browser, for example, bundling it with the company's Windows operating system jeopardizes sales of competing browsers, such as Netscape's Navigator.

Achieving rapid market acceptance

Generally, we observe different take-off patterns for new technologies. Figure 1 shows some possible market penetration scenarios. The least desirable scenario is retarded market penetration – this is every marketing manager's nightmare. The newer the idea or the more "discontinuous" the technology, the more likely such a scenario becomes. The slow take-off for fax machines is one such example (*see* Figure

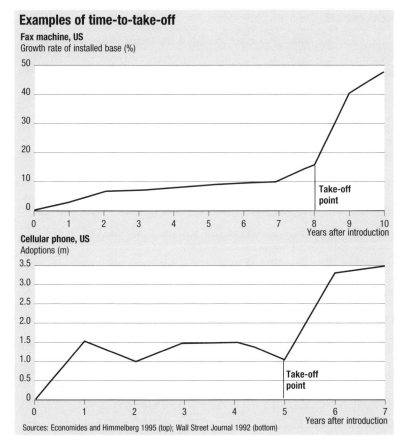

Examples of time-to-take-off

Fax machine, US
Growth rate of installed base (%)

Take-off
point

Years after introduction

Cellular phone, US
Adoptions (m)

Take-off
point

Years after introduction

Sources: Economides and Himmelberg 1995 (top); Wall Street Journal 1992 (bottom)

Figure 2

2). The network externalities issue was especially vexing here: people did not want to invest in a fax machine until they were sure that enough other people had one.

Slow take-off is seen in sales patterns for other technology products, such as high-definition television, VCRs and digital cameras. A recent analysis showed that the average time to take-off for consumer durable products was 18 years before the Second World War and six years afterwards. VCRs are an interesting example of slow take-off. The technology was developed by Ampex in the US in the late 1960s and initially called cartridge television. Yet it was the VHS format that eventually won the day and led to widespread household penetration, though not until the mid-1980s. Table 1 provides data on technology adoption for different products 15 years after their introduction; the penetration levels are not always impressive.

The marketing manager generally wants to accelerate take-off for a technology. The objectives underlying this may include:

- to capture demand before market windows close and competing technological solutions appear
- to pre-empt competitors and discourage market entry
- to leverage patents while they are still valid and competencies before they are imitated
- to recuperate investments on research and development and move rapidly down the cost curve.

How fast do technologies take off?		
	Year of introduction	Penetration level after 15 years (%)
Major appliances		
Clothes washer	1908	23
Refrigerator	1911	3
Freezer	1929	3
Room A/C	1932	1
Electric clothes dryer	1939	7
Microwave oven	1957	1
Housewares		
Vacuum cleaner	1908	33
Blender	1946	9
Electric tin-opener	1956	46
Electric knife	1963	42
Consumer electronics		
Radio	1920	72
Black and white TV	1939	63
Color TV	1954	38
Automated tellers (ATMs)	1970	60
Desktop videoconferencing	1981	10
Source: based on Bayus 1992		

Table 1

On the demand side, the customer's expectation of benefits from an emerging technology grows as more information becomes available and uncertainty is resolved. The company can perform strategic actions that will reduce the perceived risk of an emerging technology and reduce the hurdle of adoption for early users.

The following key strategies can accelerate take-off: aggressive market penetration, ensuring product compatibility, pre-announcement of new products, and marketing alliances.

Aggressive market penetration

These entail low pricing and high resource commitments to distribution, advertising, the sales force and promotional activities. The objective is to move quickly from initial sales to technophiles to broader mainstream markets. Such strategies are pursued in order to benefit quickly from cost reductions through experience-curve effects and economies of scale. They may also discourage other competitors from taking an equally strong stance towards the target market.

In the 1970s, as the concept of experience-curve effects was promulgated, penetration pricing became a key strategic issue, with notable successes (such as Texas Instruments in calculators) and failures (such as Texas Instruments in digital watches). In the 1980s penetration strategies were often attributed to Japanese companies, which tended to price aggressively to gain market share with the objective of long-run rather than short-run profits.

Over time, penetration strategy has come to be thought of in broader terms than pricing. Today it is usually coupled with big resource commitments to advertising, sales and distribution, as was seen in the launches of Sony's Playstation and Microsoft's Windows 95.

Examples of emerging consumer technologies

High-definition television (HDTV)
A television display system with resolution that is four times higher than conventional television, thus allowing clarity on a large screen.

Digital television
Digital transmission allows compression of multiple channels onto a frequency band, thus increasing programming choice.

Video on demand
A service delivering a specific movie (ordered by the customer) directly to the customer's television via an information network.

Smart cards
An extension of stored-value cards with magnetic stripes that are used mainly to add or subtract cash. Smart cards use an "electronic purse" with information stored on computer chips to facilitate transactions.

Desktop videoconferencing
Enables video-based interaction between users. Callers' and receivers' pictures are sent via small cameras and data and images can be shared – all on the computer screen.

Network computers
Inexpensive computers without high levels of built-in intelligence. Data are stored in and accessed from a network.

Digital cameras
Digitized images are captured and stored in memory chips and can be downloaded onto a computer.

Digital video discs (DVDs)
High-resolution replacements for analog VCR cassettes that offer superior sound and picture quality.

Product compatibility

Compatibility can be pursued by designing new products to be consistent with the installed base or by endorsing moves towards standardization. Strategic issues related to compatibility are especially important when network externalities characterize an industry. The main incentive for achieving compatibility is the opportunity to eliminate inter-technology competition and, consequently, the uncertainty over which technology will dominate. The pursuit of compatibility may also allow a company to charge higher prices. Consumers are willing to pay a premium for compatibility that allows them to access a larger network or to assemble a system that is closer to their ideal configuration. One of the reasons for the slow sales of digital video discs (DVDs) may be the fact that issues of standards and compatibility are not yet resolved.

Pre-announcement of new products

In much the same way as car manufacturers stimulate interest when they announce a new model before it is actually in the showrooms, technology marketers can gain attention and prepare consumers for new products. If consumers have an inkling that a new-technology product might be useful for them, they may delay current purchases and wait for the new product. "Leapfrogging" may occur, whereby consumers decide not to buy an existing technology in favor of the pre-announced next generation. The net result is that the manufacturer may enjoy quicker and easier initial sales. New product pre-announcements are a common occurrence in the software industry, although not all of them make it off the drawing board (hence the term "vaporware").

Marketing alliances

Perhaps more than in other industries, launching a new technology product requires a range of assets and competencies that rarely exist or can be developed rapidly within a single company. The challenge for technology marketers is to acquire such competencies fast. A practicable option is to form an alliance with rival companies (horizontal alliance) or with companies that have adjacent positions in the value chain (vertical alliance).

Alliances are co-operative agreements among companies to achieve a common goal by pooling specialized resources. An example from the medical technology industry was the agreement between Ohmeda and Hewlett-Packard to create and distribute the Component Anaesthesia System, which ran from 1994 until last April. Another is the co-marketing of the cholesterol-lowering drug Lipitor by Warner-Lambert and Pfizer.

The potential advantages of alliances are:

- faster and broader access to markets – through its alliance with Pfizer, Warner Lambert has rapidly penetrated the market with Lipitor
- access to marketing expertise – biotechnology companies, for example, have borrowed marketing skills when forming alliances with pharmaceutical companies
- shared risk of market participation – Smith & Nephew, for example, has formed an alliance with Advanced Tissue Science to develop and commercialize orthopaedic implants
- increased marketing scale effect – for example, Gateway 2000 recently formed a co-marketing agreement with Corporate Software & Technology, whereby each will cross-sell the other's product
- crystallization of market power, by locking customers in to a technological specification shared by alliance partners – this is ultimately how Matsushita won the VHS battle – by licences and alliances to lock in a product standard.

New entrants and incumbents

The strategic options for marketing a new technology depend on whether a company is a new entrant or an established competitor in that area of technology. Many market incumbents are slow to change and many successful rivals are new entrants but there is no conclusive evidence as to which is most likely to succeed.

A critical asset controlled by incumbent companies in high-tech industries is their installed base. By leveraging this, an incumbent could be more effective than a new entrant in achieving fast penetration for new products. However, empirical evidence indicates that incumbents tend to be too committed to their existing products and hence reluctant to market aggressively innovations that could cannibalize them. Many companies fall by the wayside as technology changes. Incumbents, therefore, should not delay the introduction of a new technology, even at the risk of cannibalization. IBM's tendency to sit on technologies such as the reduced instruction set chip was one reason for its upheaval in the mid-1990s.

New entrants face the challenge of creating a customer base while risking an incumbent's reaction. One option for a firm new to a technology category is to pre-announce the launch of its new product. This will reduce customers' switching and learning costs. The attendant risk of cannibalization is smaller for new entrants than incumbents. A new entrant could also ensure that its product is compatible with products already on the market, again reducing switching costs. Finally, a new entrant should consider an alliance with a company already identified with the technology category. The possible benefits are greater market reputation and access to complementary marketing assets.

Summary

Companies are constantly challenged to reduce both product development cycle times and market penetration cycle times. Here **Sabine Kuester**, **Elisa Montaguti** and **Thomas Robertson** explain how marketers can achieve rapid sales take-off for new technologies. This enables companies to pre-empt competitors and achieve a quicker return on investment. Possible strategies include aggressive pricing and promotion, ensuring compatibility with the existing product base, pre-launch announcements, and marketing alliances. However, it is important to recognize that market incumbents have different strategic options from new entrants.

Suggested further reading

Bayus, B.L. (1992) "Have diffusion rates been accelerating over time?" *Marketing Letters*, 3, 215–26, July.

Economides, N. and Himmelberg, C.P. (1995) "Critical mass and network size with application to the US fax market," Discussion Paper EC-95-11, Stern School of Business, New York University.

Golder, P.N. and Tellis, G.J. (1997) "Will it ever fly? Modeling the takeoff of really new consumer durables," *Marketing Science*, 16 (3), 256–70.

Hamel, G. and Prahalad, C.K. (1994) *Competing for the Future*, Harvard Business School Press, Boston, MA.

Moore, G.A. (1991) *Crossing the Chasm*, Harper Business, New York. (The "chasm" of the title lies between innovating technophiles and mainstream consumers.)

Von Braun, C.-F. (1997) *The Innovation War*, Prentice Hall, Englewood Cliffs, NJ.

Zangwill, W.I. (1993) *Lightning Strategies for Innovation*, Lexington Books, Lexington, MA.

Evaluating demand for innovative products

by Paul E. Green and Abba M. Krieger

All retailers face the difficult task of creating an attractive mix of products and services that will provide customers with the best choice of both brands and price points. Retailers must try to determine what combination of price and features customers are seeking and how best to package them. Indeed, product assortment and price are the two areas customers consider most important when shopping.

Determining the optimal product mix is a constant challenge. If the retailer carries too narrow a range of products, shoppers are likely to go elsewhere. If the retailer carries too many products, the store will end up carrying unsold inventory. This article is intended to help retailers find the best mix.

There are, of course, other issues. Retailers must also price their products competitively and provide a suitable range of prices for their customer base. When we examine the first of these tasks alone, we can see how complicated things can become.

If a competitor raises or cuts the price of a product by 5 per cent, do we match the move? Do we match it exactly or in part? When we offer a new product with additional features, how do we determine what the new features are worth when compared to the older product? And when we have an assortment of competing products, how should we set prices among the various goods? If we change the price of a specific product, how can we predict how that will affect our market share? And, of course, how can we predict how our competitors might react?

When a company markets many products that compete with one another, as well as with other products in the marketplace, this complicates matters further. As an example, assume that a store manager carries, among other goods, seven different brands or models of electric mixers. The manager wants to determine what the ideal mix of brand and price should be for the store. Display and selling space in any store is always limited, so the manager wants to determine whether profits can be enhanced by reducing the number of mixers. Among the questions the manager must address are:

- if a specific mixer were to be removed from the store's offerings, which of the other models would be likely to gain the most share?
- would that increase or reduce profits?
- for each mixer option, what is its associated price elasticity?
- how much flexibility does the manager have in adjusting prices to enhance the line's overall profitability?
- are there brands currently not carried that the manager might want to add to the line?
- if all seven models are to be kept, how should the manager set prices to maximize the expected return?

How do returns differ by market segment?

In research we carried out for such a retailer we went through the entire line of mixers, deleting each in turn, determining the impact and then restoring each to the line. In this way we were able to show the best combination of pruning and price optimization. Often a drop in market share caused by eliminating certain products can be more than offset by an increase in margins.

Moreover, if the Brand A mixer has, say, a 10.6 per cent market share and we eliminate it from the line, what happens to its market share? Do customers simply buy the competing product closest in price? Do they stay with the brand but move to the next product up or down the line? Or do they go elsewhere to find the product?

Finding answers to these questions provides invaluable information about the value of the brand, the competitiveness of a particular product and one's pricing strategy. We found, for example, that when we eliminated the Brand A mixer, 4.2 per cent went to one model from Brand B, but the remaining 6.4 per cent were split among three different models from Brand C. Clearly Brand A was most competitive with Brand C.

Price elasticity is another variable that retailers need to understand. What would happen to the market share of the Brand A mixer if we moved its price from a low of \$17.97 to a high of \$21.97? What is the optimal price? Our research demonstrated highly varied elasticities across brands. We found that the store manager could maximize the expected return on Brand A by cutting its price (\$19.97) by approximately one dollar. Conversely, we found that with another product, Brand D, the manager had set the price too low and could maximize the store's return by increasing the price from \$21.92 to \$24.11. The important fact to keep in mind is that the optimal price can change in response to whether the product is carried separately or in combination. In other words, the optimal price for the Brand D mixer is \$24.11 by itself but when the store also carries Brand A, the optimal price is actually somewhat higher.

The final question we addressed for the retailer was that of pruning the line. Dropping a product is not simply a question of determining which item is the lowest and slowest seller. We found that the retailer could actually benefit overall through higher margins by dropping a product that had a reasonable market share relative to the other products.

This approach to product assortment and pricing is based on conjoint analysis, a technique that goes well beyond traditional product concept testing and shows the product (or service) mix that maximizes sales or profits. Conjoint analysis focuses on the specifics of each product: price, brand equity, features, warranties, technical services and so on. Where conjoint analysis can be most effective is in the testing phase for new products. Here we define "new products" not merely as line or brand extensions but rather as highly innovative products, of a type that has not previously existed. Testing consumer acceptance is extremely difficult in this situation because there is rarely anything physical that people can examine, nor are there comparable products in the marketplace against which they can judge the new product.

EZPass: a conjoint analysis case study

Our work with seven regional transportation agencies in the New York/New Jersey metropolitan area provides a good example of conjoint analysis in practice. Our brief was to investigate the potential for adopting an electronic toll collection device – to be called EZPass – for the major highways and bridges in a densely populated, heavily traveled area.

At the time of our study, such schemes were already in use in several parts of the US. Electronic toll collection eliminates the need for drivers to wait in line to go through a manual toll collection booth. A driver's vehicle has an electronic transceiver that emits a tuned radio signal. Receivers in specially designated toll booths read each driver's unique signal and debit an account set up for the purpose by the driver.

The seven agencies that we worked with realized that they would need to co-operate to make the idea successful since the regional highway system was highly integrated. Accordingly they created a task force that was charged with identifying the best configuration of service attributes for each participating agency's commuters. It then had to compare the configurations among agencies and determine what product and service attributes would provide the best mix for a widely divergent population.

The task force developed a long list of attributes which was ultimately refined to seven issues that concerned commuters:

- How many accounts are necessary/how will statements be received?
- How does one pay for an EZPass account and where?
- How many lanes will be available for EZPass users and how are they controlled?
- Can the tag be transferred to another vehicle?
- Is there a separate charge for the tag/are there other service charges?
- What is the cost per use of EZPass/are there any savings for using it?
- What other possible uses for EZPass might there be (for example, parking, fuel purchases and so on)?

The participating agencies were committed to implementing the EZPass system, so the task force was not asked to address the issue of demand for the system. Indeed, the essence of the problem was not all that different from that faced by the retail store manager trying to determine the optimal configuration of electric mixers.

The agencies realized that setting priorities for service attributes and investigating level-preferences within attributes through the use of conjoint analysis could provide them with the information they sought. It was particularly important to estimate the part-worths that commuters assigned to various attribute levels, where different levels would incur significantly different operating costs.

The task force had the same problem faced by a business or other organization that is trying to develop a new product or service: it wanted commuters to participate actively in the creation of the EZPass system. Yet since this was a new product with which commuters were completely unfamiliar, how could they understand it well enough to make useful decisions about the overall service? More simply, how was the task force to demonstrate a non-existent product to potential users?

Its solution was to produce an 11-minute "infomercial" that explained how EZPass could alleviate the worst traffic congestion problems that commuters faced each day. But then the task force faced the problem of how to reach an appropriate sample of commuters to view the video. It was not feasible to gather a group together in one setting or even in several settings. Each agency wanted representative samples from each of the geographic areas and constituencies that it served. Once the task force had selected its sample, it prepared survey kits which were then mailed to each respondent. Each kit contained the video, along with the survey form and instructions.

Among the most complicated tasks was how to define combinations of attributes and attribute levels. Each participating agency had its own perspective on how to set attribute levels. But survey results showed a consistent and common thread: respondents were far more concerned with the number of lanes that would be available to EZPass users and how those lanes would be controlled than they were with the cost of the service. The message to the task force was clear: focus on the primary benefit of the system – reduction of traffic congestion – and don't be concerned with aspects that most users regard as less important.

Only after conducting this initial research did the participating agencies realize that it was important to determine demand. Setting up EZPass lanes, ordering large quantities of transmitters for users and installing the computer system would require a substantial investment. Hence the task force needed an accurate estimate of the overall demand for the system. Subsequent experience has provided ample evidence for an accurate estimate of demand: the rate of use has been running at over 40 per cent of regular commuters and full implementation is expected in two years.

Conclusion

Decisions about pricing and attribute designs are critical for both products and services. Conjoint analysis is increasingly used to help in making these decisions.

In the high-technology field, IBM used conjoint analysis to help design its Risc 6000 computer workstation. AT&T used it in designing and pricing the first mobile telephone system to use the new "honeycomb" transmission system. It has also been applied to the design and pricing of – among other products – photocopiers, computer printers, electronic games, cars and cameras.

Conjoint analysis is also used to design basic consumer goods such as foods, beverages and toiletries. Products' physical and chemical characteristics are varied to determine the influence of taste, smell, appearance and convenience of use on consumers' preferences.

In the service sector, conjoint analysis has been applied to airline services, credit cards, banking, insurance, telecommunications, advertising copy and municipal services. In the tourism industry, it has been used to design everything from complete hotel facilities, to holiday packages, time-share units and theme-park amenities. It has even been applied to state lottery games.

In sum, since its first commercial applications in the late 1960s, conjoint analysis has become an established set of techniques for measuring the trade-offs that people make when selecting everything from toothpaste to political representatives. Along with such allied techniques as multidimensional scaling of buyer perceptions and cluster analysis for market segmentation, it is an essential part of the marketer's toolkit.

Summary

Successful retailers need to find the best mix of products and the most appropriate range of prices to attract and satisfy their customers. The challenge becomes even more complicated when several competing products are displayed on the same shelf. In this article, **Paul Green** and **Abba Krieger** describe how conjoint analysis can be used to solve problems of this type. Researchers using this technique systematically adjust the product mix and prices until they arrive at an optimum line. Surprisingly, the best strategy may sometimes be to drop products that have a reasonable market share. But conjoint analysis need not be confined to consumer goods; the authors provide a case study to demonstrate how it can usefully be applied to innovative services.

Managing learning to lock in consumers

by Vikas Mittal and Mohanbir Sawhney

As internet usage explodes, we are witnessing the biggest land grab since the settling of the Wild West. This time the settlers are marketers and the real estate is in the minds of consumers. According to John Perry Barlow, co-founder of the Electronic Frontier Foundation, "in the information economy, attention is the monetary unit." Marketers of information products are realizing that the battle for eyeballs is fought and won before the battle for profits even begins.

Information economy companies such as America Online, Amazon.com, E*Trade and Yahoo! have astronomical stock market valuations, largely based on the customer relationships they control. America Online is valued at over $21bn and Yahoo!, whose 1997 revenues were a mere $67m, boasts a market capitalization of $12bn.

Consumer attention is valuable because time is a finite resource. While the array of information product offerings on the internet is growing exponentially, the time that consumers have to spend on them is limited. Despite the intense competition for their attention, consumers are willing to invest very little time to learn about new offerings. As the cost and difficulty of attracting consumer attention escalates, marketers of information products need to think strategically about how they manage it, especially in the early stages of customer relationships.

From attention to retention

Most consumers will try a new information product once but very few products they try become part of their daily lives. The proliferation of offerings on the World Wide Web has only aggravated the situation. Consumers can surf and bookmark hundreds of websites to which they never return. Marketers of information products are finding that the real battle is not for consumer attention – which is hard enough to attract – but for consumer retention. How can they win this battle?

When consumers are exposed to a new information product – an online bookstore, say – they need to learn about how to use it as well as about the content that it offers. If the learning experience is not carefully designed, consumers will tend to experiment haphazardly and learn little about how the product works or what they can get out of it. Oblivious of this problem, many information product marketers gleefully count the footprints of wandering passers-by as their "customers." But how many of these customers have developed loyalty because of what they have learned?

To understand consumer learning, it is useful to consider a financial analogy. The time that consumers possess to learn about new information products is analogous to financial capital. We define this as "learning capital." Just as consumers can invest their financial capital in a portfolio of financial assets, so they can invest their learning capital to learn about new products. The "return" that consumers get from their investment is the satisfaction that they derive from using the product. The "risk" that they incur is the likelihood that the new product turns out to be inferior to alternatives and thus a waste of time.

The rationale for this analogy comes from two assumptions. First, the amount of time consumers can allocate to learning is limited. Second, consumers are willing to learn about new products and services to improve their return on time invested. Learning is like buying an option to use a product. The value of learning is then the option value of using the product. If consumers decide to use the product that they have invested in learning about, they are effectively exercising the learning option. Conversely, if they abandon the product, they are effectively letting the option expire.

Although time is a useful metric for consumer learning capital, the amount that consumers bring to a learning situation may differ, as may its cost. Extending the financial analogy, if learning capital is a bank account, the cost of learning capital is the interest earned on the deposit. Marketers must understand why consumers' "learning accounts" vary in order to segment their customer base.

Factors that determine the amount of learning capital that consumers have include:

Perceived risk and return

Different product categories have different levels of perceived economic, psychological or social risk and return. Consider a website for buying cars and a website for renting movie videos. Consumers will generally allocate more time to learn about the car site because the financial stakes are higher. The greater the possible benefits of using a product, the more learning capital consumers will invest.

Consumer involvement

Consumers' involvement with a category is strongly correlated with the time they allocate to learning about it. The return on time invested in a category is higher when the consumer's involvement is high (if it is important for their hobby, say).

Consumer knowledge

Experts or novices in a category are likely to invest less learning capital than consumers with moderate knowledge. People with little or no knowledge are likely to be easily discouraged and give up, whereas experts are likely to expend little learning capital because of the diminishing returns to incremental learning. Consumers with an intermediate level of knowledge are likely to spend most time learning to leverage their existing knowledge base.

Another set of factors determines the cost of drawing upon learning capital:

Competing demands on time

Consumers differ in the demands that are placed on their time. For example, busy executives have little time to research new information. The same is true of working parents, who have to juggle work and family. However, while there is a correlation between financial opportunity cost and learning capital cost, there are important exceptions. For example, the financial opportunity cost of homemakers' time may be relatively low but their learning capital may still be expensive because of competing demands from children and housework.

Quality of available alternatives

The return that investors expect from a new investment depends on the return from competing assets. The quality and quantity of available alternatives determines the "status quo" return that consumers get from their time. As the quality of information products increases, consumers are more satisfied with their alternatives and less willing to experiment to improve upon the status quo.

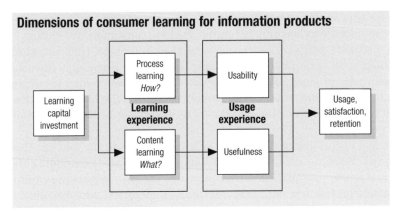

Dimensions of consumer learning for information products

Figure 1

Two types of learning

Consumer learning can be thought of along two dimensions – process-orientated learning and content-orientated learning. The quality of the consumer learning experience is determined by the quality of both dimensions (*see* Figure 1). **Process-orientated learning** involves learning about the features of a product and how to use it. For example, when learning about a Yellow Pages website, you may want to know how to search the address database, how to define search parameters and the scope of the search, how to use keywords and so on. Process-orientated learning determines consumers' ability to use a product effectively and hence their opinion of how usable it is.

Content-orientated learning, on the other hand, refers to learning about the information residing in a product. Whereas process-orientated learning focuses on the journey, content-orientated learning focuses on the destination. In the Yellow Pages example, content-orientated learning may include finding out about the comprehensiveness of the listings, the depth and breadth of information about each business, and its accuracy. Content-orientated learning determines consumers' evaluation of how useful a product is.

In designing high-quality learning experiences, marketers are faced with a difficult trade-off between emphasizing process or content. Clearly, the relative importance of the two will depend on the learning context (*see* Figure 2).

On the process dimension, information products can be either "complex" or "simple." For example, using personal finance software such as Quicken or a Yellow Pages website such as Bigbook.com is a relatively complex process, whereas using e-mail or a web browser is relatively simple. Learning experiences for products with complex processes should emphasize search, navigation and usability. Similarly, on the content dimension, products can be "content-rich" or "content-poor." An online bookstore such as Amazon.com or a financial information product such as Microsoft Investor are content-rich, whereas word processing software or e-mail software are relatively content-poor. By understanding where their products fit into this scheme, marketers can design learning experiences to match the learning context, thus enabling consumers to maximize their return on learning.

Learning and loyalty

Having expended learning capital on a new information product, consumers move from the learning phase to the usage phase. Generally, their willingness to learn

Understanding differences in consumer learning contexts

	Content-poor application	Content-rich application
Complex process	Word processing Tax software E-Yellow Pages	Yahoo.com Amazon.com Microsoft Investor
Simple process	E-mail Web browsing Paper Yellow Pages	Online magazines Video games Physical bookstore

Figure 2

The consequences of learning

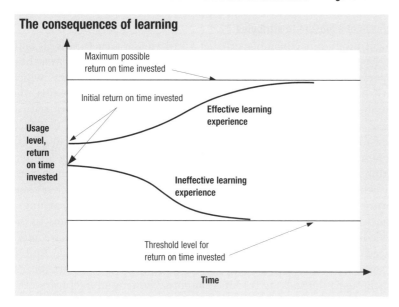

Figure 3

and experiment diminishes dramatically after the learning phase. Continuing the financial analogy, we propose that consumers evaluate the quality of usage in terms of "return on time invested" ("Roti"). The better their learning, the higher is their initial Roti (*see* Figure 3).

The initial Roti is critical. If it is satisfactory, consumers will use the product more and more regularly and derive even more satisfaction as their expertise increases. This initiates a virtuous circle, eventually resulting in customer retention. On the other hand, if the initial Roti is low, the level of usage and satisfaction declines. This sets off a vicious circle, until the Roti declines so far that consumers cease using the product.

Both content- and process-orientated learning contribute to consumer lock-in by creating sunk costs. For example, someone who reads a Sherlock Holmes story invests at least a little time in its content. If the reader goes on to read more stories, he or she becomes increasingly locked in to the world of Holmes through content-orientated learning. Similarly, someone who takes the time to learn how to use America Online (AOL) to chat with friends and do other activities on the internet, has invested time in process-orientated learning. The resulting knowledge locks the consumer in to AOL, whether or not AOL provides the best offering.

Switching from the status quo information product, about which these consumers have developed elaborate knowledge structures, entails a substantial effort. Knowledge structures are remarkably stable and change-resistant, even when change offers potential benefits. Learning-based lock-in can be a source of sustainable competitive advantage for information product marketers. As their knowledge structure becomes richer, customers see more and more interrelationships among product features and become more likely to continue using the product.

The learning experience

Marketers can design effective learning experiences by managing the order in which consumers sample features, the set of features they sample and the product vocabulary they need.

Managing the sequence of exposure to attributes

In learning about a product, a consumer creates a knowledge structure with both content and process elements. The attributes that comprise this mental representation vary in importance. Consider 3Com's Palm Pilot personal organizer, which uses the "Graffiti" alphabet for handwriting recognition. In learning Graffiti, the alphabet, the numbers from zero to nine and basic punctuation are more critical than mathematical symbols and sophisticated punctuation. Recognizing this fact, Palm Pilot has two templates for learning Graffiti – the basic and the advanced. The manual recommends that people use the basic template until they are familiar with the basic alphabet. By managing the exposure sequence so that consumers first learn about central, basic attributes, Palm Pilot allows them to anchor their knowledge structure and build upon it, thereby leading to more effective learning.

It is also important to match the difficulty of the initial set of attributes to the consumer's knowledge. A mismatch can seriously hinder learning. If newcomers are first presented with difficult attributes, they may be discouraged. And if consumers with some knowledge are presented with a sequence of basic attributes, they may regard the learning task as trivial. Computer game manufacturers take this into account by allowing users to select for themselves their skill level.

Managing the attribute set for context relevance

A complex word processing package or a complex website may have hundreds of features. But not all of them are equally relevant to a given consumer's usage context. The greater the context relevance of an attribute, the greater should be the level of exposure to it during the learning process. For example, a consumer who is going to use a word processing package only for writing letters need not learn about clip art or drawing functions. But someone who plans to use the package for desktop publishing may need a high level of familiarity with these features. Marketers can use consumer research to measure an attribute's relevance for specific segments and design learning experiences accordingly.

Managing the consumption vocabulary

Every new information product requires consumers to learn a new set of concepts, terms and metaphors. For example, to use Microsoft's Windows operating system, consumers need to learn the meaning of "icon," "desktop," "folder," "file," "format," and so on. Once they have acquired such a vocabulary, consumers are better able to anticipate and articulate their consumption experiences. Marketers can enhance the quality of learning by ensuring that consumers learn the vocabulary they need to get the most out of the product. Further, marketers should strive to make new vocabulary consistent with consumers' existing vocabularies so that the learning needs are reduced. Clashing metaphors may hinder learning.

Implications for marketers

Encourage learning capital investments
To promote learning-based lock-in, marketers should offer incentives for consumers to invest learning capital in their products. Such incentives might include limited-period trials of full-featured products or unlimited trials of limited-functionality products. Once learning-based inertia has been created and switching barriers are in place, marketers can start charging a premium. This strategy has been followed effectively by online editions of *The Economist* and the *Wall Street Journal*.

Create specialized learning capital
To create sustainable advantage, marketers should create learning capital that cannot be leveraged outside their offerings. For example, in learning Palm Pilot's proprietary Graffiti alphabet, consumers make an investment that cannot be leveraged if they switch to another personal organizer.

Leverage learning capital for cross-selling
Marketers seeking to expand a market via cross-selling should leverage the costs that consumers have already sunk into learning about their existing products. For example, Microsoft has gained significant leverage from the learning investments that consumers have made in Word. Subsequent products – Powerpoint, Access, Excel, FrontPage and Internet Explorer – have had significant overlap in process-orientated learning.

Preserve learning capital investments
If a new entrant attempts to nab market share from an incumbent whose product consumers are very familiar with, a strategy of extreme differentiation may well backfire. Customers are unlikely to want to dismantle their existing knowledge structure. Assimilating oneself to rather than contrasting with the incumbent is likely to be a more successful strategy as it protects consumers' learning investments. The same logic applies to one's own products. Marketers who frequently change user interfaces should realize that they are destroying their customers' stock of learning capital.

Design targeted consumer learning experiences
Consumers differ in how and why they want to use a product, as well as in the knowledge that they bring to it. Marketers should therefore create learning experiences that are "context aware." Currently, most learning programs assume that "one size fits all."

Understand consumer learning through contextual inquiry
End-user research should inform the design of learning experiences. But marketers need to go beyond superficial market research techniques. They need to conduct extensive ethnographic research, which involves observing consumers in their everyday environments. Companies such as Intuit and Microsoft invest heavily in usability labs and "follow-me-home" programs that aim to discover the problems that consumers have with their products. These investments pay off handsomely in terms of improved usability and usefulness and, eventually, in terms of customer retention and loyalty.

Summary

As internet usage grows ever more rapidly, marketers know that they must compete fiercely for customer attention. But can they convert attention into retention? According to **Vikas Mittal** and **Mohanbir Sawhney**, the key is learning: marketers need to persuade customers to invest time in learning about their information products. Once customers have sunk their "learning capital" into a product they will be more reluctant to switch to competitors' offerings. They will also be more likely to see a satisfactory return on the time they have invested in the product when they start using it. Marketers of information products must therefore design effective learning experiences for consumers; this involves carefully managing the order in which people find out about product attributes, matching the learning experience to the user's requirements and ensuring that any new technical vocabulary meshes with existing knowledge.

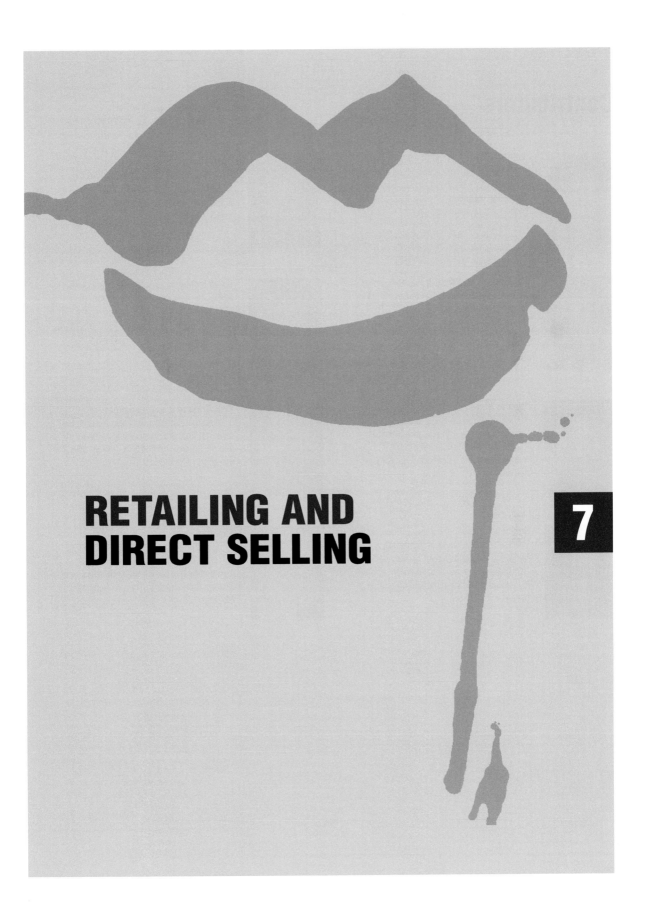

RETAILING AND
DIRECT SELLING

7

Contributors

Jagdish N. Sheth is the Charles H. Kellstadt Professor of Marketing at Goizueta Business School, Emory University. His areas of specialization include marketing theory and global competitive strategy.

Jagmohan S. Raju is associate professor of marketing at the Wharton School of the University of Pennsylvania. His research areas include pricing, retailing and corporate advertising.

Rajendra S. Sisodia is Trustee Professor of Marketing at Bentley College, Boston. His research focuses on the impact of information technology on marketing strategy.

Dawn Iacobucci is professor of marketing at the J.L. Kellogg Graduate School of Management, Northwestern University. Her research interests include service marketing and models for dyadic and network interactions.

Thomas W. Gruen is assistant professor of marketing at the Goizueta Business School, Emory University. His research interests include relationship marketing, the management and valuation of customers, and category management.

Kent Grayson is assistant professor of marketing at London Business School. His research focuses on issues of authenticity and deception in marketing, and on network marketing ("pyramid selling").

Stephen J. Hoch is the John J. Pomerantz Professor of Marketing at the Wharton School of the University of Pennsylvania. His research interests include retail strategy, decision support systems and consumer behavior.

Richard Berry is a former chief executive of a major UK direct selling business and is currently director of the Direct Selling Association. He is also the author of *Direct Selling: From Door-to-Door to Network Marketing* (Butterworth-Heinemann).

Contents

Introduction

Retail companies occupy the boundary between the manufacturer and the consumer, and are thus key players in the marketing process. An important theme of this module is the substantial changes that the retail sector has undergone in the 1980s and 1990s: these include closer relationships between retailers and suppliers (exemplified in "efficient consumer response" initiatives), the associated growth in "scientific retailing" through category management, and the advent of online shopping. Other issues considered are the increasing success of – and possible manufacturer responses to – retailers' "own label" brands, and the elements of superior customer service. The module concludes with a discussion of the traditional alternative to the retail channel, direct selling.

The changing face of retailing

By Jagdish N. Sheth and Rajendra S. Sisodia

The marketing function depends heavily on the presence of intermediaries between the producer and the consumer. These intermediaries provide convenient access to products for a wide range of customers. As well as serving as product conduits, intermediaries also serve as information conduits. Often, producers have little or no direct contact with end-user customers and must rely almost entirely on intermediaries for information about them. Likewise, intermediaries often carry information for end users from producers.

Retailers are perhaps the most important type of intermediary, situated at the point of direct contact with customers. The retailing function adds value in a number of ways, most of which are difficult for manufacturers to replace. These include: breaking bulk (breaking caseloads into smaller quantities); providing an assortment of products so that customers can go one-stop shopping; creating an inventory buffer between producers and consumers so that products are available when desired; and providing support services such as display, demonstration, credit, delivery, assembly, repair, and return and warranty services.

The retailing sector is huge, representing over $2,200bn a year in revenues in the US alone (approximately 30 per cent of gross domestic product) and employing about 25m people in that country. Worldwide, it is estimated that retailing accounts for about $7,000bn in annual revenues.

Over its long history, the retailing function has changed, often reacting to changes in consumption patterns (for example, the rise in the proportion of expenditure allocated to services), demographic shifts (for example, the migration from inner cities to suburbs) and technological forces (for example, the widespread use of credit cards). Today, it is going through another round of changes, the scale and scope of which are likely to exceed those that have come before.

Indications are that the retailing sector in most developed countries is overbuilt. In the US the square footage devoted to retailing rose by 216 per cent between 1966 and 1993 while sales (in real terms) rose by only 50 per cent. At the same time, the amount of time spent shopping has been declining. It has been estimated that the average amount of time spent by a typical American in a shopping mall has declined from seven hours a month to about two and a half hours over the past 15 years.

Time pressure, coupled with the general sameness of much retailing, has led to a change in people's perception of shopping: from something regarded as fun and entertaining to an activity that is now generally considered a tiresome burden to be dealt with as expeditiously as possible. As a result of these factors, the retailing sector is experiencing a shakeout. The number of bankruptcies has been rising, reaching approximately 13,000 a year in the US.

"New-style" retailers

A number of "new-style" retailers (such as Wal-Mart and Carrefour) have emerged in recent years. These account for much of the new wealth creation in the retailing sector, while conventional retailers have been responsible for huge declines in shareholder value.

The new retailers have adopted a business philosophy and operating style that includes the following elements:

High levels of investment in information technology (IT) and the establishment of close electronic links with upstream partners

Rather than monitor the inventory of each item themselves, the new retailers move much of the responsibility for ensuring product availability to suppliers. Suppliers accomplish this by monitoring sales at the point of sale on a real-time basis through computerized links. They then automatically replenish stock when inventory levels run low. Payments are made through automated bank-to-bank transfers to suppliers, eliminating a lot of paperwork.

A more rational approach to pricing and sales promotions, with an emphasis on "everyday fair pricing"

Instead of having large and predictable price variations, the new retailers attempt to provide a "fair" price all the time. The objective is to assure buyers that they need not wait for a sale to get a reasonable price on the products they want to buy.

A reduction in the number of suppliers

As this occurs, the share of business for each remaining supplier increases. Rather than rely on new suppliers to increase variety, retailers encourage existing suppliers to add variety and offer a fuller line of products. This enables them to leverage existing logistical systems more effectively.

Greater market power, arising from retail concentration and intense customer loyalty

Successful retailers have to be treated by manufacturers as customers rather than intermediaries; without their support, the manufacturer is effectively barred from a sizeable portion of the market. Wal-Mart, with over $120bn a year in annual sales, and Toys R Us, which controls over 25 per cent of toy sales in the US, are gatekeepers to large and loyal markets of consumers that rarely shop elsewhere.

Retailer–supplier partnering

Dramatic gains in distribution and marketing efficiency are realized when manufacturers and retailers work together. Partnering between these two groups is a major departure from their traditionally antagonistic relationship; it recognizes that both are part of a single process – which can be greatly streamlined and simplified – for distributing products to customers. These so-called "channel partnerships" have been adopted in such diverse categories as household goods, personal care products and home furnishings.

Inventory is pulled through the system rather than pushed down, allowing companies to provide greater product availability for customers with lower average levels of inventory. This is reflected in Black & Decker's distribution philosophy of "sell one, ship one, build one."

Partnering thus provides the advantages of vertical integration without the attendant drawbacks. It has its roots in the "quick response" movement in the clothing industry. In the grocery business, it is known as "efficient consumer response" (ECR). A report by Kurt Salmon Associates for the US Food Marketing Institute estimated that ECR had the potential to reduce inventory by 41 per cent and save $30bn a year in the US grocery industry.

Central to partnering arrangements are the enabling technologies of bar-coded product identification and electronic data interchange (EDI), along with the re-engineering of business processes both within and across companies in the value chain. These systems improve efficiency and customer service primarily by replacing physical assets with information. They reduce the retailer's inventory while providing a supply of merchandise that closely matches consumers' actual buying patterns. Resources that were formerly tied up in inventory can be directed elsewhere – to increased advertising, or the bottom line, for example.

The result is a win-win-win outcome. Consumers consistently find the merchandise they want (often at lower prices); suppliers increase sales, lower costs and cement ties with retailers; and retailers gain increased sales and inventory turns.

Electronic shopping

Beyond facilitating of channel partnerships, technology is affecting retailing through the substitution of electronic shopping for store-based retailing. For many time-pressured customers, shopping online or via a catalog for next-day delivery provides greater time value than a trip to the mall.

US consumers spend $3bn a year on items from TV shopping networks, $10bn a year shopping over the Internet and $60bn a year on purchases from mail-order companies such as L.L. Bean. While this still represents a very small portion of the retailing sector, recent growth trends indicate that electronic retailing is poised to enter the mainstream.

The World Wide Web, even in its current narrowband mode, shows the vast potential of technology. In 1997, $6bn worth of cars were sold over the internet in the US, while Dell Computer alone was selling its products at a pace of $6m a day towards the end of the year. America Online reported sales of $150m in December 1997 alone, much of that in categories such as clothing that have thus far seen little internet shopping activity. While electronic grocery shopping remains tiny, Anderson Consulting projects an astounding $85bn a year by 2007.

It is a well-established dictum of retailing that the "total shopping experience" must be considered in order to assess the strengths of different retail formats. Electronic shopping is typically more cost-effective than store-based retailing (according to researchers, it can lower costs by around 25 per cent). However, other factors must also be evaluated; these include the number of alternatives that can be made available, the social and recreational dimensions of shopping, the amount of information that customers need and the amount that can be readily provided, and the type of product.

In an award-winning recent paper in the *Journal of Marketing*, Joseph Alba and his co-authors (see Suggested Further Reading) suggest that successful electronic retailers will seek competitive advantage in one or more of the following areas:

- distribution efficiency
- assortments of complementary merchandise
- collection and use of customer information
- presentation of information through electronic formats
- unique merchandise.

Alba and his colleagues suggest that catalog retailers are the most vulnerable to electronic shopping. While it has some of the same limitations as catalog retailing, such as delivery times, electronic shopping can provide customers with much more information than catalogs.

The authors also suggest that electronic shopping is ideal for retailers with strong reputations for high-quality, unique merchandise but incomplete market coverage (for example, Nieman-Marcus, Harrods, Gump's and Saks). Chains such as Sears, which already have extensive market coverage, have less to gain from electronic retailing.

To prevail, store-based retailers will have to emphasize merchandise that has predominantly experiential attributes (that is, it must be seen directly, touched and so on), promote the non-informational benefits of shopping (such as entertainment and socializing), and treat electronic shopping as a complement to their in-store business.

The Alba paper also outlines the conditions under which manufacturers would have an incentive to disintermediate – that is, to bypass retailers and deal directly with customers. Manufacturers with strong brand names and the ability to produce complementary merchandise – such as Levi Strauss – are most likely to consider this. However, they should carefully consider the impact on their relationships with intermediaries.

In situations where the advantages of electronic shopping are very strong, store-based retailers would be ill-advised to try to counter the trend. Rather, they should devote their efforts to developing strategies to take advantage of the opportunities offered by electronic shopping.

Retailing as entertainment

Retailing, entertainment and recreation are converging. Entertainment companies, such as Walt Disney, Warner Bros, Discovery Communications, Sony and Viacom are moving into retailing in a big way, while retail developers are moving rapidly to add entertainment options to their new and existing developments. Such moves are clearly related to the perceived threat from electronic shopping.

Shopping as entertainment and as a social experience has long been an inherent part of retailing, especially in advanced economies. However, the entertainment and social aspects have not usually been explicitly emphasized. In fact, cinemas and other forms of entertainment in shopping malls have generally been considered a financial drain, taking customers away from stores and leading to lower sales per square foot.

In the rediscovery of the link between shopping and entertainment, there is a much more explicit focus on using entertainment as a way to differentiate the retail experience from conventional and electronic retailing. Some new retail developments incorporate nightclubs, zoos, virtual-reality rides, comedy clubs, target ranges, musical revues and stadium-style cinemas. Retailing is also converging with learning. Customers can develop expertise in new areas and parents can make their limited time with their children more meaningful.

Customers come to such stores not just to buy products or learn skills but to browse, socialise and be with other people. They also spend more than in a traditional mall; in a Los Angeles development called CityWalk, sales are about $500 per square foot compared with about $203 for the average mall.

The manufacturer's view

From the perspective of producers, some of the key issues in retailing are: a move towards "hybrid" distribution systems in which a larger number of short channels replace a small number of long channels; the growing prominence of non-traditional retailers; and the increased pressure producers are bringing to bear on retailers to adopt technologies such as EDI and ECR.

Most producers in the past tended to distribute their products either indirectly (via intermediaries) or directly (selling to end users without using middlemen). Now both types of producer are moving towards the simultaneous use of direct and indirect distribution. The aim is to provide the greatest market coverage in the most cost-effective way.

Companies that previously sold only through indirect channels are now adding direct channels (for example, IBM Direct, Xerox Direct). Airlines are adding direct channel options for end users through their websites. Such moves are being facilitated by the rising power and falling cost of IT.

At the same time, many companies are finding that it is uneconomical for them to service smaller indirect accounts; they are now in the process of "outsourcing" some of their retailer customers. In some cases, smaller retailer customers are being outsourced to larger distributors. One packaged goods company, for example, is asking some of its retailers to become "master distributors" and take on smaller retailers as customers. In moving to such complex hybrid marketing channels, companies face a number of areas of potential conflict with distributors. Preventing and managing such conflict is an important factor in the success of these arrangements.

Owing to greater demographic diversity in most markets as well as rising mobility, producers are finding that traditional retailers do not adequately cover many of the locations where customers wish to shop. Increasingly, shopping occurs in the home and in public places such as airports. Non-traditional retailers are stepping into the breach and producers need to include these in the mix in order to achieve greater market coverage.

Finally, the search for efficiency and productivity is leading manufacturers to press retailers of all sizes to integrate IT into their operations, especially for the sake of vertical information flows.

The future

The mammoth retailing sector will experience major shifts and severe dislocations in coming years. Conventional retailers, especially those that are mid-sized, will be squeezed from all sides: from larger players with better economies of scale; from smaller players with more focused selection or a greater emphasis on convenience; from electronic retailers that have few physical assets but are rich in information; and from entertainment- and education-orientated players that offer a more vibrant consumer experience.

Some of the key trends we see for retailing – in addition to electronic shopping and the melding of retailing with entertainment – include:

More polarization in size

We expect retailers to be very large or very small; relatively few will be mid-sized. As in most industries, retailing will be characterized by a handful of giants and a large number of specialists.

More emphasis on services

In the US the share of revenues at shopping malls from services rose from 48 per cent in 1980 to 60 per cent in 1996; this trend will continue. The services that will grow will be those that cannot be delivered by electronic or other means directly to the home and those that have a substantial social component (that is, their value is enhanced by experiencing them in groups rather than singly).

Greater focus on older customers

With the ageing of populations in most developed countries, most buyers have less need for physical products and more desire for services (including entertainment, education, travel, healthcare and financial services). Few retailers currently focus on mature customers; this will change as the needs of older buyers are better understood.

More outdoor shopping centers located in central urban areas

Many existing enclosed malls are "demalling" and opening up to the outside. Newer developments are mostly clustering in city centers, often with active municipal involvement.

Repurposing of malls

Many malls – especially those linked to hotels – will be converted to convention centers or be occupied by fully fledged universities. Other malls will be converted to office space.

Limited globalization

Rather than full-blown globalization of the retail industry, we expect to see regional internationalization. The primary reason is that the supply function is not sufficiently globalized. Global retailers would therefore have to deal with different suppliers in different parts of the world, erasing much of their scale advantage. Retailers will prefer to try to dominate a particular area (because of shared costs) than to spread out thinly around the globe.

Conclusion

Historically, retailing's primary emphasis was on transactions that resulted in the movement of merchandise. In the future, it will increasingly emphasize services, and transactions will be peripheral to the experiential elements of shopping and consumption (*see* Figure 1).

Past retailing was based predominantly on a gravitational model, in which store locations were the primary driver of customer shopping behavior. Such a model placed clear time and place constraints upon customers; transactions could only occur at the store during specified hours. In the future, such constraints will be self-defeating. Retailers must gain the ability to allow transactions to occur at any time, in any place.

The trend towards disintermediation is still in its early phases but it will result in massive dislocations. It will also cause major growth in support services for companies that deal directly with larger numbers of customers. For example, growth in small package shipping will be likely to exceed by far that in bulk shipments or the building of warehouse space.

Another important consequence of this trend is likely to be "reintermediation," or the emergence of new types of intermediaries that will capture the value-creating opportunities that will be spawned by the confluence of new modes of consumer–producer interaction. Examples of such intermediaries may include rating services, automated ordering services, services based on consolidating small orders from numerous consumers into more economically viable quantities and so on. Market specialists might emerge who will orchestrate the offerings of numerous

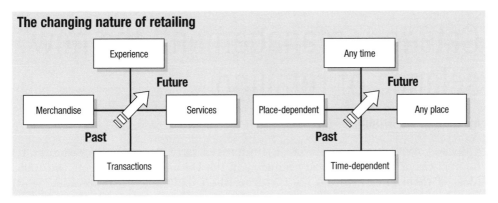

The changing nature of retailing

Figure 1

suppliers around the specialized needs of a single customer.

For today's retail intermediaries, the challenge is whether they can adapt to the emerging realities in a way that ensures their continued relevance and thus prosperity. They must identify a value-adding role for themselves in the new landscape of producer–consumer relationships and create a blueprint for moving towards a new business model.

Summary
Retailers play a critical role in the marketing process. Not only do they transfer goods from producers to consumers, they also channel information back from consumers. The importance of retailing is underlined by its immense size; in the US alone it accounts for some 30 per cent of gross domestic product. Yet the sector is currently in the throes of massive change, say **Jagdish Sheth** and **Rajendra Sisodia**. "New-style" retailers, using IT to facilitate close relationships with suppliers, are threatening more traditional formats; online shopping is giving consumers the prospect of more cost-effective shopping; and – partly in response to the online threat – moves are afoot to package retailing as entertainment or even education. The authors predict that mid-sized players have most to fear, as the market will become polarized between retail giants and niche businesses.

Suggested further reading
Alba, J., Lynch, J., Weitz, B., Janiszewski, C., Lutz, R., Sawyer, A. and Wood, S. (1997) "Interactive home shopping: consumer, retailer, and manufacturer incentives to participate in electronic marketplaces," *Journal Of Marketing*, summer.

Sheth, J.N. and Sisodia, R.S. (1997) "Consumer behavior in the future," in Peterson, R.A. (ed.) *Electronic Marketing and the Consumer*, Sage, London.

Category management: the new science of retailing

by Thomas W. Gruen

Efficient consumer response (ECR) initiatives have dramatically reshaped the practices of the retail grocery industry in the US and Europe during the 1990s. Most of them have involved restructuring the supply side of the retailer, which includes the creation of a paperless information flow between channel partners (using electronic data interchange) and more efficient physical replenishment of stores. The latter has reduced the amount of inventory in the channel, cut the number of times a product is handled and given rise to more efficient practices in areas like direct store delivery and cross-docking.

While the supply side of ECR generally goes unnoticed by the consumer, there is also a demand side – termed "category management" – that directly affects shelf-presentation, promotions, pricing and product assortment. Category management is defined by the Joint Industry Project on ECR as "the distributor/supplier process of managing categories as strategic business units, producing enhanced business results by focusing on delivering consumer value."

Category management is considered the "new science of retailing" for three basic reasons. First, it involves a systematic process that has been shown to be robust in various retail situations across the US, Europe, South Africa, Australia and Latin America. Second, it emphasizes decision-making based on complex analyses of consumer data, scanner data and market-level syndicated data. Third, category management replaces the brand bias that stems from a supplier's interest in maximizing market share with a more objective view based on the consumer's desires.

Background and strategy

The ECR initiatives, developed initially in 1993 for the US grocery distribution channel, identified several inefficient practices that were adding $30bn to the cost of the supply chain without creating consumer value. The ultimate goal of ECR is a responsive, consumer-driven system in which channel members focus on the total supply system in order to reduce costs and inventories while improving the consumer's choice.

Strategically, category management organizes the retail grocery store into a set of 150–250 interrelated product categories, each with its own role and sales/profit/asset/productivity objectives. The Joint Industry Project on ECR defines a category as "a distinct, manageable group of products or services that consumers perceive to be related and/or substitutable in meeting a consumer need."

In using category management, the retailer seeks sustainable competitive differentiation and advantage by competing on a category-by-category basis. The retailer manages each category as a strategic business unit. The goal is to design the category's marketing mix so as to provide more value to customers than they could obtain by purchasing through an alternative retail format.

Before the adoption of category management, grocery retailers had responded to the erosion in margins by increasing the frequency and size of price promotions, by requiring manufacturers to pay "slotting fees" for new products and by effectively padding margins at the expense of suppliers. This shortsighted approach took little account of consumers, whose loyalty accordingly decreased.

The Joint Industry Project on ECR in 1993 was a distress call by the grocery industry to replace inefficient and misdirected practices with an improved set of customer-value-adding practices. The Partnering Group formally developed the category management business planning process adopted by the US ECR consortium, and this information was published as the *Best Practices Category Management Report* in 1995.

By providing greater customer value on a category-by-category basis, grocery retailers sought to counter the assaults of a variety of alternative retail formats. For example, sales of pet products were being lost to "category killer" pet superstores, and sales of health and beauty products were being lost to the deep-discount drug format. Club stores were taking share in economy-size items, and mass-merchants such as Wal-Mart were taking general merchandise share.

In each case, the alternative formats offered a greater perceived value to the consumer, even though the consumer had to suffer the inconvenience of visiting an additional store. While grocery retailers have been major beneficiaries of category management, it has been a "double-edged sword," as it has also been successfully adopted by drug, mass merchandise and convenience stores.

Although initiated in the US, category management practices have been quickly adopted in Europe. Parallel work sponsored by ECR-Europe produced best practice reports for category management and efficient assortment. In Europe supply-side initiatives have been complicated by the diversity of different national cultures, languages and systems, but the demand side of category management has matured more quickly than in the US.

An eight-step process

While there are variations, the eight-step approach developed by The Partnering Group has been adopted as best practice by the ECR consortia in the US, Europe and Brazil. Each of the eight steps is described below and shown in Figure 1.

Category definition

The retailer begins the category management business process by assigning products to categories. A category is ideally defined by consumer usage; typical examples are haircare products, petfood, soup and yoghurt. Another factor is packaging. Thus shelf-stable juices, refrigerated juices and frozen concentrated juices are three distinct categories.

From the total store perspective, every stock-keeping unit (SKU) will ideally be placed in a category. From a practical perspective, retailers will begin to incorporate category management one category at a time, so the assignment of SKUs to a specific category will occur on an incremental basis rather than at a single time.

Category role

Each category is assigned a "role" that it is to play in the store's total category mix. The *Best Practices Category Management Report* suggests a set of four consumer-based category roles.

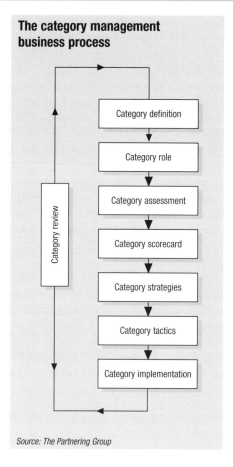

The category management business process

Category definition

Category role

Category assessment

Category scorecard

Category strategies

Category tactics

Category implementation

Category review

Source: The Partnering Group

Figure 1

1 *Destination categories* are those that the retailer uses to help define itself as the store of choice by offering superior consumer value. For example, a retailer may choose coffee, pasta, paper, bread, soft drinks and certain perishables among its destination categories.

2 *Routine categories* are those that the consumer regularly purchases at the store. Examples could be juice, milk, cereal, detergent and petfood.

3 *Occasional/seasonal categories* are purchased less frequently and could include condiments, cleaning supplies and suntan products.

4 *Convenience categories* are ones where the consumer knows that a greater selection and lower prices might be obtained elsewhere, but the value provided by the retailer is enough to make it not worth the cost of visiting another outlet. Examples of convenience categories could be car products, natural foods or confectionery.

A category has no fixed role, only that assigned by the retailer. The retailer must organize categories into a balanced "portfolio" of roles in order to manage each according to its expected return and to achieve the company's strategies and goals.

Category assessment

This stage includes a detailed assessment of the category's subcategories, segments, brands and SKUs on the basis of consumer, distributor, supplier and

Resources for category management

Several resources are available for managers involved in category management. First, the Joint Industry Project on ECR has published the *Best Practices Category Management Report* and the *Efficient Assortment Report*, both written by The Partnering Group. These publications, as well as updates and related reports, are available through the Food Marketing Institute in Washington, DC.

Parallel best practices and efficient assortment reports for Europe are available through ECR-Europe.

The Food Marketing Institute has published a series of five implementation guides on category management written by Robert Blattberg of the Center for Retail Management at Northwestern University, USA.

market information. Category assessment uses a variety of analytical tools designed to determine the category's strengths, weaknesses, opportunities and threats. Ideally, the analysis compares store-level scanner data with market-level data obtained from a syndicated data service such as Nielsen, IRI or GFK.

Spreadsheet-based templates are normally used for this analysis. Figure 2 shows an example of a quadrant analysis of the subcategories in the frozen concentrated juice category. The y-axis of the share-growth quadrant chart represents the store's market share relative to the relevant market area. The x-axis shows the recent growth performance of the store relative to the relevant market area. In the example, two subcategories, orange juice (FCOJ) and drinks/ades/punches (Dr/Ade/Ph) have a lower market share and lower growth than the overall market. Alternatively, variety juices (VarJc) and mixers have a higher share and higher growth.

The contribution-to-margin (CTM) quadrant analysis shows the relationship between the amount of sales of each subcategory and its gross margin level. Gross margin return on investment (GMROI) analysis measures retailer inventory asset performance, showing the relationship between gross margin profitability and annual inventory turns.

These charts, along with other assessment tools, each provide a unique insight into some aspect of the category's (and its components') performance. Each suggests possible ways to improve the category's performance.

In Figure 2, the quadrant charts show that the mixer subcategory performance may be enhanced through price increases and lower inventory levels. In the FCOJ subcategory, given the high number of turns indicated on the GMROI chart, the category manager may consider adding some additional SKUs to enhance its growth and market share. For the Dr/Ade/Ph subcategory, the manager may consider more aggressive pricing and cutting some slow-moving SKUs. Final determination of actual tactics (for example, which SKUs to add or delete) will occur only after similar quadrant analysis has been made at the brand and SKU level.

Category scorecard

This is used to establish performance measures for the category business plans. What is measured depends on the category's role and the strategies used. However, a common set of measures includes market share, sales, GMROI and net profit. The scorecard disciplines and structures the category management process and provides a means of aligning category managers' incentives.

Frozen juices and drinks
Share-growth quadrant: subcategory analysis

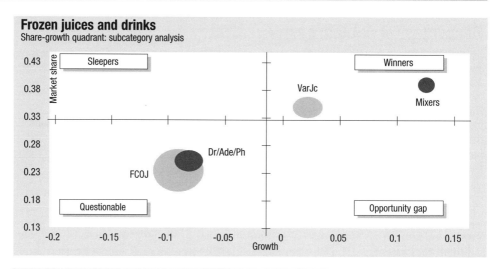

Frozen drinks and juices
Contribution-to-margin quadrant: subcategory analysis

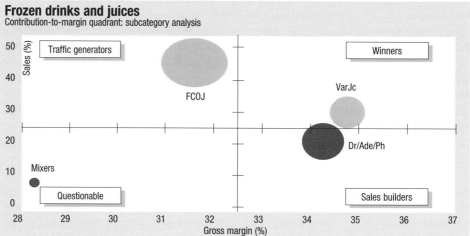

Frozen drinks and juices
Gross margin return on investment quadrant: subcategory analysis

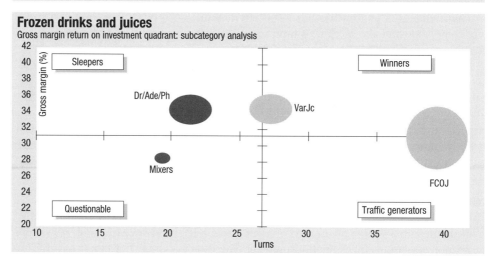

Figure 2

Obstacles to implementation

The consensus is that the major obstacles to category management are not technological or financial but organizational. One challenge surrounds the basic organization and habits of channel members, and a complementary challenge concerns individuals' skills.

Traditional retail organizations have been fragmented into sections responsible for merchandising, buying, promotion and pricing, with the emphasis placed on the functional skill set required for the task. Category management requires integration of these skill sets for each category. Not only does this necessitate a change in the retailer's structure, but personnel must also be retrained to take a "team approach" to enhancing category performance.

Category plans are based on recent data and any delay in implementing the plans will quickly render them obsolete. Implementation can be slowed by a retailer's traditional structural obstacles, but often there is also a basic distrust of the category management approach – retailers will be cautious until they can see results. Therefore, retailer trust must be gained by successfully implementing category management in a few key categories.

Overall, my own research has shown that the planning process is much more developed than the implementation process. Overcoming the barriers to implementation requires a strong commitment on the part of retailers' senior management. It also requires substantial reorientation and/or retraining of current personnel, together with new measurement and reward systems along the lines of the category scorecard.

Category strategies

Marketing, product supply and in-store service strategies must be determined for each category. Typical category marketing strategies are traffic building, transaction building, profit contribution, cash generation, excitement generation, image creation and turf-defending. These help shape the category's marketing mix.

Category tactics

Once the strategies have been selected, a detailed plan is developed showing what needs to be done to the category. This includes plans for both the demand and supply sides of the category. On the demand side, optimal product assortment, pricing, shelf presentation and promotion tactics are set out, while the supply-side plans include product procurement and distribution.

Category implementation

While the tactical plan focuses on what needs to be accomplished, the implementation plan covers who carries out the category plan, when and how. This includes assignment of responsibilities, a timetable and provision of the necessary resources.

Category review

During the execution of the plan, the category is regularly monitored, measured and modified.

Fact-based decision making

Category management is considered a "scientific" approach to retailing because of its reliance on data-driven, fact-based decision making. This approach has been made possible by the use of information technology and has been enhanced by decision-support software developed by industry consultants. It has greatly changed the role of both the buyer and the seller.

Category management is necessarily intensely data-driven and analysis-dependent. Even the simplest category assessment that uses a Pareto analysis to rank profit or volume sales of a category's SKUs still requires accurate store-level sales data. Category assessments seek to integrate the store's scanner data with market-level sales data (supplied by data services) and consumer information from manufacturers in order to identify "opportunity gaps" for sales, profit and return on investment.

Collecting, standardizing, managing and analyzing these huge volumes of data from multiple sources requires a commitment of hardware, software and personnel. Category management transforms the mass of data that retail scanning collects into useable information.

Category management has been made much less complex as software programs capable of integrating these various data sources and automating the fundamental analyses have been developed. The goal has been to reduce the time required to conduct a category review and to standardize the information that managers use. These programs are available through consultants or data providers, though several of the larger branded goods companies, such as Procter & Gamble and Coca-Cola, have developed their own analysis tools based on TPG's Best Practices Category Management model.

One of the most significant results of the fact-based decision making approach is a change in the role of the retail buyer. Category business planning establishes the assortment, facings and placement of SKUs based on what the information suggests will be the best way to satisfy the consumer. Thus traditional buying is relegated to a logistical role, working to minimize distribution and inventory while ensuring that there is enough stock to keep the shelves filled. Category management effectively extends these responsibilities into total management of the assets deployed within a category.

An objective approach

Another reason why category management is seen as "scientific retailing" is that it involves a partnering approach between retailers and suppliers. This requires that both partners view the marketplace through a set of objective lenses in order to serve the consumer.

Previously, suppliers and retailers took a more adversarial position. New products would find their way onto the shelves when accompanied by slotting fees, rather than being driven by the needs of the target customer. Merchandising would be based on the amount of money given to the retailer, rather than on consumer value. Pricing was based on gross margin rather than on true profit. This created a haphazard approach that was aimed at propping margins rather than creating a loyal customer franchise.

The requirement for objectivity on the part of the supplier can be seen when the supplier plays the role of "category captain." In this situation, the retailer selects one supplier in the category that it views as being most capable in category management. The category captain works with the retailer to create a plan for the entire category, including competitors' brands and private label brands.

In essence, the retailer places the well-being of the entire category in the hands of a single supplier. This changes the fundamental role of selling. Instead of seeking to gain market share at the expense of competitors' brands, the category captain hopes to benefit by increasing the size and performance of the category, so all brands (including the captain's) will benefit.

Efforts on the part of the captain to produce a biased report are likely to reduce the anticipated category's performance, and this will show up during the business planning process. Using objective data and adhering to the eight-step category management process delivers the business plan that will best build the category relative to the target consumer segment.

The category business planning process often leads to a reduction in the number of SKUs that will be carried. The category captain must remain objective even if some of its own SKUs are eliminated. Category assessments in the US and Europe result, on average, in a recommendation to reduce 10–15 per cent of SKUs in a category (although a few do result in the addition of SKUs). Research has shown that in some categories up to 25 per cent of SKUs can be eliminated (or "delisted") without reducing customer satisfaction. In fact, satisfaction should increase because the retailer has an easier time keeping in stock the items that the segment most values. In addition, consumers find it easier and less confusing to make purchases.

Summary

Efficient Consumer Response (ECR) is best known as a supply-side initiative that helps retailers control inventory levels and efficiently replenish their stock. The demand side of ECR, known as "category management," is less familiar but it can also be a crucial element in a successful business strategy. In this article, **Thomas Gruen** provides a step-to-step guide to the implementation of category management and explains how it can offset brand "bias" on the part of suppliers, change the relationship between retailers and suppliers and lead to a stronger relationship with consumers. Category management can be a significant departure for retailers – it requires different functions to integrate their skills, for example – so a strong commitment on the part of senior management is essential.

Are private labels a threat to national brands?

by Stephen J. Hoch and Jagmohan S. Raju

Walk into any supermarket today and you will find all the national brands that you see advertised on television and in the newspapers. But occupying an increasingly prominent space among the major brands are private label goods. These "store brands" were once thought of as the products stores sold exclusively to price-conscious shoppers. Shoppers who had higher incomes and who were concerned about quality would always select the national brand over the store brand. Or so store owners and manufacturers thought.

Strong growth in the sales of private label goods has sent managers of national

The future

Consumers have shown an increasing penchant for high quality at lower prices. This provides opportunities for both national brands, which have historically had the edge on quality, and for private label goods, which have had the edge on price. As both the real and perceived quality of private label goods increases, a growing number of customers are likely to choose them.

Relatively slow growth in consumer spending on fresh and packaged food, as well as continued consolidation in the highly fragmented food retailing industry means greater competition and shrinking margins for retailers and manufacturers alike. In many countries, the trend is towards a smaller number of retailers controlling a larger percentage of the market; these are the players that will have the resources to develop successful private label programs.

Successful national brands will be those that distinguish themselves from private label goods. This means continuing to build value for the brand itself. The well-established formula has never been more apt: solve an important consumer problem with a high-quality product and then aggressively communicate the benefits the product offers through strong advertising.

National brands are well along the road to establishing stronger links with their retail customers. That trend will continue. Retailers know that they need national brands, so they will want to maintain strong relationships with their suppliers.

Although the success of a private label program depends on the retailer's actions, national brands too can strongly influence where private label products will go in the future. The more benefits the national brand can offer to the retailer, the less likely it is that the retailer will divert resources to promoting private labels. National brand managers should not focus on price; rather, they should focus on the many benefits their product offers to both the retailer and the consumer.

brands scurrying to develop new methods for competing successfully against them. National brands are in a delicate situation: the stores that mount successful private label programs are also the national brands' major customers.

Where once consumers bought private labels only out of economic necessity, store owners have found that shoppers are now purchasing these goods because they are perceived to have a level of quality comparable to national brands. They also tend to be between 10 and 30 per cent cheaper than comparable national brands.

Where national brands once tended to focus on the consumer and pay little attention to the retailer, brand managers now understand that the success of any product is dependent upon the manufacturer, the consumer and the retailer. Retailers and manufacturers of branded goods are trying to determine how best to work co-operatively and in competition with one another at the same time.

Private label goods captured 13 per cent of supermarket sales revenue in the US in 1991. While that may seem a relatively small number, it represents sales worth almost $50bn. In our recent research, we found that, on average, private labels are priced 21 per cent below comparable national brands. In many categories, private label goods are dominant. For example, private label frozen green beans and hard cheese account for more than 50 per cent of sales. We found that retailers earn a gross margin on private label products that is 20 to 30 per cent higher than on national brands.

Private labels have performed significantly better in Europe and Canada than in the US. In Germany, for example, private label sales rose from 13 to 23 per cent between 1982 and 1990. Table 1 provides a breakdown of store brand penetration by country.

Private label penetration by country				
Country	PL share (% units)	Pop/km2	% large stores (≥3000m^2)	Top 3 retailers' market share (%)
Switzerland	41.2	155	36	80
UK	37.1	228	70	45
Germany	21.8	225	40	47
Canada	21.0	3	50	25
Belgium	19.8	325	56	58
United States	17.6	25	70	17
France	16.4	103	76	38
Netherlands	16.3	363	31	47
Denmark	15.1	118	37	77
Sweden	10.7	19	38	95
Finland	8.0	148	27	75
Spain	7.7	77	35	20
Italy	6.8	19	26	11
Austria	6.3	91	26	56
Norway	5.0	13	19	86
Ireland	3.6	50	53	43
Portugal	2.3	113	43	41

Source: A.C. Nielsen 1994

Table 1

There is a significant qualitative difference between private label programs in the US and those in Europe, where private labels often offer greater quality and choice than in the US. Both Europe and Canada have large national retail food chains, with far greater concentration than in the US. In the US, for example, the largest food retailer is Kroger; although it is large – with more than $20bn in annual sales – it has only about 6 per cent of the domestic market for food sales. Recent merger and acquisition activity in the grocery industry may signal that the US will move towards the European model. Alternatively, the continued elimination of manufacturer trade restrictions in the European market may in fact move the food retailing sector along a path more like that in the US, with regional retailers holding smaller shares of the overall European market.

Our research indicates a strong link between private label sales and overall economic conditions: when times are tough, consumers tend to buy more private label goods; when the economy is strong, they buy national brands. When market share for private label goods is plotted against an average income index, a mirror image is revealed: as income goes up, private label market share goes down and when income drops, private label market share goes up (*see* Figure 1).

We have also found that in areas where there is a higher concentration of elderly people, large households, or women working outside the home, there is a greater price sensitivity and a greater tendency to purchase private labels. Conversely, when household incomes are high consumers tend to be less price sensitive and private label goods tend not to sell as well.

Interestingly, we have found that higher education levels are generally associated with lower price sensitivity, but also with higher sales of private labels. We surmise that the better-educated consumers are better informed about the quality of private labels relative to national brands.

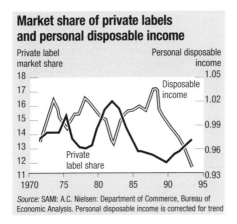

Market share of private labels and personal disposable income

Source: SAMI: A.C. Nielsen: Department of Commerce, Bureau of Economic Analysis. Personal disposable income is corrected for trend

Figure 1

Quality *and* price

It is the combination of price and quality that distinguishes private labels from national brands. Whereas customers may once have sought quality with little regard for price, or low prices at the expense of quality – thus enabling national brands to focus on quality and private labels on price – now they seem to want high quality at an affordable price. Consumers have the economic resources to afford national brands but their price consciousness leads them to demand the prices normally attached to private labels. This poses a challenge for manufacturers and retailers alike.

National brands have historically staked out quality as their turf. Quality has two components: (1) the average level of quality of one product compared with another and (2) the consistency of the quality of a product over time. Manufacturing and processing technology account for much of the quality level of any product.

National brands once had the edge on consistency of quality over the long term. Increasingly, however, private label manufacturers can match or exceed the quality of branded goods and assure a consistent level of quality across their range. It is in these situations that national brands face their greatest competitive threat.

Once consumers realize that private labels are of as high a quality as a national brand and that the quality is consistent, they will not hesitate to turn away from the national brand. After all, the consumer is getting what he or she wants at a price that is, on average, 20 per cent below that of the national brand. To be sure, consumers are willing to trade off quality for lower prices but only to a limited extent. Our research has shown that the effect of price is inconclusive.

Competing with private labels

The growing success of private labels is shifting the balance of power away from national brands towards the retailer. Yet all is not lost for the national brand. A key concern for retailers is when to give limited shelf space to private label goods. National brands provide retailers with advertising and marketing support, such as coupons and other promotions, whereas retailers have to develop their own support for private labels. Where retailers have strong private label programs, they often use that fact as leverage in bargaining with national brands for better terms, prices and product availability. Because private labels provide a higher gross margin for the retailer, national brands have to offer more inducements to maintain shelf space.

National brands have their own leverage. They typically provide support and investment in market growth that retailers cannot afford in the case of private label goods. Retailers of private labels have to take on responsibilities that are normally handled by the manufacturers of national brands. The retailer must invest in inventory, packaging, display space, special promotions and advertising.

The average grocery retailer carries tens of thousands of different items; managing a private label program for every good or category is clearly out of the question. Therefore they will concentrate their efforts on goods that provide both greater sales revenue and higher gross profit margins. National brand manufacturers can compete aggressively by increasing advertising and promotional support and by improving product quality.

Private label goods tend to be less successful where there are a lot of competing products. Compare, for example, the shampoo market, where there are more than 1,100 different products, with salt or sugar, where there are few variants. The greater the variety in the market, the more difficult it will be for the private label to capture significant market share. The manufacturer of the national brand will want to examine its market carefully and constantly to determine what niche it has and how consumers perceive its products.

Consumers have become increasingly knowledgeable, sophisticated and demanding. They want a balance between quality and price. The key word in retailing these days is "value." Consumers are able to make informed quality judgments and to determine which product provides the best value. Where manufacturers of national brands have clearly staked out their turf and where there are many variants of a product, private labels are far less likely to succeed.

Advertising still plays a strong role in creating an image of quality in the minds of consumers and in helping to build brand loyalty. Retailers spend a lot of time and money in building loyalty to their stores. National brands could engage in more co-operative advertising, marketing and promotion with retailers. The national brand manufacturer has to become each retailer's partner and not just sit back and think of itself as the supplier. The manufacturer can provide significant marketing support for retailers attempting to project an image of quality, while it can also work to ensure that its goods are sold at a competitive price that also provides the retailer with a fair margin.

Retailers are in constant contact with their customers and can make changes in their product selections and displays virtually instantaneously in response to feedback. They can piggyback off promotions run by national brands in order to promote their own labels. Retailers also have complete control over product placement and promotion. If a product does well, the retailer can react immediately to boost sales further. If it does badly, the retailer can reposition it or eliminate it from the line-up. National brand managers must understand the growing power that retailers have and the need to work co-operatively with them.

Performance of store brands has improved dramatically in the fastest-growing segment of the retail market: discount mass merchants such as Wal-Mart. If such retailers continue their aggressive move into traditional food retailing, and combine that move with their commitment to private label goods, this will pose a competitive threat to national brands. National brands will have to respond with a higher level of advertising and promotion to convince consumers that they offer better value.

Retailers frequently use national brands in their advertising to draw customers to their stores. Our research has shown that retailers who use such strategies generally carry more national brands, have deeper assortments and offer generally lower prices across the board. These strategies, of course, work against the store's private label goods. This underlines the difficulty of the balancing act retailers must perform to maximize revenue and gross margin in each product category.

Our research has important lessons for any industry where there are products that are both private label and national brands. As long as there is the possibility of outsourcing, there is the possibility that private label goods will grow at the expense of national goods. The consumer often shows little brand loyalty and is willing to try something new. National brands, however, tend to have the resources to develop new and improved products much faster than private label manufacturers. Most national brands have large, sophisticated research departments, as well as large advertising and marketing departments. This gives them a considerable advantage.

Price is not the driving factor in the success – or lack of success – of private label goods. The biggest obstacle they have to overcome is branding. Nationally branded goods tend to assure consumers of their quality; private label goods historically have not had that advantage. A 1990 Gallup poll reported that 85 per cent of consumers considered quality to be "very important" in their purchasing decisions, whereas 73 per cent considered price to be "very important." On this evidence, quality is the single most important purchasing criterion for most shoppers. National brands have to focus on their image of quality, even as they become more price competitive.

The best pricing strategy for retailers is to maintain a medium-sized price gap between national brands and private labels. With a very large gap, higher-margin national brand sales suffer and, at the same time, the retailer gives away too much private label margin without a big enough increase in private label sales to compensate. More importantly, the retailer gains little in terms of a better overall price image since price image is driven more by national brand than private label prices.

With a small gap, national brand sales do increase but decreases in store brand sales more than cancel out those gains. The lesson is that both national brand manufacturers and retailers would be better off if they spent less energy competing on price. National brands should pursue a strategy based on product innovation, along with strong advertising and marketing to support their products; retailers ought to concentrate on running their stores more effectively and retaining their installed base of loyal customers.

Summary

Private labels – or "own brands" – are flourishing. They account for over half of all sales in some categories, are often cheaper than national brands and tend to provide greater margins for retailers. Most worryingly for national brand managers, many private labels are now competing on quality. Here **Stephen Hoch** and **Jagmohan Raju** argue that the best strategy for national brands is strongly to promote their image of quality – which most consumers value over price – while pricing themselves competitively. A national brand can also increase its advertising and promotional activity, effectively forcing retailers to give it more space. Alternatively, a brand can advertise and market in co-operation with a retailer; such partnering arrangements help retailers project an image of quality and ensure a better deal for brands.

Suggested further reading

Dhar, S. and Hoch, S.J. (1998) "Why store brand penetration varies by retailer," *Marketing Science*, 16, 208–27.

Hoch, S.J. (1996) "How national brands should think about private labels," *Sloan Management Review*, 89–102, winter.

Raju, J., Sethuraman, R. and Dhar, S. (1995) "The introduction and performance of store brands," *Management Science*, 41, 957–78.

Golden rules for customer service

by Dawn Iacobucci

According to recent economic statistics the service sector represents at least two-thirds of the global economy. Service industries include the "purer" services, such as hotels, restaurants and consultancies, as well as "mixed" industries in which the core purchase may be a product, but one that is purchased with a large service component, such as car dealerships or mortgage brokers.

With competition intensifying due to deregulation, privatization and industrial restructuring, managers are increasingly seeking to provide added value for customers and to enhance their competitive advantage by offering better customer service.

One starting point on the road to superior customer service is to gain a better understanding of the fundamental characteristics of services. Services tend to be *intangible, produced and consumed simultaneously*, and *heterogeneous*. Each of these qualities has implications for the marketing and management of customer service.

Services are intangible

The service encounter is often described as an "interactive performance," in which the consumer and front-line service personnel obtain value from one another. The customer emerges from this exchange having been processed in a manner that may not be tangible.

The intangibility of services has a number of managerial implications. For example, it has been suggested that advertisements for services should provide symbols, or tangible cues, as concrete signals of abstract attributes. An instance of this might be Prudential's rock, symbolizing solidity.

The main area of academic inquiry relating to intangibility has been its effect on customers' evaluation of the service they receive. Several conceptual models of customer satisfaction and service quality start from the assumption that evaluation is a comparison between the customer's actual experience and his or her prior expectations – if the experience exceeds the expectations, the models predict satisfaction. (Professor Richard Oliver at Vanderbilt University in the US has researched in this area.) The expectations that encounters are compared with are thought to be developed through communications from a company (for example, advertisements) or from other customers (word of mouth).

Building on such analysis, academics are trying to develop further models of real practical use. Professor Roland Rust (again at Vanderbilt University), for example, advises companies to measure "return on quality" (ROQ) to assess the financial effectiveness of initiatives intended to enhance customer service and satisfaction.

Certain actions or modifications of the service delivery system will indeed please customers more than other actions, so the challenge is to identify the qualities that customers value. Companies can meet this challenge if they only think to listen to what their customers are telling them.

Professors Eugene Anderson and Claes Fornell at the University of Michigan have begun to demonstrate a promising relationship between indicators of satisfaction and macroeconomic statistics such as the US consumer price index. Both indices may be suggestive of customers' sense of economic well-being, or satisfaction may eventually serve to diagnose the state of the wider economy. This research suggests that the very simple and mundane human interaction involved in service encounters (the front-line employees' competence and empathy) has a direct impact on a company's and a country's bottom line.

Researchers are also beginning to understand that satisfaction and dissatisfaction are not opposites. Professor Vikas Mittal at Northwestern University in the US has demonstrated that satisfaction and dissatisfaction are similar in that both are nonlinear functions whose increase or decrease in value is consistent (that is, they are monotonic). His research also shows that greater and greater efforts to enhance satisfaction eventually yield diminishing returns. However, satisfaction and dissatisfaction differ in that reducing dissatisfaction appears to matter more than improving service for already satisfied customers.

For about a decade we have all been instructed that "it costs more to acquire new customers than to retain our current customer base." Mittal's research indicates that our greatest danger is in losing a customer. We should do whatever is necessary to retain a customer. Beyond retention, attempts to satisfy current customers further are futile and cost-inefficient. We therefore need to segment customers with respect to their dissatisfaction thresholds.

Finally, academics are finding that evaluations of quality or of satisfaction do not affect repeat purchasing and loyalty as much as perceptions of value. Value is typically defined as some comparison between quality or satisfaction and price (which has both economic and psychological components, including search and purchase efforts). Stronger customer service is expected when paying higher prices and poorer customer service may be tolerated when paying lower prices: customers value value.

Services are simultaneously produced and consumed

The consumer is often involved in the co-creation of a service, so the production and consumption of services usually requires his or her presence. As a result, the services marketing manager must consider the physical environment of the service shop, as well as the front-line employees who help create a string of "moments of truth."

The customer usually does not see goods being produced. The manufacturing plant and its workers and distributors have no immediate impact on customer satisfaction. For services, however, customers usually come to the point at which they are "made." As a result, the physical environment of the service delivery system plays a significant role in the customer's evaluation. An office can provides tangible clues to the quality of service. For example, a lawyer's office can imply that the legal mind is messy and disorganized or that the lawyer is highly successful and enjoys the luxury of large overheads.

From retail services arose the age-old claim that "location, location, location" is what matters, and indeed, site access is important. Access also implies being open for business at convenient times. The simultaneity of production and consumption is also behind another aspect of services – they are perishable. The flight that lifts off with empty seats can never retrieve those seats for future use.

The closest approximation services managers have to inventories is queuing. But this solution may not be desirable to customers. Laundry detergent, athletic shoes and cars do not mind being stored for long periods of time. But people do.

An even greater challenge posed by simultaneous production and consumption is the customer's encounters with the front-line staff. A surly overseer in a chemical plant is irrelevant to the customer. But a surly physician prescribing, or pharmacist dispensing, or cashier charging directly affects the customer's experience.

Researchers are finding more and more empirical support for the view that employee satisfaction and customer satisfaction are interrelated. Professors Leonard Schlesinger, Earl Sasser and James Heskett at Harvard University have long warned that a key to customer retention is keeping one's employees satisfied. Specifically, if the front-line jobs are well designed and management is selective in hiring and generous in training and remuneration, employees will be capable and loyal. Their lower turnover will contribute to profitability (less resources devoted to hiring and training) and to customer satisfaction because of their extended experience.

With more knowledgeable front-line personnel, customer satisfaction will rise. There will be fewer service failures and greater opportunities for customization. Clearly, the customer retention that results will contribute to profitability through repeat purchasing, positive word of mouth and reduction in the resources directed towards acquiring new customers. In addition, customer satisfaction reciprocally contributes to employee satisfaction – working with happy customers is a happier employment experience.

The fact that a large component of services is interpersonal, between the customer and service provider, contributes to the challenge of managing and marketing services. Even competent, well-intentioned front-line employees can have moments of poor judgment.

The front line serves as an intermediary in the relationship that the company wishes to forge with its customers. Indeed, a common complaint and cause of "burn-out" among front-line employees is the role conflict they frequently experience – wishing to please the customer but having to follow bureaucratic rules or wishing to do a good job but wanting the customers to go away. Professor Kent Grayson at London Business School has talked about the roles that service employees play. An important part of front-line professionalism is to play the role of the helpful service provider, regardless of one's momentary state. With extended and repeated contact, a truer sense of a relationship between two persons can develop. But in the typical short-term, one-off marketplace transaction we function as "customer-role" interacting with "service-provider-role."

Service encounters are heterogeneous

The fact that services are co-created by two dynamic and fallible humans also leads to services being described as heterogeneous. Service provision varies across customers and across front-line employees at multi-site or even same-site locations. Different employees have different skills and attitudes and different customers have different needs.

Heterogeneity, like cholesterol, can be good or bad. Good heterogeneity is the opportunity in the interactive service encounter to tailor the service to suit a customer's individual needs. Bad heterogeneity is error. Just as variability in the market is considered financially risky, so variability in services makes people perceive them as riskier purchases. One's computer may be manufactured with nano-precision but one's sushi will never be prepared quite the same way twice.

A marketing tool gaining some momentum among the better providers in many industries is the service guarantee. This can reduce the perceived riskiness of a purchase and can provide an indication of the quality of service to be expected. After all, the customer reasons, how could a company offer a guarantee unless it was confident that it would not require frequent redemption?

Many value-added aspects of customer service are easily matched by competitors. As these additional services diffuse throughout an industry, they no longer serve as points of competitive distinction but rather, in customers' eyes, as commodities. Expectations rise and customers come to demand even more.

On the surface, it would seem easy for competitors to match service guarantees. The point of distinction, however, is that they are not easy to sustain. A "me too" provider whose quality does not match the leader cannot afford to offer a competitive guarantee. Guarantees also provide a clear means of feedback to the company. In the vast majority of instances, a customer receiving poor service simply complains to friends, family and colleagues. Corporate headquarters never learns of the problem nor is able to pursue the opportunity to try to design out future errors.

The collective wisdom regarding service recovery currently seems to be "empathy plus one." In other words: be sure to have a caring and understanding attitude towards the customer's complaint and situation; fix the problem; and (over)compensate for the mistake by doing something beyond what the customer paid for. We marketing academics have to admit that we cannot offer more substantial advice on the topic of service recovery than this. It seems to reduce to the universal moral exhortation "do unto others ..." Still, if it were observed, customer service would indeed improve.

No matter what the situation, the front-line employee must maintain a professional role and treat the customer with dignity. Most customer complaints in service industries address neither a failure of the core service nor its price but instead focus on the incompetence and poor attitude of front-line staff. For example, the frequent business flyer can be understanding when global weather patterns or mechanical malfunctions produce delays. However that flyer becomes irritated when no explanation is given or the front line is brusque or rude. Customers can, of course, be obnoxious – perhaps increasingly so. But the front line must be trained to remain collected and not reciprocate. Such difficulties are inevitable when one deals with people. Yet it is precisely the "people" factor that makes services so interesting and challenging to manage.

Summary

Offering and delivering superior customer service is an important way in which companies have sought to respond to growing competition. In this article, **Dawn Iacobucci** looks at the characteristics of service businesses – their intangibility, heterogeneity, and the fact that they are simultaneously produced and consumed – and considers the implications for managers. Issues include strategies for dealing with both satisfied and dissatisfied customers (is there any point, for example, in enhancing service for contented consumers?), the importance of employee satisfaction and the value of service guarantees. The author admits that the best advice on the last of these is to stick to the golden rule: "Do unto others as you would be done by."

The strategic advantages of direct selling

by Kent Grayson and Richard Berry

Direct selling is the use of salespeople to sell and supply goods to private individuals, usually in their home or workplace. Although one of the oldest distribution methods, it has been overshadowed by other approaches in most modern economies.

The growth of mass manufacturing and brand advertising in the early 20th century, for example, meant that many consumer-product organizations turned to mass distribution systems as a more efficient means of reaching the market. More recently, the mass marketing of products via catalogs, direct mail and telephone (sometimes called "direct marketing") has been facilitated by the development of advanced database marketing techniques.

But neither retail distribution nor direct marketing is without problems. For example, the power of retail chains has grown to the point where they can present considerable barriers even to well-established brands. And consumers – who every day are bombarded by a growing number of advertising messages – are becoming immune to the sales pitches they face when watching television, traveling to work or opening their post.

Direct selling is an approach to distribution that is not as vulnerable to some of the problems associated with standard channels. At least this has been the experience of successful direct-selling companies such as Amway, Herbalife, Mary Kay, Betterware, Weekenders, Oriflame and Kleeneze. Today, companies such as these use direct selling to move more than \$18bn worth of consumer products in the US and more than \$10bn in the European Union every year. These figures have encouraged a number of managers to consider direct selling as a primary or secondary channel of distribution for their products.

One-to-one or one-to-many?

One way to distinguish between direct-selling organizations is to see whether their salespeople tend to engage in one-to-many or one-to-one selling. With one-to-many direct selling ("party plan" selling), several customers and potential customers are invited to group product presentations. Those who attend are often friends and acquaintances who are interested not only in the products being offered but also in the socializing that occurs. These presentations are often made in a home environment and have a casual, festive atmosphere. In contrast, one-to-one direct salespeople present their products not to groups of customers but to individuals or couples. As with one-to-many selling, these presentations often occur in a home environment, especially if the salesperson seeks customers by going "door to door." One-to-one salespeople also arrange individual appointments, which may occur in any number of locations, including restaurants, pubs or workplaces.

Direct-selling companies tend to emphasize one type of selling over another. This is often dictated by the type of product being sold. For example, one-to-many selling is obviously a good forum for products that are interesting or fun to demonstrate, such as cosmetics and skin-care products. Once one or two people decide to make a purchase at a party, others are likely to follow.

More pedestrian items, such as household products, tend to be sold via one-to-one contacts, where products are displayed via a catalog rather than a demonstration. One-to-one selling also tends to be more appropriate for more expensive items such as vacuum cleaners and water filters. This is because customers often require more individualized sales pitches before making a larger purchase.

The salesperson's skills also play a role in the type of selling that occurs. One person may be particularly good at individualizing a sales pitch and may therefore prefer one-to-one sales encounters. Another may have excellent demonstration skills and may therefore initiate home party sales events – even for products that other salespeople find difficult to demonstrate.

Single-level or multi-level?

Another way in which direct-selling organizations can be distinguished from one another is by the way in which the company's management and sales supervision are organized. Some companies – "single-level" sales organizations – have one or two levels of managers (for example, a vice president of sales and regional sales managers) whose responsibilities include the recruitment, training and supervision of salespeople. Single-level direct-sales companies operate like many standard sales organizations because their respective organizational structures are similar. In contrast, "multi-level" direct-sales organizations depend on their local salespeople to recruit, train and supervise the sales force. Salespeople are motivated to do so because they earn commissions on the sales of anyone they recruit, and on the products sold by their recruits' recruits, and so on. Companies that depend on their salespeople to recruit and train are called "network marketing" or "multi-level marketing" organizations because their salespeople benefit from the number of productive sales levels they build.

Because of this, network marketing salespeople generally must be good at selling not only the benefits of a product line but also the advantages of building a sales business using the line. The most successful network marketers must also have good training and sales management skills. Although individuals in single-level organizations may on occasion be rewarded for recruiting others, they are not rewarded for the activities of their recruits' recruits, their recruits' recruits' recruits, and so on.

The manufacturer's view

Every marketing tool has pros and cons, and direct selling is no different. Its strategic advantages depend on the organization's goals and the strengths and weaknesses of its human resources.

There are three key issues that a consumer product manufacturer (or service provider) should consider when gauging the strategic opportunities of direct selling.

Initiating the sale

Consumers today are becoming more skeptical of advertising messages, in part because they are inundated with them every day. Consumer researchers have found that even children know that advertisements should be treated with a degree of skepticism. In contrast, research has also shown that face-to-face and word-of-mouth communication is often a more credible source of product information – especially when it comes from someone already known by the consumer.

In both single- and multi-level organizations, customers are strongly encouraged to tell their friends about the company's products or services. In so doing, direct-selling organizations can in many ways sidestep the resistance that dogs other forms of promotion and distribution.

However, not everyone is comfortable when social relationships are used as a basis for building commercial relationships. Some view this as taking advantage of friendships or tainting a personal relationship with a profit motive. In part because of this, direct selling is seen by some customers as an unwelcome personal intrusion.

A recent study by Wirthlin Worldwide showed that 42 per cent of the US public have a positive attitude towards buying from a direct selling organization. Half of those people bought from a direct seller who was previously known to them. Those with negative views – mainly those without personal exposure to direct selling – expressed concern about being put under pressure to buy. To counteract this potential resistance, direct salespeople often take an approach to selling that is different from most other salespeople. In fact, many direct salespeople would prefer not to be called "salespeople." Instead, they see themselves as product enthusiasts who are simply sharing the benefits of a product with friends, just as they might recommend a good book or film.

Building consumer relationships

As evidenced by the explosive growth in loyalty programs over the past decade, marketing practitioners have been paying greater and greater attention to building long-term relationships with consumers. Besides reduced selling costs, this gives a company the opportunity to learn more about individual consumers and therefore to tailor market offerings to their needs.

However, as emphasized recently by Susan Fournier, Susan Dobsha and David Glen Mick in the *Harvard Business Review* (January/February 1998), many companies do not truly understand consumers as individuals and do not truly tailor their market offerings to each individual consumer. Relationship marketing is not simply a matter of using a consumer's name in a direct-mail letter and remembering his or her birthday. Instead, it requires a deep understanding of the consumer and an ability to adapt the market offering to suit his or her needs.

Direct selling offers companies the opportunity to develop true relationships. Unlike television commercials and direct-mail packages, individual salespeople can interact with consumers, which means hearing and responding to their needs and desires. They are also in a good position to see the same customers time and again. This combination of interactivity and repeated encounters gives direct salespeople the ability to implement relationship marketing in spirit, not just in name. In a recent survey of network marketing salespeople implemented by London Business School and the UK's Direct Selling Association, a strong link was found between the strength of a salesperson's personal relationships and his or her success as a salesperson.

Unfortunately, staff turnover in direct selling is high (although not necessarily higher than some standard retail environments) and when people leave they often take with them the relationships they had with their customers. Many companies counteract this by using database technology, not only to support their salespeople but also to provide a back-up sales contact for customers whose salesperson has left the business.

Power and control over the distribution channel

As consumer-product manufacturers well know, retailers have grown dramatically in size and power over the past decade. Many retail chains are attractive brands in their own right, with sophisticated approaches to marketing and with their own ranges of private label products or services. Now it is the manufacturers who must be willing to make concessions – such as trade discounts – for the privilege of being made available in popular outlets. In fact, many small consumer-product companies cannot meet the high-volume demand at these outlets and therefore cannot use them.

Powerful retailers will often decline the opportunity to sell a new product or brand because they can earn greater profits using their space to sell more established brands. To satisfy retailers that a product will be popular with consumers, companies often need to make a commitment to invest heavily in advertising. Many manufacturers are still asked to pay "slotting fees" to retailers, which are payments for guaranteed shelf space for a particular product. It is easy to see why many organizations – particularly start-up companies – do not have the funding, capacity or volume to warrant attention from major retailers. Direct selling is one way in which companies can circumvent the costs and barriers associated with distributing through these organizations.

When compared with managing relationships with retailers, the management of a direct-selling channel raises rather different issues of power and control. This is primarily because the scope of direct-sales management is in many ways much larger than that of retail sales management. A company that needs to influence a force of hundreds or thousands of salespeople requires different skills and systems from one that has to negotiate with 10 or 20 retail buyers. Furthermore, because retail salespeople work on-site, they can be monitored and managed much more closely than direct salespeople. These challenges are heightened in the case of network marketing direct-selling organizations, whose salespeople are independent contractors rather than formal company employees.

Many direct-sales companies seek to manage their sales forces by developing standardized training programs and holding sales meetings and training seminars. However, there remains a greater potential for variability in how a product is marketed and sold than is the case with other types of sales force. This can be a benefit because it allows direct salespeople to tailor the market offering more closely. But direct-selling companies are more vulnerable to the possibility that salespeople will market products in a way that does not support company strategy or is unethical.

The salesperson's view

Because direct-selling companies depend so heavily on their salespeople, these organizations can be successful only to the extent that becoming a direct salesperson is appealing. Fortunately, this holds considerable attraction for many individuals; in particular, it offers many of the advantages of launching one's own business but without many of the disadvantages.

Low start-up costs

Becoming a direct salesperson requires little or no capital. Because no shop or staff are needed, direct salespeople need not worry about rental or payroll. Furthermore, large inventories are not necessary. A new salesperson will usually buy no more than is required for personal trial and sales demonstrations.

In the UK the direct-selling code of business conduct forbids companies to ask for more than an initial £200 investment. Many start-up kits cost a fraction of that. Most direct-selling companies also provide their salespeople with marketing materials, many of which must be purchased, but generally at a cost that is lower than that of producing materials from scratch.

The drawback is that low start-up costs sometimes mean lower initial commitment. People often join direct-selling organizations not as a career choice but only to earn extra money over the short- or medium-term. Easy entry and low commitment mean easier exit. The result is high industry turnover. In most direct-selling businesses, maintaining a sales force of 1,000 means having to recruit between 1,000 and 1,300 new recruits annually – and for companies selling the most expensive products, that number can rise to 4,000.

Independence

Although teleworking and job sharing offer some flexibility for corporate employees, such progressive employment schemes often allow less personal freedom than direct selling. Direct salespeople can work either part-time or full-time. They can choose to work on days and at times that are most convenient for them. They are not supervised for most or all of their working day.

Direct selling is more likely than other types of business to attract individuals who are not committed to selling full-time. For example, many individuals use direct selling as a way to augment their full-time income. Others – for example, stay-at-home parents – pursue their direct-selling business as a part-time secondary activity.

The LBS/DSA study mentioned earlier found that, on average, network marketing direct salespeople commit only 10 to 15 hours a week to their business. The study also showed that the most successful individuals commit an average of 40 hours a week, but these individuals are relatively rare. These figures suggest that direct-selling companies must recruit many more individuals than other types of selling organization. If every new recruit works only half-time on the business, it will take two new recruits to match the market coverage and sales potential of a full-time salesperson.

Easy access to training and support

Almost by definition, individuals starting their own businesses must be extremely self-motivated. They must seek out their own training and advice. They must learn by trial and error, which means having to live with the consequences of mistakes. And they must often rely only on themselves to keep a positive attitude when times get tough.

While direct salespeople also must be self-motivated, they benefit from systems established by the company whose products they sell. Like those starting a well-known franchise, direct salespeople are often provided with company-sponsored training programs. They are also usually asked (at least at first) to follow pre-established systems for running a successful business, systems that "de-skill" the selling process.

In single-level direct-sales positions, people are formally supervised by a company employee. In multi-level organizations, salespeople must be introduced to the business via a sponsor, and because the sponsor benefits from new recruits' sales, he or she is strongly motivated to supervise, motivate and train them appropriately.

Salespeople – at least those in multi-level organizations – appear to take full advantage of the training opportunities available. In the LBS/DSA study, only 20 per cent of respondents did not attend a training session during the previous year and 40 per cent attended a training session at least every other month. Furthermore, these sessions pay off. The study showed a strong association between number of training hours and salesperson profitability.

Ironically, however, the existence of formalized supervision in direct-selling companies sometimes puts them in an awkward position. Starting any new business is always risky – direct-selling or otherwise. When independent entrepreneurs fail to overcome these risks, they often have no one but themselves to blame.

But in direct selling, an individual's poor performance can be attributed to a sponsor's poor supervision or a company's inadequate training. Thus, the supervisor and the company can become easy targets when a direct-selling business fails, even if the failure was caused by the direct salesperson's inability to sell, self-motivate, organize, or manage time.

Summary

Direct selling can be a lucrative strategy. In the US alone, companies using it shift goods worth over $18bn a year. Here **Kent Grayson** and **Richard Berry** outline some of the organizational options available, together with the potential benefits and drawbacks. Companies can either establish a "single-level" direct sales force, in which company managers supervise salespeople, or a "multi-level" force, in which local salespeople are responsible for recruitment and supervision. In turn, salespeople can adopt a "one-to-one" or a "one-to-many" approach to selling; which is best depends on the product and the individual salesperson. Direct selling offers companies the potential to build close customer relationships, and to exercise direct control over distribution, while salespeople gain some of the benefits associated with setting up a business but at much less risk.

SECTOR
MARKETING

8

Contributors

 **Patrick Barwise** is professor of management and marketing at London Business School, where he is also director of the Centre for Marketing and chairman of the Future Media Research Programme.

 **David Soberman** is assistant professor of marketing at INSEAD. His research interests include information marketing and the organization of distribution.

 **Sean Meehan** is professor of marketing and strategy at the International Institute for Management Development (IMD), Lausanne, Switzerland.

 **Jehoshua Eliashberg** is the S.S. Kresge Professor of Marketing at the Wharton School of the University of Pennsylvania.

 **James C. Anderson** is the William L. Ford Distinguished Professor of Marketing and Wholesale Distribution, and professor of behavioral science in management at the J.L. Kellogg Graduate School of Management, Northwestern University.

 **Philip Parker** is professor of marketing at INSEAD. His research focuses on marketing strategy, international management, pricing, new product diffusion and forecasting.

 **Gregory S. Carpenter** is associate professor of marketing at the J.L. Kellogg Graduate School of Management, Northwestern University. His research focuses on competitive marketing strategy.

Contents

Introduction

Understanding the theory is one thing; seeing it in practice is another. Here we look at how businesses in different sectors are meeting the challenges of marketing. Professional service firms, for example, have achieved considerable success less through discrete marketing campaigns than through a pervasive culture of customer focus. And companies in business-to-business markets are having to learn how to differentiate their products to avoid the "commodity trap." Other issues discussed in this module are forecasting in movie marketing, the problems of information overload for marketers, and the paradoxes of information pricing.

Professional service firms: unsung masters of marketing

by Patrick Barwise and Sean Meehan

The top accounting firms, law firms and management consultancies are among the best-managed businesses in the world. Examples of such professional service firms (PSFs) are the "Big Five" accountants, law firms such as Clifford Chance, Baker McKenzie and Skadden Arps and consulting firms such as McKinsey, Bain and the Boston Consulting Group. At the top end of their respective markets, these businesses are global, fast-growing and very profitable. Within the business community, they have built powerful brands based on strength in depth across many industry sectors and technical specialities.

Given their size and complexity it is hardly surprising that they are heavy users of the leading-edge thinking that is their stock-in-trade. As such, PSFs make an intriguing case study. What drives their success? What is marketing's role? Little hard evidence is available to address these questions. However, we find PSFs speak with one voice when explaining their success. Three sets of factors dominate these explanations:

- Integrity. You must be seen as valuing integrity above all else. However, we believe it is completely overrated in this context. Integrity is a given, not a point of differentiation.
- Strong methodologies, sector knowledge and technical expertise.
- People and infrastructure.

Two patterns stand out. First, most of the major players are working to very similar formulas. They have grown at broadly uniform rates in recent years on the back of a surging market. Aside from the impact of mergers and acquisitions – motivated by economies of scale and scope – relative competitive positions have remained fairly constant, despite much rhetoric to the contrary.

Second, marketing is seldom mentioned as contributing to success. In fact, "marketing's" reputation within these firms is fairly mixed. Our assessment, however, is that marketing in its broader sense has made a major contribution and that PSFs are masters of market orientation (*see* "Do you value customer value?," p. 23). That is, they have a "client first," highly competitive culture and are outstanding at sensing – and responding to – market signals. This apparent contradiction can be best understood in the context of the development of marketing practice in PSFs.

The marketing overhead

"Marketing" came into the vocabulary of PSFs along with the relaxation of regulations preventing advertising and unsolicited direct contact with non-clients. In the UK this was in the early 1980s. In response, many firms established a marketing services department that focused on communications (press relations,

The future winners

The winners in the new global market will be the PSFs that have been most able to leverage their market knowledge and strategic marketing expertise. They will have defined distinct and valuable positions in the minds of buyers in their target markets. They will have overcome deeply held prejudices about marketing's value and have addressed the three critical priorities: segmentation, organizational alignment and branding.

This, then, is the paradox about PSFs and marketing. They are still at an early stage in learning how to do some aspects of functional marketing, such as brand communications, that have long been associated with fast-moving consumer goods powerhouses such as Procter & Gamble, Mars and Nestlé. At the same time they are past masters at marketing in the broader sense – that is, in terms of closeness to customers, competitive orientation and responsiveness to market signals.

direct mail, advertising, seminars and conferences) and supporting the sales process (in particular, large bids).

Specialists – often from fast-moving consumer goods companies – were brought in to run these activities. Typically they would report to a fairly junior partner whose main qualifications for the job were a good track record for selling new work and a reputation as a creative thinker. These new resources were rarely if ever leveraged by senior management to influence strategic thinking. The prevailing attitude to "marketing" was at best tactical. Why?

The traditional PSF view is that its *raison d'être* is billable client service. Everything else is "overhead." Without any direct client service responsibilities the newly arrived marketing specialists were an "overhead." Marketing was to be carefully managed and all related expenses and new initiatives subjected to close scrutiny. In practice, the early marketing services departments added far more value than most traditionalists realized. At a minimum they reined in random and ill-planned expenditure which reflected two PSF syndromes: "pretty it up" and "let's do a brochure."

"Pretty it up" reflects some partners' expectations of marketing people – specialists who could turn dull-looking documents into something a little more glamorous. "Let's do a brochure" is the call to arms of a partner when given a marketing responsibility, say for an office or service line. Eager to show initiative, the partner reaches for what he or she believes to be low-hanging fruit. Unfortunately, these projects turn out to be difficult, time-consuming and politically sensitive. Worse still, the marketing objectives are often unclear and the initiative uncoordinated with other activities.

These attitudes made life frustrating for marketing pioneers. At the same time, they found among their new colleagues an extraordinary commitment to the voice of the market. Client interests were paramount and market sensing and responsiveness highly honed.

Client first

Working with PSFs, one cannot help but be impressed by their devotion to serving clients. We see three main drivers of this dominant value: close customer contact; measurement and reward systems; and leadership.

Customer contact

Seventy to 80 per cent of employees in a PSF spend most of their time solving client problems. Mostly this is in direct face-to-face contact with the client. Further, career progression – however far – does not mean less client contact. This contrasts with the situation in manufacturing, where most employees have no direct customer contact and senior managers spend only 15 per cent of their time with customers. Even in other service businesses, such as banks, airlines, architects and advertising agencies, the amount and quality of customer contact time are far lower than in PSFs.

Measurement and reward systems

Client contact drives PSFs' measurement and reward systems. Most veterans of PSFs can recall clearly their first exposure to the time sheet during their induction program. The time sheet is the key to the "time and billing" system. It allows the firm to track the extent to which anyone is "utilized" – that is, working on fee-paying assignments. In at least one firm the practice of publishing the utilization rates of the top and bottom 10 per cent at each level has had a defining effect on the culture.

A related measure is the "recovery rate," the extent to which the hours spent on an engagement can be turned into fees actually paid by the client. Its effect is to focus the engagement on delivering services highly valued by the client. In turn this encourages spending time with clients to really understand their business.

Leadership

These systems would count for nothing without leadership. Every chief executive has the opportunity to set the organization's priorities. As PSFs' leaders are almost always home-grown it is not surprising that "client first" rings out at every opportunity. Mike Cook, chairman of Deloitte & Touche in the US, is credited with popularizing the idea that "clients are gold and prospects are silver."

Superior market sensing

PSFs have thousands of partners and senior client service staff in the marketplace every day. At least 60 per cent of their time is spent working directly with clients. Another 15 per cent is spent at seminars and conferences interacting with clients, prospects, competitors and other industry figures. The rest is spent on management and training.

To illustrate how this level of market access can be leveraged we refer to a case from the mid-1980s, of a managing partner in a global consulting firm who asked a young marketing analyst to undertake a competitive review. Weeks later the analyst returned with profiles generated from press coverage, copies of bids and discussions with recent hires from the target competitors. In summary, the firm's competitors were global, growing fast, successful in winning new work, recruiting heavily and had many blue chip clients. But this was not news – the partner knew that those were the very characteristics that had made these firms his competitors.

To him, a competitor review should not describe competitors today but rather competitors' strategies. These, he argued, could be revealed by listening and watching carefully. He had wanted the analyst to leverage the thousands of hours a week that people were spending outside the firm. The partner subsequently sent a message that he expected people to find out as much as possible about four or five specific competitors over the next two months. They were to keep this in mind when talking to clients and non-clients in airport lounges, on flights and at industry meetings. He reasoned that many weak signals might, when pulled together, reveal an emergent strategy.

His experiment worked – partners started to listen much more actively to the market and were encouraged to share information about market events that could not yet be interpreted as trends. The partner exploited the latent resource all firms have by sensitizing people to the process of continually refining their own model of the market.

A global superleague?

One of the biggest drivers of growth among the larger PSFs has been the globalization of big business. It has created unprecedented demand for the delivery of a broad range of services worldwide. The initial response of dispatching staff on an ad hoc basis was inadequate, as was the establishment of multiple locations populated mainly by American and British professionals.

Globalization has required the PSFs to invest on a scale not contemplated in their earlier economic models. This has resulted in consolidation. The "Big Eight" accountants became the "Big Six" and then the "Big Five." In the world of consulting, what we know as Gemini today was created by bringing together the MAC Group, United Research and CAP Gemini Sogeti. In law, however, most fees are generated from work based on a domestic code. Although some consolidation has taken place within national markets, combinations such as that which led to the creation of Clifford Chance have generally been resisted.

Today there are five broadly based accountancy practices, about ten management consultancies and at most ten law firms that can credibly claim to be global. As the multidisciplinary practice takes hold, we may see further consolidation towards a "premier league" of perhaps a dozen global firms offering a combination of audit, tax, legal, strategic and information systems consulting. The challenges of holding such firms together will, given their diverse antecedents, be tremendous. Competing domestic and global pressures will reduce the independence of national partnerships (which have very fragmented client bases). This, we predict, will precipitate a further restructuring.

The main constraint is that a firm cannot be all things to all people. The market shakeout will therefore result in a superleague of high-powered firms which combine economies of scale and scope with a tight focus on service lines offered and market sectors served. The challenge facing PSFs now is how to adapt to face this future. This is likely to involve three classic tools of marketing strategy: segmentation, organizational alignment, and branding.

Segmentation

Sector or industry is the most common factor used by PSFs to segment the marketplace. This is in response to the increasing complexity of client business and to the fact that clients prize sector knowledge. However, aligning the practice has been problematic.

In the past, with agendas dominated by the interests of the national partnership, large PSFs felt obliged to have representation across all industry sectors. This, it was felt, would boost credibility. This philosophy has served the firms well so far but may be incompatible with the requirements of the global PSF. Other more creative bases have been used with varying degrees of success. Dividing the market by company ownership, size and growth rate has proved a worthwhile predictor of the value a PSF can hope to add. So also is management's attitude, a characteristic exploited by Arthur Andersen in the mid-1980s.

Andersen's research showed that it was seen as (among other things) innovative, creative and efficient. However, it was also seen as pushy, aggressive and arrogant. Andersen decided that these negatives should not be hidden: they were a valid part of its personality that might be valued by the younger, more entrepreneurial, high-growth companies it really wanted to do business with. Subsequent research confirmed that such companies would associate such values with dynamism, confidence and capability.

Organizational alignment

The traditional PSF was structured along service lines (for example, audit, tax, asset valuation). The realignment to the market has been evolutionary. At first firms created special interest groups (SIGs) comprised of professionals from each division. SIGs were responsible for targeting companies involved in specific sectors. SIGs initially focused on publishing newsletters, presenting seminars on topical subjects and (alas) producing brochures.

The next phase was to reorganize within divisions to reflect the firm's sectoral strengths and ambitions. The divisions were subdivided into groups dealing with highly specific sectors (for example, financial services). This forced individuals to specialize – to give up clients outside the sector. The new organization was a matrix defined by the divisional (for example, tax) and sectoral axes. The dominant axis was still the division and this reduced the impact of the reorientation.

The most recent phase has been the empowerment of the matrix's sectoral axis, supported by increasing investment in infrastructure and "knowledge manage-ment" to ensure that organizational learning is exploited efficiently. This last phase is clearly required by PSFs with global ambitions. Critical mass is no longer an issue – on a global basis these larger firms will have a sufficiently strong practice to serve the global players in the main sectors. As the economic demands of national partnership are unlikely to optimize the investments in products, services and people required to serve global clients, many PSFs serious about being global have begun the difficult transition to financial integration of their practices.

Branding

Although measuring brand value has proved difficult and controversial, it is undeniable that a brand that clearly positions a product, service, or firm in the minds of the target audience is a significant source of advantage. Volvo, Coca-Cola, Heinz, Levis, Marlboro, McDonald's and Nike are examples of brands that are clearly positioned relative to their competitors.

Owing mainly to the intangibility of the services provided and the difficulty clients have in comparing offers in advance of delivery, PSFs have generally found it hard to achieve distinctive brand positioning. An important exception is McKinsey, which owes its premier position in the market to the foresight of its founders – they established a new category and, using law firms as a model, taught corporate America what management consulting was all about. The rest became "me toos."

In accounting, the Big Five as a group are a megabrand clearly distinguished from all others. But within the Big Five, despite extensive advertising, the market finds it hard to distinguish between firms. One view is that efforts to create clearly positioned brands have failed because of the diversity of services offered and sectors served. As long as firms continue to serve many distinct segments, it is hard to fashion a positioning with meaning for buyers in these disparate markets. In contrast, value-based consultants Marakon, who advise companies like Coca Cola, Dow Chemical, Nordstrom, Boots and Lloyds TSB, have avoided this trap by staying focused on their expertise; they are only known for one thing. This strategy works: last year Marakon's revenues per consultant were tied with market leader McKinsey.

Despite the difficulty of establishing a differential positioning, brands are already crucial in PSFs (as in other services) for communicating quality and credibility. Clients are more likely to buy services from a well-known firm and will pay a premium to do so. Also, the top firms' brand names are crucial in recruitment: MBA students will almost invariably join the most prestigious consultancy if they have a choice.

When the next wave of restructuring is complete, brands may be even more important in signaling a firm's capabilities. The major PSF names may become umbrella brands, with increasing emphasis on subbrands serving distinct sectors. The challenge will be to ensure that the subbrands carry some core values that connote the umbrella brand.

However great these challenges, we must not underestimate the ability of PSFs to overcome them. In the words of *Chicago Tribune* journalists James O'Shea and Charles Madigan, authors of a recent warts-and-all book about the top consulting firms, "The greatest attribute of the American management consulting industry is its ability to market itself."

Summary

The world's leading professional service firms – such as PricewaterhouseCoopers, McKinsey and Clifford Chance – are highly profitable, growing fast and have powerful brands. So what part has marketing played in their success? According to **Sean Meehan** and **Patrick Barwise**, such firms have benefited less from the efforts of their marketing departments than from a pervasive culture of customer focus. These businesses are highly responsive to their customers and acutely sensitive to the market. The authors also discuss the likely impact of globalization on the main players in the professional service market.

Suggested further reading

Maister, D.H. (1997) *True Professionalism: The Courage to Care About Your People, Your Clients, and Your Career*, Simon & Schuster, New York.

O'Shea, J. and Madigan, C. (1997) *Dangerous Company: The Consulting Powerhouses and the Businesses They Save and Ruin*, Times Books (US) and Nicholas Brealey (UK).

Quinlan, F.H. (1998) "Carving out a niche is key," *The Times*, August 6.

Spar, D.L. (1997) "Lawyers Abroad: The Internationalization of Legal Practice," *California Management Review* 39 (3).

Escaping the commodity trap in business markets

by James C. Anderson and Gregory S. Carpenter

In many business markets, customers are perceiving fewer and fewer differences among competitors' offerings. The main reasons for this are the quality management movement in production and the greater availability of comparable alternatives from international sources. As a result, customers are making an increasing number of purchase decisions on the basis of price alone – the definition of a commodity market. They are pressuring suppliers to reduce their prices and provide additional price discounts. In industry after industry, suppliers are finding that although their sales revenues are growing, it is often at the expense of profitability. This article will explain how suppliers can forestall or reverse this trend.

Suppliers often conclude that they are in a commodity business simply because they think narrowly about the core product or service. The personal computer, hospital supplies or letter of credit that the customer purchases may be nearly or exactly the same across suppliers. But the market offerings that companies purchase are typically more than just the core product or service. They contain supplementary services, programs and systems that enhance the value of the core product or service and that provide additional value to customers.

Before concluding that they are in a commodity business, suppliers need to look more closely at market and internal data to determine exactly what differences there are between their offerings and their competitors'. Specifically, they should estimate the value that customers receive, validate their pricing and estimate their share of customers' business.

Estimate the value that customers receive

Value is the worth in monetary terms of the technical, economic, service and social benefits a company receives in exchange for the price it pays. It is always assessed within some context; typically it is a comparison of an offering's value with what the customer is currently using or with the next best supplier's offering.

To estimate the value that a customer receives, the supplier gathers comprehensive data on how its offering adds value or reduces costs in the customer's application. At the same time, suppliers should investigate how much changes in their market offerings would be worth to customers. They should also weigh service and social benefits, which can be significant sources of value.

Consider, for example, safety glasses. These provide the technical benefit of protecting workers' eyes from infrared and ultraviolet light and foreign substances. They provide the economic benefit of fewer lost days due to injuries and lower insurance premiums. To obtain these benefits, workers must wear the glasses; however, some younger workers feel that the glasses make them look "dorkish" and hence do not wear them when they should. Taking a more comprehensive view of value, Dalloz Safety Products has designed a line of safety glasses that look like designer sunglasses. They have contoured wraparound frames that come in a variety of colours, with lenses in a selection of tints. Since workers actually enjoy wearing such stylish protective eyewear, workplace compliance is no longer a problem.

Validate market pricing

Understanding competitors' prices is often difficult in business markets because of problems in determining comparability. A supplier should investigate what supplementary services are included in a competitor's price. Unfortunately it may be in the customer's interest to dissemble about a competitor's pricing and offering. An additional difficulty is the increasing use of a variety of off-invoice discounts, such as year-end rebates or bonuses.

Suppliers must gather data from the field on the range of prices that customers are paying for market offerings. They should also seek out disconfirming as well as confirming evidence on competitors' pricing moves. For example, if a salesperson reports that a competitor has cut the price of its market offering, a supplier should seek not only other instances of price cutting but cases where the competitor did not reduce the price of its offering. Such data will provide a finer-grained understanding of variations in competitor pricing.

A supplier must also gather data about its own prices. Off-invoice rebates or allowances, whose size may depend on the amount of business that the customer has done with the supplier during the quarter or year, make it difficult for a supplier to know at the time exactly how much it is gaining from a given transaction. Monitoring transaction prices enables a supplier to learn the extent to which exceptions are being made to pricing policy. One supplier discovered that 67 per cent of its business was done on the basis of non-policy requests – transaction pricing that deviated significantly from established pricing policy.

Estimate share of customers' business

What percentage of a customer's total purchase requirements for a particular product or service does a supplier obtain? Although most companies in business markets have some estimate of their market share, far fewer have estimates of their share of each customer's business in the markets they serve. Yet "share of customer's business" is much more diagnostic in that it pinpoints accounts that see the supplier's offering as superior to competitors' and suggests sources of differentiation.

Suppose that a supplier has a 20 per cent market share. It is unlikely that each customer in the market is purchasing 20 per cent of its requirement from the supplier. Rather, some customers are purchasing nothing from the supplier whereas others are purchasing more than 20 per cent of their requirements. What differentiates large-share customers from minor-share customers and what sources of differentiation would be possible if the customer were to give the supplier a share of 100 per cent?

Sources of differentiation

In business markets where the core product or service is seen as a commodity, it may be extremely costly or difficult to differentiate it in a way that customers would perceive as significant. But by considering more broadly how they might deliver value to customers, suppliers can identify significant sources of differentiation. Some valuable strategies are discussed below.

Create knowledge banks

A supplier can search for knowledge that would be valuable for customers to have,

A gradual process

Just as differentiated offerings did not become commodities overnight, suppliers cannot rebuild commodity offerings into differentiated offerings overnight. So our emphasis has been on changes that, over time, will reduce the amount of their business done solely on the basis of price. We recognize that price will be likely to remain important to customers but the changes we have discussed should decrease the emphasis that customers place on it.

Value assessment provides a deep understanding of customer requirements and preferences, and what it is worth for suppliers to fulfil them. Superior knowledge of value

also provides suppliers with a means to get an equitable return for their efforts and to judge to what extent they are getting such a return.

One senior manager we spoke to during our research suggested that a good motive for rebuilding differentiation is that there is no fun to be had in selling only on price. When there is market pressure on price, his business unit tries to respond creatively by demonstrating that it has something different to offer, something that provides better value than competitors' offerings.

So why not have some profitable fun?

yet is difficult for customers to acquire by themselves. An example is how the customer's ways of doing things compare with those of competitors. Allegiance Healthcare, a leading distributor of hospital supplies, has built a best-practice database from the experiences of 100 leading hospitals. The database details the activities performed and resources consumed in each of 30 procedures that together account for 80 per cent of the hospitals' surgical operations. Armed with the information on the database, Allegiance's clinical consultants can work with customers to identify deviations from best practice in order to reduce costs and improve productivity.

Build leveraging expertise

A supplier can search for problems that a number of customers experience, with a view to investing in expertise that could be used to provide solutions. In doing so, it should be able to provide superior solutions to customer problems and differentiate itself from competitors.

GLS Enterprises, a distributor of composite materials and elastomers, recognized that it could leverage its expertise in environmental, health and safety regulatory compliance as a value-adding service for its customers, which are mostly small and medium-sized companies. GLS monitors the Federal Register and writes bulletins alerting customers to regulatory changes and reminding them of existing standards. It supplies a regulatory compliance manual, audits compliance at customers' sites and helps smaller customers to prepare their annual toxic chemical release inventories and air emissions statements. Without GLS's assistance, these customers would find it difficult and costly to keep up with regulatory changes. Senior managers welcome GLS's support, because failure to comply with regulations can lead to criminal prosecution.

When corporate customers buy personal computers (PCs), they often want to install software that is specific to their companies, in addition to software from companies such as Microsoft. To do this typically takes an hour or two, has a total cost of between $200 and $300 and is a bother to both the user and the company's PC support staff. Dell Computer recognized that it could build expertise that would enable it to put an end to this costly nuisance. It created a high-speed, 100-megabit

Ethernet at its factory that can instantly download a tailored mix of software onto major customers' computers.

Change the customer's frame of reference

Customers that focus on the core product or service tend to see price reductions rather than total cost as the way that suppliers set themselves apart from one another. Suppliers that can change the customer's frame of reference to total cost have greater opportunities to add value, reduce costs and differentiate themselves. As an example, Boeing has 100,000 Dell PCs. Dell has 30 employees on site at Boeing, who work closely with Boeing managers in configuring their network. The Dell personnel are regarded more as Boeings' PC department than as a PC vendor.

In exchange for all of a customer's business, suppliers sometimes are able to change how they do business with the customer. For example, a coatings supplier was willing to put a technician on site to oversee the painting process and to quote a price per coated object rather than the customary price per litre of coating.

Selectively work together in ways that align business interests and goals

Often the customer and supplier have to work together to produce superior outcomes. Collaborative risk- and gain-sharing agreements are possible arrangements. In these, the supplier works with the customer to improve the customer's performance and, while exposing itself to potential losses, receives an agreed-upon share of any gains.

Allegiance is a company that uses such agreements. Its managers believe that Allegiance's clinical consultants can help the typical hospital to reduce operating costs by about 20 per cent. Often these savings come in the form of improved supply management, product standardization and increased product utilization. But the more efficient a hospital becomes in its use of supplies, the fewer the products and services it purchases from Allegiance. Rather than promoting the wasteful use of supplies, Allegiance is willing to trade its expertise for an equitable share of cost savings. Thus it proposes risk-sharing, gain-sharing agreements with its strategic hospital customers.

Once an agreement is signed, Allegiance puts its consultant on site to work on improving the customer's whole supply management process. At the end of the first year, cost savings are audited. The hospital and Allegiance split the savings 50:50. Each year thereafter the hospital gains a greater portion of the savings. On the risk side, Allegiance must not only keep the hospital's costs from rising above the baseline established from the previous year, it also needs to discover cost savings great enough to cover the expense of participation, which is substantial.

Construct flexible market offerings

No matter how precisely a supplier segments a market, some residual variation in the requirements of segment members will remain. Even though customers within a segment may be essentially the same in some of their requirements, they remain different in others.

In the past, suppliers have either ignored or been unable to deal with this. They have chosen instead to provide offerings consisting of "standard" bundles of products and services designed to meet the needs of the "average" customer within each segment. Worse, in many instances suppliers have provided the same "vanilla" offering across all segments. As a result, some customers have paid for services they did not need, while others have not had the depth of service they required, even if willing to pay extra.

Rather than ignore residual variation, perceptive suppliers take advantage of it by building flexibility into their market offerings. They do so by first constructing "naked solutions" for each market segment – the bare minimum of products and services that all segment members uniformly value. Importantly, they are sold at the lowest profitable price. In turn, naked solutions are wrapped with options that are offered separately for segment members that value them.

The return on differential value

Rebuilding differentiation in a commodity offering does suppliers no good if they cannot obtain an equitable return on the value provided. However, this does not necessarily mean that they have to charge more. Gaining a greater share of customers' business and "co-operative pricing" provide greater profitability by lowering a supplier's costs. Small price premiums or "pocket price" improvements and value-adding services offered for a fee allow suppliers to realize a higher price.

A greater share of customers' business

Suppliers might seek to have customers give them a greater share of their business as a reward for providing superior value. After all, customers must buy their requirements from someone, so why not from a few suppliers or even just one? This is especially effective when the supplier can offer some compelling benefit in return – as in the previous coatings example – and can alleviate concerns about continuity of supply and single sourcing.

Co-operative pricing

When customers simply demand lower prices, a supplier that wants to do business with them needs to work with them to find ways to reduce it. With "co-operative pricing," the supplier and customer work together to detect "minimum" performance specifications that are unnecessarily restrictive in the customer's application and that can be relaxed in exchange for a lower price. Thus two companies might trade longer lead times, fewer product variations, fewer delivery locations or less technical support for reduced prices. In each case, the supplier may retain part of the cost savings as incremental profit and pass the remainder on to the customer as an incentive to change.

Small price premiums or "pocket price" improvements

On occasion, suppliers can realize small price premiums for differentiation initiatives. A pigment supplier, for example, was able to get a premium of half a cent per pound for providing its pigment in slurry form rather than in 50-pound dry bags. This change made it easier for coatings customers to handle the pigment, since it was already liquid and there were no dust hazards for workers or bags to dispose of.

Suppliers can also improve profitability by monitoring transaction pricing, which involves realizing the greatest net price for each individual order. To monitor transaction prices, the supplier first constructs a "pocket price waterfall," which refers to all terms, discounts, rebates, incentives and bonuses that a customer receives for a given transaction. These waterfall elements are then subtracted from the list price to produce a "pocket price," which refers to the revenue the supplier actually realizes from the transaction.

Analysis of pocket prices reveals which customer segments receive the greatest discounts, how willing customers are to pay, and whether salespeople are exercising their pricing authority appropriately. Reducing the number of pricing exceptions can dramatically improve profitability. McKinsey consultants Marn and Rosiello contend that a 1 per cent improvement in price, assuming no volume loss, increases a supplier firm's operating profits by 11 per cent.

Value-adding services, for a fee

Many supplier managers believe that to differentiate themselves from competitors, they must give away value-adding services for free. This is not necessarily the case, provided that they can persuasively demonstrate that their service offers substantially greater value than competitors' services. For example, although Dell estimates that loading a tailored mix of customer software at the factory saves the customer $200 to $300 per PC, it charges only $15 to $20 for the service.

Summary

Business-to-business markets are increasingly operating as commodity markets. That is, customers perceive few differences among suppliers' offerings and hence make purchase decisions solely on the basis of price. This puts severe pressure on suppliers to cut prices, which harms profits. According to **James Anderson** and **Gregory Carpenter**, a supplier's smartest response is to differentiate its offerings in a way that customers will value. Possible strategies are to build knowledge or expertise that can be used to provide solutions for customers (perhaps via partnering arrangements), to persuade customers to focus less on the core product's price than on overall value, and to ensure that products and services are flexible. The authors also explain how suppliers can obtain an equitable return for providing such superior value.

Suggested further reading

Anderson, J.C. and Narus, J.A. (1995) "Capturing the value of supplementary services," *Harvard Business Review*, 75–83, January–February (On the virtues of flexible market offerings.)

Anderson, J.C. and Narus, J.A. (1999) *Business Market Management: Understanding, Creating, and Delivering Value*, Prentice Hall, Upper Saddle River, NJ. (A thorough discussion of value and its assessment.)

Carpenter, G.S., Glazer, R. and Nakamoto, K. (1997) *Readings on Market Driving Strategies: Towards a New Concept of Competitive Advantage*, Addison-Wesley, Reading, MA.

Gleckman, H. with McWilliams, G. (1997) "Ask and it shall be discounted," *Business Week*, October 6, 116, 118. (On the way that customers are pressuring suppliers to reduce prices and provide additional price discounts.)

Magretta, J. (1998) "The power of virtual integration: an interview with Dell Computer's Michael Dell," *Harvard Business Review*, 72–84, March–April (Describes Dell's experience of building leveraging expertise.)

Marn, M.V. and Rosiello, R.L. (1992) "Managing price, gaining profit," *Harvard Business Review*, 84–94, September–October.

Information overload and the new dealers in data

by David Soberman

"To boldly go where no man has gone before" (Gene Roddenberry, 1966)

It is hard to imagine better words to describe the effect that the information revolution will have on the life of marketers than those of Gene Roddenberry, the creator of *Star Trek*.

Marketing has always been the art of magically combining knowledge about customers and competitors with corporate capabilities to generate profit. While the information revolution has certainly increased our ability to collect, store and even sort information, the major implication for marketers of information technology is its ability to convert information into knowledge.

Farewell to gut feel?

In many industries, a critical ingredient for success has always been experience, and knowledge of how the market works and responds to different initiatives. Designing promotional programs requires industry-specific knowledge about the trade and how consumers respond to various incentives. If one wanted to name the process by which such knowledge is obtained, "trial and error" might be most appropriate. This approach, while not providing a basis for an industry theory, certainly provides managers with distinct lists of "should" and "should not" strategies.

The situation faced by managers of companies in new industries is quite different. Frequently, there is little knowledge within the company as to how the market will respond to initiatives. In addition, some mature industries – such as airlines and the music business – have undergone radical changes as a result of technological innovation. In such circumstances, it can be quite risky to base decisions on past experience. Managers in both of these situations frequently used to depend on "gut feel." They would extrapolate experiences from other industries or other markets and make educated guesses about the likely evolution of new or fast-changing industries.

However, with the information revolution, this approach is no longer good enough: the age of gut feel has passed. Marketers have a plethora of tools at their disposal to obtain a detailed picture of market development, tools that go right to end-consumers to get the answers. These tools include market research techniques such as multi-dimensional scaling, factor and cluster analysis and conjoint analysis (some of these are described in "Forecasting: principles that work," (*see* p. 49). Such tools have been around in some form or another since the 1960s; why then were managers ignoring them and continuing to use gut feel through the 1980s? The answer lies in economics.

Before the availability of the personal computer and user-friendly software packages, these procedures, while easy to describe, were very difficult and expensive to use. Only sophisticated market research companies with access to mainframe computers could provide the required services for companies tackling a new or changing product category. Thus, while these tools were used in industries with large marketing budgets, such as soft drinks, beer and tobacco, their penetration in small and medium-sized businesses was minimal.

Today, however, the personal computer (PC) and software for analyzing market research data have made many of these procedures relatively accessible and affordable. For example, a small industrial supplier can conduct a conjoint analysis of its customers cheaply and gain critical information on which to base decisions. Even when these procedures are contracted out to private market research companies their cost is a fraction of what it was several years ago. As a result, the bar has been raised for everyone in competitive industries. A company in a new or changing industry cannot afford to depend on gut feel in order to survive and prosper. Some degree of understanding and application of modern market research techniques is a *sine qua non* for success.

How much is too much?

While information has become vastly more important, it is also true that managers are receiving much more of it (even if it is for reasons as simple as receiving data on warehouse shipments on a daily rather than a monthly basis). In fact, many managers will tell you that the biggest problem that they have is information overload. A recent IBM paper estimated that in the oil and gas industry, 60 per cent of professional time was spent on clerical activities such as locating, collecting, collating and manipulating information rather than analyzing it.

On the one hand, this development seems to go against conventional wisdom, which dictates that the more information you have about a given situation, the more likely you are to make good decisions. But then again, as pointed out by Herb Simon in 1951, an innate characteristic of the human mind is its limited capacity for processing information, a characteristic which he termed "bounded rationality."

Essentially, this theory suggests that when people have too much information to process, they will stop processing and apply rules of thumb, or heuristics, to make decisions. This suggests that when there is too much information we can observe a regression to gut feel and rules of thumb that have always worked before. In other words, unless a company learns to limit and filter the information acquired on its market, performance and competitive activities, it runs a risk of reducing rather than improving its responsiveness and profitability. This area is sensitive and a company must pay strict attention to information flow given its limited managerial resources.

The pattern of information flow is neither natural nor positive. If it is not controlled, it can and often will flow in a manner that causes damage. There are four basic steps that a company needs to take to ensure that marketing managers have information that is sufficient, relevant and diagnostic for the decisions that they need to make:

1 A company must clearly define the responsibilities of each manager in its marketing department. Through discussion with each manager, it must isolate the three or four questions that need to be answered to make effective decisions. In the past, companies could allow marketing managers to develop these questions more independently since the information-gathering stage was less critical. Today, marketing information comes from all parts of the company so that total company involvement is now important in identifying key questions.

2 The marketing department must identify the kind of information necessary to help answer the manager's questions. Some information may be currently available within the company while other information may require the assistance and input of a market research company.

3 The cost of obtaining this information must be determined in order to decide whether or not a research project can be pursued. The cost must be balanced against the expected gain to be realized through improved decision making. When the cost exceeds the benefit, the manager must return to Step 2 to see if there are cheaper sources.

4 The benefits of information for decision making need to be evaluated through regular feedback and performance measurement. Quite simply, one needs to conduct regular audits of the marketing department to verify that expenditures on market research and analysis are justified.

The key point here is that to be successful in managing products or services of any kind, the marketing department needs to develop an information management strategy that flows from the questions it wants answered. If the marketing department (and the company as a whole) does not take control of information gathering and information flow, the process has the potential to sap scarce managerial resources as well as to obscure the information that is truly important.

To avoid the trap of information overload, there are three simple rules for a marketing department:

1 Just because the department has always conducted a certain kind of study or research does not mean it should be repeated each year without question (managers need to confirm that they are in fact using the information to make their decisions).

2 Managers need not read reports or analyze data simply because it comes across their desk. Managers tend to believe that they should read anything that comes across their desk because it must concern them. Most reports do, in fact, concern them; but, in this day and age, to read and review all information that affects one's business is a recipe for disaster. The problem is that there is an enormous amount of information flowing around most organizations. A manager who reads everything that he or she receives will find that it consumes an enormous chunk of the average working day. One of a marketing manager's key responsibilities is to manage the flow of information and focus on the things that are important.

3 Marketing managers need to orient the rest of the organization to provide information that is useful for decision making. Accordingly, staff in production, research and development and sales must have an appreciation of what marketing is trying to do so that they can provide the information needed.

The model marketer

Given the picture sketched above, what kind of people should we expect to see working in a marketing department? Marketing needs people with the audacity to cancel reports that are no longer used. This may be difficult because other members of the organization may have a vested interest in the continued production or purchase of certain information. Marketing people also need to have the ability to sort through mounds of information, find what is important and discard the rest. Finally, they should be able to sell an information "vision" to the rest of the company.

Traditionally, many businesses staffed their marketing department with salespeople who had shown strong planning potential, and people from advertising agencies. Such people generally knew the business well and had the ability to sell a "vision" to the rest of the company. However, few of them had strong information analysis skills. Many large companies now staff their marketing departments with business administration graduates who, in general, are taught to think strategically, to take action (so they probably would not have difficulty in cancelling a superfluous report) and to sell their ideas.

Nevertheless, few business administration programs recognize the importance of information analysis; students now spend much more time in marketing courses discussing cases rather than conducting analysis. It is becoming ever more important for students to be heavily exposed to information and data so they can develop the skills necessary to evaluate information for its usefulness against specific criteria.

Dealers in data

The information revolution has greatly enhanced opportunities for marketing companies. It is enabling them to understand their consumers better, to deliver better products or services to them and to monitor their satisfaction after purchase. The benchmark for excellent performance in most categories is higher now than it ever was before. The abundance of information has created opportunities for new kinds of services and activities that were not possible in the past.

Nevertheless, it is not possible for all companies with active marketing departments to capitalize on all the opportunities provided by information technology. It is mainly independent companies or entrepreneurs that have capitalized on the opportunities afforded by information and technology. As a result, the sector of companies that sell information products to other businesses has expanded rapidly.

Until the late 1970s, there were two main categories of marketing information companies. The first comprised companies that sold syndicated survey data, such as A.C. Nielsen and IRI. These companies collected data through retail audits or household surveys, prepared and analyzed it and sold it to manufacturers and service providers. This activity became very lucrative because in many industries it was the only way to obtain information on competitive performance on a regular basis. It should be noted that retail audit information is now collected through scanner data and therefore is much more accurate than it was in the past. In addition, some households are now "wired," enabling researchers to analyze the correlation between retail activity and household purchasing behavior with far more precision than before.

The second category consisted of market research companies that conducted research on a project-by-project basis for large manufacturers. The three main types of research performed by these companies were focus group research, in-depth interviews, and surveys.

The first two types of research provide mainly qualitative information that is useful for investigating problems that are ill-defined or for testing and developing creative advertising. These methods remain indispensable today because feedback is obtained quickly and is relatively cheap. None the less, the information provided is not quantitative and is relatively unhelpful for making important financial decisions.

The third type of research is quantitative and can be used to assist in making financial decisions. However, it is expensive to conduct and requires considerable time to execute – statistically relevant results cannot be obtained quickly, regardless of whether the survey is carried out door-to-door, in the street, by telephone or by mail. None the less, this type of research remains very important.

Recently, opportunities for new market research services have appeared as a result of the information revolution. The companies that offer these services are the "new kids on the block."

The two main areas of rapid growth are:

1 the collection of massive databases on loyal customers; generally these are drawn from frequent flyer/buyer/user programs
2 the active collection of data on people through general surveys, electronic inquiries, or even internet activity that can subsequently be used to implement marketing activities.

There has been a large increase in the number of businesses and products that offer frequent-consumer programs. Many of these programs, such as the ones operated by airlines, are wholly owned and operated by individual companies. There are also schemes, such as air miles, that are run by independent operators and that offer bonuses for purchasers across a large number of categories.

These programs give suppliers an opportunity to tailor offers to individual customers and to increase the value that a customer obtains by being loyal. However, it is difficult to determine whether they have been effective in increasing profits for marketers. On the one hand, loyalty programs are designed to make customers more faithful, thus allowing suppliers to increase prices (net of loyalty program benefits). On the other, the competitive effects of loyalty programs may cancel each other out and simply increase overall operating costs. This outcome is most common when customers have the opportunity to belong to several schemes. It would be interesting to ask airline executives today whether their frequent flyer programs are truly generating the benefits that were envisioned when they were created in the early 1980s.

The second area where there has been a huge increase in activity is in the collection of consumer information by electronic means. In some cases, independent entrepreneurs actively gather information; in others, companies leverage information that they accumulate as a by-product of other activities. One of the most successful "new kids" is Icom, a Canadian database marketing company (*see* boxed extract below).

These market researchers provide businesses with effective methods for converting marketing dollars into trial for new brands and into loyalty and volume-building programs for established brands. The primary benefit of new information-based marketing services is better targeting and less money spent on people who are already users or who are not interested in the category.

This approach has significant implications for marketers. Activities that used to be associated with substantial wastage and poor response, such as couponing, can become much more attractive with better targeting. Companies may shift funds away from mass-marketing activities due to the higher impact that direct marketing activity can deliver. The key to success in the future, even for a packaged goods producer, may be knowing the name of each of one's customers and engaging in a regular dialog about his or her needs.

How Icom taps the power of data

One company that is thriving on the information explosion is Icom Information and Communications, based in Canada. Serving clients such as Procter & Gamble, Johnson & Johnson, Nestlé, Unilever, Lexus and Reader's Digest, Icom epitomizes target marketing in the information age.

The company aims to find innovative and cost-effective ways to target individual consumers and has become one of the fastest-growing database marketing companies in North America. It collects detailed product usage and purchase profiles from more than 20m households through proprietary census-scale surveys and houses the resulting mass of individual consumer information in a specialized database using advanced data scanning, interpretation and computer storage technologies. This information is then used to construct a range of data and communications products for marketers. The company also provides database design services.

To help marketers "narrowcast" a range of messages, samples and coupons to relevant segments of the database, Icom has automated the process of syndicated mailings, where the contents of each mailing are tailored to the habits of each target household. According to Alan Levine, Icom's co-chief executive, information technology has allowed the company "to create the economies of scale associated with traditional mass marketing while achieving the persuasiveness of one-to-one selling."

But individualized mailing is only one of the possibilities created by the explosion in information-based marketing. Accordingly, Icom is working in a number of new areas. Its statisticians and programmers have developed a program that can track brand usage among consumer segments with specific media habits. The company is also developing a series of new information products that link consumer purchase habits to retailer-specific shopping behavior. The initial response to these products, says Levine, indicates that there is a substantial market.

Things to come

So with all the changes that have already occurred in marketing due to information technology, what can we expect in the future?

First, continued advances should be expected in terms of the types of information products that will be available to marketers. At present, most databases are used in isolation for different marketing initiatives. The linking of databases is still rare because of technical difficulties. As technology improves, this will become easier and more common. Linking a frequent buyer database with a syndicated mailing database (for example) would provide significant opportunities for marketers.

Second, there will be growth in the number of consumer-orientated information companies. At present, there are very few companies that offer consumers guidance on shopping and other activities – by pointing them towards the best prices or performance in the market, for example. For marketers, this development will intensify price competition when products offer equivalent performance. It may also bring about a quicker end for products that do not perform to industry standards.

Finally, many industries will be rationalized because of the increased competition resulting from advanced shopping technology. We need only think of the pressure placed on local bookstores by new internet competitors such as Amazon.com. New businesses will arise to build expertise in the specialized communication channels that are used to interact with consumers. For example, the distributor of the future may specialize in providing a range of products and services through the internet or via interactive shopping channels. Traditional companies such as Nestlé and Adidas will have to deal with these new distributors and exploit the opportunities they provide to reach a growing number of customers.

Summary

Advances in information technology are revolutionizing marketing. Where managers used to rely on "gut feel" to estimate the impact of new initiatives – and to avoid the cost of market research – now software enables them to analyze data cheaply. But the problem, says **David Soberman**, is information overload; this can be so overwhelming that managers revert to gut feel in order to cope. Marketers must therefore learn to say "no" to irrelevant information and must ensure that the rest of the organization knows exactly what information is needed. The author also discusses the rise of new types of market research companies.

Suggested further reading

"Engineering dimensions," Professional Engineers of Ontario, November/December 1997, 25–31. (The paper from IBM indicating the amount of time wasted by managers chasing information.)

A critical problem for movie marketers

by Jehoshua Eliashberg

With an average production cost of more than \$50m and associated average marketing costs of more than \$25m, a Hollywood film has to gross more than \$100m in the US simply to break even (that is, after giving cinemas their share of the revenue). One would therefore expect the film industry's marketing to be state-of-the-art, using the latest perspectives and practices. In the present author's view, however, it lags behind the consumer packaged goods industry and other businesses in some important respects.

In general, the industry has been reluctant to embrace the use of predictive techniques and decision support systems. Managers are skeptical of the ability of modern tools and models to predict audience response. Often they rely on judgment, historical cases and conventional wisdom. For example, one widely accepted piece of industry wisdom is that critics have the power strongly to affect box office receipts at the start of a movie's run. The argument is that when a film is newly released, viewers have virtually nothing else to go on when they decide whether to see it or not. Yet as we shall see later, the importance of critics lies elsewhere.

Marketing movies

As in many other industries, the key components in an effective movie marketing strategy are analysis, design and execution. Of these, the first is fundamental.

Analysis requires studios to segment and target the audience in new ways. Summer moviegoers, for example, are becoming older and more educated and accordingly require more serious and sophisticated types of movies. *Saving Private Ryan*, for instance, is believed by Steven Spielberg's DreamWorks company to have attracted people who had not been to the movies in years.

Viewing target audiences in terms of traditional demographic variables – such as age and gender – may lead to overly narrow and possibly misleading conclusions. Segmentation and targeting could be improved significantly by using "psychological" variables such as lifestyle, interests, personal and social aspirations and tendency to seek sensation.

Designing a positioning strategy based on such variables and executing it through appropriate media vehicles – television spots, the internet and cinema trailers, for example – has the potential to boost initial audiences significantly. Unfortunately, the movie industry underexploits this potential, in part because it focuses too much on the role of the critic at the film's launch.

The role of the critic

Moviegoers' behavior and their decision whether and when to attend a movie can be broken down, in principle, into two basic time intervals: the time it takes the moviegoer to decide to see a particular movie, and the time it takes him or her to act on that decision.

The first time interval can be influenced by word of mouth and – via an appropriate marketing strategy – by the studio. The second depends on factors such as how much free time the moviegoer has, the number of other films he or she wants to see, and whether the movie is on nearby. The role played by film critics in the decision-making process is less apparent.

The pattern of box office receipts, however, may indicate whether the critic should be seen as an "influencer" or a "predictor" of a film's performance. If critics were actually able to influence box office revenues, we would expect that influence to be most noticeable when a film opens. As more people see a film, the critic's influence should diminish because information from other sources becomes available. Word-of-mouth information from friends could dissuade someone from seeing a movie regardless of good reviews – or could persuade someone to see a film that has been panned. Thus *Hook* did well at the box office despite mostly negative reviews, while *Gettysburg*, a movie universally praised by critics, did not fare well.

The evidence we found is intriguing: reviews tend to be correlated with cumulative performance but not with opening box office revenues. Although it is impossible to disentangle causality and correlation completely, we can estimate the correlation between critics' reviews and box office performance for each week of a movie's life. We found that the impact of reviews is actually greater in the later weeks of a movie's run than in the opening weeks. Our findings therefore support the view that critics are predictors rather than influencers. Most studios, however, have a strong belief in the influencer model. Accordingly they sponsor screenings and make direct contact with reviewers in the hope of garnering good reviews. Film-makers tell horror stories about how films were dropped following bad reviews.

Strategic implications

Which of these models one subscribes to – the "influencer" or the "predictor" – has substantial implications for marketing. And the debate is not just of relevance to the film industry. After all, some companies spend a lot of time and money trying to sway opinion leaders.

If critics are influencers, a studio should use them as part of the marketing campaign. For example, if a studio expects a movie to receive mostly negative reviews, it will not want to offer previews. If, on the other hand, it anticipates positive reviews, it should schedule the preview immediately before the release to maximise the influence of the influencers.

A different approach is called for if critics are predictors. Studios should hold previews well in advance of the release. If the reviews are negative, studios should then have time to make changes to the film (by re-editing it or restoring cut scenes, for example) or to the marketing strategy (bypassing cinemas and releasing the film on video first, say). Positive reviews may have segmentation and positioning implications. Critics would, in effect, assist in determining the appropriate marketing budget and strategy for a film.

The influencer perspective suggests that quotations from critics should be used in advertisements for films. There are three reasons for this. First, the quotations persuade moviegoers to see the film. Second, they help publicists gain favor with critics, because each quote helps to boost the critic's reputation. Third, quoting may encourage some critics to make favorable comments to get self-publicity.

The predictor perspective suggests that quotations may be desirable but that advertising should focus on other information. It suggests that trying to influence critics does not provide significant benefits. Reviews can, however, provide valuable predictive diagnostics. Critics who broadcast to or write for a particular market segment might accurately predict a film's success or failure within that group. Correlating viewers' or readers' demographic and psychological variables with critics' reviews could enable studios to predict which groups or geographical areas will like a film.

As noted earlier, our data support the theory that critics are predictors rather than influencers at the aggregate box office level. This has managerial implications. First, trying to persuade film critics is a costly distraction; instead, management should focus on the film itself. Second, prescreenings should focus on critics who represent particular audience segments. Analysis of their responses will enable studios to segment target audiences more precisely and to position the movie correctly. In addition, better predictions of box-office performance will be obtained. With accurate predictive tools, studios may be able to fix a small problem before it becomes big.

Summary

One of the biggest challenges for marketers is the "experiential" product – one whose quality is hard for the consumer to assess without actually experiencing it. A sector that confronts this problem in particularly acute form is the film industry. Yet according to **Jehoshua Eliashberg**, Hollywood's marketing departments rely too much on questionable conventional wisdom. In particular, he argues, they tend to treat critics as influencers of a film's opening revenues, whereas research suggests that they should instead be regarded as predictors of its long-term performance.

Much of the information in this article first appeared in "Film critics: influencers or predictors" by J. Eliashberg and S. Shugan in the *Journal of Marketing* (April 1997). Other sources are listed at www.ftmastering.com

How is information priced?

by Philip Parker

Everyone seems to be talking about the "information age" and how knowledge is changing the nature of traditional products and services. According to an article in *Business Week* (November 7, 1994), for example, "with the dawn of the Information Economy, the traditional split [between goods and services] does not make sense."

But what exactly are information products and services? And do traditional competitive strategies apply to this industry? Recent research provides rather counter-intuitive answers: companies selling low-quality information can make the highest profits, whereas high-quality information sellers struggle to survive. For the low-quality sellers, textbook competitive strategy is simply inapplicable.

To clarify this conclusion, I shall first define what is meant by information products and services, then describe the structure of competition in information markets and summarize some case studies.

What is information?

In what follows, it is appropriate to think of a consumer who buys information to make a decision. Knowledge or information products take a variety of forms: industry reports, consulting services, educational programs and professional opinions given by medical, engineering, accounting, financial and legal professionals among others.

The information services industry also includes database services such as Dun & Bradstreet Business Information Reports and IMS International Sales Territory Reports and Consumer Reports. A doctor's recommendation to a patient to follow a particular treatment, like a strategy professor's recommendation to a company to enter a new market, are both information products.

By the early 1990s, the US Department of Commerce estimated that professional fees for information-orientated products and services reached over $375bn annually in the US alone. This multi-billion-dollar industry exists for one simple reason: information asymmetries. Consumers are uncertain and lack knowledge. They then shop for information suppliers who know more than they do and a transaction takes place. Knowledge, as it were, is tradable.

The structure of competition

Who makes the most money in information markets? Figure 1 summarizes the implications of a game-theoretic model proposed by Miklos Sarvary of Stanford University. There are two knowledge-sellers in the model. Two perceptional dimensions distinguish the two sellers: (1) the sellers' perspectives and (2) the quality of the information they provide.

Let us define these terms. What is a "perspective?" It is useful to think of two doctors: one is a homeopath, the other is a traditional general practitioner. A patient with a headache might visit the traditional doctor and explain his problem, and the doctor, after examination, might feel that the patient is stressed and should take a few days off work. The same patient might also visit the homeopath

The structure of information "competition"

	Different perspectives (sellers come from different "schools of thought")	Same perspective (sellers come from same "school of thought")
Low quality (high uncertainty; low reliability; low information accuracy)	**Highest profits** • Consumers buy from both sellers • Competitors sell **complements** • Low price competition	**Moderate profits** 1–2 reports purchased
High quality (high certainty; high reliability; high information accuracy)	**Moderate profits** 1–2 reports purchased	**Lowest profits** • Consumers buy from one seller • Competitors sell **substitutes** • Severe price competition

Figure 1

and explain his predicament, and the homeopath might also recommend that the patient take a few days off work. Despite the two doctors giving exactly the same advice, they are nevertheless seen as coming from two fundamentally different schools of thought. Perspective is not "what you know or say" but rather "your perceived methodology."

One key factor in describing competition in knowledge markets is the correlation in perspectives across sellers. Two homeopaths have similar perspectives – that is, their knowledge is perceived to be correlated. A homeopath and a traditional doctor have different perspectives – their knowledge is uncorrelated.

What is "quality?" Quality is related to the reliability or accuracy of the information being sold. High-quality information is extremely accurate. Low-quality information is inaccurate. Where does quality come from? It may come from the competence of the seller. In competitive markets, competence is unlikely to drive long-run quality since a company (for example, a consulting company) can always hire competent employees, or fire incompetent ones. A more interesting source of quality is the environment. Consider a company selling forecasts of car demand. A five-year forecast for China will be less accurate and less reliable than a five-year forecast for the UK. Similarly, consulting companies are more likely to provide low-quality forecasts for new product categories not because they are less competent than managers or other people but because the market for new products is highly uncertain.

Table 1 illustrates this for cellular telephones in the US. The forecasts were made in the mid-1980s for the year 1990 and beyond. The estimates vary from 430,000 to 40m subscribers. The actual size of the market by 1990 was 5.2m subscribers and no forecaster came close to this number. The prestigious companies that made these forecasts were no more incompetent than the others; they simply used different methodologies with different assumptions. The accuracy, reliability and quality of the information provided was none the less low.

Who makes money in knowledge markets?

Figure 1 reveals possible outcomes for two report-sellers facing a manager who might be willing to buy decision-making information. Consider the case when both sellers offer highly accurate information (such as industry statistics) and both come from exactly the same "school of thought" (both sellers are twins raised by the same

Cellular subscriber projections in the 1980s				
Source	Date of projection	Population included	Date projected for	Number of subscribers (m)
Yankee Group	1985	Total market	1990	0.43
Shoesteck Associates	1983	Urban pop.	Potential	0.53
Shoesteck Associates (a)	1987	n/a	1995	9–12
A.D. Little	1980	Total market	1990	1
A.D. Little (b)	1985	n/a	1994	3
Cellular Business Systems (c)	1985	n/a	1993	3.8
BCG	1985	Total likely	1990	1.2
Link Resources	1984	Total market	1990	1.4
EMG	1985	Total market	1990	1.8
Business Comm. Co. (d)	1985	n/a	1993	1.3
Lehman Brothers	1982	Top 90 markets	1989	2
Dean Witter	1982	Total market	1990	2.1
IRD	1980	Total market	Cellular	2.5
RRNA	1985	Total market	1990	2.6
Goldman Group (e)	1988	n/a	2000	9
DLJ	1985	Top 90 markets	1990	2.6
Leigh	1982	Urban pop.	1990	3
Arthur Andersen	1984	Total market	1990	7
AT&T (f)	1985	n/a	2000	30–40
		Actual market	**1990**	**5.2**

Sources: Telocator, February 1986, pp. 22–27; (a) Telephone Engineer and Management, July 1987; (b) Washington Business Journal, April 1 1985; (c) Charlotte NC News, June 17 1985; (d) New York Times, June 23 1985; (e) Cellular Business, January 1988; (f) Peoria Illinois Journal Star, May 26 1985.

Table 1

parents and both graduated from the same university, where they were room-mates). In this situation the manager will purchase from only one of the two sellers. The two will fiercely compete for this market. Prices will fall towards marginal costs and neither will be very profitable. Why? Because the two are selling perfect substitutes. *Profits are low for high-quality information-sellers.*

Now consider the case where the consumer is making a $100m investment decision in Indonesia. The market is highly uncertain. Forecasts will surely be inaccurate given the high levels of uncertainty (look again at the cellular telephone forecasts in Table 1).

One of the information-sellers has developed a complicated econometric model of the industry and is selling demand forecasts in the form of an industry report. The other company is also selling demand forecasts in a report but it has a socio-political perspective: it emphasizes that it forecasts demand using a Delphi procedure, interviewing politicians and analyzing sociological trends in Indonesia.

How many reports does the manager buy now? It turns out that the manager will buy both reports and the two sellers will charge near-monopoly prices. *Companies selling low-quality information make high profits!* Again, low quality does not arise from incompetence. The two companies may, in fact, employ the most competent people on the planet. But their high profits are driven by the fact that the decision-maker is facing great uncertainty and the sellers offer different perspectives. The products they are selling are complements.

The intuition behind Figure 1 is the following. Consumers facing important decisions may find it beneficial to purchase from several information-suppliers. This is most likely to occur when the reliability of information is low and the sources of information are independent from each other. Information products in this case tend to be complements and, as a result, competition between sellers is mild. In the opposite case, information is reliable and/or sellers' sources are highly correlated. Consumers are satisfied after consulting a single source. In this scenario, information products are substitutes and sellers tend to undercut each other's prices to attract consumers.

Implications

Fundamentally, what is the difference between toothpaste and information? In toothpaste markets, consumers do not buy two brands, squeeze both tubes onto the same brush and then brush their teeth. But in high-value-added knowledge markets something of the sort actually happens. The final product is a blend of multiple inputs that act as complements. In toothpaste markets low-quality brands do not have higher prices. In information markets the opposite can be the case; consider the difference in price between accurate industry statistics and forecasts generated by management consultants.

This suggests that the competitive strategies recommended in most business-school texts are unlikely to be applicable to knowledge markets where consumers face high uncertainty and sellers offer multiple perspectives. In these markets knowledge products sold by companies are not substitutes but complements. Complementary strategies (as opposed to competitive strategies) are appropriate in these cases. For example, in uncertain markets a knowledge-seller would prefer to have a competitor (the fact that traditional medicine exists increases the value of homeopathic medicine – both types of doctor end up charging higher prices). And given that apparently competing information-suppliers really complement each other, a strong case can be made for allowing them to merge or collude – this could drive information prices down!

What is the implication for information-suppliers? A number of companies have supplied highly accurate information to managers (for example, A.C. Neilsen, Information Resources, Dun & Bradstreet, Reuters, Dialog, Reed Elsevier). Some of these sellers are starting to face direct competition from their own primary suppliers and are finding it hard to maintain their margins. Their competitors have identical perspectives.

To reverse this trend they will either need to develop alternative perspectives or reposition their businesses to high-uncertainty markets. Who is currently serving managers facing the highest levels of uncertainty? Mostly strategy consulting companies (for example, McKinsey). Indeed, many consulting companies will refuse to respond to proposals from potential clients if the problems described are too "simple." Similarly, in the publishing world the highest-priced publications (per page) are industry studies that forecast highly uncertain markets (for example, China) or industries facing uncertainty generated by factors such as deregulation (for example, telecommunications and electric utilities). Traditional data provided by trade associations on historical trends are more accurate but of less market value.

Summary

The market for information is huge. In the early 1990s, professional fees for information products and services stood at $375bn a year in the US alone. Yet a lot of the most expensive information is also the least accurate – a forecast of the Indonesian car market is likely to cost more but be less reliable than statistics about the current UK car market. This is because when information is of high quality, buyers are indifferent as to the source, so companies selling it are forced to compete on price. But where knowledge is less certain, buyers see sellers as offering complementary products and competition is muted. Here **Philip Parker** discusses the nature of information markets and the implications for competitive strategy.

Suggested further reading

Sarvary, M. and Parker, P.M. (1997) "Marketing information: a competitive analysis," *Marketing Science* 16 (1): 24–38. (A more detailed discussion of Sarvary's model of information markets, which first appeared in his INSEAD thesis.)

NEW MARKETING MEDIA

9

Contributors

David Soberman is assistant professor of marketing at INSEAD. His research interests include information marketing and the organization of distribution.

Eric J. Johnson is the David W. Hauck Professor of Marketing and professor of psychology and of operations and information management at the Wharton School of the University of Pennsylvania. He is also founder and director of the Wharton Forum for Electronic Commerce (ecom.wharton.upenn.edu).

Patrick Barwise is professor of management and marketing at London Business School, where he is also director of the Centre for Marketing and chairman of the Future Media Research Programme.

Albert A. Angehrn is professor of information and communication systems at INSEAD, and the director of INSEAD's Center for Advanced Learning Technologies (www.Insead.fr/calt).

John Deighton is professor of business administration at Harvard Business School. His research centers on how digital technologies are shaping the practice of marketing.

Robert V. Kozinets is assistant professor of marketing at the J.L. Kellogg Graduate School of Management. His research interests include popular culture and consumer behavior, and consumer behavior on the internet.

Mohanbir Sawhney is assistant professor of marketing at the J.L. Kellogg Graduate School of Management, Northwestern University. His research interests include marketing strategy for technology companies and cross-functional coordination in product development.

Contents

Introduction

There is widespread belief that we are moving from an industrial age into an information age. This module considers some of the implications for marketers of this profound social change, as well as the likely impact of new technologies such as digital television. In particular, we look at how the internet is transforming business: the reduced cost of reaching customers means that manufacturers can bypass traditional intermediaries ("disinter-mediation"); detailed information about consumers' online shopping behavior can easily be collected, and advertising targeted accordingly; and the growth in "online communities of consumption" is changing the balance of power between marketers and consumers. Companies that establish websites to try to profit from such developments, must make full use of the medium's interactivity, instead of creating mere online brochures.

Into the upside-down age

by David Soberman

"Through the unknown, we'll find the new" (Charles Baudelaire, 1857)

Long before the semiconductor and even longer before the information revolution, Baudelaire in *Les Fleurs du mal* wrote prophetically of the magic of the unknown. These words have always rung true but they are particularly apposite for today's marketer. You can hardly get past the second page of a business newspaper without reading of new and exciting services that are going to be the basis of marketing in the 21st century. You might read about companies such as Videotron, which is making huge investments in the Quebec market place to offer interactive shopping through its cable television network, or about how Great Universal Stores, the venerable catalog retailer, is trying to modernize by transforming itself into a direct-marketing company. In a brief 20 years the information age has descended upon us and no one has felt the changes more than the executives and managers who manage some of the world's largest brands.

In this article, we shall discuss the implications of the information revolution for marketing managers, with specific emphasis on how the information revolution is changing society and the way people live, work and play. In-depth understanding of consumers is the cardinal first step in providing them with something they are willing to buy.

The information revolution and society

The information revolution really started in the late 1970s with rapid increases in computing power that resulted from advances made in microchips and semiconductors by companies such as Motorola and Intel. It has been accelerated by numerous other factors, including advances in computer operating systems, software, communication (fiber optics and satellites) and the internet.

The information revolution, of course, is not simply the start of a new product category, the personal computer – it is a change that is affecting the way society is organized and the way we communicate with each other. To understand this change, it is helpful to put it into the context of other technological advances and their impact on society:

- *The steam engine* made society less "rural." As early as the 17th century, inventors toyed with the idea of an engine powered by steam but it was not until James Watt patented his steam engine in 1769 that the concept became a practicable source of power for industrial applications. Ultimately, this machine and other inventions in the early 19th century led to the industrialization of society. This created a need for people to live much closer together to provide the labor required by the newly created factories.

- *Mass production* made society less "individualistic." Mass production and the automation techniques pioneered by Henry Ford and other US car manufacturers early in the 20th century meant that huge advantages could be gained by producing large numbers of very similar products. This led to rapid increases in the standard of living and the power of industry but also to significant homogenization in consumption patterns. For example, as early as the 1920s, Americans from the shores of the Pacific to the capes of New England were all driving identical black Ford Model Ts.

■ *Mass media* has given society "common knowledge." One of the most significant effects of the arrival of mass media was that people in several countries or even continents could watch the same news, the same entertainment and the same sports events.

A cynical observer might say that while mankind has made tremendous technological advances since the early 19th century – making us healthier and happier – the net effect on the organization of society has been to make it more homogeneous. People now live much closer together, dress similarly and consume and think about the same things.

The information revolution has the potential to reverse many of these trends:

■ It will allow people to return to rural life because work, play, learning and shopping can be done in the confines of a small rural community or even the family home. People are no longer obliged to travel to a factory or office to earn their living. For example, I know of a young computer programer who works for the office of a Tel Aviv company from her home in the French countryside. While this example is somewhat extreme, it is clear that much valuable work can be performed working on a computer in the family home.

■ It will reverse the homogeneity in consumption created by mass production and automation. Companies can now use technology and information to customize product offerings for each and every consumer. The computer that this article is being written on has been tailored to my individual needs in terms of power, controls, communication devices and capacity. There is probably no other computer in the world that is exactly the same. This would have been unthinkable even 20 years ago.

■ Information technology and communication will splinter the mass media "global village" envisaged by Marshall McLuhan in the 1960s. Evidence of this splintering can be seen in television, where the rapid expansion of choice has led to much lower ratings for top-rated programs. Of course, new lines of communication will appear as like-minded people trade products, ideas and information among themselves with no regard for the geographical distance between them.

Perhaps the best phrase to capture the impact that the information revolution has had on society is "upside down." It would seem that information has the ability to turn the world upside down and to undo many things that we might describe as typical of 20th-century society.

Implications for marketers

So far so good – but what are the implications for practitioners of marketing? A good place to start is to consider the three reversals just described.

If we agree that the information revolution means that a greater number of people will be working at home, doing less commuting and perhaps living further from major centers, we envisage a society that is becoming more heterogeneous (at least in the short term). This presents tremendous problems for marketers: marketing is predicated on the grouping of people into like-minded segments with similar needs. The idea is that companies can orient themselves to serve one or more of the segments profitably by tailoring a product or service package.

For this approach to be effective, segments must first be large enough to warrant a customized offering and second, a company must serve enough segments to be profitable. In this context, increased heterogeneity is a serious issue because:

- the existence of a greater number of distinct segments means that it will be much more difficult to provide a tailored offering for each segment
- it is going to be increasingly difficult to identify the needs of each segment, since the splintering of society will make the finding of people representative of each segment more difficult
- the needs of the segments, given the greater overall heterogeneity in society, will be much broader and more differentiated.

The response to these problems must be to *gather* more and better information on customers. The successful business will understand the new heterogeneity and be able to design an approach to the market that recognizes the changes.

A second challenge for marketers stems from consumers' expectation of products that are tailored to their individual needs. In some sense, companies such as Dell and Panasonic are creating a problem for all manufacturers. In the past customers always wanted products that simply provided good value for the price paid. This in large part explains the popularity of products from Volkswagen cars to McDonald's hamburgers. However, customers knew that they were getting a standardized product that was essentially identical to the product bought by both the customer served before and the customer served after them.

Dell (in personal computers) and Panasonic (in bicycles) have certainly obtained a short-term advantage over the competition by providing customized products; however, in the long run, customers will expect customized products and service from every competitor across a number of categories. Successful companies will have to recognize and respond to this change in expectations.

A successful company will not just be obliged to *gather* information on its customers, it will have to develop effective strategies to *use* the information. These strategies will involve difficult decisions, including choices that go beyond issues of customized manufacturing and/or service. Companies will have to develop strategies for knowing which things to customize and how they should be customized for each of the target segments that they choose to serve.

Finally, the splintering of the media creates a tremendous challenge for the mass marketer in many traditional categories.

One of the principal tools that a marketer must control and manage in order to run his or her business profitably is communication. The mass media (broadcast and print) remain the primary vehicles that marketers use to communicate important information about their products and services.

In the past marketers who managed products with broad appeal could depend on mass advertising to reach a broad target audience. The techniques of advertising on these media have been well honed since the early days of television. It is safe to say that there are many organizations that can provide creative and effective ways of raising awareness or communicating the information that consumers need in order to make product decisions.

However, a new range of problems faces marketers today:

- Media fragmentation means that they cannot depend on the mass media to deliver a message to a broad population. Instead, several complementary channels are required.

267

- The cost of producing creative material is expensive, and approaches that were appropriate for network television often do not work on alternative channels (or media).

- The importance of regular television and radio remains high but alternative channels, such as interactive television and the World Wide Web, are becoming important in reaching a significant number of consumers (close to 40 per cent of the US population has access to the Web). There is little expertise among advertising companies as to how these media can best be used to communicate with consumers.

While the splintering of the media tends to make a mass marketer's life more complicated, it may be a boon for niche marketers. In the past, niche marketers had significant problems in communicating with consumers because mass media were too expensive given the size of the audience they wished to reach and their sales volume. Frequently they had to depend on communication mechanisms such as specialized magazines, word of mouth and public relations.

Now, however, niche marketers can reach specialized markets efficiently through specialized channels. For example, a manufacturer of car spoilers can afford television advertising on the Men and Motors speciality channel. Similarly, a gay bar can advertise on channels that target the gay community. The proliferation of channels has also led to an increase in the amount of speciality programming. Thus surfboard manufacturers, garden supply companies and golf club manufacturers can find shows that target their specific market, making the per unit message affordable.

The principal skill that both mass marketers and niche manufacturers will need to be successful is the ability to analyze the mass of information available on their potential customers. A mass marketer must learn to identify a target market that is both worth entering (from a volume and profit perspective) and attainable (from a communication perspective).

Having a product or service that a customer desires is no guarantee of success. A marketer must also identify the appropriate media and message to tell that customer what he or she wants to know about it. In contrast, a niche marketer needs to become skilled in using media such as television, which in the past were too expensive.

Learning how to gather, use and analyze information is not easy. But marketers must do so if they are to meet the new and exciting challenges created by the social changes outlined in this article. Only by becoming familiar with the unknown through the advanced use of information will marketers be able to meet the new demands that people have.

Summary

The information revolution promises to reverse many of the social trends that characterized the 20th century. "Unconventional" jobs will be more common, as telecommuting enables people to work away from big cities; consumers will increasingly demand customized products; and the mass media "global village" will fragment into a multitude of smaller communities. Clearly, says **David Soberman**, this has important implications for marketers. A more heterogeneous market means that marketers must become skilled at gathering information in order to be able to target smaller segments. At the same time, they must be able to use this information to tailor their offerings accurately. Finally, a more splintered media is changing the rules for niche manufacturers and mass marketers alike.

Digital media: cutting through the hype

by Patrick Barwise and John Deighton

If you ask any senior marketer about the main marketing issues facing their business over the next five years, the chances are that "new media" or "digital technology" will be high on their list. Digital technology is affecting marketing in many ways. As with other functions, people in marketing and – especially – sales are increasingly using information technology for everyday communication. Over the past three years the main development has been "intranets" – corporate information systems using open internet standards. Other developments include the near-ubiquity of e-mail, the growth of audio and video conferencing, and the increasing use of mobile technology.

The growth of electronic markets is also blurring the historical distinctions between industries and changing the competitive rules for many businesses. "Extranets" use internet technology to move information between a company and its customers, suppliers and other partners at much less cost than the electronic data interchange (EDI) systems used hitherto. The increasing pace of change and the greater "connectedness" of electronic markets mean that today's partner or customer may be tomorrow's competitor and vice versa.

We here focus on a third set of issues, closely related to these two but falling more within the specific realm of the marketing function. This is the impact of new, digital media on marketing communications and, in some cases, distribution. Specifically, we focus on new media such as digital television and the internet, which depend on consumers having access to the necessary technology.

In consumer markets, most homes do not yet have access to digital technology, although this is changing fast, especially in the US and Scandinavia. Most of the access there is is via online personal computers (PCs). Future access devices may include digital televisions (DTVs), digital radios and "third-generation" mobile phones. DTV's supporters claim that it will revolutionize the way viewers (and therefore advertisers) use television and accelerate the take-off of consumer electronic commerce.

Consumers will need to invest money and time in these technologies. The companies behind them will have to ensure that they provide real benefits and minimize the barriers to adoption for consumers. Both the benefits and the barriers are likely to differ significantly from those influencing the adoption of digital technology in business markets. In particular, entertainment and relaxation – the main motivations for most consumers' use of existing media – are likely to be key drivers, while key barriers include slow transmission, trust and privacy issues and problems with the user interface.

We are potentially at the threshold of a revolution in marketing. Digital media are raising the scope and power of interactive marketing onto a new level, combining individual addressability, instant response, round-the-clock availability, global reach and unprecedented opportunities for the consumer to shop around and access information. But marketers need to cut through the hype and focus on consumer benefits and practicalities.

The access issue

The proportion of consumers connected to the internet varies greatly between countries. The percentage penetration is highest in Finland but in absolute terms the largest market by far is the US, boosted by unlimited free local telephone calls (*see* Table 1, p. 273).

Internet penetration figures by households, however, tend to understate the size of the consumer markets that can already be reached by the internet. First, those who are online tend to spend more money than the average, especially on computers, books, music and so on. Second, many consumers have access to the internet at work or college.

No one knows how fast online PCs and other digital technologies will penetrate the consumer market in different countries. Estimates vary widely. Nor are the different devices equivalent as marketing channels. PCs will still be mainly used for information-intensive applications controlled by a full keyboard. DTVs will be used more in company with a simple remote keypad, and mostly for watching television. Digital radios and mobile phones will have small screens and keys and still be mainly used for music, messaging and chat.

Despite the uncertainties, a reasonable assumption is that interactive, screen-based digital media will be in most homes in the US (and one or two other countries, such as Finland, Sweden and Norway) by about 2005, and perhaps two to three years later in most other developed countries.

Home use of the internet today is so bedeviled by slow transmission rates that disillusioned users talk of the "world wide wait." The full promise of the digital future will not be realized without some solution to the bandwidth problem. Two contenders are the cable modem and ADSL transmission over normal telephone lines. The *New Yorker Magazine*'s communication writer, Ken Auletta, has termed high-speed internet access "a sort of digital Panama Canal."

In North America enough progress has been made to allow informed conjecture about the timing of that breakthrough. In December 1995 a suburb of Toronto, Newmarket, became the first to be sold cable modem access to the Web at speeds about 500 times faster than conventional telephone-based service providers could offer. For an installation charge of C$99 and a monthly charge of C$39.95, homes could buy the service from Rogers Communications, Canada's largest cable television provider. Three years on, 10 per cent of the 16,000 homes in Newmarket with access to cable television are subscribers to the service, a number which is half of the homes with any internet access at all.

Several US consortia are rolling out cable modem services. The two largest are @Home, a joint venture of AT&T, Cox Cable and Comcast, and Roadrunner, a joint venture of Time Warner, Microsoft and Compaq. Since broad commitment to the roll-out began in mid-1996, the service has spread until it is now available to 15 per cent of North American homes. To date, only about one per cent of these homes have subscribed.

Pursuing the Panama Canal metaphor, the take-off of electronic commerce is hampered by slow digging. Two diffusion curves are operating: the suburb-by-suburb roll-out of upgraded cable pipes, and the slow build-up of demand in each suburb once it has been upgraded. At the present rate, it will be ten years before 50 per cent of North America has access to the service and longer before even 5 per cent of North America has taken it up. The roll-out may accelerate, however, as competitors to the cable modem arrive (ADSL service began to be offered in late

1998). And penetration of suburbs may occur faster as "network externalities" emerge: as with all communication technologies, the benefits of adoption increase as more people have the technology.

DTV

DTV has already been launched in several countries, with early success in the US and France. In the UK, DTV is being launched on terrestrial (ONdigital), satellite (BSkyB with British Interactive Broadcasting – BIB) and cable (CWC, NTL, Telewest) platforms. At least in the short term, much blood will be spilt by the broadcasters but for marketers the result should be to increase greatly the number of UK homes that can be reached via digital technology.

However, there are big uncertainties. How many DTV homes will have interactive technology? Will the various platforms have compatible standards? Will they provide free access to third parties? BIB is currently talking about a "walled garden" using proprietary standards, which suggests not.

On the question of whether, with hundreds of television channels, broadcasting will become "narrowcasting," the jury is still out but the initial evidence is negative. It is clear that most channels will have specialized content, as is already true of multichannel cable television. With more channels, content will become even more specialized – not just sport, movie and music channels but channels for particular sports, movie genres and music styles. But the evidence is that, first, such channels will attract very low viewing figures and second, their audiences will not be strongly segmented. In other words, most of the *content* of DTV will be "narrowcast" but the *audiences* will not.

Of course, there will be some differences: viewers of music channels tend to be young, viewers of sports channels tend to be male and so on. We will also see more "masthead" programming, explicitly linked to specialist print media. But these differences are unlikely to be sufficient to persuade advertisers to pay a premium per viewer compared with the main networks. In fact, cable audiences currently sell at a lower cost per viewer than network audiences, because of the restricted number of homes able-to-receive and because their audiences tend to be heavy viewers of television in general. We see no compelling reason why this should change significantly as we move from, say, 50 channels (the current US average) to 200 or 300.

Some DTV supporters claim that its interactivity will make television viewing a more active and involving experience. Viewers will build their own schedules, choose camera angles during football matches, drill down for more information during news programs and so on. This assertion is not easy to test directly, but the indirect evidence from interactive television trials and from previous research on television viewing habits is largely negative. People watch television at a fairly low level of involvement most of the time.

Again, we expect some change at the margin. Interaction can increase viewers' enjoyment of game shows (competing against others in the home or studio) and sport (team news, match statistics and so on). Television viewing may also decline because of competition from other activities and because the "leisure society" is as elusive as ever. In the long term, as the technology improves, we may see an increase in "time-shift" viewing (watching a program after transmission), from less than 5 per cent today to, say, 10 or 20 per cent.

None of this represents the kind of revolution predicted by some digerati. Such predictions rely on the implausible assumptions that there will be abundant good programming and that many viewers will choose to spend hours per week, year after year, positively interacting with their televisions.

For marketers, then, DTV is unlikely to provide highly targeted audiences or much scope for revolutionary interactive commercials. It will, however, provide "phoneless direct-response TV," potentially a significant change. Already about half the television commercials in the US are "direct-response," in the sense of inviting the viewer to call a freephone number. Many also include a web address. However, the process of getting in touch – being held in a queue, reciting personal details and so forth – is often troublesome. Interactive DTV will eliminate most of this hassle, assuming that the consumer interface is well designed.

In the longer term – 20 years, say – television advertising could change more radically. Historically, which commercials viewers see has always depended on which programs they watch. But in future, only the dog-owners (known from their loyalty card transactions) would see dogfood commercials and only high-net-worth retirees would see commercials for certain financial products, regardless of their program choice.

So, although DTV *channels* will not deliver strongly segmented audiences, if and when most (valuable) viewers are individually addressable, television could become a highly targeted medium for direct marketing. However, the practical problems (such as scheduling and privacy) are severe.

Other media

Other existing media will survive, or even thrive, with the digital revolution. But, as with the advent of media such as radio and television, they will need to adapt to new roles.

Digital radio will develop steadily as the cost of equipment comes down, starting in upmarket new cars. Music sales will gradually go online, although in the short term this will involve postal delivery of a physical product such as a CD or DVD (digital versatile disc).

Books, too, will increasingly be ordered online but will be mostly delivered as print-on-paper, as now. People do not like to read large amounts of text on-screen and today's digital technology is mostly more expensive and less convenient than print. The exception will be reference books, especially encyclopedias.

For similar reasons, digital interactive media such as the internet are not well adapted for most *display* advertising but have huge potential for *classified* advertising. This is because the internet has limited scope as a "push" medium like television – most users are irritated by commercial messages pushed onto their screens – but has great power to help users "pull" information if they are looking for a particular thing. With the development of "agent" software and with more and more products available online, the web's "pull" power will increase even further.

One implication is that those media that rely on classified advertising sales for much of their revenue – trade and consumer magazines, local newspapers and Yellow Pages – need to respond to this threat. Their best response is to embrace the new medium and combine it with their existing service. This will not always succeed, since the internet is no respecter of existing market boundaries, but the established print media have brands, market knowledge and other advantages.

The likely impact on national newspapers is unclear. Digital technology allows readers to tailor products as they please (the "Daily Me") but there is little evidence that many will bother to do so for their personal newspaper. Professional newsletters are a different matter: many professionals are already using personalized systems on the web for current awareness. Meanwhile, most major newspapers are publishing at least part of their (current and back-issue) content online but are struggling to find the right business model. The challenge is to persuade online readers to pay when they have so much access to free information.

Web advertising

Much of the advertising on the web is for the medium itself – for example, for internet-related businesses such as Microsoft, IBM, Excite and Yahoo! – not for the other products and services that ultimately will justify its existence. But web advertising is growing fast, now accounting for about one per cent of all US media advertising.

How do advertisers compare the cost and benefits of Web advertising with those of other media? The usual quantitative measure for advertising media is cost per thousand audience member impressions (CPM). CPM rates for the Web currently lie between television and print. Because CPM counts simply how many times an advertisement appears on a website, it does not take advantage of the medium's ability to detect viewer response. As a result, "clickthrough" advertising has become popular. When advertising is priced per "clickthrough," the advertiser pays only when a response is elicited.

Internet access by networked personal computer		
	Homes linked to the internet (%)	Internet access cost (20 hours/month)
United States	25	$30
Germany	10	$65
United Kingdom	10	$55
France	4	$50

Table 1

Advertisers also take many qualitative factors into account. The web scores highly for measures such as audience selectivity, prestige and the ability to change content quickly.

Websites command a range of CPMs, depending on audience size and quality. It is common to distinguish two main kinds of site: search engines and destinations. Search engines are the sites that users visit to find other sites. They provide advertisers with large volumes of traffic but are not selective and therefore tend to earn low CPMs. Destination sites contain the content that users are searching for. They deliver lower levels of traffic but audiences are more homogeneous.

A third category of advertising site is the "start page" or "personalized home page." These sites enable users to select a number of features – perhaps a Dilbert cartoon, the Philadelphia weather forecast and last night's basketball scores – to appear each time they start a web session. Examples are Netscape's "My Start" page launched in 1996, Microsoft Network and IBM's infoSage. Customized start pages may provide both high volumes of traffic and the opportunity to target advertising. They are therefore likely to be the next competitive battleground after search engines.

Overall, however, display advertising on the Web is unlikely to supplant existing media for customer acquisition. The real power of digital media will be for one-to-one relationship marketing with existing customers, especially in business-to-business markets. The challenge in consumer markets is to use these media in ways that benefit, rather than irritate, the consumer.

Summary

Marketers are right to be both nervous and excited about the prospects for digital media, say **Patrick Barwise** and **John Deighton**. Some of the more revolutionary changes predicted by techno-enthusiasts, such as the end of passive television watching, look wide of the mark but print, radio, direct mail and the telephone will all need to adapt to survive. Display advertising will evolve, while classified advertising is likely quite quickly to go "bi-media," with both print and digital access to ads. The main opportunities to exploit growing consumer access to digital media will fall to direct marketers – that is, those who have historically addressed consumers individually via the telephone and mail. Almost every business needs to strengthen its capabilities at this kind of database/relationship marketing.

Suggested further reading

Barwise, P. and Ehrenberg, A. (1988) *Television and its Audience*, 2nd edn, Sage, London.

Barwise, P. and Hammond, K. (1998) *Media*, Phoenix, London ("Predictions" series).

Fournier, S., Dobscha, S. and Mick, D.G. (1998) "Preventing the premature death of relationship marketing",
    Harvard Business Review, January/February.

Future Media Research Program (1997) *Consumer Adoption of Electronic Commerce*, London Business School.

Peppers, D. and Rogers, M. (1993) *The One-to-One Future*, Piatkus, London.

Schor, J.B. (1992) *The Overworked American: The Unexpected Decline of Leisure*, Basic Books, New York.

The new middlemen in the networked economy

by Mohanbir Sawhney

The purpose of marketing is to maximize the value of exchanges between buyers and sellers. These exchanges are facilitated by channel intermediaries, who add value by reducing the cost of transactions. According to transaction cost theory, companies organize themselves in ways that minimize their transaction costs. Companies use mediators because mediated transactions are more cost-effective than non-mediated transactions. If companies find that they are better at performing channel functions on their own, they will choose to deal directly with their customers. This phenomenon, called "disintermediation," is hailed as one of the defining characteristics of the coming networked economy. Companies such as Amazon.com, Dell, E*Trade and Travelocity are held out as the future of mediation.

If the pundits are to be believed, middlemen will be roadkill on the information superhighway.

But matters are more complex than the simplistic logic of disintermediation would suggest. First, disintermediation is not an "all or nothing" phenomenon. Disintermediation can occur at the level of individual channel functions. When this happens, traditional mediators are not eliminated but are reduced to performing fewer functions. Channel functions can be unbundled and performed by specialized mediators.

Further, disintermediation may not reduce the total cost of the transaction because it shifts some channel functions to customers. Customers need to search, evaluate, negotiate and configure products on their own, in the absence of mediators. To reduce the total cost, new mediators will be needed to assist customers in the search and negotiation process leading up to the transaction.

Finally, disintermediation takes a conventional view of products and markets. It operates within definitions of industry boundaries that are becoming meaningless as industries and markets converge. To rethink mediation, we need to redraw the boundaries of industries and markets.

The networked economy will spawn entirely new forms of mediators. Many of these companies will have no parallel in the pre-digital ("analog") world and will have little or no physical presence. The new mediators will be made possible by networked commerce and they will make networked commerce possible. In the long run, they will replace traditional mediators and enable the creation of business designs that will be dramatically more efficient.

The future of mediation

To understand the new mediators and the future of mediation, we need to consider three different aspects of the internet. Taken together, they paint a clear picture of the future of mediation in the networked economy.

Disintermediation: the net connects

The internet is revolutionary because it connects companies with companies, companies with customers, and people with people without regard to time, space and hardware/software platforms. Companies can connect with their trading partners through the internet at far less cost and with far more flexibility than proprietary electronic data interchange links.

General Electric's Trading Process Network, which connects GE with its suppliers via the internet, dramatically reduces the cost and time of purchase transactions. Ingram Micro, a computer wholesaler, uses the internet in managing the inventory of computer resellers such as CompUSA.

Customers can connect with companies to gather information, evaluate or configure products, place orders and get technical support. Dell has become a leader in electronic commerce by using the web to connect with its customers for configuring, ordering and providing technical support for its products. Cisco sells 64 per cent of its products, handles 90 per cent of its software upgrades and 70 per cent of its customer support queries over the internet, resulting in a saving of over \$385m in 1997.

People can connect with people to form communities of commerce. These may bring buyers together (examples include the Grocery Network, Manufacturing Marketplace, Oil Online, PlasticsNet and VerticalNet) or may bring buyers and sellers together for transactions in which the price has to be negotiated (examples include FastParts, FairMarket, Onsale, eBay and the Virtual Garment Center).

Improved connectivity dramatically reduces the cost of communication and co-ordination in exchange transactions. In a networked economy, companies can bypass mediators who have traditionally facilitated the flow of information and goods between companies and their customers. Disintermediation is beginning to take hold in many industry sectors. Companies such as Travelocity (travel), Insweb (Insurance), Wells Fargo (retail banking), Schwab (investments) and Amazon.com (book sales) are reaching out directly to their customers, eliminating retailers and other channel intermediaries.

Deconstruction: the net separates

If we look deeper at disintermediation, it becomes obvious that for every mediator that is eliminated, several mediators are created. Amazon.com sells books directly to customers but it uses Ingram Books for warehousing, UPS and Airborne Express for fulfillment and America Online for real estate to advertize its presence. AutobyTel.com takes purchase requests for cars over the internet but the orders are fulfilled by traditional dealers. In all such cases, the internet enables the separation of information from the physical product, and of the core product from complementary products.

Most products consist of a physical component and an information component. When consumers buy a camera or a car, they buy information about the product too. Further, most complex products are bought along with complementary products and services. A computer requires software, a camera requires lenses and a car is sold with a warranty, financing and optional accessories.

In the analog world, information is often bundled with the physical product and the core product is often sold along with complementary products. Vertically integrated mediators provide bundled flows and bundled offerings. For example, car buyers rely on car dealers for information, negotiation, financing, spares, warranties and delivery. The bundling of functions and offerings offers "one-stop shop" convenience to consumers, who would otherwise have to deal with several providers.

But bundling also involves significant compromises because vertically integrated middlemen are often not the best or lowest-cost providers of particular flows or particular complementary products. Car dealers, for example, often use new car sales as a loss leader to sell higher-margin accessories, financing and extended warranties.

In the networked economy, information channel flows can be unbundled from physical channel flows in time and in space. Customers can search for information, evaluate, negotiate, pay for and take delivery of products at different points in time and from different providers. Just as the videocassette recorder allowed consumers to separate the transmission and the viewing of television programs, so the internet allows customers to separate channel flows in exchanges. This means that integrated mediators can be replaced by a combination of specialized "market*space* mediators" who manage information flows, and a set of specialized "market*place* mediators" who manage physical flows. For example, car dealers are coming under attack from specialized providers of car information, car insurance, extended warranties, financing, negotiation services and used cars. Deconstruction of channel flows offers significant advantages to consumers because they can mix and match "best-of-breed" flow providers.

But deconstruction has drawbacks. It places much greater demands on customers' time. Instead of dealing with one vertically integrated mediator, consumers now need to deal with a whole host of specialized mediators. They need to search, evaluate and assemble information from a variety of providers. And they need to perform this search process on the internet, where information is poorly organized and of uncertain quality. So while consumers gain by finding lower-cost, more specialized service providers on the internet, they lose in terms of higher search and evaluation costs. Higher search costs translate into higher marketing and customer acquisition costs for service providers. Clearly, deconstruction alone is an unsatisfactory view of the future of mediation.

Metamediation: the net realigns

To achieve the promise of frictionless commerce, deconstructed channel flows and offerings need to be reassembled in ways that reduce the search and evaluation costs for customers. A new breed of mediating institutions is emerging to inform and advise customers and to simplify their dealings with product and service providers. These mediators, which I shall call "metamediaries," dramatically improve the efficiency and effectiveness of transactions in the networked economy. They also redraw the boundaries of markets by creating metamarkets, which have no parallel in the physical world.

The concept of metamarkets stems from a simple yet profound insight – customers think about products and markets very differently from the way products and markets are bundled and sold in the physical marketplace. This misalignment arises because customers think in terms of *activities*, while companies think in terms of *products*.

Activities that are logically related in people's minds may be spread across very diverse industries, and very different service providers. These related activities constitute a metamarket – a cluster of cognitively related activities that customers engage in to satisfy a distinct set of needs. The boundaries of metamarkets are defined by activities that are closely related in cognitive space, not by the fact that they are created or marketed by related companies in related industries.

Consider the activities associated with home ownership. From an activity perspective, customers view home buying, home financing, home maintenance, home repair and home improvement to be logically related. This cluster of activities can be viewed as the "home ownership metamarket." However, in the marketplace, homeowners need to deal with estate agents, banks, mortgage companies, newspapers, plumbers, electricians, gardeners, cleaning services, home improvement stores, architects and interior designers to perform these activities and to satisfy this set of related needs. In doing so, customers need to search for, evaluate and negotiate with a large number of service and product providers. Figure 1 illustrates this discontinuity between cognitive space and the marketplace in the context of the car metamarket.

Metamarkets can be constructed around major life events – childbirth, education, career changes and retirement, say – and major assets. Such assets include homes, cars, boats and financial assets.

The conditions that are essential for a viable metamarket are:

- there is a rich set of related activities that are clustered together
- these activities are important in terms of their demands on customers' time and their economic impact
- to perform these activities, customers need to assemble information from many

The car metamarket

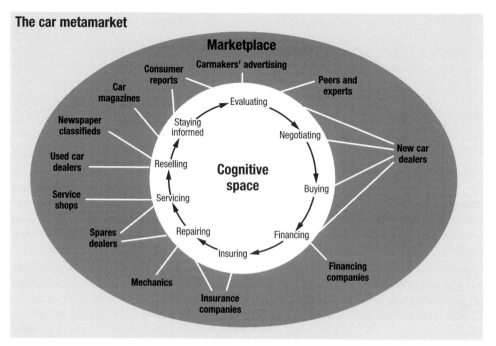

Figure 1

fragmented sources

- to perform these activities, customers also need to deal with many product and service providers across several industries
- vertically integrated middlemen who currently provide channel flows are inefficient and the buying experience is unpleasant.

Meet the metamediary

Once we have grasped the concept of metamarkets, it becomes easy to understand what metamediaries do. Metamediaries are trusted third parties that operate on the internet (the "marketspace") to realign the marketplace with the way customers mentally bundle activities. Metamediaries make metamarkets possible by assembling the products and services in a metamarket into a seamless bundle. They serve as a single point of contact between buyers and sellers in a metamarket.

Unlike channel intermediaries, metamediaries do not represent providers of products and services. Rather, they represent customers in their dealings with product and service providers. They empower customers and facilitate exchanges but they do not participate in the actual transactions. They do not make money by advertising, subscription or transaction fees. They recapture value by collecting a referral fee from partners for every connection they make between a customer and a provider.

Metamediaries are not aggregators in the traditional sense. Aggregators bundle product and service offerings from the provider perspective, while metamediaries bundle activities from the customer perspective. Consider an aggregator such as Insweb, which bundles information on a variety of insurance products from a number of insurance providers. Insweb aggregates information on home insurance, life insurance and car insurance. But customers may think about home insurance

Metamarkets and metamediaries		
Metamarket	**Activity cluster**	**Metamediary**
Childbirth	Prenatal care, labor and delivery, feeding, health and safety, nutrition and feeding, child development, work and family, family finances	BabyCenter **www.babycenter.com**
Wedding	Wedding planning, scheduling, invitations, registry, honeymoons, wedding-related travel	The Wedding Channel **www.weddingchannel.com**
Gardening	Information, tools and supplies, design, tips, gardening community	Garden Escape **www.garden.com**
Home ownership	Home buying advice, valuations, listings, financing, rentals,	Home Shark **www.homeshark.com**
Auto ownership	Reviews, buying advice, dealer pricing, reliability ratings, financing, extended warranties, spares and parts, used sales, new sales	Edmunds **www.edmunds.com**

Table 1

as part of the "home metamarket," life insurance as part of the "wedding" or "parenting" metamarket and car insurance as part of the "car metamarket."

Metamediaries are emerging in a variety of areas (*see* Table 1). One contender for the metamediary role in the car business is Edmund Publications (www.edmunds.com).

Edmund's has created a valuable information franchise by giving away information about new and used car pricing, dealer cost and holdbacks, reliability, car-buying advice and car reviews. It attracts over 80,000 visitors to its site every day and has been ranked as one of the most popular car sites on the internet. Over time, Edmund's has channelled this traffic to a number of partners that provide specific channel flows: Autobytel.com for negotiation and dealer search; CarFinance.com for financing; Price Auto Outlet for off-lease used cars; J.C. Whitney for spare parts; Geico for insurance; and Warranty Gold for extended warranties. Customers can visit the Edmund's site to gather information, negotiate, evaluate, finance, purchase, insure and buy spares in a single place. It makes its money by referring car buyers to a small set of strategic partners that provide specific channel flows and complementary products.

By providing a single point of contact between the car-buying community and the car-selling community, Edmund's has realigned car-related products and services to mirror the set of activities that constitute the car metamarket (*see* Figure 2). This makes transactions more efficient for customers and marketers alike. It reduces search costs for customers and customer acquisition costs for marketers. It also brings buyers together into a community, where they can exchange advice.

The death of friction?

Metamediaries such as Edmund's can eliminate billions of dollars of transactional inefficiencies. Consider the numbers. About 15m new cars and light trucks were sold at an average price of $20,000 in the US in 1997. Almost a third of the retail

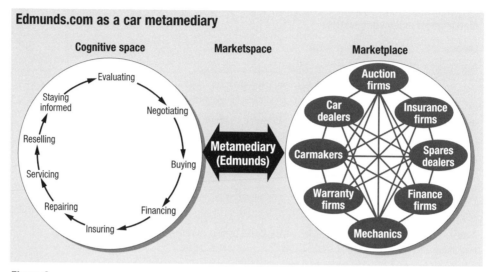

Figure 2

price ($6,700 per car) was the cost that marketers incurred in promotion, distribution and dealer incentives, giving a total transactional cost in excess of $100bn. Car dealers alone spent around $5bn in consumer advertising, as did the three main US carmakers (General Motors, Ford and Chrysler). Consumers and dealers spent $15bn in classified advertising. Billions more were spent by insurance companies, financing companies and suppliers of spares.

In 1997, Edmund's referred over 500,000 customers to car dealers through Autobytel.com. Edmund's has estimated that it reduces the dealer's cost of acquiring a qualified car buyer from $300 to $40. If these figures are accurate, Edmund's could have accounted for savings of well over $100m for car dealers. Edmund's also refers thousands of customers every month to its other business partners, who in turn offer car loans, extended warranties and insurance at rates that are 15 to 30 per cent below the market. The company also has the potential to reduce classified advertising spending by bringing buyers and sellers together in a common forum. All these numbers are likely to grow exponentially as more households come online and use the internet for car transactions. Chrysler estimates that one in four car purchases in the US will be made over the internet by the year 2000.

While the evolution of metamediaries involves both disintermediation and reintermediation, it goes well beyond these concepts. Edmund's has effectively redrawn the boundaries of the car market. In doing so, it has inspired a host of specialized mediating institutions. Conventional mediators (car dealers) are left with a reduced set of functions, such as offering test drives and servicing cars. It is not difficult to visualize even these flows being eliminated by the emergence of multi-brand test-drive outlets and multi-brand service and repair outlets (*see* Table 2).

The battle for cognitive real estate

By providing a single point of contact between customers and marketers, metamedaries do more than reduce transactional efficiencies. They also gain control over the customer relationship. They operate as the "switchboard" through which every exchange transaction is routed between buyers and sellers.

The future of mediation in the car market

Today
- Classified advertisements in local newspapers
- New car dealer and used car dealer network
- Dealer consolidation by carmakers
- Dedicated brand-specific used car dealers
- Integrated value chain – test drives, negotiating, buying, financing, servicing, repair

In future
- Direct nationwide buyer–seller transactions
- Direct consumer sales, test drive and service outlets
- Virtual and physical consolidation by aggregators
- Multi-brand physical and virtual used car dealers
- Deconstructed value chain – specialized providers co-ordinated by metamediaries

---

Table 2

This switchboard function will become ever more powerful as the community of buyers and the community of sellers grow, setting off a virtuous circle of increasing customer traffic, increased attractiveness to product and service providers and even more attractiveness to customers. By positioning themselves at the center of this growing web, metamediaries can control valuable "choke points" in cyberspace.

Metamediaries can also increase their embeddedness in their webs by creating connections among buyers, as well as among sellers. For example, Edmund's has created a discussion area called "Edmund's Town Hall," where tens of thousands of buyers discuss a variety of subjects related to cars. Such user-generated content is a powerful source of sustainable competitive advantage.

On the supplier side, Edmund's is creating links between suppliers, such as the financing by CarFinance.com of spares sold by J.C. Whitney or the combining of financing by CarFinance.com with used-car sales from PriceCarOutlet.com. These horizontal linkages among suppliers increase the embeddedness of Edmund's and allow sellers to cross-sell and create new bundled offerings that would have been extremely difficult to set up in the physical marketplace. In the networked economy, such relationships are a valuable asset that metamediaries can continue to leverage into other partnerships. In building strong customer relationships, metamediaries are effectively acquiring "cognitive real estate" in customers' minds. This real estate corresponds to the most important activities that people carry out and the most valuable assets that they hold. But the area that is commercially viable is limited; the race is on to stake a claim.

Summary

As place and time become increasingly irrelevant in the networked economy, vertically integrated mediators will find their franchises eroded by specialized mediators. These will offer better products and services at lower costs than full-service mediators. But in doing so, customers will be faced with a dizzying array of specialized product and service providers. **Mohanbir Sawhney** argues that this will in turn result in the emergence of "metamediaries," who will reassemble the offerings into bundles that are logically related from the customer's perspective. Metamediaries will reduce customer search and evaluation costs, and dramatically improve the efficiency of networked commerce transactions. Ultimately, they will make frictionless commerce possible.

How e-commerce is shaping new business models

by Eric J. Johnson

We hear every day astonishing predictions about the impact electronic commerce is going to have on the global economy. internet stocks, and indeed all things internet, are skyrocketing (and sometimes collapsing just as suddenly). These trends make the area of electronic commerce complex and problematic for managers. You may find yourself uncertain as to what path to take, yet convinced that if you do not proceed aggressively, current or new competitors will race by you and dominate the nascent electronic market. A growing number of businesses are moving forward but most are moving with more than a degree of trepidation and uncertainty.

A historical view

It is often instructive to look backwards in order to understand the future more clearly. By looking at historical analogies we can see in retrospect the key benefits and difficulties in the relationship between new technology and business models.

One analogy that strikes a number of observers as relevant is the introduction of broadcast radio. Much like electronic commerce, its early practitioners were essentially technologists rather than business professionals. The history of radio saw many fortunes made (and lost) as it got off the ground and established itself.

Westinghouse was among the first companies to start broadcasting to create a "pull" demand for radio sets which they thought would generate profit, but it took David Sarnoff (pioneer of radio and television broadcasting in the US) to develop the industry's first profitable business model. He realized that the same program could be broadcast over many different radio stations and in doing so the cost of the programming could be amortized over many stations and listeners, lowering production costs and increasing the quality of programming. This changed fundamentally the costs of reaching a mass audience. Indeed, for the first time advertisers could communicate their messages throughout the nation.

From a business model perspective, electronic commerce is best understood by looking at its effects on the costs of communicating with customers. Just as the advent of mass advertising generated new business and new business models, electronic commerce is doing the same now. The key to understanding these new business models is to understand how the adoption of information technology (IT) by customers radically changes costs, in some cases by considerable orders of magnitude.

To understand this better we need to look at the activities that take place in a traditional channel of distribution (whether business-to-business or business-to-consumer). The basic activities we shall examine are:

- companies communicating to consumers through advertising, sales calls and so on
- customers talking to companies through market research, consumer complaints and so on

■ customers finding other customers (the lower cost of which in electronic channels is perhaps their least appreciated aspect)

Will advertising be more efficient?

Consider the carmaker who is trying to reach potential car buyers. People are in the market for buying cars only occasionally, say once every three years. The normal channels, such as buying a full-page advertisement in the local newspaper or in a magazine are wasteful because at any point in time many, if not most, readers are not in the market for a car. In contrast, if we were to go to any search engine and type the word "car" we would find along with our results a banner advertisement for a car manufacturer, retailer or online car buying service. The person doing the search is actively seeking information about cars and is therefore a much more likely prospect.

Much advertising on the internet today is placed through advertising networks such as Flycast and DoubleClick. These networks can track the response rate to a particular banner advertisement across a large number of sites. This opens up an enormous number of possibilities for improved advertising efficiency. First, an advertiser can easily determine which advertisements are most effective in generating traffic ("click-throughs") and which sites provide the best placement. Second, these networks can monitor how many times an individual has seen a banner ad and can control the number of exposures. If a customer has seen my advertisement five times and not taken any action, for example, I can conclude that he or she is not interested in my offering. I can then either revise my advertisement to try to stimulate interest or drop it.

Thus web advertising can be more efficient because it talks to people when they want to be talked to and allows them to control the amount of information that they are given. Web advertising is comparatively inexpensive, with cost per thousand currently ranging from about $5 to $80. Since this efficiency comes at about the same cost as the equivalent magazine or broadcast advertisement, it looks as if advertising effectiveness is increasing and costs are decreasing by a considerable order of magnitude.

One area where advertisers are finding large savings is in communicating new events and products to customers. Imagine a very good assistant in a bookstore who watches what customers buy and asks them how well they like it. This assistant could provide great customer service by recommending books that other customers, with similar buying patterns, have liked. He or she would build loyalty to the store by providing the customer with significant added value. Unfortunately, in the typical large retail setting such assistants are relatively expensive and cannot easily service large numbers of customers.

Now consider the recommendations generated by a company like Amazon.com, which has software that looks at purchase patterns across customers to make recommendations, and then sends (with customers' permission) e-mail to suggest new purchases. This is like receiving a customized catalog from a retailer, yet the cost is much less than the assiduous assistant – or even a more typical mass mailing – and the response rate is higher. Another example of the web's potential for reducing the cost of communicating with customers is the replacement of telephone technical support and call centers with Web pages that perform the same function.

Listening to customers

Most current tools for customer research are relatively slow, expensive and often discontinuous, because they are applied sporadically – at product launches or at times of crisis. Focus groups can cost tens of thousands of dollars and the cost of conducting extensive survey research often runs well into six figures. Tracking studies are rare. Electronic commerce provides an unprecedented opportunity to listen to and understand customers far more effectively and cost-efficiently. It does this both by explicit data collection and by less intrusive implicit data collection. Explicit collection relies on customers' answering questions. Online surveys, one obvious example of this, have broader geographical reach and can be conducted more quickly than conventional surveys.

At Wharton we conduct the Wharton Virtual Test Market, an online panel of over 10,000 internet users recruited through banner advertising, links from Wharton's learning partner companies' websites, and word of mouth (or, in many cases, "word of mouse"). Participants have each completed a 40-question survey about their experiences online and about shopping on the Web, and over 80 per cent have agreed to participate in future studies. In return, they are entered in draws for small cash prizes. The total cost of participation and recruitment has been less than $2 per respondent, a figure which is around ten times cheaper than physical market research. Over 15 per cent of the respondents are from outside the US, from countries as diverse as Australia and Belarus. When we have contacted respondents for further research, we obtain high response rates and quick turnaround.

As exciting as explicit data collection might be, implicit data collection is the real advantage of the Web. Imagine that you ran a store that recorded not only everything purchased by your customers but also which products they considered but did not buy. In many ways the Web is like this store: it is as if customers wear video cameras on their heads, through which we can see what they look at while they consider whether to make a purchase. Websites can record which pages customers look at and which ones they ignore and can give researchers a rough idea of how long each page is examined.

Consider, for example, what this means for an online retailer of compact discs. Such a retailer, in principle, can observe not only what a customer buys, which discs he or she browsed, whether or not he or she sampled online content, and whether there is any systematic difference between the discs considered and bought and those considered but rejected. The retailer might discover, for example, that someone who bought a Bruce Springsteen CD actually looked at information about three others by Springsteen. A follow-up e-mail offering a discount on any two Springsteen CDs might be particularly effective in persuading this customer to make further purchases. Consider too the value this information might have for other businesses whose products have links with the CDs. An example might be a company promoting a Bruce Springsteen concert, who might use this information in selling seats (particularly luxury boxes). Of course, major issues arise concerning privacy rights and informed choice on the part of customers.

Taken together, advances in explicit and implicit data collection are the beginning of the end of marketing research as we know it today. Online commerce now provides us with the opportunity for continuous marketing research, in which we constantly watch and listen to customers as part of the normal course of doing business.

Customers and fellow customers

If you have an obscure hobby and access to an online service, you are probably seconds away from finding hundreds if not thousands of people who share your passion. Online newsgroups serve as meeting places for everyone from camera collectors to competitive flower arrangers. The much hyped concept of the online community arises from these self-organizing groups of kindred spirits.

From a marketing perspective, it is as if consumers have already done their own segmentation. Again, this is a story of cost reduction. The cost to customers of finding other customers drops radically. One intriguing example of this is online auctions such as eBay, which currently has over 800,000 items on sale. EBay performs two functions: it provides a central meeting point for collectors, and a mechanism for tracking the reputation of sellers. After each sale, the buyer gets to rate their satisfaction with the seller, whose cumulative rating is accessible online. In time, prospective buyers can know quite a bit about each seller and can thus shop more confidently. The ultimate attraction, of course, is higher prices for the sellers. Because eBay brings together a larger set of potential buyers, sellers often realize higher prices on line then they would at a local antique show.

The reduced cost of customers finding other customers has a drawback too (at least from a business perspective): a dissatisfied customer can easily find others. The result can be word-of-mouth communications that reach tens of thousands of potential customers virtually instantly. There are already a number of websites run by dissatisfied customers. A quick search reveals sites organized by customers for businesses ranging from Hewlett-Packard to Snapple.

The power of the internet community was clearly revealed by the Pentium flaw incident that affected Intel in late 1994 and early 1995. The floating point flaw, first reported by a mathematics professor at a small US university, was amplified first through technical online user groups and eventually via e-mail through Pentium flaw jokes. Intel, which at first announced a very limited trade-in program, was caught unawares by the breadth of consumer reaction. Within weeks, it announced a widespread recall and a two-year write-off of more than $400m to cover the cost.

What this means for marketing

Whenever the costs of business functions change by a considerable order of magnitude, new ways of doing business result. Electronic commerce is substantially reducing the costs of communicating with customers, listening to customers and finding fellow customers. In many cases, reduced costs mean that producers are finding it cheaper to go directly to customers instead of using intermediaries such as distributors and physical retailers. This effect, known as "disintermediation," particularly applies to channels that essentially provide information.

Consider the travel industry and its intermediaries, travel agents. Currently the channel provides mostly information to customers; the only physical product, an airline ticket, is being replaced by electronic ticketing in many cases. Some airlines have seized upon this as a profit opportunity. United Airlines, for example, has set up a website that allows customers to book tickets for over 500 airlines through existing online reservation systems, but via a friendly user interface. Similar sites are being operated by most major airlines. The goal is to replace the travel agent and to collect the fare commission, which until recently was the lower of $50 or 10 per cent of the ticket price.

For the consumer this new service has tangible benefits: it is available 24 hours a day and provides more information than the typical travel agent can over the phone. The display shows more flights and includes other details such as the percentage of times the flight arrives on schedule. From United's cost perspective, the key benefit is an increase in revenue. According to published reports the cost of booking a transatlantic ticket through a travel agent is between $70 and $80. The online cost is about $20. In addition, United gains information about flights taken with competitors and about hotel and car rental bookings (both of which are available via its online service). And United is likely to experience an increase in customer loyalty as experience with the system grows.

Another consequence of the reduced costs associated with electronic commerce is the emergence of new intermediaries and markets. Because the costs of finding buyers – and sellers – have been markedly reduced, new marketing channels and suppliers are developing. One example is PriceLine, an online service that allows people to bid for flights. Users specify a range of times and dates and the bid is then either accepted or rejected. PriceLine provides a value-added intermediary service, running what is, in essence, an auction between airlines and potential flyers to help airlines realize incremental revenue by filling every available seat. Notice that running this auction without the reduced costs provided by IT would be impracticable. Many airlines are trying to increase incremental profits themselves by using e-mail to offer last-minute fares on lightly traveled routes. There are many other examples of new intermediaries filling market functions that were too expensive to serve before. EBay, mentioned above, is one, and others include Flycast, which is making a market in online banner advertising, and Metal Exchange, which conducts business-to-business markets in the steel industry.

Conclusion

The key impact of electronic commerce upon business models will be through greater efficiencies. The most important thing to remember is that this change will not be incremental but rather, in many cases, quite radical. Order-of-magnitude changes in cost represent irresistible incentives for organizational change.

Success in marketing in this new world will go to those who best understand how technology will change business models. The result will be new channels characterized by disintermediation or the presence of new intermediaries. Changes in cost are the driving forces that will make electronic commerce happen and the result will be a much leaner and more efficient marketing function.

Summary

New technologies give rise to new businesses and new business models. This happens because they drastically reduce the cost of certain functions. In the case of electronic commerce, says **Eric Johnson**, it is the cost of communicating with customers that has plummeted. Advertising is becoming more focused and more cost-effective; market research is becoming faster and more detailed; and the presence of online interest groups offers the prospect of ready-segmented markets. Markets that essentially consist of flows of information will undergo disintermediation and new intermediaries will spring up to perform market functions that would formerly have been too costly.

Towards the high-tech, high-touch website

by Albert A. Angehrn

As early as 1994, managers worldwide started getting bombarded with statements such as "If you're not an active internet citizen by the mid-1990s, you're likely to be out of business by the year 2000." Today, European surveys confirm that it is extremely hard to find executives who will admit publicly that their company is not engaged in – or at least planning – exciting internet initiatives. When asked how they think their companies have gained from using the internet or their corporate intranets, European executives report enhanced corporate image as the main benefit, followed by added efficiency, improved quality of products and services, improved employee relations and a strengthened customer base. To a lesser degree, increased sales, higher profits and closer ties with suppliers or distributors are also reported as tangible benefits.

Just looking uncritically at these data might make us very optimistic about the health of our companies and public organizations. Reality, obviously, is a little different. As we all know, surveys do not always capture reality, although they can be good for measuring social pressure, like that imposed by the media on naturally technophobic managers (and people in general). Furthermore, mental habits, deeply rooted business models and practices as well as organizational structures do not change fast.

Change *is* taking place, but we are still in an early stage of development. Has the internet only succeeded in becoming the new (admittedly efficient and entertaining) toy of marketing managers and researchers? Or has it really stimulated new marketing models and approaches? Above all, are traditional marketing approaches sufficient to leverage the dynamics of a global marketplace in which information barriers between economic agents (companies, regulators, governments, suppliers and customers) are falling, virtual communities are emerging to influence market trends, and increasingly sophisticated services are being distributed to any destination immediately and inexpensively through global communication networks? Is a "paradigm shift" already happening in marketing or are companies just upgrading their technological infrastructures?

Old wine in new bottles

Analyzing companies' Web presence might not be enough to gain a full overview of their internet strategy. internet strategies do not necessarily focus on marketing, but can aim, for instance, to improve internal processes, increase the performance of "back office" processes or reduce internal or external transaction costs. Nevertheless, websites at least reveal a company's and its marketing managers' attitude towards the internet as a global market communication medium.

A systematic analysis of the web presence of corporations and institutions worldwide confirms that it is hard to find companies that do not have, or are not constructing, a website. These may be very diverse in appearance, but most of them actually have something important in common: they belong to the "brochure"

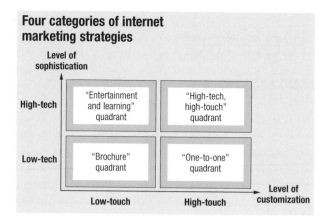

Four categories of internet marketing strategies

Figure 1

category illustrated in Figure 1. Figure 1 shows four categories that can be used to classify commercial and public websites. These categories represent different degrees of sophistication and customization in companies' internet marketing strategies. The level of sophistication of corporate websites reflects the degree to which specific characteristics of the medium are exploited, while the level of customization reflects the degree to which the internet is used to provide individualized services.

Let us look first at the "brochure" quadrant, into which most sites still fall. Such sites reflect the low-commitment, low-cost (and consequently low-return) strategy adopted by the vast majority of companies. For these companies, the internet is just another medium for relatively untargeted and unsophisticated one-directional messages about themselves and their products and services. Besides being a case of filling new bottles with old wine, there is no evidence that such sites, even if well advertised on television or elsewhere, contribute much more than traditional brochures to performance improvements in marketing.

Fortunately, not all marketing managers are so unimaginative. Over the past few years, rapid advances in hardware, network and software technologies have enabled some to discover the richness of the internet as a medium and a technology. Some companies have graduated from the unimaginative "brochure" quadrant to the more sophisticated "entertainment and learning" quadrant. Web technology makes it possible for them to transform unattractive brochures into sophisticated, interactive multimedia entertainment experiences that they can distribute at low cost to attract market attention.

Moreover, connecting database technology to traditional websites makes it possible to transform a passive brochure into a marketing tool that can be used to capture important market data in large amounts and at low cost. Such data might include information about who visits the site, how they access it and whether they call again.

Internet marketing strategies falling into the "entertainment and learning" quadrant still do not go beyond traditional models but they at least represent an attempt to take as much advantage as possible of the internet. Such strategies treat the internet as a new support technology to improve the effectiveness and efficiency of existing marketing strategies and practices. The resulting websites attract the attention of innovation- and entertainment-hungry online consumers, exploiting the rapid spread of virtual "word-of-mouth." But do they create customer loyalty? Do they go as far as possible in exploiting the internet as a vehicle for learning about customers and market trends?

Beyond the brochure

Only a few websites today reflect the intention of marketing managers to experiment with the possibilities for customization opened up by internet technology. Such "high-touch" sites require a major rethink of the internet, as not just a new opportunity to broadcast commercial messages but as an individual relationship-building vehicle. What companies target here is what non-customized sites – whether high- or low-tech – do not appear to guarantee: customer loyalty.

High-touch websites are still rare. These are the sites that welcome you personally as soon as you enter ("Hi Albert. Why didn't you visit us last week? Don't you like the industry report you've been reading every week anymore?"). They change their structure and content to match the needs of each customer, whose profile, habits and preferences are stored and updated dynamically.

A certain degree of customization can be reached through relatively simple software that enables the user to indicate personal parameters to determine the appearance of the site. But more advanced technologies, such as distributed 3D and agents, are enabling managers to experiment with new forms of internet marketing.

A visit to such sites, located in the "high-tech, high-touch" quadrant, can take the form of a walk through a virtual store in which customers are welcomed by "sales avatars" (computer- or human-controlled entities with a "human" appearance). These are able to recognize returning customers, to welcome new ones, to engage in dialogs with visitors and even to have customers meet (or "bump into") each other to discuss a specific product.

Current research is helping us to understand how people in general, and consumers in particular, behave in such virtual environments, where the social dimension is reinforced by a feeling of being "present" – with others – in a common space that can be tailored more flexibly and naturally (by moving objects) than traditional websites. The same research is producing guidelines for the design of such "high-tech, high-touch" virtual spaces, and new metaphors for providing product and company information are being explored.

For example, the first experiments with internet-based, three-dimensional virtual shopping environments that could be accessed simultaneously by different users used the familiar shop metaphor. More recently, shops have been replaced by beaches, in which a new line of swimwear can be more appropriately introduced to customers, or by offices and other environments in which customers meet and interact with avatars controlled by people (or, increasingly, computers) in the front office. Such sites bear little resemblance to "brochure" sites. They reflect a more mature exploitation of internet technology and a new "mass customization" approach to communicating and building relationships with customers.

New models of marketing

In a 1994 report, the European Round Table of Industrialists, an association of chief executives whose companies have a combined turnover of some 550 billion euros and more than 3M employees worldwide, challenged European managers with statements such as: "Information highways will make a greater impact on society than railways, electric power and the telephone." Today, the impact of the

The evolution of the website

Studies conducted in the banking sector back the idea that companies' internet marketing strategies evolve along a path that starts with first-generation websites in the "brochure" category. At the present stage of evolution, some of these have become second-generation websites in the "entertainment and learning" quadrant; a few have evolved into third-generation websites in the "high-touch" quadrants (*see* Figure 2).

First-generation banking websites are good examples of the non-committal "brochure" approach. Since then, more sophisticated sites have offered the experience of visiting a virtual branch. Now banks that are experimenting with third-generation sites aim to exploit the internet totally. They are extending highly personalized services to every customer. Visiting a bank site might soon mean entering the (virtual) office of your personal (virtual) banker – who might have sent you an e-mail reminder – so the two of you can discuss the impact of the (real) recent Russian crisis on your investment portfolio.

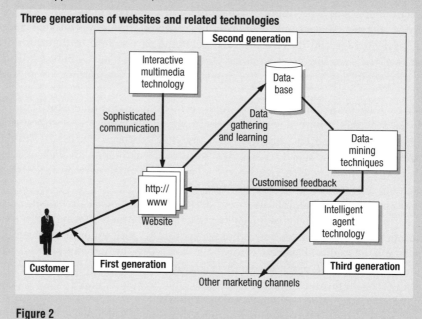

Three generations of websites and related technologies

Figure 2

internet on communication patterns and styles around the world has become evident.

These changes have deep implications for marketing studies, techniques and strategies, as communication is at the core of establishing and maintaining relationships. A parallel might be the modification or elimination of axioms underlying a mathematical theory. Under such conditions it is unlikely that cosmetic changes and minor adaptations will be enough to enable players to identify new opportunities and threats in time. More forceful questioning of dominant models and practices is now necessary, together with a willingness to explore new business models even if they depart from the "good old ways."

The good news is that the price of participating in the rapid innovation cycle we have just entered is not very high. The bad news is that the price of departing from mental models we have used successfully for years is usually high. If learning new tricks is not always easy, unlearning old ones is certainly harder.

Summary

Over the past few years, companies have been exhorted to jump aboard the internet or risk being left behind. Thus there are now few companies that do not have a website. Unfortunately, says **Albert Angehrn**, most of these are little better than online corporate brochures that fail to take full advantage of the technology that is available for mediating interactions with customers. The best corporate websites are both "high-tech" and "high-touch": they combine sophisticated multimedia and data-capture mechanisms with a high degree of customization to build durable relationships with customers. Although a lot of research is being undertaken into the dynamics of such virtual spaces, marketers still face the difficult task of developing new mental models of their discipline.

How online communities are growing in power

by Robert V. Kozinets

In the past three months, it is estimated that over 11m people worldwide – most of them in the US – participated in "virtual communities" of one type or another. The longer internet users spend online, the more likely they are to begin using – and to continue using – virtual communities as a source of information and interpersonal communication.

These gatherings have variously been termed "virtual," "online," or "computer-mediated" communities. internet pioneer Howard Rheingold defines them as "social aggregations that emerge from the net when enough people carry on ... public discussions long enough, with sufficient human feeling, to form webs of personal relationships in cyberspace." With 51 per cent of internet users using the web daily, and exponential growth rates around the world for new users, it seems certain that there will be prodigious growth in the quantity, interests and influence of virtual communities.

Virtual communities have a range of cultural effects, including influencing consumer behavior. In fact, many of these groups are structured around consumption and marketing interests. "Online communities of consumption" are a specific sub-group of virtual communities that overtly deal with consumer interests. They may be defined as "affiliative groups whose computer-mediated interactions are based upon sharing enthusiasm and information about a specific consumption activity."

Four types of community

Online communities of consumption comprise four different kinds of social sites –

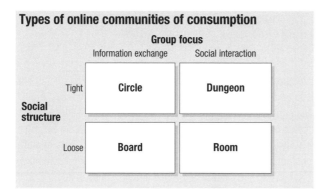

Figure 1

"dungeons," "rooms," "circles," and "boards." These differ in the amount of social structure their members exhibit when interacting ("loose" versus "tight") and in the type of focus that the group has (geared towards either information exchange or social interaction). Each type of community provides a wealth of opportunities for the astute marketer.

Dungeons

A "multi-user dungeon" (Mud) is a virtual environment where players of "dungeons and dragons" fantasy games meet. I use the related term "dungeon" to encompass any computer-generated environments where people socially interact through the structured format of role- and game-playing. Dungeons contain consumers who are focused on technologies that facilitate fantasy and play.

Computer games such as id Software's Quake owe much of their success to the collectives of game- and role-players who shared secrets, software and camaraderie in online dungeons. Besides directly marketing games, software, books and related goods to inhabitants of dungeons, strong brand-building activities can also be pursued. The new values that characterize dungeons can form the basis of new value propositions. Their cutting-edge, ever-evolving lexicon of symbols can provide the raw material for new marketing ideas.

Rooms and circles

I use the term "rooms" to refer to computer-mediated environments where people socially gather together, interacting in real time without the overt structure imposed by fantasy role-playing. The process – also called IRC, or "internet relay chat" – is analogous to a party-line telephone call. "Circles" are links of related homepages, interest-structured and information-orientated collections of related consumption interests.

Both rooms and circles are themed in ways that make them very attractive to marketers. They can be defined by geographical areas (for example, Asia, Brazil, Chicago), by educational categories (for example, first-year students, particle physics, Camille Paglia's works), by important issues (disarmament, dealing with Down's syndrome), by sex, by sexual orientation, by religion, by occupation or by more overtly consumption-related themes.

Smart marketers are already taking advantage of the opportunities afforded by such self-segmentation. "Do you have a Web site?" the web-page at Amazon.com asks. "If you do, you could jump into the world of electronic commerce today by

Go online, young marketer …

Some virtual communities of interest

- Dejanews newsgroup: www.dejanews.com Contains archives of board-type newsgroup postings that are individually searchable (via the "browse groups" function); from this database one can even "profile" the interests of individual message posters
- For a brand-loyal online car community, see rec.autos.makers.saturn
- For an online community of bicycle riders, see rec.bicycles.soc
- For a sampling of the exchanges and interests of sports collectible collectors, see rec.collecting.sport.basketball
- For stock and mutual funds purchasing try misc.invest.stocks
- For cruise travel, try *rec.travel.cruises*
- For the official Simpsons web-page, see www.thesimpsons.com/simpsons

- For a circle of unofficial websites devoted to The Simpsons, see www.clarityconnect.com/webpages/aceohe arts/simpsons.htm
- For a room in which to chat about The Simpsons, see www.wnol.com/wnol/simp-sonschat.html
- For a "family-safe" room to chat in, try www.worldvillage.com/wv/chat/html/chat.htm
- For a slick and stylish "alien abduction" themed chat room, try www.cygnuschat.com/index2.htm
- For a fantasy dungeon devoted to magic and mysticism, try www.netwalk.com/~mystical/Main%20Page .htm
- For a science-fiction dungeon devoted to Martian topics, try www.marsmud.com

joining the Amazon.com Associates Program." Offering circle members a commission on any books it sells to others through "advertising" on their websites, the online bookseller seeks to benefit from their "native expertise."

Boards

Perhaps the most directly consumption-related communities are "boards." Boards are online communities organized around interest-specific electronic bulletin boards. Board members read and post messages that are sorted by date and subject, and also respond to discussion threads.

There are boards devoted to pop groups and films. Others discuss beer and cigars, cars and cameras. There are even boards devoted to discussions about Taco Bell and McDonalds. Very often, within groups not specifically devoted to a consumption topic – such as parenting or environmental groups – the discussion revolves to a significant extent around available products and services.

The race is on for contemporary marketers to understand and build connections with these online communities of consumption before their competitors. The inter-activity of the internet and the accessibility of the information it contains are behind a fundamental shift now taking place in the way people think about purchases.

Revolutionary implications

There is a classic "80–20" rule in consumer marketing: approximately 80 per cent of most products and services are consumed by only 20 per cent of their customer base. For example, in the US beer market, 16 per cent of beer drinkers consume 88 per cent of the beer. The segment encompassing these so-called heavy or loyal users is usually at the heart of any successful marketing effort.

As internet usage proliferates and the constitution of online communities

The cyberconsumer's manifesto

Feeding on the wire, a new breed of consumer is evolving from the old. According to some scholars, the trends in marketing reflect an accelerating shift in human evolution, a move from a purely organic form of life to one captured by the eerie term "cyborg." Through advanced information technology, the senses and tastes of the average consumer are being extended through millions of interactive nodes.

Keeping pace with the monumental changes in consumers' everyday information and communication needs, marketers must adapt to and facilitate new "cyborg-friendly" forms of marketing. The following principles may provide guidance for millennial marketers.

Speak to the group identity

Collective online responses mediate the tastes of individual consumers. Hence you are not speaking to the group, you are speaking through the group. While directing your language at individuals, keep group identities and processes clearly in mind.

Follow the fragments

Study the fractal-like micro-segments and niches in online communities of consumption in order to understand the critical differences and similarities that coexist within an ostensibly unified market.

Follow the spotlight

Scan for where interest flows and link to the symbols that provide personal meaning and garner attention. Successful marketing directed at online community members will give them meaning and inspiration that is relevant to their shared consumption identities.

Consider pay-for-attention marketing

Offer online community members incentives such as contests and prizes in exchange for their permission to tell them more about a product or service, and to learn more about them.

Consider giving it away

Establish reasonable limits related to brand identity and then give away things that can be easily copied. Giving things away allows consumers to become brand champions who customize corporate symbols into their lives and enables marketers to build loyalty and trust.

Beware the revolution

Organizing online is an empowering experience for consumers, so be ready to have your management decisions, your ethics and your quality revealed to the world. Abusing the privacy and trust of online communities is a surefire way to fail in the new medium.

becomes more representative of the mainstream, virtual communities are going to be the place to find many of the loyal users. While access may become simple, the marketer's job overall will become considerably more complex as revolutionary changes are occurring in the consumer–marketer relationship.

The messengers are becoming the medium

Loyal consumers are increasingly creating their tastes together, as a community. Online, loyal consumers evaluate quality together and negotiate standards. Individuals place great weight on the judgments of their fellow community-of-consumption members. Collective response influences their consumption and tempers their judgment of marketing communications. For example, on The Official X-Files Home Page (www.thex-files.com), fans of the popular television series not only debate the merits of each episode, they also discuss the most recent licensed merchandise. The board generates excitement, instils awareness and mediates consumer demand.

Far from simplifying things, virtual communities make the marketer's life even more complex. Power is shifting from marketers to consumer communities. Increasingly, marketers will need to realize that they are communicating not with one but with many. "The customer" will need to be seen as an agglomeration of communicating consumers, who draw on each others' knowledge and experience to evaluate communications.

The mass market completely dissolves online

Online communities of consumption are heavy user groups, the virtual equivalents of the 20 per cent who consume 80 per cent. To a considerable extent, they come to the marketer already self-segmented by intensity of interest. But however united they may seem, within that consumption segment there will be a multitude of niches, micro-segments and micro-micro-segments. Community members endlessly reorganize themselves into increasingly identity-specific "factions."

For example, stratified groups of coffee fans in the alt.coffee newsgroup will debate the merits of various strains of coffee beans, of methods of preparation, of coffee machines and of brands. The best way for marketers to handle such diversity is to segment judiciously, while simultaneously uniting at the symbolic level that unites brand identity with consumer identity. Product loyalty is inevitably based on the need to believe and belong. In the midst of the clutter and the semiotic assault of the information age, a key way for marketers to stay strategically focused will be to concentrate on brand identity and global positioning.

Paying attention and pay-for-attention marketing

Attention marketing is based on the notion that the scarcest commodity in the information age is not time or information but human attention. Smart marketers must focus on the attention of the global market and of its multitudinous segments. Accordingly, marketers should go where the interest flows. Quite often this will lead to strong brands, be they household brands with strong identities – such as Marlboro or Levis or Coca-Cola – or the branding of entertainment and leisure products such as films. Consumer marketing must be linked to symbols that provide meaning and attract attention. The more marketing provides online community members with some meaning related to their shared consumption identities, the more those consumers will become and remain loyal.

"Pay-for-attention" marketing is one way to build this loyalty. Such marketing implies that the old models of marketing as an unsanctioned interruption of television or radio broadcasts, or as an imposing billboard, are giving way to a model in which marketers must offer online community members something in return for permission to tell them about a product or service. For example, eyewear-maker Bausch & Lomb's online "The Eyes Have It" sweepstakes (www.yoyo.com/games/eyes) involve online consumers in a "trivia game" in which they can win a cruise. In the course of the "game," players learn more about Bausch & Lomb's products, while revealing information about themselves.

Power to the people

Pay-for-attention marketing and demanding, united consumer groups imply that power is shifting away from marketers and flowing to consumers. While consumers are increasingly saying "yes" to the internet, to electronic commerce and to online marketing efforts of many kinds, they are also using the medium to organize consumer resistance. Circles, dungeons, rooms and boards have all been used as forums for fomenting and organizing acts of consumer dissent. As online communities build ties between devoted, loyal consumers of products, scrutiny of and wariness towards the marketers of those products heightens.

The more members communicate with one another through the internet, the bolder they feel about challenging marketing. Sony's efforts to market its recent Godzilla remake using a corporate "fan" board backfired when fans overwhelmingly used the forum to gripe about the movie. In the end, the company shut the board down.

One of the most infamous examples so far of friction between marketers and online communities has been the so-called "foxing" incident. Fans of Fox Broadcasting television shows, such as The Simpsons, had gone to considerable effort to create their own non-profit web homepages dedicated to the shows. In 1996, the network, which is owned by News Corporation, began a "crackdown" on these "unofficial" sites. Fans were sent "cease-and-desist" letters, demanding that they remove trademarked pictures and sound clips from their sites. Fans rallied quickly. They organized letter-writing campaigns and boycotted licensed merchandise. Apparently, Fox and its licensees felt the effects, because they seem now to have ceased and desisted from their legal actions. The result, though, is a tarnished relationship, and the possibility of more consumer resistance to come.

Virtually forced to give it away

As the "foxing" incident suggests, there is little doubt that issues of information trade and copyright are going to be contentious in the age of instantaneous replication and transmission. Information-related products such as software, movies, music, newspapers, magazines and education used to be considered "non-fungible" – it was difficult to replace one item with another. This is no longer the case.

The US has been trying to establish strong legal protection for intellectual property through the General Agreement on Tariffs and Trade and the World Trade Organization. Technical means of protecting it, such as new forms of encryption, and stiff penalties for those who pick the digital "lock" on a piece of intellectual property, have been proposed. But controlling copies of easily copied goods in a digital world is a complex challenge, particularly because people who take copies often change them in subtle ways before rebroadcasting them.

A simple marketing rule emerging in the digital economy is that networks are what build value, and networks are often created by giving things away. That was the pattern that led to the early success of Netscape, Eudora, and countless other shareware and freeware standards. Even Microsoft has followed this strategy for its internet Explorer.

Remember that the goal is not to control the information but to use it wisely to build solid relationships with products or brands. Virtual communities offer an excellent venue for the marketing research that underlies these relationships and for building a subscription or membership base.

Within limits, giving things away that can be easily copied is perhaps the wisest marketing strategy. Giving things away allows marketers to build loyalty and trust and allows a company to make its margins on things that are difficult to copy.

When dealing with virtual communities, use a light touch. Guard brand identity but provide members with the raw materials they need to construct a meaningful community – and remember that community-building is a creative activity. Treat members as your partners in promotion and distribution. Provide channels for them to become your heralds and champions and they may well reciprocate in a "virtually overwhelming" way.

Summary

The growth of "virtual communities" on the internet has been rapid. Many are overtly structured around consumer interests and hence are of vital interest to marketers. In this article, **Robert Kozinets** describes the four main kinds – "dungeons," "rooms," "circles," and "boards" – and considers some of the revolutionary implications for marketing. These include market fragmentation and a shift in power from marketers to consumers, who create their tastes consensually in online groups. As human attention becomes an increasingly scarce commodity, marketers will need to "pay" for it and to build networks by giving products away.

INTERNATIONAL MARKETING

10

Contributors

Arvind Sahay is assistant professor of marketing and international business at London Business School. His research interests include marketing strategy, technology and innovation, technology licensing and strategic alliances, new product development and international marketing.

Philip Parker is professor of marketing at INSEAD. His research focuses on marketing strategy, international management, pricing, new product diffusion and forecasting.

Jill G. Klein is an assistant professor at INSEAD. She specializes in marketing management, with a focus on consumer decision-making in international markets.

Richard Ettenson is currently visiting associate professor of marketing at the Graduate School of Business, University of Chicago, and associate professor of marketing at Bond University School of Business, Australia.

Andrew John is affiliate professor of economics and political science at INSEAD.

Jerry Wind is the Lauder Professor and professor of marketing at the Wharton School of the University of Pennsylvania. He is also director of the SEI Center for Advanced Studies in Management

Tim Ambler is senior fellow at London Business School, where he teaches global marketing and doing business in China. His research interests include measuring marketing performance, how advertising works and relationship marketing.

Chris Styles is a lecturer at the University of New South Wales, Sydney, where he leads a research program investigating East–West business partnerships in South-East Asia. His other research interests include brand management and strategy development.

Contents

Introduction

In this final module we look at the art of marketing products and services overseas. For marketers in multinationals, the key challenge is to create a strategy appropriate for many national markets; typical dilemmas are whether to launch new products market by market or everywhere at once, and whether to adopt a standard marketing mix worldwide (although global variations in climate and terrain are likely to make absolute standardization impossible). Truly global strategic thinking – which requires companies to envisage new business and organizational models – remains a rare commodity. Also discussed in this module are consumer boycotts (particularly those motivated by international animosities) and the difficulties faced – and solutions adopted – by small and medium-sized enterprises considering exporting for the first time.

Finding the right international mix

by Arvind Sahay

International marketing can be broadly divided into two areas:

1 market entry issues and building a presence in international markets
2 situations where companies operating in global markets already have a presence in the markets in which they are interested.

Multinational companies such as Coca-Cola, General Motors, Philips, Hyundai, Sony, Daimler-Benz, Glaxo-Wellcome, Motorola, Hewlett-Packard, Microsoft, Infosys and others tend to have a presence in most if not all of the markets that interest them. For such companies, the issue – which this article will focus on – is more one of managing the international marketing mix than of international market entry.

What are the principal issues facing a marketer who has to plan on an international scale? Generally they are the following:

- How does one develop a product for international markets? Should a new product launch be simultaneous in all markets (a "sprinkler" model) or sequential (a "waterfall" model)?
- Given the rhetoric of leading thinkers such as Theodore Levitt, who support standardization, how far should a company standardize its product and other elements of the marketing mix and how far should it adapt to individual markets?
- If it chooses to adapt, how does a company avoid potentially damaging inconsistencies among different markets? Or is there no drawback in having differences in product features and brand positioning across countries?
- More generally, should the marketing mix as a whole be standardized or adapted to each country or market?

These are critical questions. Without a coherent marketing strategy that integrates actions across all a company's markets, it is easy to fall into a multidomestic pattern of operations that does not take advantage of the possibilities that arise from co-ordinating actions across different national markets. In its extreme form, a multidomestic strategy treats each national market as a separate entity to be managed in isolation.

New product development

If a product has been developed for one geographical market, taking it to other countries sometimes requires little extra intellectual effort in terms of new product development – as in the case of pharmaceuticals – but at other times it is a daunting challenge.

The same medicine tends to be used for the same ailments whatever the country. Some countries do put up regulatory entry barriers for "foreign" medicine, and distribution systems can be very different but the product that is distributed is the same – except perhaps for packaging and branding.

Consumer tastes in cars, however, are very different in North America, the UK, Germany, Italy, Japan and India. A "global" car that does not have country-specific differentiating features will fail. The manufacturer, therefore, has to find the balance between designing a separate car for each market – which would be exorbitantly costly – and designing one car for all markets. Nissan was a pioneer in this area. It reduced the number of different chassis designs from 40 to eight for cars meant for 75 different national markets.

Ford went one better when it used cross-national teams – in the US, Italy and Japan – to design the Mondeo/Contour. The designers took a modular approach, where different components were mixed and matched to provide the features required for different markets. This greatly reduced the number of different types of components (and suppliers) required without substantially affecting the number of options available to consumers.

Some companies, however, do develop the same product for all markets regardless of existing local preferences. Companies such as Kellogg have succeeded in changing consumption patterns. Breakfast cereal was unknown in France 20 years ago. Today it is common. Kellogg ignored the research that said cereal would not sell in France.

There is a spectrum of new product development strategies. Firms sometimes customize a product to every market; at other times they offer one standardized product everywhere; and sometimes they compromise and settle in the middle.

A theme that runs across many international product development activities is that concepts coming out of one national market are frequently used in others. For example, Procter & Gamble's Tide detergent in the US uses surfactants developed for use in the Netherlands and enzymes developed for use in Japan. New product development that co-ordinates efforts across national markets leads to better products and services. Such opportunities are not normally available to a company that operates only in one country or is only just entering a new country.

The advent of the internet and intranets has the potential to accelerate the process of mining all markets for relevant information and for features that can be included in new products. Unilever has four global research laboratories that develop products for their different national markets while providing inputs for global products. The laboratories co-ordinate their efforts by looking at the possibilities of melding product ideas arising from different countries. Motorola's software development establishments co-ordinate their efforts in working on different modules of the same project.

Finally, companies develop products in different countries in markedly different ways. Japanese companies, for example, tend to believe much more in getting new products to market and then gauging the reaction to them. The product itself may have been developed with reference to observations of present and potential customers rather than conventional market research. US companies, on the other hand, tend to use more formal market research methods. And for German companies, product development schedules tend to be more important.

Product launch

Toshiba launched the Digital Video Disk (DVD) in Japan in November 1996, in the US in March 1997 and in Europe in autumn 1997. However, Intel launches its latest PC chips practically simultaneously in all countries. On the other hand, while more than a million cars are expected to be sold with car navigation systems as standard or optional in Japan in 1998, cars with this feature sell in very small numbers in the US and Europe and have yet to reach developing countries. Clearly, companies decide on different launch strategies for different categories of products. Can we infer some general rules? To do so, we first need a typology of products and services in relation to the consumer.

One criterion is whether the product is purchased separately by the consumer or is a component in another product or service. A second criterion is the amount of promotion needed to get the product off the ground. A third is the price of the product. It has been suggested that a product that provides desired benefits can quickly become a mass-market item in developed economies if it costs less than $300. However, even at those levels, it is unlikely to become a truly mass-market item in developing economies. Other criteria are the complementary products or services required for a successful launch and the stage of the product category's life cycle in the country in question.

Research carried out by the present author suggests that, in the case of an "inter-mediate" product/service purchased by organizations, simultaneous launch is more likely, at least in countries at the same stage of development. For consumer products, the evidence is less conclusive. On balance, companies are more likely to adopt a sequential approach, as exemplified by DVDs, car navigation systems and razors.

Evidence also suggests that companies choose to have multiple layers of brands. Some brands are global while many others are present in only one country. For example, out of the 560 brands that Nestlé had in 1995, 250 were present in only one country and only 19 were found in more than 50 per cent of the countries where Nestlé operates.

In terms of pricing, the more the price of a consumer product exceeds $300, the greater the likelihood that the launch will not be simultaneous in all developed-economy markets. Higher-priced products are more likely to be bought by the segments of the population that are innovators or early adopters who do not mind price-skimming strategies (see below). Research also suggests that the "waterfall" model is preferred over the "sprinkler" model when:

1 The life cycle of the product is relatively long
2 Many markets have unfavorable conditions such as slow growth
3 A weak competitive climate exists in many markets.

When a new product is launched at different times in different countries, adoption rates tend to be higher in "lag" countries than in the "lead" country. Potential adopters in lag countries have had more time to understand and evaluate the innovation than their counterparts in the lead country. Depending on the infra-structure, the rate of penetration may also be higher in lag countries. Over time, products tend to improve in quality and decrease in price due to scale economies.

Standardization versus adaptation

The launch decision also includes marketing mix decisions. In 1991, when Citibank introduced its credit card in the Asia-Pacific region, it launched it sequentially and tailored the product features for each country while maintaining its premium positioning. The promotional, pricing and distribution strategies also differed from country to country.

As one of the most internationalized banks, Citibank faces a peculiar problem. In the US, Citibank is a mass-market banker; its clientele includes a wide swathe of the middle class, although it does have high-income individuals as well. However, outside the US, Citibank has positioned itself as a provider of premium retail banking services for people with high incomes. In the UK, for example, individual account holders need to have a minimum annual income of $50,000; in India, the limit has been a minimum balance of $7,500. Ninety per cent of Citibank's private banking clients are in Asia. Thus, its US positioning is inconsistent with its positioning outside the US. (Later we shall see whether Citibank should do something about this.)

As a contrast, consider Rolex. The genuine Rolex watch is the same certified chronometer anywhere in the world; its positioning – as the timepiece for the elegant high achiever – is the same around the world, as is the advertising message. One will always find a Rolex in an upmarket distribution outlet and at a premium price. Or consider Unilever's Lifebuoy soap, which has different ingredients in India compared to East Africa. However, Unilever positions the soap in the same way in both markets – as an inexpensive everyday soap that has antibacterial properties and protects health.

Clearly, it is possible to have a completely standardized international marketing mix. It is also possible to have some elements that are the same across countries and others that are adapted to each country. Here we shall discount the extreme strategy of adapting all elements of the mix. So how can an international marketer decide whether to standardize or adapt the marketing mix? One possibility is to apply the product launch criteria already noted:

Is the product purchased separately by the individual consumer or is it a component in another product or service?

If the product is purchased separately by the consumer, then prescriptions are harder to come by. Culture-bound products are more likely to have an adapted marketing mix than culture-free products. The marketing mix for the DVD has been largely the same in Japan, North America and Europe. (Culture-bound products are those that are heavily influenced by a country's culture. Clothing, food, home decorations and so on are products that have a larger likelihood of being culture-bound.)

Additionally, products that are positioned at the higher end of the spectrum in terms of price, prestige and scarcity are more likely to have a standardized mix. These segments are relatively homogeneous around the world. Mass-market consumer products, on the other hand, are more likely to be positioned differently in different markets.

If the product is purchased by an organization as a component for its own products, then there is a greater likelihood of having a successful standardized marketing mix. While there could be differences in sales force strategies or pricing levels across countries, the basic positioning will depend on the component's function in the end product.

How much promotion is needed to keep the product before target customers in the markets of interest?

In general, products that are bought directly by the consumer tend to need higher levels of advertising/promotion than products that are components in other consumer goods. For products that are bought directly, evidence suggests that developed economies need higher levels of "share of voice" on different media to maintain consumer awareness. These messages need to be tailored to national markets, making a standardized marketing mix less likely. Components, however, are more likely to have a standard mix.

If the product is a consumer product, by how much is it priced above or below $300?

For a higher-priced product, the chances are that it is relatively new and that the target segment consists of innovators or early adopters – people who tend to adopt new products first, regardless of price. Companies use price skimming, as this is called, because these consumers tend to be price insensitive. Thus, the more the price of a product is above $300, the greater the likelihood that the pricing strategy is a skimming one, product features are changing fast and availability is selective in all markets. This line of reasoning assumes that innovator and early adopter populations are likely to be similar across countries.

Below $300, as the product begins to move into the mass market, different segments open up. These segments are more likely to differ across countries, leading to a greater likelihood of mix adaptation across countries. The lower the price, the stronger this tendency is likely to be.

Are complementary products/services required for market success available?

Many products and services, such as computers, cars, medical services and so on, require the presence of complementary products and/or services to be successful in the marketplace. Others, such as foods, textiles, toys and so on, require fewer "complements" for the consumer to derive benefits. Different international markets provide varying levels of complements. Products that do not require complements can have marketing mix elements that are independent of other products – which allows greater flexibility in adapting the mix to individual markets. Products that do require complements, on the other hand, have less flexibility.

At what stage is the life cycle of the product category in the country of interest?

If one country is at a different level in its development cycle compared to another, the product category life cycle in question is also likely to be at a different stage. Cars are a mature product in the US, Western Europe and Japan; they are in the late growth stage in South Korea; and in the very early growth stage in India.

In western Europe, for example, cars are as much a lifestyle product as a means of transportation, even in the mass market. Advertising reflects this and features of the product/service package are rarely dwelt on. In India, by contrast, while a car is a status symbol in many places, fuel consumption, reliability and price are more important than lifestyle appeals as determinants of purchase behavior in the mass market. Promotional messages in India have to account for this.

To return to the question of Citibank, how can it solve any potential problem arising from its inconsistent positioning – given that it is in for the long haul and cannot realistically be expected to shut down operations in some countries?

Inconsistency in positioning need not be a problem if consumers in the Asian markets are not aware of Citibank's positioning in the US. If upscale Asian consumers are aware of the US positioning and it is a problem, one approach that can be used (and which Citibank has adopted) is to move into the "middle" markets in Asia with a different set of products. Over time, such moves should lead to a more consistent positioning for Citibank across all its markets.

Since Citibank's product is a consumer service offered in markets with different levels of infrastructural development and consumer requirements, product differentiation in terms of features is inevitable, as are pricing and distributional differences. However, by expanding its offering to include the mass market and by simultaneously keeping its offering for elite customers differentiated, the company can project a uniform image around the world.

Summary

In these days of increasing global integration, the task many international marketers face is not so much market entry as managing the marketing mix in different national markets. Is it better to standardize or to adapt it across different markets? According to **Arvind Sahay**, a number of factors should be considered, such as whether the product is aimed at the "innovator" or "early adopter" segment (likely to be fairly uniform across countries), whether it is a component in or a complement to other products or services, and what stage of development targeted countries have reached. The author also discusses the issues of product development and product launch and suggests some strategies for dealing with inconsistent international positioning.

Suggested further reading

Samiee, S. and Roth, K. (1992) "The influence of global marketing standardization on performance," *Journal of Marketing*, 56 (2), 1–17.

Kalish, S., Mahajan, V. and Muller, E. (1995) "Waterfall and sprinkler new-product strategies in competitive global markets," *International Journal of Research in Marketing*, 12, 105–19, July.

Why markets will not converge

by Philip Parker

"The earth is round, but for most purposes it's sensible to treat it as flat. Space is curved, but not much for everyday life here on earth" (Ted Levitt, 1983)

In the early 1980s, the influential US academic Ted Levitt argued that the time had come for marketers to adopt standardized global strategies. Global differences in consumer preferences and tastes were "vestiges of the past." To marketers facing pricing, production/distribution, communications and product design decisions, the question of whether or not they can find consumers willing to buy a product that is the same around the world is moot; the answer has to be yes. But does this mean that Levitt was right? Are consumer tastes and preferences converging on a planetary basis across cultures?

To answer this question, we need to know if consumers' utilities, preferences and incomes are converging. ("Utilities" in this context means the value people assign to particular products.) Despite strong anecdotal evidence to the contrary, this article will argue that convergence has not occurred and will not occur in the future. This is not due to cultural diversity but to physioeconomic forces.

Physioeconomic theories, unlike micro- or macroeconomics, take account of *physiological* and *physiographic* ("physical-geographic") factors when modeling the differences between cultures. Such theories treat human physiological reactions as the drivers of variation in social and economic behavior across countries.

As information ubiquity and economic liberalism increase worldwide, the physioeconomic prediction is that behaviors will remain divergent on a planetary basis because of adaption to different environments. However, they will converge over time in countries with similar physioeconomic characteristics (climate and terrain, for example).

Physioeconomics

Physioeconomic theories seek to explain global variation in economic behavior. They date back at least to the work of the French political philosopher Montesquieu (1689–1755) and the Scottish economist Adam Smith (1723–90). The physiological aspects of these theories help in explaining global variations in the way people consume and work, whereas the physiographic aspects relate to variations in national production and assets.

The basic thesis of physioeconomics is that all human behavior is constrained by unchanging physiological laws. These laws prevail irrespective of racial, religious, ethnic, cultural, sociological or economic origins and situations. They affect people's physiological and psychological needs, which in turn affect culture, social structures and economic activity.

Figure 1 (*see* p. 311) summarizes the basic model behind physioeconomic theories. It is important to understand that the factors that influence behavior – broadly either "climate" and "terrain" – do so indirectly. They are behind the causal physiological and physiographic mechanisms that vary from one country or culture to another. These mechanisms are reviewed below:

Physiological mechanisms

Many differences in human behavior superficially attributed to culture or genetics are the result of physiological differences across populations.

Thermo-regulation

Humans need to maintain a constant core body temperature of 37°C wherever they are. Therefore their physiology constantly adjusts – via secretions of hormones, neurotransmitters and other chemicals – in order to maintain this temperature.

In the short run, thermoregulation may cause shivering (which generates internal body heat) or sweating (which allows heat loss through evaporation); in the long run, it involves acclimatization. Failure to balance incoming and outgoing heat may result in result in illness or even death by hypothermia or heat stroke. The metabolic adjustments that the body makes to maintain the right temperature ultimately also affect basic needs and preferences.

Acclimatization

This is a long-term adjustment that ensures physical comfort in particular climates. Each climate has a temperature/humidity threshold which, if passed, causes physical discomfort or illness for people acclimatized to that particular climate. In hotter climates, physiology adjusts to allow people to endure higher temperature/humidity levels before feeling discomfort. People living in the tropics, for example, feel less discomfort than tourists visiting the tropics, just as

Scandinavians, say, feel less discomfort than tourists coming from the tropics to Scandinavia. Thresholds are set by both average climatic conditions and seasonal variations. People living in places with very cold winters and very hot summers experience the highest levels of discomfort all year round.

Other physiological and psychological mechanisms

As well as the temperature-related factors just described, the diseases that people face, together with their immunity to them, are also affected by environment. Recent studies have also demonstrated the role of climate in psychology. For example, the nearer people live to the poles, the lower their level (on average) of the neurotransmitter serotonin. Abnormal levels of serotonin are associated with mood disorders such as depression and violence.

Physiographic effects

Certain activities require particular climatic or geographic conditions. Some sports, for example, can only be practised in particular geographic areas (for example, ice fishing, skiing). Certain diseases – such as malaria – are confined to areas that have not had frosts over the past 10,000 years. Virtually all animal and plant species are geographically bounded by prevailing climatic conditions (for example, oak forests and their fauna); this in turn affects the economics of human consumption.

Some activities are directly bounded by terrain and/or the severity of climate. The economics of mining vary according to the existence of mineral reserves; elevation and the amount of sunshine prevents the cultivation of certain crops. Such *exogenous* constraints – including rainfall – affect the supply of and demand for various goods and services, certain cultural traits, economic development patterns and even vital statistics. Exogenous factors include all non-human natural resources.

Endogenous factors, on the other hand, include any of human origin, including population, culture, religion, language, economic policies and social systems. Figure 1 includes "endogenous climate," which encompasses such things as air conditioning, heating and greenhouse effects. This is critical in the exploitation of certain physical resources.

Physioeconomics and determinism

Physioeconomics is not deterministic. Philosophies of determinism hold that all events, actions and decisions are the inevitable consequences of factors that are independent of human initiative or genius. But physioeconomic mechanisms do not directly cause behavior at the individual level. In the case of suicide, for example, sociologists have discarded climate as a factor in cross-national suicide rates. Climate is rarely, if ever, directly linked to particular acts of suicide, which instead are brought on by mental illness or personal circumstances. There is still a possibility, however, that climate affects a person's propensity to commit suicide given a specific circumstance.

Can we identify physioeconomic effects?

Given all the above, Levitt's "flat earth" conjecture can be evaluated by answering two questions:

1 are physioeconomic effects actually present, and
2 to what extent does the variance they account for decline over time?

The physioeconomic hierarchy

To grasp how far variations in behavior are driven by physioeconomic factors, a variety of statistical procedures can be used. Figure 1 illustrates the results of a filtering ("step-down") procedure based on the physioeconomic framework.

Physioeconomic framework

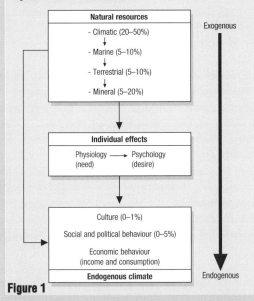

Figure 1

Natural historians recognize a causal hierarchy whereby certain natural phenomena are necessary conditions (and historical precedents) for others. The sun, or "solar climate," is the ultimate ("most exogenous") factor in natural history. Physical climate (continental and oceanic formation) follows. Climatic forces cause variations in the world's marine biology, vegetation and zoological resources. Each level in the hierarchy is a necessary condition for the next: culture depends on the existence of terrestrial life, which depends on the existence of marine life, which depends on a particular climate. Minerals are considered after these (though this is debatable) because many are formed by climatic processes that may also involve animal or plant life; and their measurement or extraction certainly comes after the rise of animal life.

Beyond these purely exogenous factors, difficulties arise in establishing hierarchies in human-generated factors. For the sake of illustration, Figure 1 follows a hierarchy generally accepted by historians with respect to current social systems. Modern religions, for example, are generally more exogenous than modern languages, which are in turn more exogenous than current economic policies, political systems or social institutions.

This framework can be used to assess any activity

via sequential filtering. The behavior in question (caloric consumption, say) is first filtered for solar climate. The resulting residual – that part of the behavior not correlated with solar climate – is in turn filtered for physical climate, and so on. This process is like that used in time-series studies that attempt to measure the short-term effects of policy on economic behavior that varies according to season.

The advantage of the sequential filtering process is that it directly measures the explanatory power of each element along the hierarchy. For example, we can estimate the extent to which a "Protestant work ethic" explains labor productivity beyond variance explained by exogenous elements – the "work ethic" may itself be explained by climate. Similarly, we can test whether religious affiliation (Catholic or Protestant, say) affects suicide rates after we control for exogenous geographic effects (Catholic countries are more concentrated towards the equator).

Solar climate is measured as absolute latitude squared (to account for the earth's curvature). Measures of physical climate include elevation and total land area. Marine life is measured using coastline length. Similar measures are used for land and mineral resources. Cultural measures include measures of the five largest world religions, number of religious groups and use of major colonial languages. Political and economic measures include dummy variables for alternative regimes (for example, communism, right-wing dictatorship, democracy).

For each level of the filtering hierarchy, Figure 1 indicates in parentheses the percentage variation that each explains across 30 cross-national measures. These include measures frequently used in demography (for example, mortality, fertility, population, population growth), sociology (for example, crime, suicide) and economics (for example, manufacturing, mineral extraction, consumption of durables, caloric intake, aggregate output, savings). These averages should be seen as typical of many, but not true of all, behaviors.

Regardless of how "culture" is defined – by national group, religious group, linguistic group – the percentages are relatively constant. A few behaviors – for example, short-term inflation rates across countries – are not explained by the hierarchy.

Across the various levels in Figure 1, solar climate generally explains the largest variances in behavior; over 70 per cent of the variance observed across the behaviors just mentioned are explained by exogenous factors, including income per head. Cultural variables explain little variance beyond that already explained by natural endowments. Controlling for climatic effects, for example, religion does not have an impact on labor productivity or "work ethics."

Certain philosophers, climatologists and geographers, dating back to Hippocrates (469–399BC), argue that the curvature of the earth (solar climate) is the single most important factor behind global variations in everything from religious doctrines, education and child rearing to folklore, music and even language. Unlike other species, humans are highly adaptable and respond to physiological adjustments – caused by climatic change – through consumption and industry.

With respect to the first question, solar climate alone (absolute latitude squared) has a stronger correlation than income per head with many economic behaviors that are usually thought of as "development driven." In the examples that follow, statistical correlation coefficients are given in brackets (1 = perfect positive correlation; –1 = perfect negative correlation; 0 = no correlation).

Behaviors that are uncorrelated with income per head but are explained by solar climate include milk consumption per head (.53) and cereal consumption per head (.57). Behaviors that are better explained by solar climate than income per head include flour consumption per head (.35), coffee consumption per head (.75), cigarette consumption per head (.33) and suicide rates (.62). Behaviors that are equally well explained by solar climate and by income per head include average population growth rates (–.50), number of major diseases (–.52), literacy rates (.46), percentage of homes with piped water (.66), telephones per head (.65), egg consumption per head (.54), beer consumption per head (.56), steel consumption per head (.65). In general, the correlations are higher when the data are limited to European countries or to industrial countries located in very different climatic regions.

While aggregate levels of consumption have clearly not converged around the world, neither have forms of consumption. Many consumption behaviors reflect an adaption to climate – for example, the use of tile floors in hot climates and carpets in cold climates.

There is an inverse relationship between the amount of calories that people eat and ambient temperature. Some 80 per cent of food consumption is required simply to maintain the body's temperature. The hotter the climate, the less one eats, especially of foods that require a lot of energy to digest, such as meat proteins. The colder the climate, on the other hand, the greater people's preferences for alcoholic drinks, which provide lots of calories (but cause dehydration). The greater, too, the need to install heating and to wear heavy or layered clothing. The fact that Mars Bars contain more fat and sugar in polar European countries than in Mediterranean countries is also ultimately explained by thermoregulatory effects.

Climatic effects may also explain differences in the physiological utility of physical labour; the same level of physical work has greater utility in temperate or polar regions than in equatorial or hot regions.

Physiological adaptations across populations affect dietary preferences (caloric/protein intake), housing preferences (heating, insulation, architecture) and clothing preferences (light versus heavy); overall they influence 30 to 50 per cent of total household consumption in developed economies and up to 90 per cent in less developed economies. Climate must therefore have a substantial impact on aggregate measures of behavior that incorporate these items (for example, cross-cultural measures of aggregate consumption or income per head).

While the non-convergence of both product attributes and consumption levels seems apparent for "thermoregulatory" products, physiological adaptations across climates also explain the strong correlation between solar climate and "psychological" products (such as entertainment products). The demand for the mental distraction provided by such products is higher towards the poles.

Physiological adaptations also account for the fact that seasonal affective disorders (winter depression) are stronger in temperate or polar climates than in equatorial climates. People residing closer to the poles are more likely to experience depression and suicidal thoughts. Suicide and mood disorders rise in the winter months in temperate or polar climates and peak towards the end of winter or in early spring, when cumulative hormonal imbalances are greatest.

Is behavior converging?

As for the second question – is variation in consumption/production behaviors declining? – physioeconomic theory predicts that such behaviors will diverge on a planetary basis but converge in countries with similar climate and terrain. This may account for the differences in economic performance between countries, a subject that has long been debated by economists. Some 70 per cent of variances in observed income can be explained by variances in natural endowments. Countries such as Chad, for example, are underdeveloped mostly because of their lack of natural resources and their equatorial or desert climates; economic policy failure is less important.

If Levitt's conjecture is true, variance explained by physioeconomic factors should be declining to zero. But data that adjust for purchasing power parity and that go back as far as the 1950s show that such variance has been increasing. As information ubiquity and democracy progress, economic planning approaches its optimal level within each country. As this happens, it will be physioeconomic factors that will increasingly explain differences across countries. By the late 1980s, solar climate alone explained over 60 per cent of the variance of income per head across countries.

The gradual increases in variance have occurred while consumption and income levels have substantially increased across both polar and non-polar countries. Strong climatic effects (high variances due to physioeconomic factors) do not mean that countries will remain underdeveloped. Absolute levels of behavior have shifted over time for all countries. Furthermore, signs of optimal adaptation to equatorial environments – in the form, say, of dress and architecture – are sometimes mis-attributed to poverty.

Consequences for economic planners

The acceptance of physioeconomic explanations for cross-country variances calls into question current measures of economic development. When comparing countries' "relative development" or economic performance given their exogenous endowments, one finds that the resulting national income differences are relatively small compared to absolute levels (they are within a few thousand dollars, say, rather than tens-of-thousands of dollars).

Many "less developed" countries (for example, Costa Rica) have higher economic performance, given their endowments, than the United States. We can conjecture that if Americans were to inherit Africa, they would do no better in developing Africa with their culture or social system than current Africans have done with theirs; similarly, if Japan were to have been located on the equator, its social system would perform only slightly better than Indonesia's (instead of being better by several orders of magnitude, according to absolute measures of development).

By focusing on these filtered measures, therefore, one may be able to identify "relatively successful" countries; the policies of these countries may prove useful in countries with relatively poor performance or those with similar endowments. Tropical countries, for example, may benefit from studying social and economic policies in Costa Rica or the Cayman Islands, which have relatively high economic performance given their natural endowments. Similarly, development efforts undertaken by the World Bank or by private voluntary organizations may be erroneously labeled "unsuccessful" because observers concentrate on absolute, rather than filtered, measures.

Current studies generally fail to recognize fundamental cross-country differences in both physiological and psychological utility ("basal utility") for a number of human needs, including food, clothing, housing, energy and entertainment. Cross-country data, including those limited to industrialized countries, indicate that part of the observed variances in development can be explained by climatic adaptation to maintain basal utility. For certain measures of development (for example, aggregate consumption per head), holding all countries (or climatic regions) to some absolute standard, regardless of where that standard was established, can be problematic.

Consider caloric intake. European data spanning several decades indicate substantially lower caloric consumption in warmer countries than in colder countries (probably because of thermoregulation). These levels have remained relatively constant over time, despite large increases in real income per head. Similar observations can be made about many other climate-affected behaviors.

If we are interested in measuring development from a general utility perspective, differences in basal utilities should be taken into account. Two different levels of absolute consumption may generate similar levels of utility, the difference being due to thermoregulation. For example, Belgians consume some 50 per cent more calories per head than people living in Bermuda (3850 versus 2545, respectively); it is difficult to imagine that all of this difference is due to economic performance or that Belgians receive that much more absolute utility from their diets.

While economic development measures might be adjusted to account for basal utility differences across countries, such adjustments run the risk of overestimating the development of those countries with the lowest absolute values on the original scale. An alternative is to place more emphasis on measures not subject to basal utility shifts, or indirect physiological or psychological mechanisms.

International studies (by companies or governments), for example, will give poor estimates of global food shortages if they use temperate-climate standards, which are likely to overestimate global needs (given the fact that more people live near the equator than in temperate climates). Policies such as food subsidies that are based on erroneous estimates may harm local farming economies.

Filtered measures can give realistic indications of the likely impact of policies on countries with different endowments. Likewise, the influence of ethnic, religious, language or cultural differences on social behaviors can be measured (or be identified as confounding or irrelevant) using approaches that incorporate physio-economic variables. By using filtered measures we can identify "relatively successful" rather than "absolutely successful" policies, which can be inappropriate or misleading.

Conclusion

Today, any given product can be found anywhere on the planet. Convergence theories have strong anecdotal support. In contrast to 20 years ago, for example, the average French high school student of today appears virtually identical to American students of the same age in terms of clothing, eating and entertainment preferences.

Such anecdotes support the prediction that countries converge towards similar behaviors provided that they have similar climates and terrains. But if we expand the sample to countries with highly dissimilar physioeconomic characteristics (Chad and Finland, say), we find behavioral differences that can be explained by human adaptation.

Filtering economic data for physioeconomic factors clearly reveals that countries may develop, in equilibrium, differing levels of behavior. These levels may reflect, in large part, physiological and physiographic effects rather than economic policies, culture or social institutions (which are also influenced by physioeconomic forces).

The physioeconomic framework responds to calls to expand the use of non-traditional variables in comparative studies of culture and economics. For example, neoclassical theories of growth fail to account for all the variance observed across national groupings. Inclusion of physioeconomic variables might go a long way to resolving such difficulties.

The fact that physioeconomics seems to disprove Levitt's "flat earth" thesis has substantial implications for marketers. If consumers' preferences for different products and modes of consumption are a function of something as fundamental as physiology, then in the long run there will be limits to strategic uniformity. For example, however hard marketing departments work, or however much they spend, adult alcohol consumption per head will not converge across all countries (and for more than simply cultural reasons).

However, physioeconomics does suggest many alternative ways of segmenting markets. If convergence is to be expected in countries with similar climate or terrain, such factors should at least be used alongside economic measures such as income per head. Perhaps most importantly, physioeconomic factors need to be weighed when companies decide which markets to move into. Typically the most attractive markets are those that have high latent demand and are relatively accessible (see "Choosing where to go global: how to prioritize markets", p. 17). But latent demand has a substantial physioeconomic component – measuring it just on the basis of factors such as income per head or penetration per head may be badly misleading.

Summary

In Module 1, **Philip Parker** explained how managers should select the best markets for their companies to move into. In this article, he examines the question of whether companies will ever be able to adopt standardized global strategies. The answer depends upon whether consumers' tastes and preferences are converging over time. According to purely economic theories, there is no reason why they should not. But if one takes physioeconomic factors into account – such as climate and terrain, and the way people physiologically adapt to them – convergence starts to look unlikely. The nearer one lives to the equator, for example, the less utility there is in physical labor or in consuming calories. The importance of physioeconomic factors is underlined by the fact that they correlate more strongly than economic factors with many supposedly "development-driven" activities. In the end, global strategies may be constrained by the simple fact that the earth is a globe.

Suggested further reading

Levitt, T. (1983) "The globalization of markets," *Harvard Business Review*, 92–102, December.

Parker, P.M. (1995) *Climatic Effects on Individual, Social, and Economic Behavior: A Physioeconomic Review of Research Across Disciplines*, Westport, CT, and Greenwood Press, London.

Parker, P.M. (1997) *Cross-cultural Encyclopedia of the World*, Westport, CT, and Greenwood Press, London.

How should companies respond to boycotts?

by Jill G. Klein, Richard Ettenson and Andrew John

The use of boycotts as a coercive marketplace tactic has increased in recent years and is expected to rise further. One reason for this is that consumer protests are proving more successful than in the past, both because those who organize boycotts are adopting more sophisticated tactics and because more consumers are supporting and joining organizations with explicit social and political agendas.

Boycotts are the conceptual opposite of relationship marketing. They sever the link that has developed between a business and its customers. As previously discussed in this book, relationship marketing currently generates keen interest among marketers because the cost of obtaining new customers far exceeds the cost of retaining current customers. Managers who allow their company to become a boycott target risk not only losing loyal customers but also encouraging those customers to form relationships with competitors.

In addition to loss of sales, boycotted companies suffer other serious negative consequences. Boycotts can severely disrupt the planning, implementation and analysis of the company's everyday marketing activities. They require managers to redirect significant resources to crisis management activities and to contend with the deleterious effect a boycott can have on the morale of employees, suppliers and other stakeholders.

Types of boycott

The usual conception of a boycott is as follows. A company commits some act or has some business practice that arouses the wrath of some of its customers. These customers then organize and decide not to purchase the company's product or service. The customers have the avowed aim of placing market pressure on the business in order to bring about the end of the offensive practice. An example was the boycott of tuna, which was aimed at getting companies to change their fishing practices so that dolphins would not be caught in nets.

Although some boycotts fall into such a category, many do not. Many consumers have no real intent to change the company's behavior but are simply motivated to avoid the product by anger or guilt. An animal lover may refuse to eat veal or foie gras, not to change farming practices but simply because he or she would feel uncomfortable or guilty about eating these foods.

In some ways, such private motivations to engage in boycotts make more sense than boycotting to change a producer's behavior. Consumers surely realize that an individual's actions are almost certainly insignificant to a company, even if it may be influenced by a large number of consumers acting together. Furthermore, there is a free-rider problem: any individual consumer would presumably prefer that others bear the burden of putting pressure on the company.

Boycotts, then, need not be driven by a desire to influence a producer's behavior. Even more strikingly, a business may find itself on the receiving end of a boycott through no fault of its own. Many boycotts trace their roots not to a company's current behavior but rather to the behavior of people with little or no connection to its activities. In particular, there is a class of boycotts fueled by international animosity, where consumers avoid a particular country's products because of the current or past behavior of its government. The US World War II veteran who refuses to buy a Sony television is doing so because he remembers Pearl Harbor, not because he dislikes Sony's business practices.

If we shift attention away from "traditional" organized boycotts and focus on individual consumers' motivations, we obtain a richer conception of the phenomenon. Developing ideas of marketing academics Craig Smith and Monroe Friedman, we can distinguish between *direct* boycotts, which stem from a specific act by a producer, and *indirect* boycotts, which are motivated by the actions of entities only peripherally linked to a producer. We can also distinguish between *instrumental* boycotts, which are intended to bring about change, and *expressive* boycotts, which are based on the desire to express anger or to avoid guilt.

Thus we arrive at a two-by-two categorization of boycotts. There is the *direct, instrumental* boycott, of which a good example might be the boycott of Nike by people trying to change its overseas labor practices. There is the *indirect, instrumental* boycott, such as the recent Australian boycott of French goods aimed at stopping France's nuclear testing in the south Pacific. There is the *indirect, expressive* boycott, exemplified by the Holocaust survivor who does not wish to purchase goods produced in Germany. And there is the *direct, expressive* boycott, which includes, for example, individuals who wish to express outrage towards Nike but do not expect to have any impact on its decisions.

Our taxonomy should really be thought of as categorizing individual motives rather than boycotts themselves. As our Nike example illustrates, different people may participate in a boycott for different reasons and indeed an individual may have multiple motives. Recognizing exactly why people are boycotting a company is the first step in formulating an effective response.

Strategic options

Our research (*see* boxed extract) indicates that producers may be victims of boycotts through no fault of their own and perhaps without even being aware of the fact. International animosity is only just beginning to be recognized as a factor affecting purchase decisions in the global marketplace. Yet there is evidence to suggest that, if levels of animosity towards a producer nation are high, traditional means of influencing consumer behavior and increasing market share (such as brand advertisements or price promotions) will not be appropriate or successful. After all, the

The animosity model of foreign product purchase

In a series of recent international studies, we examined animosity towards current or past national enemies and its effect on consumers' attitudes towards imports.

The city of Nanjing was the site of a massacre of Chinese civilians by the Japanese during December 1937 and January 1938 (*see* Iris Chan's *The Rape of Nanking*, Basic Books, 1997). This episode remains significant in contemporary Chinese history. Nanjing is thus a location where we might expect to find international animosity.

We surveyed consumers – aged 18 to 92 – in Nanjing and measured their evaluations of Japanese product quality, their willingness to buy Japanese products, their animosity towards Japan and their actual ownership of Japanese products. We found that animosity towards Japan was a powerful predictor of a refusal to buy Japanese products. Thus consumer animosity is leading buyers in Nanjing to participate in an indirect, expressive boycott.

Consumer animosity is distinct from consumer ethnocentrism, which is the widely held belief that it is wrong to purchase foreign products because to do so is damaging to the domestic economy. Our findings make allowances for this – that is, the negative influence of animosity is above and beyond such general ethnocentrism (*see* Figure 1). In addition, consumers who are ethnocentric also tend to denigrate foreign products, believing them to be inferior to domestic goods. In contrast, Chinese consumers who harbor animosity towards Japan are quite willing to acknowledge that Japan produces high-quality goods. Consumers avoid Japanese products simply because of their anger towards Japan's past actions.

These findings were replicated in a study we conducted in the US. US consumers who are still angry with Japan due to World War II are less willing to purchase Japanese products. As in China, the effects of animosity are above and beyond the effects of consumer ethnocentrism and independent of evaluations of Japanese product quality. We are currently studying attitudes towards the US held by consumers in Hiroshima.

Our findings represent a departure from traditional marketing wisdom. Practising marketers and researchers typically assume that consumers' evaluations of a product's quality are the key

The animosity model of foreign product purchase

Figure 1

determinant of purchase decisions. This assumption is obviously valid in many contexts; indeed, it gives managers the rationale for focusing on micro-level marketing activities intended to influence consumer brand choice and satisfaction. Our research reveals, however, that there are circumstances in which product quality is simply swamped by animosity.

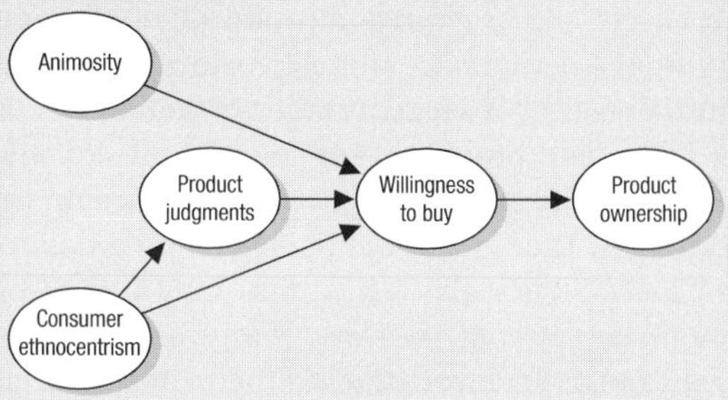

We extended our work by considering an indirect, instrumental boycott. Specifically, we surveyed Australian consumers about their purchases of French products during and after the French nuclear tests in the south Pacific in 1995–96. In the absence of direct access to the French government, Australian consumers attempted to express their indignation and to put pressure on France to desist by identifying indirect or surrogate boycott targets. These included French companies (for example, Air France and Peugeot) and French product categories (for example, French wines).

The boycott certainly had an impact: there were reports of sharp drops in the sales of French goods throughout Australia. At the height of the protests some consumers even boycotted French restaurants and bakeries that displayed signs clearly indicating that they were locally owned and operated. As in our other studies, we found that animosity was a significant predictor of participation in the boycott. Further, despite the severing of relations with French marketers, Australian consumers did not denigrate the quality of French goods. Perceptions of French product quality remained generally unchanged.

Jill Klein and Richard Ettenson

problem is not that consumers think the products are bad. They just dislike the place where the products are made.

A key message of our research is that an effective response to a boycott is possible only if managers understand what motivates the protest. Faced with a boycott stemming from international animosity, marketing managers need to know if consumers are acting out of anger (an expressive boycott) or out of a calculated desire to put pressure on a government (an instrumental boycott) or both.

The best strategic response to an indirect, expressive boycott is probably to decouple the product from its country of origin in markets where animosity is likely to be high. This can be done by downplaying the "Made in ..." aspect of the product or by developing hybrid products. Animosity can also be addressed directly by (cautiously) attempting to improve perceptions of the country and to address the sources of international tension.

When faced with an indirect, instrumental boycott, other options are also available. First, companies might find it worthwhile to put pressure on their government. (Whether or not the Australian boycott played a role, the French government did cut short its series of tests.) Second, a company might try to dissociate itself from the offending act and could even take a public position against its government's behavior (which could, of course, entail a completely different set of costs).

Direct boycotts, unlike those just discussed, respond to something the producer has done. This is a critical difference because a company faced with a direct boycott usually has the option of ending the offensive practice. Whether or not a company chooses to respond in this way, its actions should still depend upon what is motivating participants in the boycott.

Capitulating to the boycott is a managerial option that should be taken seriously. The public may have a point – perhaps the act to which it objects is indeed unethical, inappropriate, or unwise. If so, managers should look beyond the bottom line. And even if, after due consideration, managers decide that the boycott is unfair and that their customers are wrong, it may be easier and more profitable to give way.

There may be circumstances, however, where managers feel that giving in to a boycott would itself be an unethical act. For example, a company might decide to continue to sponsor a controversial television program in spite of a boycott because managers view the boycott as censorship.

If the company does capitulate, its problems are not over. It still has to win back its old customers. If the boycott was instrumental, then the most important next step is to get the word out to consumers and show that the company is responsive to their concerns. With luck, consumers will be happy that the company has changed its ways and will be easy to win back. If the boycott was expressive, then it may take still more work to regain old customers. Even after the company has changed its behavior, consumers may remain angry.

If a producer decides not to accede to the boycotters' demands, then it can only hope to regain customers by changing consumers' attitudes. Again, the best approach depends upon whether motives are expressive or instrumental. In the face of an expressive boycott, a company can try and explain its behavior. For example, Nike has tried to convince customers that working conditions in its factories are good.

In the face of an instrumental boycott, another tactic is to try and convince customers that the boycott simply will not work. This could be achieved by taking public actions that commit the company to continuing its current practices. To take the example of the sponsorship of a television program, the company could sign a long-term contract to continue its support. This strategy is risky because it may simply anger consumers – the boycott may become expressive rather than instrumental.

Summary

Not all consumer boycotts are alike. Different people have different motives for joining them and managers need to understand this if they are to react effectively. Moreover, as **Jill Klein**, **Richard Ettenson** and **Andrew John** demonstrate, businesses can sometimes be targeted through no fault of their own but as the fallout from international hostility. The prudent marketing manager no longer worries only about product and service quality. Monitoring deeper feelings towards the business and its home country may be critical in preserving customer relationships.

Strategic thinking in the global era

by Jerry Wind

Conducting business on a global basis is difficult under the best of circumstances. In turbulent markets affected by political and economic unrest such as the Asian crisis or by the information revolution and environmental change, continuing to follow the same marketing strategy is extremely risky. Companies therefore need to examine their ways of doing business, and the concepts and methods they use, then decide what to keep, modify, delete and, most importantly, add.

Changes and challenges

New manufacturers and new products are appearing everywhere. Close to 200 countries are vying in the world marketplace and global trading companies, such as the Hong Kong-based Li & Fung, use integrated global supply chains to offer products that are significantly cheaper than many of their competitors'. This means constant challenges for even the most competitive companies, regardless of location. We have only to look at the economic crisis in Asia to see just how quickly things can change, yet the changes also offer enormous opportunities. Changes include:

- globalization of business, including increased global competition and the emergence of regional and global customers and resource markets

- rapid and radical developments in science and technology, in particular in the fields of computing, telecommunications and information sciences (consider the impact of cellular phones and the internet)
- shifting industry boundaries and competitive structures, including mergers and acquisitions of unprecedented magnitude and strategic alliances within and across traditional industry groups
- changing demographics, together with changing popular values, expectations and behavior
- increased scrutiny of business decisions by government and the public, with greater focus on the ethical dimensions of these decisions
- increased deregulation, privatization and co-operation between business and government
- changes in business practices – for example, downsizing, outsourcing and re-engineering
- changes in the social/business contract between companies and their employees, customers and other stakeholders.

The issue of brand equity adds to this complexity. Companies devote a lot of time, energy and money to building the value of their brands. But how can you effectively maintain brand values and market globally to an international consumer base? What compromises will be necessary? How should you determine which aspects of your brand have value not only across different countries but across different segments within countries? Technology is another tricky issue. It has been one of the driving forces in the global economy over the past decade, yet countries differ in how they embrace it and in the benefits they seek.

The most important problem facing any large business today is how to build a truly global service organization that draws on economies of scale, yet meets unique and constantly changing local demands. How can your organization become more service-orientated and market-driven, more nimble to capitalize on emerging opportunities, and less bureaucratic to allow effective implementation?

Thinking global

There is no place that should not be considered by successful global companies. The realities of a finite organization may mean that you concentrate on limited import and export initiatives at first, but you always have the option of forming strategic alliances in specific countries or regions, or on a global basis. Furthermore, at every stage of development you should ensure that the whole organization thinks globally about each link in the value-added chain.

At the local market level, the key marketing question is: what are the optimal strategies to capture the local market (while achieving economies of scale and scope across countries)? Answering this question requires managers to determine the optimal positioning, branding, product and service offerings, pricing, communications and distribution within the company's overall marketing strategy.

Companies must also address a number of cross-country questions, including:

- what is the optimal portfolio of countries by mode of entry and segment?
- what new market entry strategies should be considered?
- how important is simultaneous global launch and what is the optimal schedule of entry?
- what is the optimal design for an integrated global supply chain – including

global sourcing and manufacturing facilities – and how should it be implemented?

■ how should the company capitalize on local government policy, tariffs and trade restrictions?

■ how should the company capitalize on opportunities for barter, offset and counter-trade?

History lessons

What general lessons can we glean from previous experience?

First, most companies tend to underestimate the market strength of their competitors and especially of new competitors from outside the traditional boundaries of the industry. How long, for example, did it take banks to recognize that their real competitors were not other banks, but the mutual fund complexes, Quicken, and possibly Microsoft and other new players in electronic banking?

Many companies, meanwhile, even those that are customer-orientated in their home market, tend to ignore market heterogeneity in other countries and fail to customize their product and service offerings accordingly. Others tend to stampede into new cultures without taking the time to learn about exactly how those cultures differ from their home country. Yet it is essential that everyone within an organization respects the different cultures and working practices found within each country; companies cannot expect to force results to happen at the same rate in different areas.

Is global strategy an oxymoron?

Few companies have strategies or organizational structures that can truly be called global. Far too many companies develop products or services for a general – average – global market; few develop products for specific domestic market segments as part of an "umbrella" global concept. A surprisingly small number of companies have high-level marketing teams that include executives from various countries. And only a handful of companies have effective processes for knowledge transfer across countries. Your company should be a microcosm of the global marketplace. The diversity of your own organization will help your company understand better the diverse needs, tastes and wants within the global economy.

Nor do many companies have a global knowledge base about consumers or competitors. Without addressing this concern, companies thinking about electronic commerce are putting the cart before the horse. Companies that do not understand their consumers and do not know what current competitors are doing in the marketplace – as well as what potential competitors are planning to do – cannot possibly hope to succeed.

With the exception of large multinational businesses, most companies tend to focus on the developed markets of North America, Europe and Japan. Too often they ignore the 86 per cent of the world's population who reside in countries whose gross domestic product is less than $10,000 per head. Yet these countries offer enormous opportunities for those who understand the needs of their various market segments and make the effort to tailor solutions.

The global enterprise of the future

Successful global enterprises in the 21st century will have 12 interrelated characteristics. They will have flatter, less hierarchical, more cross-functional organizations; empower the individuals and groups within them; have a global perspective; be networked (as part of a group of companies that together deliver the entire value chain); base themselves on information technology; be customer-driven; focus on their stakeholders; steer themselves with reference to a corporate vision, with shared values and culture; be time competitive; create value (beyond the assurance of quality); be innovative and entrepreneurial; and be flexible and knowledge-based.

These businesses will have to create and implement a new marketing paradigm to reflect the interrelated characteristics of the new organization and capitalize on advances in the science of marketing. This new approach establishes marketing as a business philosophy rather than just one of the business functions. As such, its concepts and methods should be as relevant to the chief executive and the board as they have traditionally been to the brand manager.

At its core is the question of how marketing can, together with the other business functions, create value for customers and other key stakeholders. Marketing needs to become the "eyes and ears" of business, providing early warning of external change and insights into how to address it. This requires that marketing's concepts and methods should themselves be adjusted constantly to reflect these changes, and that corresponding changes are made to the organizational architecture.

The new marketing strategy process

We begin with the most essential question: who are our customers and what do they need and want? From there we can move on to the next question: what product and service offerings will meet the target segment's needs and offer sustainable competitive advantage?

Answering these two questions will allow us to address the third question: which strategies and programs, resources, capabilities and processes will be required to develop and implement the product or service solution? A global organization has to answer these questions both on a local level and for each regional and global market segment it seeks to attract.

Another critical component of marketing strategy is constant innovation. This requires effective mechanisms for gathering information from local markets about what customers want and need and, of equal importance, what local, regional and global competitors are doing or planning. A strong network is required for gathering intelligence and there has to be an effective process for analyzing, storing, updating and accessing it.

Figure 1 outlines the process for developing global strategy. The process begins with a "Swot" (strengths, weaknesses, opportunities and threats) analysis and the development of the likely environmental scenarios. This is followed by the creation of a corporate vision that reflects both external perspectives (on what type of company will succeed in the changing business environment) juxtaposed against an internal perspective (on what type of company we aspire to be). Once the vision has been established, the next challenge is to define a new business paradigm that reflects the benefits customers seek and the value the company can create. Figure 2 illustrates what this might mean for a pharmaceutical company.

Historically, pharmaceutical companies sold drugs and resisted the pressure for discounts on the price of the drugs. Consumers, on the other hand, are not

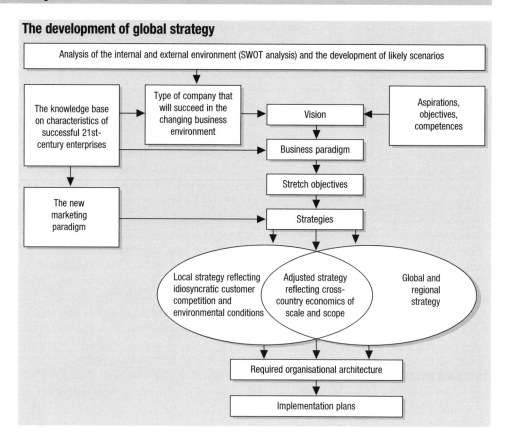

Figure 1

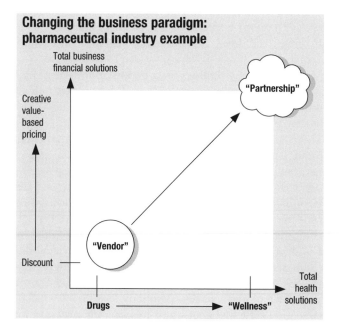

Figure 2

interested in the product but rather in a solution to their health problems. Similarly, payers – retail pharmacies, say – are interested in a solution to their business/financial problems and will reduce the pressure they apply to obtain discounts if the pharmaceutical company can help them generate more revenues and profits.

Whereas not all consumers may seek this solution and some segments may prefer other positions along the two dimensions of "health solutions" and "business/financial solutions," understanding and articulating this paradigm opens a new range of growth options for the pharmaceutical company. It changes the nature of its relationships with its clients from that of a "vendor" to that of a "partner" who shares the risks and rewards.

The next step is the establishment of "stretch" objectives. The importance of stretch goals such as "double revenues and profits in three years" or Hewlett-Packard's stretch goal in the early 1980s – "improve everything we do by a factor of 10" – is that they lead to the realization that "business as usual" will not suffice. Everyone is forced to challenge the way things are done, which leads to creative approaches to achieving the objectives.

The focus moves next to the development of strategy. Global marketing strategy and the related organizational architecture must balance global and local tensions. This is a matter of having a global concept and a corresponding local and global strategy. The company needs to blend standardization and differentiation, while focusing on both adaptation to local conditions and the achievement of cross-country co-ordination, integration and synergy. It is not the old philosophy of "Think global and act local" but rather "Think and act globally, regionally and locally."

Implementing the strategy

According to the new paradigm of marketing in the information age, traditional industry focus is replaced with focus on a truly borderless company that spans traditional industry lines. Consider, for example, the new information industry that fuses hardware, software, telecommunications, consumer electronics and other related industries.

Our geographical scope, moreover, changes from one that is split between domestic and international operations to a global one. Another important shift is from a mass-market to a "segments of one" mentality. This is made possible by the enormous advances in database marketing and mass customization in recent years, which allow companies to reach individual consumers economically with customized messages, media and even products and services.

The ability to customize can dramatically change the nature of products. Consider, for example, what will happen to the music industry as technological advances allow consumers to design their own CDs and download them from the internet. The consumer becomes part of a co-production process. This is true of all products, not just those that can be delivered electronically.

Our communications strategy will also change radically – from advertising and occasional use of public relations to integrated, interactive, customized marketing communications. If we focus on "segments of one" our advertising and marketing must have a message that captures each customer's interest and is delivered effectively through targeted media.

Reaching "segments of one" will be made easier by new modes of distribution. Increasingly, products and services will be delivered by electronic means. The internet has the potential to give customers access to a huge array of products and product information, any time, anywhere.

Pricing models will undergo a 180-degree change. We currently price our products and send them out into the marketplace in the hope that customers will purchase them at our set price. But there will be a move to more value-based pricing and, in more and more cases, customers can be expected to say what they are willing to pay. We will then have to develop products and services that deliver what the customer seeks for the price he or she specifies. Price.com, the online airline ticketing service does this and plans to expand into other products and services. WebAuction.com offers a similar benefit but with a different approach.

In the end, our business model will no longer be based on transactions but on relationships. Customer and supplier will co-operate. Our company will not sell products or services; rather, it will provide solutions to customers' needs.

Adaptive experimentation

Given the novelty of many of these strategies and the uncertainty of the business environment, management will be advised to rely on adaptive experimentation. This is because the market's response to any single initiative (such as a given level of advertising or a particular message) does not provide guidelines for better decisions in future. Only by experimenting with multilevel initiatives (such as low versus high levels of advertising or message A versus message B) can management determine the market response function and thus establish guidelines for the next set of decisions. To be effective, adaptive experimentation has to be done continuously and needs to focus on critical variables – ones that can dramatically change market performance. Managers must also ensure that the tested levels are sufficiently different (so that advertising is doubled, for example).

Organizational architecture

Organizational architecture decisions must cover:

- the organizational *culture* that will reflect the values and characteristics of successful 21st-century enterprises
- the *structure* that will allow the company to be market driven and to operate globally
- the *processes* required for creating value for all stakeholders, including the development of better, cheaper and faster solutions to customer needs
- *employees* and the competences they must have
- the *technology* needed to implement the new strategy; this encompasses databases and decision support systems and models, as well as the use of IT to "capture" clients and other stakeholders (via loyalty programs, for example)
- the *resources*, in terms of both finance and knowledge, required to implement the strategy
- the *performance measures* and *incentives* that will ensure the alignment of employees' interests with organizational objectives.

In designing an organizational architecture for businesses operating in the global information age, technological competences are a must, as are geographical scope and expertise. This requires the hiring, development, motivation and retention of a diverse workforce. The truly global company will have employees who are representative of different parts of the world, sensitive to different cultures and capable of operating comfortably anywhere in the world, using whatever IT tools are available.

Summary

Truly global marketing organizations remain rare as companies struggle to respond to changing industry structures, the cultural diversity of foreign markets, and new opportunities and challenges thrown up by information technology. Successful enterprises in the next century will have to rethink their strategies so they reflect the characteristics of modern business and recent advances in the science of marketing. In this article, **Jerry Wind** discusses some of the most important issues arising from the new marketing paradigm, as well as the changes that will be required in organizational architecture.

Suggested further reading

Mahajan, V., Wind, J. and Moraes, M.P. de (1998) "The invisible global market: strategies for reaching the forgotten 86 per cent of the world," SEI Center Working Paper.

Wind, J. and Main, J. (1998) *Driving Change*, Free Press, New York.

How SMEs enter foreign markets

by Tim Ambler and Chris Styles

Commitment and energy are critical in the shift from domestic marketing to exporting. Success depends on focusing human energies to drive the brand through to its final consumers, with blind faith sometimes as important as rational analysis.

This article, which looks at six main areas of international marketing, is based on research conducted among over 400 UK and Australian newly exporting small and medium-sized enterprises (SMEs). All had fewer than 500 employees.

Physical exporting, of course, is only one means of international market entry. For many businesses, especially those in services, local operations may be preferable. Sometimes national regulations or prohibitive import taxes may make local manufacturing the only option. Nevertheless, to keep things simple, "export" is here used for any form of foreign market entry. Similarly, the word "distributor" refers to the business partner in the new market – whatever the legal relationship.

1 Deciding to go abroad

Reasons for considering entry into foreign markets include: the desire to replicate domestic sucess elsewhere; a home market that is too small for a (specialist) product; and poor performance at home. Alternatively, as the Australians have shown, a company may be "born global" – that is, be set up with overseas markets in mind. Sometimes serendipity plays a key role. Holidays may introduce executives to contacts that are worth following up; cousins, friends and acquaintances may be looking for business opportunities.

Other people want a more orderly approach, such as the analytical framework proposed by Kellogg School academic Philip Kotler. This starts with the world as a whole – all 200 or so markets – and proceeds by economic analysis (elimination) to the choice of export countries, type of overseas partner and marketing mix. Only after all that do organizational issues emerge, such as who should be hired for export roles.

Our own research found that in 25 per cent of cases overseas distributors make first contact with an exporter. At the footwear company Dr Marten's, for example, unsolicited orders eventually resulted in formal distributorships. Personal networks are also very important at the beginning of exporter/distributor relationships (43 per cent of cases).

An exporter and importer may never have met, or the importer may have visited the factory. With unsolicited orders, creditworthiness is far more likely to determine the decision to export than marketing strategy. If customers continue to order and pay, exporting becomes part of the unquestioned way of life – as it is now at Dr Marten's. Managers may be unaware of ever making a formal "decision" to export.

The decision to venture abroad can always be rationalized, especially in hindsight, but we find no evidence that it generally arises from analysis of the company's options. To be sure, larger players tend to adopt more analytical approaches and to turn away unsolicited contacts from distributors but here we focus on SMEs.

2 The export organization

The textbook model, in essence, puts analysis first and personal contacts last. But a fledgling exporter is unlikely to have the resources to conduct an extensive analysis. A common problem when deciding on an exporting organization is that everyone is eager to provide information and advice but no one wants to do the work needed to get some movement. The amount of information and advice on offer from governments and elsewhere can be truly daunting. Those whose job it is to help exporters tend to believe they need more information when really they want less. With vast databases on hand, information is becoming more of a barrier to exports than a help.

One solution, if the exporter can afford it, is to reduce risk and maximize expertise by buying in specialist resources. Some governments provide subsidies for this. Consultants can carry out a feasibility study and recommend markets to enter. Then an external marketing organization can implement the recommendations. Only when the new international business has been proved feasible does commitment need to be made to distributors and an internal exports team recruited.

A company's entry into its first foreign market depends less on formal analysis than commitment. Success also depends on forming long-term personal relationships so managers should think hard about appointing the export team, however small, early. If external resources are to be used, managers should also consider how the relationships arising can be gently transferred in due course. Networking, enthusiasm, cultural sensitivity and other personal skills matter most.

3 Choosing markets

Most first-time exporters enter the foreign market that most resembles home. The exporter would like to keep the same products, prices and marketing mix. Choosing an adjacent market that uses the same language minimizes the "geo-cultural" or "psychic" distance. Often, though, the people living in the chosen export markets will be quick to resent the implication that they are "the same."

In recent years, improved global communications have greatly widened the choice of first export markets. Even small businesses are using modern communications to conduct long-range business. For example, a farmer in Norfolk, England, sells ducks' feet in China.

What resources should be devoted to research before the first visit? It is worth remembering that research may provide the data but not the answers. For example, if you are in the shoe business, are low shoe sales per foot good (opportunity) or bad (these people do not buy shoes)? If your competitors at home are there, does that mean that the market is attractive or to be avoided? Some SMEs, insanely to our way of thinking, devote a lot of time studying export markets' macro-economies. But why should next year's projected inflation of 6.7 or 7.2 per cent make the slightest difference to initial sales so small that they are effectively zero?

Are we tossing out analysis? No. We are counseling a balance between a limited amount of high-quality analysis and giving full rein to human, relational opportunities.

Our research indicates that the key issues are:

- The proportion of potential end-users in the population is less important than their total number. In India, for example, a small proportion of the population is still a big number.
- How easily can people afford what you are selling? Will they pay? Macro-economic indicators are less important than identifying the number of customers affluent enough to accommodate your products in their buying portfolios.
- What is the market's networking potential? Here market size does matter because the size of a network increases geometrically with the size of the market. In economic terms, what will it cost effectively to reach the end-user?
- All network links are important, but none more so than the exporter–importer link. What are the odds of finding a distributor good enough to succeed with your products yet hungry enough to want them? Most distributors are too busy – or there are good reasons why they are not.
- How culturally different is the export market? Cultural affinity is clearly a help to mutual understanding and increases the chances that what works at home will work there too.
- Most new exporters start with one country at a time but there are arguments for tackling two or three. With adequate resources, more can be learned faster. However, there is a danger that resources will be stretched too far.

Surprising as it may seem, competition, price levels and environmental factors are omitted from this list. Naturally, the new exporter must position the offering so that it is differentiated from and better than existing brands. That is basic marketing. But provided this can be done, the competitiveness of the market does not appear to be a major consideration for most SMEs.

4 Choosing the distributor

If we play down the process of choosing the export organization and the first market, the reverse is true for the choice of distributor. Better a second-rate country than a poor distributor.

An early consideration is likely to be the most appropriate type of local arrangement – although that too may be driven more by personal than economic considerations. Typically the options include the following: importer; licensee; joint venture; local manufacturing/assembly; management contract; turnkey operations; acquisition. Most textbooks present sound analytical frameworks that lay out the costs and benefits of each.

Some research suggests that companies develop each overseas market incrementally, minimizing risk at each stage. Initial export sales are made ad hoc but then, as a pattern emerges, a single importer is contracted. Local manufacturing on a licensee or joint venture basis follows and ultimately the exporter sets up its own fully fledged business in the export market.

The four main aims of this process are:

1 to control local marketing – to achieve alignment with strategic intentions and consistency across borders
2 to obtain incremental profit (that is, the distributor's share)
3 to increase corporate learning, which can ultimately feed into other markets
4 to use the strength of the exporter's leading brands to help the rest of the exporter's portfolio.

We raise these future considerations at this early stage because the step-by-step approach, while designed to minimize risk, carries a risk of its own. Why should importers – who have been through this process before – commit to an exporter who will only use them until a better option comes along? Issues of trust and commitment are crucial and reciprocal. Any company that considers progressive development as simply jumping into bed with an importer before jumping straight out again needs to review the options from its partner's point of view. Insecurity can easily derail an export drive at the outset.

Gunnar Beeth, the export consultant, suggests the following solution to distributor selection once a market (or shortlist of markets) has been chosen: first, see the retail buyers and discover which distributors are most successful and respected. Then eliminate those that have obvious conflicts with each other and woo the best of the rest. Canny as it is, this method will not work in many Asian markets, where connections need to be built up with retailers *before* they will get into meaningful discussions. These markets usually require more subtlety and more determination than others. One way or another, friendly connections need to be made.

Making contacts with potential distributors is a task that merits careful attention. It is probably the single most important key to getting started. It is a question not just of identifying the right importer but of convincing them to do business with you. This may not be easy. The chances are that the importer is attractive to you because it already has a successful business – but then your proposition will mean little to it. By the same token, you should worry about any distributor glad to accept you.

The ideal distributor has outstandingly good relationships with its customers, a small, highly focused portfolio that has space for, and is compatible with, your products, and a substantial volume of business, which is usually called "critical mass." "Critical mass" means that the distributor's portfolio is big and/or powerful enough to command the attention of (retail) buyers. It is hard to quantify. A very specialized or prestigious business, for example, may have critical mass without great volume or market share. If a new product is interesting enough, attention can be achieved when the volume of business is tiny. The more ordinary the product range, however, the larger is the market share needed for critical mass. Market share of 10 per cent is a good rule of thumb (where "market" is understood as immediate customers define it).

Key distributor choice issues are:

- What type of local arrangement is needed for this product category and situation?
- Can you commit to it for the long term? Can reciprocal trust be established?
- Does the distributor's portfolio fit your products and does it have critical mass?
- How best can you use networking – through prior contacts and market visits, say – to build relationships with the distributor you want?
- How can you ensure that the relationship becomes a true partnership? Multinationals find this difficult. Small importers do not trust managers in multinationals, who often hop from job to job unexpectedly. Conversely, small new exporters find it hard to secure already successful, and therefore large, distributors.
- Do you need a distributor at all? Maybe you can, within your own region at least, sell directly to the retailers.
- On the other hand, should you engage several? A large Chinese manufacturer of embroidery machines employed three distributors in each new market and then sacked the two that proved less successful.

Monogamy has had quite a good run, at least in some cultures, but one cannot rule out multiple arrangements. For example, an importer on the US East coast may have no operation on the West coast 3,000 miles away. Most exporters give distributors exclusivity, at least initially, to make the process of building brand equity less complicated.

5 Developing the exporter/distributor relationship

The next steps for the exporter are to develop the distributor relationship and marketing mix. The textbook sequence is to decide on the marketing mix and then appoint the distributor. Our research leads us to the opposite view. The distributor should normally have the stronger voice in determining the marketing mix and therefore must be appointed first. Reasons for doing it this way round include the fact that the distributor knows the export market better than the exporter. The distributor lives there and, ideally, is already successful. And if the distributor is to be motivated and feel accountable for the results, it must own the plan.

Clearly, both exporter and importer stand to benefit from pooling their skills. Their best interests are served by transferring "knowledge" and becoming "partners" in the venture. Not only does the exporter learn and benefit from its partner's knowledge but it is brought into the network of resources and competences that surrounds the distributor.

We are not aware of any company that has yet formalized its relationship and network formation stages through any planning and control system. Most managers would feel uncomfortable with developing human relations in such a way. That said, much the same considerations applied to internal managerial relationships until annual appraisals became standard practice.

Our research indicated that the more successful exporters communicated much more frequently with their opposite numbers – through letters, faxes, phone calls and visits – than the less successful. Of course, we cannot be sure which caused which. A visit to the home, or some other, market at the exporter's expense may well be a sound investment, not least to stress the "partnership" nature of the relationship. A visit at the distributor's expense may be an even better idea. It shows commitment and the distributor immediately has an investment needing a return.

The implications for new entrants are clear:

- Finding a distributor may initially be a matter of luck but it should not be left to serendipity alone. It should involve active networking with those with the strongest potential and interest. Whether through market visits, trade shows or other means – find out where they are and be there.
- Commit to your distributor. Work together to plan the marketing program. Co-operation and communication are both positively associated with export performance.
- Audit the relationship annually, perhaps using an experienced independent consultant as some advertising agencies now do.
- Resist the temptation to control the new distributor. Clearly you must keep a sharp eye on the cash but a control orientation is bad for relationship building and implies that you know more than them. Any exporter should be in learning, not teaching, mode until it understands the new market.

6 Finding the best mix

The conventional wisdom is that the marketing mix (product, packaging, price, promotion, advertising and distribution channels) should be modified as directed by local market research. We dispute that. Apart from mandatory items such as language and labeling, products are not usually changed for overseas markets. Whether products are tested in market research or not, general practice seems to favor trying the home product first and only making changes in the light of experience.

Earlier we said that the distributor should have the stronger say in determining the mix for the export territory. This remains true because an unconvinced distributor will be a poor champion. Inviting the distributor to visit the home market to see why it works may well be a sound investment.

Getting it right first time matters less than fixing problems as soon as they arise. Inflexible or opinionated exporters reduce distributors' motivation. The development of the mix should be seen less as a means of maximizing sales or profits than as a vehicle for maximizing two-way learning within the new partnership. Market research, for example, should be jointly commissioned to help partners share solutions rather than to resolve disputes.

Our research found no statistically significant link between changing domestic marketing strategies for the export market and performance. Exporters changed their marketing mixes very little. This pattern was found in both consumer and industrial products and across export markets.

Our marketing mix conclusions are:

- swap notes with the importer about previous experiences, then change whatever you are both confident about and what you have to
- conduct research to provide illumination for this discussion but do not rely on it
- otherwise stick with what worked at home but be prepared to change fast if you are wrong.

Summary

Moving into a foreign market is a big step for any company. So it is not surprising that many textbooks depict the process as the outcome of ponderous analysis. But according to research by **Tim Ambler** and **Chris Styles**, the process is much more haphazard for most companies. Many decisions to export are triggered by unsolicited approaches by distributors and by personal contacts. The nurturing of relationships with distributors appears to be critical in making a success of marketing overseas – so much so that, contrary to the usual wisdom, the distributor needs to be selected before any new marketing mix is decided upon.

Suggested further reading

Beeth, G. (1991) "Distributors – finding and keeping the good ones," in Thorelli and Cavusgilin (eds) *International Marketing Strategy*, Pergamon Press, Oxford.

Clifford, D.K., Jr, and Cavanagh, R.E. (1985) *Winning Performance*, Bantam Books, New York.

Emerging Exporters: Australia's High Value-Added Manufacturing Exporters, McKinsey & Company/Australian Manufacturing Council.

Kotler, P. (1997) *Marketing Management: Analysis, Planning, Implementation and Control*, 9th edn, Prentice Hall, NJ.

Onkvisit, S. and Shaw, J.J. (1990) *International Marketing – Analysis and Strategy*, Maxwell MacMillan, New York, ch. 13.

Root, F.D. (1987) *Entry Strategies for International Markets*, Lexington Books, Lexington, MA.

Terpstra, V. and Sarathy, R. (1991) *International Marketing*, Dryden, ch. 10.

Index